Y0-CXQ-051

WITHDRAWN
UTSA Libraries

HANDBOOK OF ACCOUNTING AND DEVELOPMENT

Handbook of Accounting and Development

Edited by

Trevor Hopper
University of Sussex, UK

Mathew Tsamenyi
University of Birmingham, UK

Shahzad Uddin
University of Essex, UK

Danture Wickramasinghe
University of Glasgow, UK

Edward Elgar
Cheltenham, UK • Northampton, MA, USA

© Trevor Hopper, Mathew Tsamenyi, Shahzad Uddin and Danture Wickramasinghe 2012

All rights reserved. No part of this publication may be reproduced, stored in a retrieval system or transmitted in any form or by any means, electronic, mechanical or photocopying, recording, or otherwise without the prior permission of the publisher.

Published by
Edward Elgar Publishing Limited
The Lypiatts
15 Lansdown Road
Cheltenham
Glos GL50 2JA
UK

Edward Elgar Publishing, Inc.
William Pratt House
9 Dewey Court
Northampton
Massachusetts 01060
USA

A catalogue record for this book
is available from the British Library

Library of Congress Control Number: 2012935271

ISBN 978 1 84844 816 2 (cased)

Typeset by Servis Filmsetting Ltd, Stockport, Cheshire
Printed and bound by MPG Books Group, UK

Library
University of Texas
at San Antonio

Contents

Figures

Tables

Contributors

Marcia Annisette, York University, Canada

Judy Brown, Victoria University of Wellington, New Zealand

Alex Cobham, Save the Children, UK

Clive Emmanuel, University of Glasgow, UK

Jeff Everett, York University, Canada

Sara Fyson, OECD, Paris

Cameron Graham, York University, Canada

Mohshin Habib, Swinburne University of Technology, Australia

Kevin Holmes, Victoria University of Wellington, New Zealand

Trevor Hopper, University of Sussex, UK

Mahmud Hossain, Curtin University, Australia

Monirul Hossain, East West University, Bangladesh

Kerry Jacobs, Australian National University, Australia

Christine Jubb, Australian National University, Australia

Stewart Lawrence, University of Waikato, New Zealand

David McNair, Save the Children, UK

Pala Molisa, Victoria University of Wellington, New Zealand

Nzilu Musyoki, Australian National University, Australia

Brendan O'Dwyer, Amsterdam Business School, The Netherlands

Hector Perera, Macquarie University, Australia

Chris Poullaos, University of Sydney, Australia

Kunal Sen, University of Manchester, UK

Javed Siddiqui, University of Manchester, UK

Mathew Tsamenyi, University of Birmingham, UK

Chibuike U. Uche, University of Nigeria, Nigeria

Shahzad Uddin, University of Essex, UK

Jeffrey Unerman, Royal Holloway University of London, UK

Danaa Vandangombo, Victoria University of Wellington, New Zealand

Danture Wickramasinghe, University of Glasgow, UK

Andy Wynne, Idilmat Training Solutions, Ghana

1 Introduction: accounting and development

Trevor Hopper, Mathew Tsamenyi, Shahzad Uddin and Danture Wickramasinghe

The motivation for this book lay in the difficulties of trying to publish research on accounting in less developed countries (LDCs). Editors often responded that it was desirable and worthy but should seek outlets in specialist development or international accounting journals. This infuriated us, for most of the world's population live in poor countries, their accounting needs are at least as great as if not more than in rich countries, so-called cutting-edge research was (and still is) heavily concentrated on serving large commercial and state organizations in rich countries, and although accounting policies were problematic in LDCs they were neglected by researchers.

Fortunately, over the past decade the field has been opening up. A sprinkling of accounting scholars worldwide have brought substantive contributions. Major journals, especially the *Accounting, Auditing and Accountability Journal*, *Accounting, Organizations and Society* and *Critical Perspectives on Accounting*, have pioneered work in this area aided and abetted by 'international accounting' journals and the newly launched *Journal of Accounting in Emerging Economies* and its companion *Research on Accounting and Emerging Economies*. A network of scholars is evolving through workshops like the Accounting and Subalternity Conference at York University, Canada, in 2007, and those of the British Accounting Association special interest group Accounting in Less Developed and Emerging Economies. Links are being established with accounting academics in LDCs, development studies researchers, and 'third sector' institutions such as non-governmental organizations (NGOs). However, this work is still in its infancy. Much more is required. Accounting scholars in rich and poor country universities need to build better bridges amongst themselves, and with academics in other disciplines, and transnational organizations that diffuse accounting knowledge, policy and practice in LDCs such as the World Bank, accounting professional institutions, international accounting standard setting bodies, the accounting consultancy industry and government institutions.

This book seeks to further these ends. The aspiration is that reviews of research on vital accounting topics for LDCs from leading researchers and practitioners will diffuse extant knowledge and stimulate further research and debate. The target audiences include: active and prospective researchers in accounting and related areas in rich and poor countries alike; and accounting policy-makers and practitioners in global and local institutions. The book is not definitive. The field is too under-researched and immature to claim this. Moreover, the contents are heavily weighted to accounting research in leading 'Western' journals; contributions from policy-makers and researchers in fields such as development economics and public administration, and from academics located in LDCs have not been trawled extensively. Such work is essential for future progress, but it lies beyond the scope and capacity of this book.

For some readers the contents of this book may be a surprise, especially if accounting is perceived as essentially technical and unproblematic. Our definition of accounting is not governed by that propounded by professional bodies, practice and academia in the West, which unduly concentrates on the private interests of large corporations and elites, and hence neglects many concerns of poor countries. Instead we see accounting as being involved in the accountability of all constituents in society, and providing information for planning and control directed at broader development goals. Thus accounting is not just an economic tool but also a social and political means of helping to improve the quality of life of poor people and to enable them to gain greater participation in democracies; it is present in social interaction not just formal reports, in words not just numbers, and should monitor not just financial flows but also social and environmental factors.

Our contributors, drawn from across the world, had a free hand to write on their assigned topic. The results illustrate how accounting practices and technical issues are embedded in a multitude of theoretical, ethical, political and social issues. The editors welcome further disputation about these contributions, in the hope that further debate will give more 'voice' to reformers wishing to create accounting and accountability systems that further development goals in poor countries.

ACCOUNTING FOR EFFICIENCY OR DEVELOPMENT?

Accounting is often presumed to consist of techniques that provide objective, value-free measurements that render individuals and organizations controllable and accountable. The emphasis lies on formality, legal-rational bureaucracy, and efficient resource utilization. Viewing accounting as a pre-defined technology has validity, as many of its techniques and systems appear portable across countries, whether rich or poor. Research has not discovered accounting systems unique to LDCs. However, accounting systems do not unequivocally flow from rational choice or environmental determinants but are shaped, inter alia, by other controls over production and labour, managerial choices and political conflicts within or without the organization (Chapter 12). This requires multi-disciplinary, multi-level and multi-theoretical analyses.

The contributions to this book reflect this: theoretically they span from economic and market studies to political economy and constructivism. Institutionally they span from the role of transnational organizations to the involvement of poor and marginalized beneficiaries. Throughout, an observation is that accounting is socially and politically constructed and its practice is intertwined with culture, local and global politics, institutions, and economic factors. Increased transparency and accountability are not just 'technical' issues (Chapter 2); nor can the effectiveness of accounting be judged merely by efficiency and profitability criteria. Rather it should be appraised against its contribution to broader development aims: corruption can flourish in functioning market economies, and starvation can exist alongside abundance (Chapter 13).

A common research finding is that the expectations of policy-makers instituting often predetermined and imported formal accounting systems and regulations are not met. Systems are often ignored, or used for purposes other than those intended, and users often change them. The point is that accounting practice is rooted in social process:

actors can improvise, negotiate and translate accounting systems during their implementation and usage. The formal and the social cannot be divorced. For example, accounting may appear absent in microfinance loan assessment and repayments, but in reality simple, group-based systems act as a substitute for formal conventional accounting. Such socialized systems are a form of accounting, albeit in a less conventional format (Chapter 10). Moreover, the influence of users and intended beneficiaries within social interaction should not be seen as detrimental but an opportunity to promote more inclusive and participatory systems that grant civil society and beneficiaries a 'voice' (Chapter 16). Pluralistic and dialogic systems that are sensitive to inequalities of power between constituents can further democracy. Similarly, examining corruption dynamically through an approach that incorporates social construction may have benefits. A static approach confined to supporting legal individual freedoms may inadvertently reinforce inequalities, whereas a dynamic stance that enables people to resist may better protect freedoms, further the public interest and incorporate broader social factors (Chapter 13). Failure to involve local participants and to tailor accounting systems and decisions to local circumstances can have unanticipated and unsought consequences. For example, privatizations encouraged by the World Bank and the International Monetary Fund (IMF) have encouraged management accounting systems that enhance enterprise efficiency and profitability but not necessarily development goals such as increased government revenue, more equitable income distribution, less corruption, greater employment, a better quality of working life, and more transparent and accountable governance (Chapter 12).

Too often accounting and tax policies in LDCs are dominated by fiscal and economic considerations. This can downplay the potential contributions by affected parties, especially within civil society, and the importance of social, environmental and accountability dimensions of development. Conventional accounting is business oriented. Insofar as it incorporates social and environmental factors, they are treated as 'externalities' and 'technical' issues, which brackets out the politics surrounding them (Chapter 16). For example, the social and environmental effects of mining in Mongolia and tourism in Vanuatu have been neglected. Economic liberalization that outstripped effective accountability and redistributive policies brought extensive offshore ownership and control of the economy, increased social division between white and black people, rich and poor, and foreigners and the indigenous population, and major ecological problems (Chapter 16).

A recurring theme throughout the book is that accounting in LDCs involves moral and ethical issues, especially regarding a commitment to accountability, transparency, democracy, and giving influence to civil society. Whether contemporary neo-liberal development approaches that emphasize the pursuit of self-interest and money-making can constitute moral and ethical bedrocks for contemporary policies is questioned (Chapter 13). Ethics and morals are vital given the asymmetrical power between LDCs and transnational institutions, multinational corporations (MNCs) and powerful investors (Chapter 13) which has led to LDCs' accounting systems essentially being extensions of those in industrialized countries (Chapter 4). Nevertheless, accounting institutions and the operation of accounting systems in LDCs still retain a legacy from colonialism and Cold War politics (Chapter 13), and it must be recognized that despite the current global financial crisis emanating from rich countries many LDCs have been hardest hit

(Chapter 3). Current economic problems make rich countries' ethical and moral obligations to poor ones more, not less, pressing.

DRIVERS OF ACCOUNTING CHANGE

Transnational Institutions

There are significant asymmetries of power between LDCs and external transnational institutions, especially the Organisation for Economic Co-operation and Development (OECD), the United Nations Conference on Trade and Development (UNCTAD), the World Bank, the World Trade Organization (WTO) and the IMF. Arguably, transnational institutions have shaped accounting in the global south (Chapter 4). For example, the World Bank and IMF assess whether national auditing standards and institutional environments are consistent with international standards on auditing established by the International Federation of Accountants (IFAC) (Chapter 7). Transnational institutions are complex institutions, but they shape who the key international accounting players are. These rarely favour LDCs; for example, members of the 'Big Four' accounting firms may be over-represented on transnational institutions' boards and committees despite potential conflicts of interests such as setting standards for their own work, and developing liberal trade policies favouring large financial service firms (Chapter 4). In addition, membership of international accounting and auditing standard setting bodies and representatives of transnational institutions often overlap (Chapter 4). This is worrying for LDCs whose interests may be different.

There are two views on the contribution of transnational institutions to accounting in LDCs. The first is that they work hard to achieve a level playing field and they formulate consistent standards that facilitate development and reduce risk for donors acting at a distance – whether geographical or cultural. The counter-argument is that transnational institutions shape accounting for their own purposes, making aid contingent on adoption of liberal trade agendas and associated accounting conditions, and bypass the local democratic process. Critics argue that this has negative consequences for LDCs: it may undermine traditional social norms, inhibit cross-pollination of practices, destroy convivial work relationships, and produce hybridized and unexpected arrangements (Chapter 4, Chapter 7). For example, the World Bank and IMF have made privatization policies an inescapable condition of loans (Chapter 12), and they have over-emphasized the technical at the expense of securing political consensus and goodwill when coordinating tax reforms within LDCs (Chapter 15).

Global Standard Setters

The international harmonization of accounting and auditing emanates from accounting institutions, especially the IFAC and the International Accounting Standards Board (IASB)[1] (Chapter 7). Whereas IFAC membership is open and its aims include serving the public interest and ethical concerns, the IASB is a private company and its members come largely from large accounting firms. This gives rise to concerns that LDCs have ceded accounting governance and regulation to external institutions that elevate rich country and shareholders' interests above those of other constituencies (Chapter 4). Hopefully the neglect of LDCs is becoming more recognized. Significantly, at the 2009–10 G20 summit, the World Bank stated that development of local accounting professions was essential for financial stability and consistent international reporting and the IASB should pay more attention to emerging economies, SMEs, and financial services to the poor (Chapter 2).

IFAC seeks worldwide development of an accounting profession with harmonized standards to provide services of consistently high standards in the public interest (Chapter 7). Many LDCs are members of IFAC, and they adopt its requirements of national auditing bodies on matters like audit quality, audit education, skills and competence of auditors, codes of ethics, self-regulation and disciplinary procedures, international auditing standards, and public sector auditing. However, how and whether they are enacted are shaped by local socio-political characteristics (Chapter 7). The lack of capital market monitoring allied to indigenous auditors of poor reputation and working for low fees frustrates the development of auditing to international standards (Chapter 6). Auditing standards may be adopted by LDCs because of external institutional pressures, but compliance and audit quality may remain poor (Chapter 7).

The IASB also seeks global convergence of accounting by issuing International Financial Reporting Standards (IFRSs).[2] The argument is that harmonization removes divergence and thence barriers to economic integration and trade (Chapter 8). However, Anglo-American accounting dominates standards. They presume that the legal, institutional and policy conditions that support good regulatory practice are in place. This is often not so in LDCs. Nevertheless, many LDCs adopt IFRSs, for it is cheap to do so and they lack the resources or capacity to develop standards themselves. However, if the IFRSs are not made mandatory and supported by necessary legal and regulatory changes they may not be adhered to (Chapter 2, Chapter 8). Thus in many LDCs IFRS adoption becomes ceremonial (Chapter 4) and is a signal of legitimacy: it is cheap and politically correct but may have little effect on the ground, especially in small and medium-sized indigenous enterprises (Chapter 6). For example, the adoption of IFRSs in Bangladesh was initiated by grants from transnational institutions, but implementation has been messy. Local accountants and many business people were unconvinced of their worth, and compliance has been sporadic.

Such reactions are understandable given the lack of evidence that IFRSs are relevant to LDCs (Chapter 6) or will improve the quality of accounting and auditing without legal and regulatory changes (Chapter 8). Indeed, the conceptual framework underpinning universal accounting standards may be alien to non-Western LDCs; for instance, ethics may be local not international, especially where commercial relationships are more communitarian or 'family' based, for example *guanxi* (Chapter 6). Principles-based IFRSs are not universally accepted: their scope for diversity may frustrate comparability, and cultural and linguistic differences bring different interpretations of inherently uncertain accounting expressions.

Also, universal accounting standards aimed at lubricating global trade may not be pertinent to LDCs with a more interventionist state than richer market-based economies. If capital markets are small or non-existent, and investors are unsophisticated, such complex accounting information may be unimportant (Chapter 6). Instead they want accounting data to input into centralized state models governing macro-economic policies. However, IFRSs have not been internally consistent, which can compound inequities affecting LDCs. For example, despite the universal framework of accounting and auditing emphasizing global trade and convergence, IFRSs on intra-company trade, transfer prices and global consolidation have not required economic activities and taxes paid in individual countries to be reported (Chapter 3). Paradoxically, as more LDCs adopt IFRSs, the influence of multinational corporations and financial secrecy in jurisdictions has grown. However, this, and the Anglo-American influence on the IASB, is being increasingly questioned (Chapter 3). For example, it is alleged that the adoption of 'fair value' lay at the root of the current global economic crisis (Chapter 6).

Capital Markets

The positive association of capital market development with economic growth is evident, but whether this promotes better accounting standards and development goals is less clear (Chapter 8). Financial markets may allocate capital resources better, foster technical innovation, and encourage more investment through risk-sharing and closer monitoring of managers. But on the other hand it may exacerbate income inequality, as only those with collateral or listed companies may get loans. This may lower the number of customers and inhibit physical and human capital development and thus stymie financial development (Chapter 8). If economic growth from financial developments is to reduce poverty then income inequalities must be reduced (Chapter 8).

Nevertheless, there is tentative theoretical and empirical evidence that financial reporting and economic performance are linked. The case for liberalizing LDC economies rests partly on presumptions that capital markets will demand and police the disclosure of high-quality financial information from firms. However, in many LDCs the regulation of financial disclosures by regulators such as stock exchange commissions may be weak and ineffective, sometimes because of inadequate staff skills and numbers (Chapter 7). Capital markets can be primitive or non-existent. For example, in Bangladesh excessive liquidity makes bank loans easy to obtain; and political patronage, weak bank regulation, and ineffective law enforcement lead to a 'default culture' and a stagnant market for shares (Chapter 7). Compliance with accounting regulations in LDCs is often linked to company size, profitability and multinational status (Chapter 8), possibly because such firms are more concerned with their reputation in capital markets and the repercussions of non-compliance. However, smaller, indigenous and family-owned businesses may be less concerned, especially if there is a weak regulatory and legal system governing the quality of financial reporting. If legal institutions that enforce property rights, and accounting regulation and auditing are ineffective then potential benefits from improved accounting, such as reduced agency problems between insiders and outsiders, greater managerial concerns with reputation, more public analysts' reports, and more active investors willing to exert control over firms, will not materialize. For example, a weak legal environment reduces demand for financial information but may increase demand for private information collected by analysts (Chapter 8).

Unlike the inconclusive results of liberalization on financial accounting in LDCs, there is evidence that privatizations bring quicker, more reliable, computerized management accounting controls that better link marketing and production. However, the lack of effective regulation could dissipate gains made from increased efficiency. In some instances external accountability declined, respect for consumer and employee rights was violated, financial transgressions took place, and coercive controls ensued (Chapter 12). This was especially marked in smaller, family-controlled firms subject to weak regulation. In summary, domestic capital markets may and could aid accounting reform in LDCs, but it is naïve to assume they will do so in the foreseeable future or to rely on them to meet broader development goals.

However, capital markets outside LDCs are important for LDCs. Stock exchanges in rich countries, especially the City of London and the USA, influence accounting in LDCs, especially via their demands on companies with or seeking overseas listing. This can act as a catalyst for establishing best practice and developing accounting capacity in LDCs. However, such capital markets are also major impediments to development when they act as hubs for unregulated finance and are major users of offshore financial centres with zero or near zero tax, secrecy, and regulatory environments oriented to non-residents and overseas users. Such practices are a source of lost revenue for rich and poor countries alike, but the effects are especially acute for poor countries. Illicit financial flows from LDCs to Western capital markets like London, using techniques like cross-border invoicing, can dwarf aid by a factor of eight. In addition, transfer pricing abuses by international firms listed on Western stock markets significantly reduce LDCs' tax take (though many MNCs comply, sometimes over-stringently, to protect their reputation) (Chapter 15). The financial repercussions upon LDCs of ethically dubious but not illegal practices by Western financial institutions and possible avenues of rectification are masked by the governments of rich countries retaining confidentiality of tax issues, rarely disclosing offenders and imposing low penalties for tax transgressors (Chapter 15). For example, the lack of publicly available data in rich countries concerning large-scale tax evasion through transfer pricing, due in part to IFRSs that neglect these matters, has hindered investigations of the scale of this abuse and stifled debate about it (Chapter 2, Chapter 15).

The Accounting Profession

The accounting profession in many LDCs is a curious 'hybrid' of the legacy of empire and independence struggles. The result can be a profession divided by class, race and ethnicity, and between Western and indigenous professional associations (Chapter 5). After independence many LDCs failed to establish a national accounting profession. Reasons for this include: their dependence on Western capital; institutionalization of Western training and professional bodies; a cringe factor, for example 'British is best'; the dominance of international accounting firms and professional associations like the Association of Chartered Certified Accountants (ACCA); global corporations preferring international accounting firms for reasons of reputation and location of their listing; and local elites wishing to preserve privileges and career mobility based on English language, rich country qualifications (Chapter 5).

The reliance of LDCs upon Western professional associations has furthered their dependency on Anglo-American accounting and harmonized accounting and auditing standards. This has come at a cost. The shortage of accountants in many LDCs is linked to failed local professionalization strategies. Attempts to build national professional institutes often withered in the face of competition from Western bodies and/or local associations that copied them (Chapter 5). This has inclined local accounting professionals and associations to neglect reforms tailored to local circumstances, for example improving public sector and small business accounting – vital issues in LDCs. Moreover, international trade conditions for financial services have prevented LDCs from protecting their infant accounting industries from UK and US competition, or insisting on residency for professional certification, or requiring international accounting firms to follow extraordinary compliance measures (Chapter 4). The failure to develop effective local accounting associations has contributed to the lack of competent auditors and accountants in LDCs, the low status of the accounting profession, poor accounting education and training, lack of adherence to standards, and even accountants' collusion in corruption (Chapter 7).

Several contributors are sceptical that first world professional accounting bodies can act as a bulwark against dictatorship and poverty. They note their reluctance to campaign for increased international financial transparency and monitoring of tax havens (Chapter 3), and how members' work on shifting residences arguably violates the moral and civic duties of professionals, and has helped foster corruption, undermined the state and raised systemic risk (Chapter 3). Large Western accounting firms' revenues (mainly from consulting not auditing) can outstrip that of LDC governments, and members of the 'Big Four' accounting firms dominate international accounting institutions. Consequently, LDCs have little potential influence over accounting policies (Chapter 9). There are signs of concern about this. For example, following criticisms of its neglect of LDCs, IFAC established the International Forum on Accounting Development in 1999 to promote transparent reporting, high-quality auditing, and a strong accounting profession in LDCs (Chapter 6).

Donors and Third Sector Organizations

Many LDCs depend on financial aid from external donors including the World Bank and its acolytes, foreign government agencies, and non-governmental organizations (NGOs). All donors want accounting systems that monitor whether funds granted to LDCs are used as intended, reduce the donor's fiduciary risk, and ensure better accountability, planning and control, especially in the public sector. Donors' stringent accounting requirements emanate principally from their own needs to be accountable. However, these requirements help improve governance more generally in LDCs by establishing good practice, demonstrating how development priorities can be determined by cost–benefit analysis, developing better data for decisions on development issues, and increasing civil society and stakeholders' involvement (Chapter 2).

External aid providers, frustrated by bureaucratic, inefficient and sometimes corrupt government organizations, have increasingly turned to NGOs to deliver services in fields like education and health, either by contracting with them directly or by insisting that governments dispense aid through them. The numbers, scale and scope of NGOs have dramatically increased over the past three decades. Some claim that NGOs represent a 'Third Way' of delivering development, as they are neither private enterprises nor government entities. Moreover, NGOs claim to represent, advocate for and deliver services primarily to poor and marginal people, and many seek to increase civil society involvement and influence to further increased democracy. Many have strong ethical commitments and are effective and efficient, but they can be controversial and raise unusual accounting issues. At the margins some are opportunistic and corrupt yet the regulation and financial reporting requirements under conventional accounting for NGOs has been neglected by policy-makers and researchers. This needs redress but, given many NGOs' commitment to broader social goals, their accountability needs to go beyond conventional accounting methods to money and power (funders and the state) (Chapter 4). Indeed, the worry is that conventional financial accounting systems may divert NGOs from their broader aims such as promoting learning or may fail to reflect criteria pertinent to NGOs' socio-political mission. Also, as many NGOs claim to represent, advocate for, and act on behalf of civil society, especially poor and marginalized sectors, accountability to beneficiaries and society is important. Failure in this respect opens NGOs up to charges of hypocrisy; that is, they advocate greater democracy and civil society participation in local and national governance but they do not practise it themselves. Such concerns have brought innovative and distinct accounting developments, for example a rights-based approach that incorporates downward and holistic accounting, raises social, ethical and environmental issues, and monitors whether projects are enhancing these (Chapter 9); and designing accountability systems that grant civil society and especially beneficiaries a greater 'voice', advance pluralistic democracy, and overcome differences in power, language and literacy between constituencies (Chapter 16). These are challenging tasks and may fail in the face of beneficiary incapacity, neglect by donors, differential power relations and deference, and resistance by some NGOs (Chapter 9). Nevertheless, NGOs offer exceptional possibilities for developing accounting reforms that promote development goals and democracy, unlike many state and market organizations.

Microfinance, especially microcredit, is an important and growing activity of many NGOs (although it is not exclusive to them). It raises issues that resonate with those discussed above with respect to furthering broader goals, especially with respect to empowering rural poor women and reducing poverty through self-help. The challenge of developing accountability to marginalized, poorly educated and sometimes illiterate people, and giving them voice and potentially greater power raises exciting possibilities for developing new forms of accounting to once neglected constituencies; for example, developing suitable training in basic book-keeping and budgeting, and using new technology such as the internet and mobile phone banking to ease the time and costs of transactions are exciting issues that have been neglected in accounting research (Chapter 10). Current accountability and control systems for microfinance that rely on monitoring by small groups of potential beneficiaries are controversial. As Chapter 10 argues, they constitute forms of governance that make new groups visible, calculable and economic subjects. Their danger is that they may privatize and shift the costs of control to the individual and community and present poverty as an individual and economic rather than a political issue involving the state, and leave beneficiaries open to uncertainties beyond their control. The issue is not whether microfinance is good or bad but how its administration policies combine sources of social, economic and cultural capital, as the cases in Chapter 5 illustrate. If microfinance organizations pursue financial and growth goals at the cost of the poor, neglect social and political programmes, and have weak accountability to beneficiaries, then accounting systems based on group norms may render groups such as poor marginalized women open to abuse and shame (Chapter 10). At worst microfinance may prove exploitative. The challenge is to devise bottom-up accountability and accounting systems that prevent this and meet the development aspirations of microfinance's originators.

WAYS FORWARD

It is difficult and dangerous to generalize about accounting across LDCs given the differences in local circumstances. Indeed, whether accounting helps development may be as much an article of faith as proven fact (Chapter 4). However, the contributions in this book, whilst not purporting that accounting is the salvation of poverty, infer that it is an essential cog in the development process that warrants more attention from all parties involved. Several means of improving accounting in LDCs recur throughout the chapters, namely improving accounting capacity within LDCs, adopting solutions based on local circumstances and involvement rather than externally imposed solutions based on Western ideologies and practices, strengthening the contribution of LDC states, and improving global coordination.

Accounting Capacity

The need to build accounting capacity in LDCs is generally accepted, especially by external institutions. This is a long-term project: short-term results will be few (Chapter 2). Also, it can figure low on the agenda of domestic politicians, who may lack expertise in or appreciation of accounting issues. Indeed, especially if corruption and political patronage abound, politicians may feel threatened by accounting reforms. However, strategies to reduce corruption are no longer a taboo topic in many LDCs, and greater democratization is pushing this subject centre stage. In that case, the need for accounting reform will increase.

Creating sufficient skilled practitioners with a good knowledge of accountancy and information technology requires better education and training at all levels – from technician to academic (Chapter 14). However, such education and training in universities and technical institutes of LDCs are frequently inadequate. There are shortages of places, poor and outdated premises, technologies and teaching materials, poorly remunerated staff, and little top-class research capacity. When teaching is in the local language, access to superior material in English is stymied and requires expensive translations (Chapter 7).

Given the deficiencies of accounting education it is not surprising that overseas professional bodies have stepped in to fill the gap. This has merits: syllabi are more up to date; professional examination standards are maintained; it removes professional controversies from domestic politics; and the qualifications are internationally recognized. However, it has a cost. Curricula are not adapted to the local terrain, and thus students may study say tax law in the UK rather than that of their own country, and use case studies on Western rather than domestic companies and situations. This compounds the problem of issues pertinent to LDCs being neglected, for example public sector accounting, management accounting, accounting for small businesses and micro-enterprises, and the accountability of organizations when capital markets are weak or non-existent. Also, reliance on overseas associations for giving credentials and training weakens local associations that could better represent local interests nationally and internationally, and provide training and services better tailored to local needs.

Unilateral Western Best Practice versus Local Incrementalism

It is difficult for an LDC to formulate its own accounting institutions, standards and systems. In actuality LDCs are influenced by their historical legacy of colonialism, for example whether they follow Francophone or Anglo-American systems, resident multinational corporations, international accounting institutions, and transnational institutions, often via special conditions in aid agreements (Chapter 8). LDCs' reliance on external agencies has encouraged widespread adoption of Western models. Initially these were based on central state planning and control consistent with the socialist policies of newly liberated regimes after the Second World War. However, they were also endorsed by Western development experts and financial institutions like the World Bank.

The failures of central planning, and the cessation of the 'Cold War' following the collapse of Eastern European communist regimes left fertile ground for market solutions often propagated as conditions of World Bank loan approvals (Chapter 12). However, Western accounting, auditing and corporate governance mechanisms developed in the context of developed economies require efficient capital markets, investor sophistication, and effective second-order institutions such as efficient regulators and judiciary (Chapter 7). This is often not so in most LDCs. For example, the auditing environment of Bangladesh is characterized by a relatively small number of publicly traded companies, many owned by families and with a high ownership concentration, weak incentives for companies to go public, poor perception of the skills of auditors, and an absence of appropriate monitoring and effective second-order institutions (Chapter 7).

The cultural and geographical distance of many accounting advisors has encouraged over-reliance on theoretical universal prescriptions that lack local input and consideration of local needs and constraints, for example unilateral adoption of IMF model income tax and VAT codes (Chapter 14) and 'new public management' (NPM) (Chapter 11). Macro-based analyses, say of corruption and privatization, are useful, but solutions need to be locally adapted and not follow universal global prescriptions, which too often is the case (Chapter 13). For example, macro-economic studies of privatization are useful for determining general performance outcomes (though they often are based on unreliable accounting information), but micro-studies of accounting in action are required to make sound conclusions and policies (Chapter 12). They often reveal sensitive policy options. For example, many privatized enterprises are sold to foreign investors with minimal participation by indigenous investors. However, often locals have insufficient capital, firms are family based, and domestic regulatory structures are inadequate. Political patronage and weak financial markets may encourage financial laxity, a lack of transparency and even irregular financial behaviour, whereas foreign-owned and overseas-listed purchasers may employ superior accounting practices and act as a catalyst and model for local firms (Chapter 12). Whether foreign or local ownership is conducive to improving accounting and accountability requires careful analysis according to domestic circumstances.

The failure to secure domestic inputs and consideration of local circumstances can lead to the apparent presence of sound accounting which on closer inspection is ignored and is merely symbolic and ceremonial (Chapter 4). This is also the case for taxation policies. Many LDCs have been subject to 'tax imperialism' resulting in over-complex and inappropriate policies. At one extremity this has resulted in LDCs adopting sophisticated Western practices based on accounting principles to tax multinational corporations, and at the other extremity poor people such as those engaged in micro-businesses, hawkers and peasants having to render tax returns relying on book-keeping (Chapter 14). Tax systems must be realistic: they should reflect income distribution, taxpayer sophistication, and ease of collection. Over-complex systems encourage manipulation, bribery and corruption. Simpler systems that make tax deductions at source for wage and salary earners, and presumptive taxes based on profits for large corporations and turnover for small businesses may prove more effective, partly because they avoid the need for complex accounting records or complex tax adjustments (Chapter 14).

Similarly, NPM solutions have often been conditions in structural adjustment programmes. These tend to advocate three-year budgets, a concentration on outputs not inputs, balanced budgets, shifts to pro-poor programmes, more computerization to better track expenditure and improve transparency and accountability, and more flexible decentralized planning and control. This is admirable in theory but requires: clear national aims, objectives and strategies; a comprehensive, integrated, technically effective budget system; skilled personnel with ownership and commitment; an effective steering group; sound design; capable project management; and adequate resources. The practicality may be demoralized staff, lower pay, cuts, emigration of the best staff, and ultimately more reliance on consultants. The results can be disappointing, that is, no improved macro-economic balance, no efficiency gains and no greater budget predictability (Chapter 11). Grandiose computerized and integrated public finance management systems and accrual accounting recommended by international consultants unfamiliar with the local situation have often proved too complex (Chapter 2).

Instead of costly and complex systems beyond an LDC's accounting capacity, greater building on existing systems, adapting best practice to local conditions, and establishing that new systems work in practice are required (Chapter 11). Sequenced reforms and getting the basics right may be more important than installing state-of-the-art Western systems; for example, a reliable accounting system is needed before an integrated one. Given that many accounting systems fail because of implementation problems rather than technical design issues, much more needs to be known about what works (and does not) at what stage and under which circumstances (Chapter 2). More detailed understanding of accounting change processes in LDCs is required, and reforms need to be made incrementally in the light of such knowledge gleaned from the field.

Above all, accounting reforms need to keep things simple. For example, harmonizing donors' accounting requirements can diminish the financial complexity facing domestic NGOs and government departments (Chapter 2). Similarly, tax forms and regulations written in straightforward language reinforced with detailed illustrations, websites and one-stop-shop support centres, the abolition of personal tax allowances and instead concentrating on initial tax exemptions for the poor, basing tax on accounting profit calculations to avoid tax adjustments, and flat rather than progressive tax rates can reduce tax evasion and collection costs (Chapter 14). More complicated rules and self-assessment for tax are better restricted to sophisticated, high-income sectors and large corporations.

Strengthened States

Frequently the state is viewed as an impediment to development. It is assumed that poor governance and administration by 'unprincipled' public officials lead to poor growth and poverty. Consequently many external agencies have prioritized strengthening individual and property rights, and market solutions and financial stability over community concerns and state actions. The aim has been to establish states that concentrate on regulation and infrastructure and leave non-state organizations to deliver services (Chapter 4). However, weak states may be a consequence of poverty. If so, then strengthening the state may be a key priority (Chapter 11). Given the shortages of capital and highly skilled personnel, weak markets, and LDCs' exposure to natural or economic disasters, the state may be the most effective means of planning and delivering development, including strengthening markets, and encouraging greater democracy with more civil society involvement. For example, effective taxation relies on transparent, equitable and sound government (Chapter 6). Also, given that an LDC's accounting profession may be weak then state intervention into accounting is required: reliable accounting may need mandatory laws and regulations – not self-regulation. Similarly, if courts provide weak protection then state intervention may be required (Chapter 6).

Getting governments to regard accounting as important and enforce good regulatory practices remains a problem – scandals still abound – but this is changing (Chapter 2, Chapter 7).

External institutions are increasingly recognizing the importance of states. For example, the Paris Declaration in 2005 stated that donors' accounting and funding should strengthen LDC states and not just ring-fence projects (Chapter 2). This reflected concerns that donors' policies had inadvertently weakened states, reduced their accounting capacity, inhibited better public finance management (Chapter 2) and weakened their tax systems. This has rendered LDCs prone to conflict and poor governance and can undermine the legitimacy of the state (Chapter 3). Consequently, more donors have directly placed funds into the treasury of LDCs to further state building and democracy (Chapter 3), but difficulties remain; for example, risk constraints requiring donors to use their own accounting systems have prohibited them from directly placing funds with LDC governments even when the latter have improved their accounting (Chapter 2). However, direct funding should extend beyond propping up the status quo and strengthening states to actively promoting more democracy. For example, to reduce corruption civil society needs mobilization, but locals cannot gain a voice without access to more financial information (Chapter 13).

Strengthening states and improving accounting does not mean unilateral and isolated national action but requires cooperation globally amongst interested parties. For example, it is in the mutual interest of most rich and poor countries to avoid tax competition, coordinate corporate tax arrangements and act against tax havens (Chapter 3). The latter's effect on LDCs is not clear, but pursuit of rent seeking rather than productive behaviour may encourage political corruption on the part of elites. Subjects are less willing to pay taxes if elites do not pay. There is a need for coordinated cross-national information sharing on transfer pricing and cooperation over bilateral air passenger duties with the United Nations arbitrating disputes (Chapter 15). Similarly, Western accounting professions should assist rather than compete with LDC attempts to create their own professional bodies and accounting capacity. As noted, we believe that helping reform accounting in poor countries is a moral and ethical imperative for all involved in accounting, and we hope that our book will help advance this.

NOTES

1. Prior to 2001 it was called the International Accounting Standards Committee (IASC).
2. Before 2001 these were called International Accounting Standards (IASs).

2 Accounting and development: the role of donors from policy to practice
Sara Fyson

INTRODUCTION

The quality of a country's accounting and auditing practices plays a critical role in the achievement of the Millennium Development Goals (MDGs). As a core element of a country's financial and accountability architecture, a strong accounting framework enables governments to manage their resources effectively in order to implement their development policies and deliver public services.

Multilateral and bilateral development agencies are well aware of the importance of strong accounting policies and practices for development and therefore provide significant resources and financing to this area. Interest and support from donor organizations for the strengthening of countries' accounting practices (in both the public and the private sector) are unlikely to diminish, especially in the wake of the financial crisis. It is likely that the functions that accounting provides will be in greater demand than ever given that pressures on national budgets are increasing and additional demands are being made by the public in both developed and developing countries for more transparency and accountability in public resources.

This chapter examines: the reasons for donor support towards improved accounting practices and standards; the ways in which donors support public and private sector accountancy; and both challenges and opportunities in the delivery of aid to this area.

PART I DONOR SUPPORT FOR STRENGTHENED ACCOUNTING PRACTICES: AN INTRODUCTION

Donor Support: Rationale and Practices

The International Federation of Accountants (IFAC) defines accountancy as the 'foundation for the production, audit and dissemination of high quality financial information, a means of promoting transparency and accountability, a key factor in enhancing confidence in the markets, and enhancing the effective management of public resources' (IFAC, 2010).

As this definition suggests, accountancy is critical to donors for a number of reasons, ranging from providing assurance that their funds will be used for the intended purposes, to supporting the growth of SMEs, to providing the enabling environment for broader accountability reforms in the public sectors of the countries they help to finance. This first part outlines in more detail the rationale behind donors' interest and financing in this area.

Donors engage in this area first and foremost *to support an enabling environment for a more vibrant economy and more accountable public sector*. Donors are keen to strengthen accounting systems in the public sector to ensure that government resources (both external and domestic) respond to development priorities – including better health and education systems. When policy makers have access to high-quality financial information, governments (and donors) can better report on and assess the cost–benefits of different government policies and how these can lead to better public service for those in need.

Accounting, as part of a broader financial management environment (including regulations to govern financial information and a strong internal control system), is considered a core element of accountability in the fiduciary process in both the public and the private sector. In particular, better accounting systems contribute to better monetary and fiscal policies, and decisions on allocation of funds across government, as well as more transparency and better reporting for external accountability institutions (such as supreme audit institutions and parliaments). Stronger accounting systems are a critical ingredient for better governance, as they contribute to reducing avenues for corruption in both the public and the private sector. Accounting systems provide reliable financial information that in turn can be used to analyse trends and support better planning and decision-making. The value for money and efficiency of programmes and policies can be assessed and the information provided to citizens and interested stakeholders.

For these reasons, many countries' poverty reduction strategies include plans to strengthen their public financial management (PFM) systems (including their accounting policies and practices). Donors have committed to finance government development strategies, and strengthening PFM is a critical element of their support.

Donor interest in this area is also increasing as new financing mechanisms emerge reflecting new and growing priorities. For instance, the Copenhagen Accord included a pledge to generate US$100 billion a year in climate change financing from both public and private sources by 2020. Managing this new funding source at the country level will be challenging and will require strong PFM (including accounting and financial reporting) systems to ensure the funds are directed towards the implementation of climate-change-related priorities. A functioning accounting and reporting system is one of the prerequisites to a strong PFM system (Vani, 2010).

The second reason why donors engage in this area is one which has always been at the forefront of donor concerns in the provision of aid: *reducing the donor's fiduciary risk in the implementation of the programmes which they fund*. Supporting better accounting practices at country level as part of broader PFM reforms will reduce the likelihood that donor taxpayer money will go astray. In other words, stronger PFM systems ensure that, beyond domestic resources, aid funds are managed and spent efficiently, giving donors the requisite confidence that fiduciary risk is at an acceptable level. Stronger accounting practices as well as a stronger accounting profession will ensure that donors can adequately report back to their own stakeholders (for the multilateral agencies the board members and, for bilateral agencies, national audit institutions, parliamentary committees, civil society in donor countries and so on).

Interest in reducing fiduciary risk is also increasing as donors change the way they deliver aid. Traditionally, donors have focused much of their attention and energy on ensuring countries comply with donors' own accounting practices and demands. For each project a donor is funding, the government official responsible for implementation will be required to comply with the specific donor requirements to provide fiduciary assurance that donor funds are being used as intended. This creates significant challenges, as the government official will have to spend an inordinate amount of time learning, understanding and complying with a multitude of different donor accounting requirements instead of strengthening the country's own systems.

As the international community has come to understand the costs this implies for governments, donors are increasingly being asked to provide their aid 'on budget'. A growing share of aid is therefore being placed on treasury (external financing is disbursed into the main revenue funds of government and managed through government systems). This means that donors are increasingly interested in capacity development in the accountancy profession and PFM more broadly to ensure funds provided for their projects are being spent for the intended purposes – rather than focusing on a specific project they are funding. As the World Bank notes in its Financial Management Sector Strategy, it allows the World Bank to scale up development impact by helping to improve the efficiency of all government expenditures and the management of all resources (not just those of projects). Donors, therefore, are increasingly interested in the quality of a country's PFM systems rather than the ability of government officials to learn and apply the accounting requirements of each donor. This has had implications on donors' funding priorities. For instance, PFM-related lending in the World Bank has increased: from an average of US$127 million per year in the 1990s to more than US$912 million per year in the period 2000 to 2006 (Independent Evaluation Group, 2008).

Supporting government systems also fits within many donors' broader strategies to improve governance and reduce corruption. 'Corruption' is no longer a taboo word in donor policies and strategies. Since the end of the 1990s, donors have not shied away from demanding better governance from countries which they are supporting (this is the case even for multilateral organizations whose articles of agreement request non-interference in a country's internal affairs). The World Bank's Governance and Anticorruption Strategy (GAC) endorsed in 2007, for example, includes the need to develop capable and accountable states and institutions (including in public financial management).

Donors, therefore, have two main objectives in financing stronger accounting systems in the public sector: 'supporting developing partner countries in enhancing their capacity and improving their Financial Management performance, and contributing to providing reasonable financial management assurance that financing provided by the Bank is used for the intended purposes with economy and efficiency' (World Bank, 2010, pp.6–7).

A third important reason for donor support in this area is *the development and growth of the private sector in low income and middle income countries.* Strengthening the private sector in developing countries can significantly contribute to poverty reduction through the creation of employment. Donors support the private sector as part of a country's growth strategy, including through the development of professional accountancy bodies and standard-setting institutions. Donors provide financing to improve enforcement and compliance mechanisms for corporate financial reporting and the development of legal and regulatory frameworks and institutional capacities to support the private sector. Stronger accountancy bodies supporting the regulatory environment contribute to attracting increased foreign direct investment (FDI) and enable the growth and development of the small and medium enterprise (SME) sector. Credible and reliable financial information increases the attractiveness of a country as a potential recipient of FDI. Moreover, high-quality information is also needed to facilitate access to credit and support business growth. All of these reasons lead donors to support the development of a stronger accountancy sector in developing countries.

Finally, another important incentive for donor support to this area is to *honour international commitments to strengthen accounting systems and build stronger international partnerships* for development. In 2005, over 100 countries and donor organizations reached a landmark agreement focusing not only on the quantity of aid but also on the quality of that aid. The Paris Declaration, as it came to be known, set out 56 commitments relating to how donors and developing countries can make more effective use of aid. A number of these commitments focus specifically on the efficiency, integrity and effectiveness with which the state raises, manages and expends its public resources. As part of these commitments, developing countries agreed to strengthen their PFM systems (including all components of a country's budget process from planning to revenue management, control, accounting, reporting, monitoring and auditing) and donors to using these systems to the maximum extent possible.

As outlined above, these commitments were born out of the realization that donors' traditional aid delivery mechanisms might have perverse effects. To ensure that the resources that donors provided to developing countries were used as intended, they tended to ring-fence their projects from a country's perceived weak public financial management systems. In doing so, they inadvertently weakened the systems further, creating a vicious cycle that undermined not only government systems but the longer-term sustainability of the projects they were funding. The commitments in the Paris Declaration were reached in a bid to reduce these perverse effects.

The rationale for the use of country PFM (including accounting) as outlined in the Paris Declaration included:

- increasing alignment to government priorities and so enhancing government ownership over reform programmes, and the sustainability and long-term effectiveness of these programmes;
- supporting sound budgeting and financial management of all resources (not only aid) to ensure the efficiency with which domestic resources are allocated and are accounted for;
- enhancing the sustainability of results beyond those monitored by parallel donor implementation units (which tend to undermine government systems);
- strengthening human resources (e.g. the accounting profession) for development, as donor-specific requirements can place overwhelming demands on government officials.
- facilitating harmonized practices amongst donors, as they will no longer impose different system requirements that risk overwhelming the capacity of the country they are funding (OECD, 2009).

Importantly, these commitments were monitored (donor by donor, and country by country) and communicated to donor and government publics, thereby incentivizing donors and developing countries to meet their agreed targets. The international community continued to press for progress in the strengthening and using of country systems (including accounting systems) and renewed their commitments in both 2008 and 2011 in the endorsement of the Busan Partnership on Effective Development Cooperation (see Box 2.1). These commitments have come to be accepted as one of the cornerstones of development policy as evidenced by the G20 pronouncements (Toronto, July 2010) amongst others.

BOX 2.1   THE PARIS DECLARATION (2005), ACCRA AGENDA FOR ACTION (2008) AND BUSAN PARTNERSHIP ON EFFECTIVE DEVELOPMENT COOPERATION (2011): COMMITMENTS ON THE USE OF COUNTRY SYSTEMS

The Paris Declaration (2005) and the Accra Agenda for Action (2008) set out agreements on the use of country public finance systems which were endorsed by developing countries and by donors.

In Paris (2005), donors committed to use country systems to the maximum extent possible and rely to the maximum extent possible on transparent partner government budget and accounting mechanisms. Developing countries, in turn, committed to exercise leadership over their PFM management reform process, to publish timely, transparent and reliable reporting on budget execution, and to ensure that national systems were effective, accountable and transparent. In Accra in 2008, this commitment was reaffirmed and strengthened as donors agreed to use country systems as the first option for aid programmes and ensure that 50 per cent or more of government-to-government assistance flowed through country fiduciary systems.

In 2011, based on evidence that both donors and developing countries had not reached the targets set in 2005, donors, developing country representatives (from the executive and legislative arms of government) and civil society organizations called for renewed action in strengthening and using country systems. Donors, developing countries, and civil society, for example, endorsed the Manila Consensus on Public Financial Management in June 2011, calling on:

- developing countries to demonstrate their political commitment to strengthening PFM through a credible reform programme, to ensure independent and well-resourced oversight institutions, and to increase transparency for better accountability to the public including through CSOs for all public resources, not only aid;
- donors to honour their political commitment, in coordination with developing countries, to support capacity development in PFM and domestic revenue mobilization and progressively increase their use of components of PFM systems for all aid modalities in order to contribute to achieving poverty alleviation;
- both to recognize the opportunity for climate change finance to utilize country systems to the extent possible;

- donors to harmonize fiduciary and other risk assessments based on existing PFM assessment tools;
- both to better define and monitor the outcomes of PFM reform programmes and PFM system use by development partners and to communicate to their respective publics these benefits for sustainable development outcomes;
- both to review the monitoring frameworks on the strengthening and use of country systems at country level, including capturing partial use of country systems, and results from diagnostics which were not available at the time of the Paris Declaration (namely, the Public Expenditure and Financial Accountability – PEFA – programme).

The agreement in Manila helped to shape some of the related commitments in the 2011 Busan Partnership on Effective Development Cooperation, which marked a turning point in the way in which international development cooperation is governed. This agreement highlighted the growing consensus that what matters is the effectiveness of all development resources, including but not limited to aid in the achievement of sustainable development results. It also included a number of commitments on the use of country systems:

The use and strengthening of developing countries' systems remains central to our efforts to build effective institutions. We will build on our respective commitments set out in the Paris Declaration and Accra Agenda for Action to:

a) Use country systems as the default approach for development co-operation in support of activities managed by the public sector, working with and respecting the governance structures of both the provider of development co-operation and the developing country.

b) Assess jointly country systems using mutually agreed diagnostic tools . . . Based on the results of these assessments, providers of development co-operation will decide on the extent to which they can use country systems. Where the full use of country systems is not possible, the provider of development co-operation will state the reasons for non-use . . . The use and strengthening of country systems should be placed within the overall context of national capacity development for sustainable outcomes. (para. 19)

Focus, at the country level, on establishing transparent public financial management (and aid information management systems), and strengthen the capacities of all relevant stakeholders to make better use of this information. (para. 23)

Donors are also called upon to honour international commitments to strengthen private sector accounting systems. At the G20 summit in 2009 in London, for example, the World Bank highlighted the development of the accounting profession as a critical component of financial stability. In the wake of the financial crisis, in particular, governments have called for increased globally consistent high-quality financial reporting. At the G20 summit in Toronto (July 2010), governments re-emphasized the importance of achieving a single set of high-quality improved global accounting standards and encouraged the international accounting standards board to improve the involvement of stakeholders, including outreach to emerging market economies. G20 governments also committed to improving access to financial services for the poor and to increasing financing available to small and medium-sized enterprises (SMEs) in developing countries.

Donor Support: What Does It Look Like?

Donor support to the accounting sector takes a number of forms (from technical assistance to financing capacity building and training programmes, to supporting country and regional accountancy bodies and the development of automated accounting systems). The following outlines briefly the different ways in which donors assist strengthened accounting practices in developing countries.

Most donor resources in this area are spent on capacity building projects to ensure a better enabling environment for stronger accounting systems and practices (in both the public and the private sector). Projects often include the development of a national curriculum for accounting and strengthening institutional capacity in the public and private sectors. For example, the World Bank is supporting a number of capacity building programmes in Africa. In Benin, funds are provided to strengthen the capacity of the members of the professional accountancy body and improve the national curriculum used by accounting and business schools to help increase, in the medium term, the number of qualified accountants. In The Gambia, funding is provided to train teachers and lecturers at local institutions and develop appropriate accounting and financial management curricula for local institutions. In the case of Lesotho, resources are being provided to develop an accountancy qualification system to qualify members for the country's PFM requirements. Donors provide support also to ministries of finance by providing advisory services to design and implement government accounting laws.

Donors also support regional accountancy bodies with technical assistance and funding. For instance, the Swedish Development Agency (SIDA) and the World Bank provide funding to the East and Southern African Association of Accountants General (ESAAG), a regional organization which aims to facilitate the exchange of information between accountants general to produce financial statements according to international standards, support the improvement of democratic processes through increased transparency and accountability, and strengthen the government accounting profession.

Another significant contribution to the development of accounting policies is assistance with the assessment of a country's accounting systems, practices and regulations. The ROSC A&A review, for example, evaluates a country's accounting and auditing standards and practices, using the International Financial Reporting Standards (IFRS) and International Standards on Auditing (ISA) as a basis. Beyond the application of standards, the ROSC also examines the strengths and weaknesses of the institutional framework underpinning accounting and auditing practices. Following the completion of the diagnostic, the country representatives assisted by donor staff develop an action plan for any needed reform and development. Such a diagnostic is expected to provide the foundation of capacity building efforts to strengthen financial reporting. So far, 100 ROSC A&A reviews have been completed (with 79 made public). The ROSC A&A is designed to be a collaborative effort between government representatives and donor staff to support capacity development in a sustainable manner. Similar collaborations have emerged in the field of audit, with INTOSAI (the professional organization of supreme audit institutions – SAIs – in countries that belong to the United Nations or its specialist agencies) signing a memorandum of understanding (MOU) in 2009 with 15 donor multilateral and national agencies. The MOU brings together donors that currently provide support in a fragmented manner to SAIs under a common approach to strengthening capacity in developing countries. It is also expected to facilitate donor funding and harmonize donor requirements to reduce transaction costs for developing countries.[1]

As a result of the international engagements outlined above, donors are striving to ensure that their support for this sector is harmonized, for instance with the Financial Sector Reform and Strengthening (FIRST) Initiative, which is a multi-donor grant facility providing technical assistance for financial sector strengthening. It was launched in 2002 by a number of donors (including CIDA, DFID, IMF, SECO, SIDA and the World Bank). FIRST has undertaken a number of capacity building programmes, such as the establishment of an accounting oversight board in Botswana.

Donors also provide support to international accountancy bodies that assist with the development of accountancy standards and capacity development programmes in developing countries. For example, donors provide funding and assistance to both regional and global accountancy bodies. A number of donors provide support to IFAC, the global organization which provides international standards and supports the development of accountancy bodies across the world.

Standards issued by this body are directly relevant to donor assistance. For example, the International Public Sector Accounting Standards Board (part of IFAC) issued an exposure draft (ED) in 2007 to strengthen the disclosure of financial information about external assistance received by governments in developing countries. The exposure draft, ED32, is expected to increase the transparency of financial statements of recipients and contribute to greater accountability[2]. The standard is designed to reduce the multiplicity of reporting practices that developing countries receiving aid face. Donors play a significant part in the successful compliance with the disclosure requirements, as reporting entities need access to information required to report on all sources of official assistance, including those funds that have not passed through the country's own accounting systems.

IFAC has requested further support from donors to increase the awareness of the value of audit and professional accountancy services, to reduce professional accountancy organization internal weaknesses, and to improve the capacity of these organizations to provide vital professional activities to advance accountancy reform. At the High Level Forum on Aid Effectiveness in Busan (2011), IFAC and 10 donor agencies signed a Memorandum of Understanding to Strengthen Accountancy and Improve Collaboration in order to improve the coherence of donor responses to this area and strengthen the capacity of professional accountancy organizations in developing countries.

Bilateral donors also provide funding to national accountancy bodies. For example, the UK's Department for International Development signed a strategic agreement with the Chartered Institute for Professional and Financial Accountability (CIPFA) in mid-2003 in order to raise the profile of international development issues to a broader audience.

This part has outlined the reasons and ways in which donors support the accountancy profession and accounting systems in developing countries. It has also highlighted international commitments and agreements that donors have endorsed in order to strengthen accounting in developing countries. How far have these commitments been upheld and what are the main challenges and opportunities for donor support to this area in practice?

PART II CHALLENGES AND LESSONS LEARNED FROM DONOR SUPPORT

Lack of Capacity and Awareness of the Importance of Strengthening Accounting

As part of international agreements such as the Paris Declaration on Aid Effectiveness, countries have committed to strengthening their accounting systems and practices. However, despite significant resources being spent in this area, weaknesses in countries' accounting systems remain an important challenge.

The lessons from diagnostic assessments undertaken by donors (World Bank, 2004) point to a number of reasons for continuing weaknesses in countries' accounting systems and practices.

Firstly, governments have focused much of their attention on adopting legislation mandating or allowing the use of international standards. The private sector has focused its attention on improving the skills of individuals and firms to international standards. Although this is a positive development, 'governments, for the most part, have not addressed the need to put in place proper incentives to ensure that this competence is actually applied in practice' (World Bank, 2004). Accounting scandals in both developed and developing countries show that having a good regulatory framework is a necessary but not a sufficient condition for strong accounting practice.

The second lesson is that many international accounting and auditing standards implicitly assume the existence of legal, institutional and policy conditions ('preconditions'), which are often undeveloped or absent in many countries. In such cases the assumption of their existence provides a false sense of security to government and to donors. The standards may well be adopted, but they are not implemented in practice.

Third, the lack of human and financial resources expended in this area continues to be a significant impediment to the implementation of international standards. This is compounded by the lack of awareness of the value of audit and professional accountancy services by governments. There are very few clear legislative frameworks which support government recognition of accountancy organizations, the legal establishment of a system for ensuring professional competence and capability, and effective independent oversight of the profession (IFAC, 2010).

Moreover, professional accountancy organizations in many cases are characterized by weak internal governance structures. They provide little or no guidance to enable professional activities to advance accountancy reform. In addition, in a number of countries there are very few certified accountants, because of the lack of accountancy bodies, and where these exist they may not have strong links to public sector bodies.

As a result of continuing weakness in capacity in the accountancy sector, donors remain cautious in the use of government accounting systems. Donors are particularly concerned at the ability of the government accounting system to deliver reliable and timely expenditure reports. Case studies undertaken by the Collaborative Africa Budget Reform Initiative (CABRI) show that large backlogs in closing government accounts and delays in reporting remain in many countries (CABRI, 2008).

Inadequate Aid Delivery Mechanisms

Beyond weaknesses in the systems and practices themselves, challenges continue to arise from the way donors deliver their support to this sector. The need for donors to account to their own publics in donor countries has at times led to detrimental effects on the accountancy profession in the countries. As outlined above, each donor will traditionally request that their accounting procedures are followed and financial reports undertaken for each of their projects. This leads to significantly higher transaction costs for government officials, who are faced with often conflicting accounting requirements, bureaucratic delays and significant time spent reporting to donors rather than to their own publics. In Tanzania, for instance, in the Morogoro District, officials spend 25 working days each quarter writing reports for donors instead of focusing on developing stronger national accountability structures to ensure more effective management of health systems and the planning and distribution of medical supplies (World Health Organization, 2007).

Importantly, donor incentives to show quick results and attribution for their dollar at home mean that the longer-term challenges of PFM capacity building might be overlooked. Typically, PFM reform and strengthening of the accountancy profession could take 10 to 15 years – much longer than the donor project or programming cycle. In addition, during a financial crisis, it is much more attractive for donors to highlight their support to building schools or hospitals rather than strengthening PFM systems (even if the latter are a necessary element of the former).

As outlined above, the commitments on country systems are expected to address some of these challenges. However, since 2005, results from the Paris Declaration monitoring surveys (undertaken in 2006, 2008 and 2011) show that donors have not significantly increased their use of country public financial management systems (see Figure 2.1). The 2010 target of ensuring that 85 per cent of aid flows for the government sector were captured in developing country government budgets was not met. Progress has been challenging also on putting aid on budget (including flowing through countries' accounting systems): 44 per cent of aid flows were recorded in governments' budgets in 2005, whereas by 2010 this figure was 46 per cent for those countries participating in both surveys – well below the target of 85 per cent.

The results also show that there is not always a correlation between the strengthening of a country's system and its use by donors (OECD-DAC, 2011). In fact, in some cases the opposite is true: in Ghana in 2008 the quality of the PFM system increased, but donors reduced the percentage of aid using country systems from 61 to 51 per cent (OECD-DAC, 2008).

Clearly other factors are at play in the decisions to set up parallel accounts rather than use government accounting systems (OECD, 2009). These include:

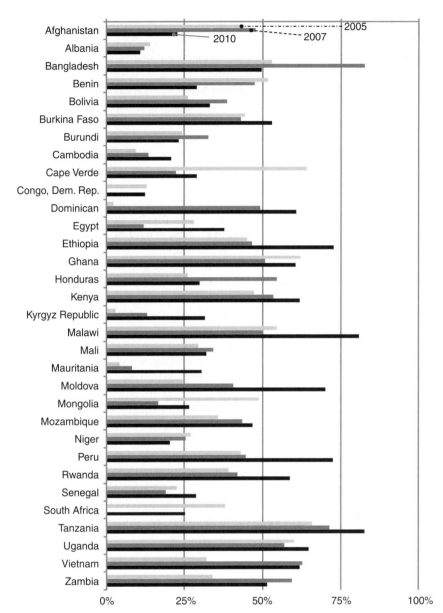

% of ODA for the government sector using partner country PFM systems
(indicator 5a)

Note: Aid using country PFM systems (percentage of total aid disbursed by donors for the government sector), 32 countries, 2005–10.

Source: OECD-DAC (2011).

Figure 2.1   Progress and setbacks in the use of country public financial management systems

- Donor legal frameworks and external accountability relations may have an impact on the donor's appetite for risk and the way in which risks are set against expected benefits (for example, if the donor's national audit institution has strong opinions on the risks and benefits of budget support).
- Donor internal incentives often preclude donor staff from taking risks in the use of a country's accounting systems rather than their own (their performance is judged on their ability to prove that resources are used as intended).
- Differences between priorities at headquarter level and field level may lead to different priorities in decisions to use country systems. In particular, there may be different levels of knowledge about country accounting systems and opportunities to use them.
- Donors are also influenced by their portfolio at the country level: donors with a focus on infrastructure, for example, will prefer project aid (and often use of their own accounting systems more readily than those providing health sector support).

The Paris Declaration survey results also show that, when disaggregating the components of a country's PFM system, donors prefer to use a country's budget execution systems more than its financial reporting or auditing systems. In 2008, in the 55 countries surveyed, 48 per cent of aid flowed through the budget execution systems, 44 per cent through financial reporting, and 43 per cent through the auditing systems. Case studies have shown that in many countries less than half of all aid is recorded and accounted for in the government's accounting system and in line with the government's classification system.[3]

The degree to which donors will use government accounting systems also depends on their choice of aid modality (whether they provide aid directly into a country's budget or whether they fund specific projects). Budget support inherently uses a government's accounting system. As a direct consequence, donors are more interested in strengthening the entire PFM system. However, for project aid, this is not always the case and may also reflect different legal traditions in the country receiving aid. In Ghana, for instance, project funds (credits and grants) are disbursed either directly by the donor or through separate bank accounts, which are not linked to the consolidated fund. In practice, less than 35 per cent of external finance (that is, only budget support) uses the treasury and other national procedures. Donors providing project support often use their own procedures (CABRI, 2008). In Uganda, although debt relief and budget support in all its forms use government accounting systems in full, project expenditures do not use the government's accounting systems. At the same time, many projects submit their accounts for audit late or use different financial years, which complicates the accounting cycle, and prevents spending agencies preparing consolidated project accounts for a given financial year. This means that most spending agencies' annual accounts prepared for audit do not cover project aid (CABRI, 2008).

Beyond decisions to use government accounting systems, development experience has shown that the ways in which donors provide technical assistance can also play a part in the success (or not) of improving accounting in developing countries. For example, it has often been noted that there is a danger of focusing on training (one-off workshops, seminars and so on) without looking at the broader systemic challenges. Technical assistance disconnected from the broader government goals and programmes is unlikely to have sustainable results on institutional capacity. Similarly, technical assistance which promotes 'best practice' unsuited to the country's political, social and institutional context will not always lead to the desired results.

The Pitfalls of Promoting 'Best Practice'

Donors play a significant part in knowledge sharing and imparting 'best practices' to developing countries. In the domain of accounting, accountancy bodies (often in part or wholly funded by donors) are an important vehicle for the transmission of good or 'best' practice.

Independent standards setting bodies such as IFAC provide guidance and direction for the reform of accounting practice through the establishment of standards: 'The individual standards, when taken comprehensively, can form a framework for financial sector improvement and point reformers in the direction of international best practice' (IFAC, 2010, p. 9). However, there are disagreements between practitioners and in academia over the transferability of best practice as defined in the OECD context and in developing countries. Research has shown that, although there are strong international standards (promulgated by bodies such as IFAC, with international public sector accounting standards – IPSAS – including for both cash and accruals), there can be a significant gap between the 'technical expertise of those who define standards and that existing in country and regional bodies' (CIPFA, 2010a, p. 30). In many cases, it is argued that national-level capabilities are too weak to develop and follow transitional paths towards standards adoption and implementation. CIPFA warns that 'these relative imbalances need to inform donors' expectations' (CIPFA, 2010a, p. 30).

Experience of PFM reforms has shown that translating approaches adopted in OECD countries has not always led to sustainable reforms in the public sector in developing countries. For example, research undertaken on the impact of integrated financial management systems (IFMS) points to significant challenges in the adoption of private sector accounting software for the public sector in developing countries (Fyson, 2009; Hove and Wynne, 2010). IFMS refers to computerized budgeting, accounting and payment operations, which most often include introducing a single IT financial system for the whole of government. Its expected benefits include integration of budget and budget execution data, thereby improving financial control, improved planning for cash, provision of adequate management reporting and improvement of data quality, as well as preparation of financial statements and reports (Hashim and Allan, 2001, cited in Hove and Wynne, 2010). Despite these perceived benefits, there are significant challenges. Research in 2003 showed that a quarter of all the IFMS-related projects were considered unsustainable, 69 per cent likely to be sustainable and only 6 per cent highly likely (Dorotinsky, 2003). One of the main reasons for this failure was the overly complex nature of these reforms, which were unsuited to the environment they were being introduced to. The experience in Ethiopia and Tanzania, for instance, showed that 'both involved extensive customization to meet user requirements. They both put into question the need for "high end" commercial off-the-shelf systems which are expensive, complex, difficult to customize and have features which have little or no use of the current or foreseeable needs of a government' (Peterson, 2007, p. 40). The transfer of such knowledge has also taken place through the use of international consultants, who may not be versed in the political, social and institutional realities of the countries in which they are introducing such

BOX 2.2   TO USE ACCRUAL OR NOT TO USE ACCRUAL?
THE ROLE OF DONORS IN REACHING DECISIONS
ON ACCOUNTING STANDARDS

Donors have a strong role to play in the transfer of good practices and knowledge sharing to developing countries. These can be transferred through technical assistance, donor-funded consultants, conditionality agreements and training programmes. One of the areas in accounting which has received significant attention with respect to knowledge transfer from the OECD to developing countries is the introduction of full accrual accounting.

Accrual accounting is expected more reliably to report government's true financial position, since under a cash basis of accounting future costs are removed from the budget, as payments and receipts are pushed back to the previous year. Accrual accounting on the other hand inhibits this by requiring that revenues are recorded when earned (rather than received) and expenditures when liability is incurred (rather than when payment is made).[4] The standard setting body IFAC argues that accrual accounting reveals the true cost of implementing government activities and as a result agencies 'can consider the cost consequences of particular policy objectives and the costs of alternative mechanisms for meeting those objectives' (IFAC, 2003, p. 9). Many public sector bodies in OECD countries have transformed their accounting basis to reflect accrual accounting (Olson, Humphrey and Guthrie, 2001). The 'accruals revolution' is notable given the rapidity with which it spread across OECD countries over a period of 10 years (Blöndal, 2003).

Donors have funded a number of significant accounting reforms in developing countries which include the introduction of accrual accounting. The widely used and recognized IMF *Government Finance Statistics Manual*, for instance, notes that: 'many countries will need to revise their underlying accounting systems to reflect the accrual accounting principles and revised classifications of the GFS system'.[5] Public financial reforms are often designed with a view to introducing accrual as the basis for accounting. In many countries, the continuation of donor funding to the broader public financial reform programmes is predicated on the move towards accrual (as part of action plans, conditionality commitments and technical assistance agreements).

Although it is heralded by a number of countries as best practice, there have been disagreements in the literature and donor guidance on the extent to which accrual should be introduced in the context of developing countries, and importantly to which degree and in what sequence. In the past decade, guidance from donor agencies has often suggested that the introduction of accrual is an 'inevitable' trend that is both 'unstoppable and inexorable'[6]. Others have argued, however, that the introduction of accrual should not be 'inevitable'. On the contrary, it should only be introduced once basic requirements have been met. In his often cited article entitled 'Why most developing countries should not try New Zealand's reforms', Schick (1998) noted that, before ' best practices' from OECD countries were introduced, a strong budget with cash controls needed to be in place alongside reliable accounting and financial reporting and the capacity to undertake compliance audits. Practice in both OECD and non-OECD countries shows the need to take a carefully sequenced approach to the introduction of accrual, especially given the significant resources (both financial and human) needed to introduce accrual.

Clearly, introducing accrual accounting can also be undertaken as a continuum and, as some have argued, 'what appears to be lost in some of these arguments is that cash and accrual accounting are not mutually exclusive concepts, but rather opposite ends of a spectrum' (Pretorius and Pretorius, 2009, p. 27). Evidence shows that it is not just a technical exercise, but must be linked with broader public sector reforms, and there need to be better sequencing in the implementation, greater accountancy skills and appropriate IT systems, and importantly better communication with parliamentarians, the media and civil society to enable stronger domestic accountability for results.

complex systems (Fyson, 2009). Another area, often discussed in the academic and practitioners' literatures, is the role of accrual accounting and its relevance for the developing country context (Box 2.2).

Accountancy bodies have called for increased awareness in the development community of the risks of over-reliance on organizations that were set up to create and champion standards for a primarily private sector accountancy profession (CIPFA, 2010a, p. 36). As they note, this is especially important in countries with weak systems and where the private sector itself remains fragile.

Donors, and donor-funded consultants, therefore, have a strong role to play both in transferring best practice and in ensuring that it is relevant to the context in which it is being implemented.

Ignoring the Political

Beyond the challenges related to the mechanisms of aid delivery and of knowledge transfer, another main challenge relates to the political nature of accountancy reform in the public sector. Experience has shown that focusing on the technical aspects of accountancy and not on how these may affect political imperatives may reduce the ability of these reforms to have a sustainable impact. In particular, without an understanding of the political dimension, it is difficult to answer the question of why some reform tools are accepted and others are not. As one practitioner noted, 'Since accrual accounting is so simple why do so many countries resist it and take forever to get it right?'[7]

Although reforms and reform components are highly technical, they also have political implications in OECD countries as well as developing countries. For example, commentators have argued that the decision to implement accrual is not merely a 'technical' decision but implies a normative (and so ultimately a political) choice (Ellwood and Wynne, 2003; Carlin, 2005; Newberry and Pallot, 2005). Accrual accounting, they argue, serves as a legitimization device for outsourcing government activities out to the private sector rather than a purely technical reform effort. In particular, Carlin (2005, 2006) shows that, in Australia (the State of Victoria), the introduction of accrual accounting led to an *upwards bias* to the assessed total cost function of government departments. Clearly, this has political implications, and when donors ignore this in the context of developing countries the results of the reform are in jeopardy.

When donors take into consideration both personal and institutional political facets of reform, they can have a positive impact on the sustainability of reform. For example, in Lesotho, the United Kingdom's development agency (DFID) financed a programme of accountancy professionalization. CIPFA (the implementer of this programme) noted that there were a number of political challenges but these were addressed as a result of the necessary commitment and leadership from key stakeholders, significantly from the Accountant General, the Auditor General and the Ministry of Finance more generally (CIPFA, 2010b).

In another example, in Ghana, the implementation of an integrated financial management system was a failure, in part because of the unfavourable political environment and the unwillingness of donors to recognize the political implications. Senior figures in the administration perceived the reform as a merely technical project foisted on government by donors; and there was little understanding of the political relevance of the reform in terms of improving transparency and accountability for the public sector. Political patronage of private business increased the possibility of corruption, and the high staff turnover in the 2000 election derailed the process (Fyson, 2009).

Another challenge which donors have faced in accountancy reform relates to the consequences of focusing attention (and funding) primarily on the ministry of finance in discussions around strengthening accounting systems. However, spending agencies are critical in the delivery of public service programmes. Case studies have shown that there is a strong need to professionalize accounting staff in the ministries, departments and agencies to ensure buy-in in the implementation of their programmes (CIPFA, 2010a).

Finally, it is important also not to lose sight of the political economy of donors having an impact on choices in the way aid is delivered to this sector. A donor national audit institution may demand accountability for each taxpayer's dollar (irrespective of the potential dangers of undermining the developmental goals), or elections in donor countries may lead to changes in policies (for instance, placing more emphasis on fiduciary risk in project delivery). These have an impact upon the view the donors will take on the importance of accountancy (including whether they will fund the strengthening of developing accounting systems and whether they will see the benefits of using those systems). Ultimately, donors need to ensure that support to accountancy is part of a broader strategy to assist in strengthening the broader PFM system. Accounting and reporting functions cannot be taken in isolation and be abstracted from the political dimensions in which they operate.

PART III   OPPORTUNITIES FOR STRONGER ACCOUNTANCY IN POLICY AND IN PRACTICE

More Coherent Donor Approaches to Supporting Professional Accounting Organizations

Despite the challenges outlined above, there has been progress in the way donors support accountancy in practice. The examples cited above show the complexity of the accounting architecture in developing countries. Donors can and do play a role in helping countries to avoid duplication and gaps and are working to ensure they reduce overloads of differing requirements placed on governments with limited capability (CIPFA, 2010a, p. 35).

Countries have increasingly become aware of the importance of accountancy to their economic growth and to the accountability and efficiency of their public sectors. Coupled with increased leadership over the delivery of aid in their country, there has been progress in the coordination and alignment of donor support. For example, Tanzania has ensured that even when donors do not provide their aid directly through a country's budget it will still be recorded in the government's accounting system. The government agreed with donors that funds not on treasury (for example, project aid) are on account, and the same mechanism can incorporate aid-in-kind into the accounts (CABRI, 2008).

In another example, the Mozambique government, together with its aid partners, has developed a way of merging all financial accounts into a single treasury account and thereby bringing all available sources of funding (including aid) under the government's integrated budget and PFM system. The government has agreed with donors (those belonging to the Programme Aid Partners group) that they will disburse at least 60 per cent of their development assistance to the government through the single treasury account. It also captures funds from the larger sector (for example, health, education and agriculture) common funds. As outlined in the case study undertaken by CABRI:

> The establishment of the single treasury account has been instrumental in the process of putting aid on budget in Mozambique and bringing its associated PFM benefits. Its creation directly addresses one of the main causes behind the phenomenon of off budgets: the lack of transparency within the treasury system, which deters donors from using local public financial management systems. At the same time it is perhaps one of the most visible manifestations of the PFM benefits brought by aid capture on treasury, given the immediate benefits the government/ treasury draws from having the number of accounts it uses for its treasury operations reduced to one. (Warren-Rodríguez, 2007)

The most important developments are those that take place at the country level such as those described above. However, donor policies are also important, as they allow donor field office staff to facilitate such progress and at the very least not undermine government leadership in strengthening its accountancy practices (by, for instance, ring-fencing projects and setting up parallel implementation units). In the Accra Agenda for Action, donors committed to provide staff guidance on how country systems can be used and to ensure that internal incentives encourage their use. There is evidence that donors are reviewing their internal procedures to accommodate increased use of country accounting systems (OECD-DAC, forthcoming).

Supporting the Accounting Profession and Regional Organizations

When it comes to the accounting profession itself, efforts are under way within international networks such as the Task Force on Public Financial Management[8] to provide more coordinated support (for both the private and the public sector) in developing countries (IFAC, 2010). A number of donors are keen to engage in these networks to strengthen harmonization at country level, to disseminate innovative and good practices and to share knowledge across countries and across donors on what works and what does not.

The Paris Declaration calls on donors to provide capacity development support that is both relevant and in direct response to developing country requests. As a result, donors as well as accountancy bodies have increasingly focused their attention on ensuring standards and practices are relevant to a developing country context. In response to criticism of capacity development programmes that were unaligned with the countries' needs, professional accountancy bodies have entered into twinning arrangements with developing country institutions. This has led to a more equal partnership around peer-to-peer and knowledge sharing arrangements. For example, the Society of Certified Accountants and Auditors of Kosovo entered into a twinning arrangement with the Royal Dutch Institute of Accountancy (NIVRA) in 2007. This led to exposure to different systems, organizations, technical expertise and policy advice through visits by NIVRA to Kosovo. NIVRA also provided support to Kosovo in terms of communicating to donors the need for financial support in this area as well as demanding increased donor coordination. The support also increased the legitimacy of the institution in Kosovo domestically, thereby improving communication and understanding around the need for stronger accountancy institutions as an element of good economic governance in Kosovo.

Donors are increasingly supporting regional organizations in their capacity to provide technical assistance (IFAC, 2010). The strength and number of regional organizations are increasing. These include bodies such as the Confederation of Asian and Pacific Accountants (CAPA), the South Asian Federation of Accountants (SAFA), the Fédération des Experts Comptables Européens (FEE), the Federation of Mediterranean Certified Accountants, the Eastern Central and Southern African Federation of Accountants (ECSAFA), the Association of Accountancy Bodies in West Africa (ABWA), the Gulf Cooperation Council Accounting and Auditing Organization (GCCAAO) and the Accounting and Auditing Organization for Islamic Financial Institutions (AAOIFI).

Regional organizations are also assisting governments, including the Association of Government Accounts Organizations of Asia (AGAOA), the Federation of Accountants-General and Auditors-General of West Africa (FAAGWA) and the East and Southern African Association of Accountants General (ESAAG). They provide significant support to accountants general through training, research and knowledge sharing. They also assist in raising awareness of the importance of accountancy, the need for a formal profession and the economic and social benefits which this can bring.

CONCLUSION

A strong accounting system as part of a broader financial management system can deliver reliable, credible and legitimate financial information, which in turn increases the transparency and accountability of the public sector. Donors are committed to strengthening accounting systems and practices in developing countries – for both developmental and fiduciary reasons. As outlined above, donors influence the funding available for this sector, the ways in which the sector is supported and importantly the ideas of good practice that are shared with developing countries.

This chapter has also shown that the ways in which donors deliver the aid to this sector have an impact upon the sustainability of any reform efforts to strengthen accounting policies and practices. International engagements endorsed by donors and developing countries have underlined the need to ensure donors use a country's accounting system to the maximum extent possible (including in the provision of project aid). Experience as highlighted above shows that, when donors do not include their aid in government accounts, the broader accountability of government is in jeopardy, as these accounts will not be able to be checked by the government court of auditors (as is the case in Burkina Faso, for instance; CABRI, 2008).

Guidelines for donor and developing countries have been produced as a result of international partnerships to strengthen public financial management in developing countries. These guidelines are based on lessons learned from experience and have been endorsed by both developing and donor countries. They include:

a. *Ensuring country leadership and ownership in the decision to support accountancy bodies.* Donors cannot always change incentives in the public sector of developing countries; rather they should be facilitating the implementation of government-led and -designed capacity development goals. Governments must take the lead in policies to strengthen accounting practices in both the public and the private sector. This includes active engagement of the government in the assessment process.

b. *Design and sequencing needs to fit specific country circumstances.* As outlined above, transplanting systems from other countries does not always work and in fact may be doing more harm than good, as expensive systems are put in place but may end up undermining capacity rather than building it.

c. *Institutional, organizational and individual capacity development needs to be taken into account.* Capacity development is not only a transfer of skills but should be viewed from a holistic or systemic perspective. Technical solutions need to be viewed in the context of political and social realities. This includes making sure capacity development goes beyond the ministry of finance and includes sectoral ministries and local authorities.

d. *Supporting a whole system approach.* The effectiveness that strengthening the accountancy profession may have will be limited unless it is linked to the broader PFM reform plans. As CIPFA notes: 'The quality of PFM depends on how well the individual organizations work, the quality of inputs provided to the system, the feedback and control mechanisms that ensure a focus on objectives, and on how well the system functions as a whole' (2010a, p. 14).

e. *The importance of communication.* Developing countries and donors need to work to strengthen the demand for stronger accounting systems, including linkages with external accountability institutions (supreme audit, public accounts committees, private sector and civil society).

These lessons are well known and remain a critical component of donor engagements at the international level. However, as outlined in this chapter, challenges remain when it comes to implementation.

Donors and developing countries were once again asked to account to the international community for how they support public finance systems at the Fourth High

Level Forum on Aid Effectiveness in Korea in 2011, including progress in strengthening accounting systems and practices. It is hoped that their response in the years to come will provide a renewed platform for international and donor dialogue and engagements on building stronger economic governance through improved accounting systems and practices.

NOTES

The opinions expressed and arguments employed in this chapter are the sole responsibility of the author and do not necessarily reflect the official views of the OECD, or of the governments of any OECD member countries or their academic institutions.

1. http://www.intosai.org/blueline/upload/intosaidonormouunterschriftene.pdf
2. Further to requests for a generally accepted accounting standard for reporting external assistance when the cash basis of financial reporting is adopted, IPSASB in 2005 issued ED 24, 'Financial reporting under the cash basis of accounting: disclosure requirements for recipients of external assistance'. However, constituents expressed some concern about the practicality of a number of proposals, outlining that the data was not available and costs of compliance would be too high. As a result, following a broad consultative process, the IPSASB developed ED 32.
3. Aid is not fully 'on accounting' if donors demand special additional financial reports (CABRI, 2008).
4. Accrual accounting is a method of accounting which records expenditures as they are incurred and income earned during the accounting period. Cash accounting on the other hand records cash payments and cash receipts as they occur during an accounting period. Accrual records transactions as they occur and distinguishes expenditure which provides economic benefits in the short term from those that will benefit the agency and community well into the future (Mellor, 1997, p. 53). The use of accrual is therefore expected to produce a 'full financial picture'.
5. IMF, *Government Finance Statistics Manual 2001* (*GFSM 2001*), Washington, DC, 1.32.
6. Jim Brumby, Presentation, PSG 2004, 'New directions in PEM: the lure of accruals', Fiscal Affairs Department, IMF, 25 May 2004.
7. Graham Scott, 'Lessons from public management reform in New Zealand: are they relevant to developing and transition economies?' Brown Bag Seminar, World Bank, 25 October 2001.
8. www.oecd.org/dac/effectiveness/pfm

REFERENCES

Blöndal, J.R. (2003). Accrual accounting and budgeting: key issues and recent developments. *OECD Journal on Budgeting*, 3(1), pp. 43–59.
CABRI (2008). *Putting Aid on Budget: Synthesis Report*, April. Pretoria: CABRI.
Carlin, T. (2005). Debating the impact of accrual accounting and reporting in the public sector. *Financial Accountability and Management*, 21(3), August, pp. 309–36.
Carlin, T. (2006). Victoria's accrual output based budgeting system – delivering as promised? Some empirical evidence. *Financial Accountability and Management*, 22(1), pp. 1–20.
CIPFA (2010a). *Public Financial Management and the PFM International Architecture: A Whole System Approach*, vol. I. London: CIPFA.
CIPFA (2010b). *Public Financial Management and the PFM International Architecture: A Whole System Approach*, vol. II. London: CIPFA.
Dorotinsky, W. (2003). *Technology and Corruption: The Case of FMIS*. Washington, DC: World Bank.
Ellwood, S.M., and A. Wynne (2003). The transition to accruals accounting. *Public Funds Digest*, 3(2), pp. 74–9.
Fyson, S. (2009). Sending in the consultants: development agencies, the private sector and the reform of public finance in low-income countries. *International Journal of Public Policy*, 4(3/4), pp. 314–42.
Hove, M., and A. Wynne (2010). *The Experience of Medium Term Expenditure Framework and Integrated Financial Management Information System Reforms in Sub-Saharan Africa: What Is the Balance Sheet?* Occasional Paper no. 9. Harare: African Capacity Building Foundation.

IFAC (2003). *Transition to the Accrual Basis of Accounting: Guidance for Governments and Government Entities*, IFAC Public Sector Committee, Study no. 14, December. New York: IFAC.

IFAC (2010). *Nurturing the Development and Growth of Accountancy*. New York: IFAC.

Independent Evaluation Group (2008). *Public Sector Reforms Evaluation*. Washington, DC: World Bank.

Mellor, T. (1997). Why governments should produce balance sheets. In *Perspectives on Accrual Accounting*, ed. IFAC-PSC, pp. 51–5, Occasional Paper 3. New York: International Federation of Accountants.

Newberry, S., and J. Pallot (2005). New Zealand public sector management and accounting reforms: the hidden agenda. In *International Public Financial Management Reform*, ed. J. Guthrie, C. Humphrey, L.R. Jones and O. Olson. Greenwich, CT: IAP.

OECD (2009). *Managing Development Resources: The Use of Country Systems in Public Financial Management*. Paris: OECD.

OECD-DAC (2008). *2008 Survey on Monitoring the Paris Declaration*. Paris: OECD-DAC.

OECD-DAC (2011). *Aid Effectiveness 2005–2010: Progress in Implementing the Paris Declaration*. Paris: OECD-DAC.

OECD-DAC (forthcoming). *Practitioner's Guide to Using Country Public Finance Management Systems*. Paris: OECD-DAC.

Olson, O., C. Humphrey and J. Guthrie (2001). Caught in an evaluatory trap: the dilemma of public services under NPFM. *European Accounting Review*, 10(3), pp. 505–22.

Peterson, S. (2007). Imperfect systems: IFMISs in Africa. Paper prepared for the World Bank and CABRI Conference on Budget Management and Public Financial Accountability, Pretoria, 11 June.

Pretorius, C., and N. Pretorius (2009). *Review of Public Financial Management Reform Literature*, Evaluation Report EV698. London: DFID.

Schick, A. (1998). Why most developing countries should not try New Zealand's reforms. *World Bank Research Observer*, 13(1), February, pp. 123–31.

Vani, S. (2010). *Prioritizing PFM Reforms: A Robust and Functioning Accounting and Reporting System Is a Prerequisite*, May. Retrieved November 2010 from IMF PFM Blog.

Warren-Rodríguez, A. (2007). *Putting Aid on Budget: A Case Study of Mozambique*. Oxford: Mokoro.

World Bank (2004). *Implementation of International Accounting and Auditing Standards: Lessons Learned from the World Bank's Accounting and Auditing ROSC Program*. Washington, DC: World Bank.

World Bank (2010). *Financial Management Sector Strategy FY11-13*. Washington, DC: World Bank.

World Health Organization (2007). *Aid Effectiveness and Health*, Working Paper no. 9. Geneva: World Health Organization.

3 The role of rich countries in development: the case for reforms
*Alex Cobham and David McNair**

INTRODUCTION

The aims of the chapter are to identify how many issues in LDCs such as governance, corruption, capital shortages and environmental degradation are exacerbated by financial policies and practices in rich countries, and to examine the case for necessary reforms in rich countries to ameliorate this. The chapter sets out the key obstacles for development which stem directly from the financial, accounting and tax policies pursued or promoted by rich countries. Most of these relate to the problem of illicit flows, which are estimated to dwarf aid received by a factor of eight or ten to one. Poul Engberg Pedersen, the Norwegian minister who opened the first World Bank conference on illicit flows in September 2009, lamented that donors tended to reverse the equation, and spend – at the very best – just one-eighth or one-tenth of the resources on illicit flows that they devote to aid.

In the following sections we will survey evidence on the damage caused to development by financial opacity and other results of rich country policies, and then address the major policy areas in turn and consider the main options to remove the obstacles to poverty eradication.

The first section summarizes evidence on the damage done, starting with the leading assessments of total illicit flows and then assessing the impact in four key areas: taxation systems; corruption; global financial instability; and environmental destruction.

The second and third sections of this chapter focus on two key areas in which rich country policy promotes and exacerbates the problem of illicit flows, and the related damage to development. One deals with corporate transparency, and the extent to which trade mispricing and other tactics can deprive poor countries of much-needed revenues. The other deals with the practices of secrecy jurisdictions, commonly referred to as tax havens, and the ways in which their deliberately created veil of financial secrecy harms developing countries.

The fourth section addresses a deeper structural issue, related to but distinct from the secrecy issues. This is the question of how the international arrangements and structures around corporate taxation give rise to a systematic bias in the distribution of taxing rights between states, with poorer developing countries on the losing side.

We conclude that the financial policies and practices of rich countries have a grave responsibility for the financial secrecy that facilitates such damage to developing countries, but that the solutions are within reach. Addressing the distribution of taxing rights is a longer-term problem, to which greater transparency can make an important contribution by raising awareness. Ultimately these are all questions of political will, but ones to which the accounting profession can make a genuine contribution.

1. THE COSTS OF OPACITY: ILLICIT FLOWS AND DAMAGE TO DEVELOPMENT

Estimating the extent of damage done to developing countries as a result of financial secrecy is, by definition, difficult. As a result, a wide range of estimates have been published by NGOs, academics and think tanks, while governments and multilateral organizations have been wary of commissioning thorough research because of data difficulties and the political sensitivities of doing so.

Even estimates, however, shed significant light on the scale of the problem for developing and developed countries alike.

Raymond Baker from the organization Global Financial Integrity estimated in 2005 that globally US$500–800 billion of illicit flows exit developing and transitional economies every year (Baker, 2005). Baker's organization has since conducted more detailed quantitative analysis for data from 2000 to 2006, which revises this estimate upwards to US$1 trillion annually (Global Financial Integrity, 2009).

Many of the countries included in the analysis are now emerging economies. However, investigation of the African region estimates that $600 billion, or nearly three times the current levels of external debt of sub-Saharan Africa, has leaked from the continent in illicit financial flows since 1975 (Ndikumana and Boyce, 2008).

More recent research from Global Financial Integrity (2009) estimates that, between 1970 and 2008, total illicit financial outflows from Africa were approximately $854 billion. Sub-Saharan African countries experienced the bulk of these illicit financial outflows, with the West and Central African region posting the largest outflow numbers. Such illicit financial outflows from Africa grew at an average rate of 11.9 per cent per year over this 38-year period. The top five countries with the highest outflow measured were: Nigeria ($89.5 billion); Egypt ($70.5 billion); Algeria ($25.7 billion); Morocco ($25 billion); and South Africa ($24.9 billion).

One particular mechanism which facilitates such illicit outflows is the manipulation of cross-border trade invoices. Christian Aid estimates that, between 2005 and 2007, abuse of the trade pricing of commodities led to $1.1 trillion in capital flow from non-EU countries into the EU and US (Christian Aid, 2009). The lost tax revenue on this non-arm's length pricing is estimated to cost developing countries $160 billion each year – more than 30 per cent higher than the global aid budget in 2008 (Christian Aid, 2008). Even powerful countries such as Germany are estimated to lose around 10 per cent of their tax base because of profit-shifting activity (Huizinga and Laeven, 2008).

The provision of financial secrecy by jurisdictions (often offshore financial centres) plays a significant role in facilitating such illicit capital movement. IMF research (Lane and Milesi-Ferretti, 2010) on 'small international financial centres' details assets held in these jurisdictions of $18.5 trillion, which the authors note is almost certainly an underestimate because of serious problems in data availability. Such small financial centres account for only around 1 per cent of world population and 3 per cent of world GDP (Oxfam, 2000), but in 1994 accounted for 26 per cent of assets and 31 per cent of profits of American multinationals (Hines and Rice, 1994).

The Financial Secrecy Index, launched in 2009 by Christian Aid and the Tax Justice Network, uses objective criteria on financial opacity and the share of jurisdictions in the provision of financial services to non-residents, to reveal that such a focus on small financial centres does not capture the whole picture – the top ten of the index includes major jurisdictions such as the USA (where states such as Delaware offer great opacity) and Switzerland. This illustrates the systemic, global nature of the pervasive problem of financial secrecy. Elsewhere (Cobham, 2012) we have demonstrated that the exposure of developing countries to the secrecy jurisdictions (the latter's share of developing countries' trade and financial flows) is generally as great as for rich countries, and quite often higher.

The damage done by developing country exposure to opacity – through both corporate structures and secrecy jurisdictions – takes multiple forms. In the remainder of this section, we focus on the impact in certain areas: taxation systems; corruption and environmental destruction; and global financial instability.

Taxation Systems

Taxation systems can be thought of as facilitating four main objectives (the 'four Rs' – see, for example, Cobham, 2005). Most obviously, taxes raise the revenue with which governments can drive human development by providing systems of health, education and social security, as well as the basis for a successful economy through regulation, administration and investments in infrastructure.

A second goal is redistribution, to reduce poverty and inequality and ensure that the benefits of development are felt by all. Generally, income taxes are progressive; corporate taxes are regressive at low incomes and then become progressive; property taxes are progressive; indirect taxes are generally regressive; and the overall picture is mixed, although structures are often regressive at low incomes (Gemmell and Morrissey, 2005) .

A third key goal is that of 're-pricing', that is, of using taxes and subsidies as appropriate to ensure that all social costs and benefits of production or consumption of a particular good are reflected in the market price. Most obviously, this may include taxing tobacco to limit damage to health, or petrol to limit environmental costs.

Finally and perhaps most importantly – although often underappreciated – is the goal of strengthening and protecting channels of political representation. These channels are systematically strengthened when the share of tax revenue in government expenditure is higher, that is, when governments rely most on tax (Ross, 2007). Indeed, the strongest relationship exists for direct tax revenues: where citizens contribute most to expenditures through taxation of personal income and corporate profits (Mahon, 2005).

Taxation is an intrinsic part of state-building, democratic development and growth. Collective bargaining around tax revenue creates a 'social contract' between members of society, who are paying taxes and voting for political parties, and officials, who are expected to raise and spend those revenues in a manner that benefits the constituents who elected them (Brautigam, 2008).

A strong 'fiscal social contract' can, in theory, legitimize elected officials and bring sustainable economic growth (Bird, Martinez-Vasquez and Torgler, 2006). Effective tax administrations can contribute to pro-poor economic growth by raising revenue for investment in human capital and infrastructure, and redistributing wealth throughout society. In fact, investors often consider strong tax administrations to be a proxy for good governance and stability (Everest-Phillips, 2008). Conversely, states with weak tax collection capacity are more prone to conflict and poor governance (Hendrix, 2007).

In the long term, state-building helps states become legitimate in the eyes of their citizens. When citizens regard tax authorities as competent, and see revenues spent on improving public welfare, they are willing to contribute (Hendrix, 2007). As Angel Gurría, secretary-general of the Organisation for Economic Co-operation and Development (OECD), has noted:

> Taxation matters for effective state-building. Bargaining between governments and taxpayers plays a central role in the emergence of democratic governance. Citizens want more responsive government. They want the state to be accountable for its actions or inaction and taxes are the vital link between governments and societies. Improved tax relationships between state, businesses and society have provided a strong underpinning for broad-based growth and state accountability. (Gurría, 2008)

For many countries in the South, an increased reliance on mobilizing domestic resources through tax revenues has other virtues as well. It is the best route toward ending aid dependency, as well as the problems caused by the harmful policy conditions frequently attached to bilateral and multilateral aid and debt cancellation.

Corruption

Many people will be familiar with the use of secrecy jurisdictions in a few high-profile corruption cases – whether that involves offshore payments to corrupt politicians by major companies, or the funnelling out of looted funds by corrupt elites.

The specific role of tax havens with regard to the laundering of the proceeds of crime is relatively well explored, not least because it has been the focus of some of the more effective international coordination efforts (see, for example, Hampton and Christensen, 2002, for discussion of the establishment in 1989 of the Financial Action Task Force, and its subsequent impact in terms of promoting anti-money-laundering legislation, at least in havens).

There is, however, little academic analysis of the linkages between opportunities provided by havens and damage done to developing countries. Torvik (2009) goes beyond the generic arguments about tax and governance to make a specific case against havens, drawing parallels with the well-established literature on the 'paradox of plenty' (the poor economic performance often associated with a country's natural resource wealth).

Torvik argues that havens distort developing countries, above all, by changing incentives. First, the balance between productive activity and rent-seeking behaviour is pushed towards the latter by the availability of secrecy, which allows the capture of higher returns to rent-seeking. This process can occur in any context, but where natural resources are also present may be particularly potent.

The secondary effects may be even more powerful, because they relate to the institutional and political context. Most narrowly, the availability of haven 'services' can support politicians' disestablishing or otherwise undermining institutions intended to uncover corruption and financial malfeasance generally. Further, politicians' incentives to move political systems towards those that make elite capture easier (that is, presidential as against parliamentary systems) will also be strengthened by haven opportunities.

Finally, if havens support the returns to narrow self-interest over broader-based progress, Torvik argues that they may increase the chances of conflict and contribute to the weakening of democratic processes.

Torvik summarizes his conclusions thus: 'The negative effects of tax havens are greater for developing countries than for other countries. There are many reasons for this. Reduced government income will have a greater social cost for developing countries than for industrialized countries. In addition, other mechanisms make themselves felt in countries with weak institutions and political systems' (2009, p. 188).

Financial secrecy can also play a role in promoting environmental damage, by creating distance between actions in developing countries and those responsible for them. One example, documented by Global Witness (2009), was the use of correspondent bank accounts in the US, Singapore and elsewhere to exploit the timber resources of Liberia in order to fund conflict and the lifestyle of its then president Charles Taylor. Opacity is also a common feature of the corporate structure of many of the companies that exploit natural resources around the globe, often in developing countries and often with grave environmental consequences.

Global Financial Instability

Financial secrecy can also contribute to instability in global markets, as the world realized to its cost in 2008. The crisis that began with banks and other financial institutions in the richest countries has spread through their economies and spilled into developing countries, undermining their sources of finance and already extracting a direct human cost. First, trade earnings have fallen sharply, with the World Bank (2009a) estimating that low-income countries' merchandise exports would have dropped by almost 15 per cent in 2009, increasing their trade deficit from 6.3 per cent to 9.2 per cent of their GDP. Second, net private capital flows have fallen around 70 per cent across all developing countries from around $1.2 trillion in 2007 to an estimated $363 billion in 2009 (World Bank, 2009b), a drop equivalent to around 5 per cent of GDP. Third, remittances to developing countries fell in 2009 by around 6 per cent, or $20 billion (World Bank, 2010).

Of course the richest countries are also suffering economically. The difference is that shocks in many developing countries will have much harsher and potentially permanent impacts. At the time the World Bank estimated that 120 million extra people would be living on less than $2 a day by 2010. The ILO (2009) estimates that global unemployment will rise to 219–241 million people, the highest on record, with disproportionately damaging effects on women. World Bank researchers Friedman and Schnady (2009) conservatively estimate that the crisis will cause an additional 30,000–50,000 infant deaths in sub-Saharan Africa alone, to say nothing of the permanent effects on a generation that a peak in malnutrition is likely to have.

What was the role of secrecy? Cobham, Hogg and Baird (2008) advance the argument that the crisis was effectively a capital account liberalization bust, following a classic boom (see Williamson and Mahar, 1998). Over a quarter of a decade or more, the richer economies engaged in competitive deregulation of financial markets. Secrecy jurisdictions took this to an extreme, exploiting the gaps left by national regulation of global finance.

The key regulatory arbitrage occurred around regulation of banks and other financial institutions, in particular that which limits the amount of assets that can be acquired as a proportion of their own capital base, in order to protect depositors from undue risk. The Basel II capital accord allows assets of $1,250 for each $100 of capital. In just one example, Stewart (2008) uncovered that the Irish holding company of now-collapsed US bank Bear Stearns held $11,900 of assets for each $100 of capital.

The crisis was driven by two key factors which allowed an unsustainable expansion of credit. One was the complexity of new financial instruments that confused investors and regulators as to the true ownership of assets and liabilities. The other was the opacity of the 'shadow banking system' – financial activities outside the traditional banking system, from hedge funds and private equity, to the structured investment vehicles and other conduits of investment banks and others, all taking advantage of regulatory arbitrage to operate out of secrecy jurisdictions.

US Treasury Secretary Timothy Geithner (then of the New York Federal Reserve Bank) estimated that just some of these activities exceeded the total assets of the entire US banking system in size: 'Financial innovation made it easier for this money to flow around the constraints of regulation and to take advantage of more favourable tax and accounting treatment' (Geithner, 2008).

The genesis of the crisis was undoubtedly complex, and attempts strictly to apportion blame likely to be ultimately futile. It does seem clear, however, that the role of secrecy jurisdictions was non-negligible at the least. An important policy response to the specific problems posed by regulatory arbitrage was the decision by G20 finance ministers in September 2009 to call for 'the setting of an overall leverage ratio, which will take into account off-balance-sheet activities, in order to limit the amount of borrowing conducted by institutions *outside the formal banking regime*' (*Financial Times*, 2009, emphasis added).

The range of damage done by financial secrecy to developing countries is broad, from global economic instability to corruption and the undermining of tax systems. In the following sections we discuss three key policy areas in which rich countries can address some of the damage done.

2. CORPORATE TRANSPARENCY

In the past decade, the role of International Accounting Standards in governing the financial reporting of listed corporations and therefore the information available to those with an interest in the activities of such companies has increased concomitantly with the influence of multinational companies in the global economy and the growth of financial secrecy provisions by jurisdictions. The framework of technical accounting standards, and the influence they exert over a broad range of stakeholders in developing countries, raises significant questions: over the legitimacy of those who establish these standards, over the definition of the stakeholder group for whom accounts are intended to be useful, and over the efficacy of the standards created.

On the international stage, the development of international norms and principles for accounting has been guided by a desire to serve a range of stakeholders. For example, the International Federation of Accountants (IFA), the global organization for the accountancy profession, sees its purpose as 'to serve the public interest, strengthen the accountancy profession worldwide and contribute to the development of international economies by establishing and promoting adherence to high quality professional standards, furthering international convergence of such standards, and speaking out on public interest issues where the profession's expertise is most relevant' (IAS Plus, 2010).

These international standards and principles include ethics standards. The International Ethics Standards Board for Accountants, a subsidiary body of IFAC, sees its purpose as 'serv[ing] the public interest by setting high-quality ethical standards for professional accountants and by facilitating the convergence of international and national ethical standards, thereby enhancing the quality and consistency of services provided by professional accountants throughout the world and strengthening public confidence in the global accounting profession'.

However, in recent years, the establishment of International Accounting Standards for most of the major economies in the world has been devolved to a body of technical experts from the accountancy profession – the International Accounting Standards Board (IASB). The board is a private company registered in the US state of Delaware, which is known for its corporate opacity; indeed it contributed to the USA being placed at the top of the first Financial Secrecy Index in 2009 (http://www.financialsecrecyindex.com/2009results.html). In practice, the board is headquartered at 30 Cannon Street in the heart of the City of London. It is arguably far more influential than the International Federation of Accountants, because of its role in establishing standards for the largest companies in the world; and yet the board is composed of technical experts who are largely drawn from the major firms that the standards are designed to regulate.

In addition, in defining the stakeholders with which the board operates, the lines are drawn tightly. The users of financial statements are seen to be shareholders and providers of capital. Other stakeholders are subsidiary to this narrowly defined group. It is not surprising then that the willingness of this board to engage in a meaningful way with a broader range of stakeholders is limited to consultations which move at a snail's pace and are defined within extremely narrow terms of reference.

The campaigning accountant Richard Murphy (2009) has compared this view of the stakeholders in financial statements with two others: the view which historically pertained in the profession, and the view from a development angle. For the former, he refers back to the view of the Accounting Standards Steering Committee (ASSC) in *The Corporate Report* (1975). The ASSC defines the following stakeholders:

- the equity investor group;
- the loan creditor group;
- the employee group;
- the analyst–adviser group;
- the business contact group (including customers and suppliers);
- the government (including tax authorities);
- the public 'including taxpayers, ratepayers, consumers and other community and special interest groups such as political parties, consumer and environmental protection societies and regional pressure groups' (p. 17).

From the development angle, UNCTAD (the United Nations Conference on Trade and Development), in a report entitled *Guidance on Corporate Responsibility Indicators in Annual Reports* (2008), identifies the following stakeholders:

- investors and financial institutions;
- business partners;
- consumers;
- employees;
- surrounding community;
- civil society organizations; and
- governments and their institutions.

The detailed definitions add further support to the view of an almost complete overlap between the stakeholders recognized by the historical view of the accounting profession and those in a contemporary international development perspective. This close resemblance highlights starkly the extent to which the view imposed by the International Accounting Standards Board is anomalous.

In consideration of the efficacy of such standards, we must evaluate their purpose. If IFRS are established by accountants for interpretation by accountants and investors, even to the exclusion of the other stakeholders noted here, then the standards should nevertheless serve the original, overarching purpose of the accountancy profession – to provide a 'true and fair' view.

In 1983 Lord Hoffman and Dame Mary Arden expressed a legal opinion over the meaning of 'true and fair', a central part of English law and a guiding principle of accounting practice since 1947 (UK Companies Act 1947). They argued that the information held in accounts must be accurate and comprehensive to within acceptable limits, though this may involve questions of degree. In the opinion of Hoffman and Arden, accounts will not be 'true and fair' unless they contain sufficient information in quantity and quality to satisfy the reasonable expectations of the readers to whom they are addressed.

These 'opinions', which received almost iconic status in their sphere of operation, were corroborated by an additional 'opinion' by Martin Moore, QC in 2008 and have guided the development of prepared accounts within the UK for the past two decades. With the introduction of International Accounting Standards (IAS), standards shifted from a principles-based system to a rules-based system. Auditors in the UK were required to comply with international financial reporting standards and, if not complying with IFRS, to prepare a 'true and fair view' (IAS Regulation 606/2002).[1] Arguably, this created increased opportunities for accountants to prepare statements which comply with regulation but yet do not represent a 'true and fair' view.

If users of financial accounts are recognized to include broader stakeholders, including civil society and tax authorities as well as other regulatory bodies, the implications for the design of standards may be profound.

Currently, listed companies are required to report their financial activities on a global consolidated basis, on the rationale that it serves the users of accounts – defined as investors and providers of capital. However, this necessarily obscures intra-company trade, which is not insignificant. In fact, it is estimated that trade between related companies within multinational groups may constitute more than 60 per cent of global trade. If accounts are to 'present fairly' or give a 'true and fair' account of a company's activity, the obfuscation of such significant information undermines the objectives of International Accounting Standards.

Arguably, this does not serve the best interests of investors, as it does not equip them to take a view on investment risk based on the policy and economic stability of operations in each of the countries in which a company operates. Significant investor groups have in fact made representation to the IASB in support of more granulated reporting.

Perhaps most important is the impact which global consolidation has on accountability at the local level. A company's stakeholders include those who are affected by its activities. As noted by the ASSC (1975) and UNCTAD (2008), these stakeholders include employees, customers, trading partners, the community in which the company operates and the government which provides the privilege of incorporation.

One particular proposal is for a standard requiring that companies report their economic activity, including tax paid, in each country in which they operate (see Murphy, 2009 for a detailed proposal of the standard; and IASB, 2010 for a discussion of the potential in the extractives industry). Such a standard could increase accountability, and the transparency afforded could expose abusive profit-shifting.

At a minimum, the information provided would give the tax authorities of poorer countries a basis on which to identify and 'red-flag' the most high-risk operations upon which to focus their limited resources. For example, the Zambian tax authority would be able to identify those multinationals recording much higher shares of their total economic activity in the country than the shares of profit being recorded there. In some cases this might well reflect entirely legitimate patterns of activity (for example, early stage capital investment in copper mining), but in some cases it would directly identify abusive practices.

In this way, a change in International Accounting Standards could give back a little power to the developing world.

3.   JURISDICTIONAL TRANSPARENCY

The globalization of capital, trade and commerce, which has been accelerated through the development and growth of multinational corporations (MNCs), has challenged the nature of taxation, the 'fiscal social contract' and 'tax morale'. The 'tax culture' or tax morale is the willingness of citizens to contribute to tax revenues. This is important, since paying tax is a social act – any rational economic model taking into account the likelihood and penalty of being caught cheating predicts a much lower level of compliance than actually seen. People pay tax as a contribution to their community, or as the 'cost of civilization', as inscribed on the wall of the US Internal Revenue Service.

Evidence from experimental economics shows that tax morale is driven by the perceived fairness of the tax system. In particular, compliance depends positively on (i) the perceived or expected level of redistribution to the most vulnerable, and (ii) individuals' expectation of others' compliance levels (Bosco and Mittone, 1997; Mittone, 2006). Tax morale is therefore undermined when some sectors or members of society do not contribute to society by paying tax, and yet benefit from the policy stability, infrastructure and services that a strong tax system brings. This is a particular problem in states where political and business elites do not pay tax and use secrecy jurisdictions or 'tax havens' to hide money offshore.

Defining Secrecy Jurisdictions

The OECD defines a tax haven as a jurisdiction that imposes no or nominal direct taxes on financial income or other mobile services. Tax havens lack transparency, do not engage in information exchange, and facilitate the establishment of entities with no substantial activities (OECD, 1998). However, this common term, 'tax haven', is also problematic. As long ago as 1981, the Gordon Report to the US Treasury stated that 'there is no single, clear objective test which permits the identification of a country as a tax haven' (Gordon, 1981, cited in Palan, 1998). While originally intended, presumably, to indicate a jurisdiction with lower rates of tax than elsewhere, the term came to be used to cover a great range of functions, many largely unrelated to taxation.

Eden and Kudrle (2005), for example, draw on the literature to identify two categorizations of havens: by taxation type and by activity. The first, following Palan (2002), separates havens into 'countries with no income tax where firms pay only license fees (e.g., Anguilla, Bermuda), countries with low taxation (e.g., Switzerland, the Channel Islands), countries that practice so-called "ring fencing" by taxing domestic but not foreign income (e.g., Liberia, Hong Kong), and countries that grant special tax privileges to certain types of firms or operations (e.g., Luxembourg, Monaco)' (Eden and Kudrle, 2005, p. 101).

The second classification, following Avi-Yonah (2000) and Kudrle and Eden (2003), distinguishes between production havens which relocate real value added (for example, Ireland in the 1990s), headquarters havens providing incorporation benefits (for example, Belgium, Singapore), sham havens providing little more than addresses for financial companies in particular (for example, the Cayman Islands) and secrecy havens whose main advantage is opacity (and which include most sham havens).

Analysis under the heading 'tax haven' tends to focus, understandably, on tax aspects. The overarching rationale for the existence of tax havens which emerges from this approach is that they provide relief, to business or individuals, from the rates of tax which would otherwise apply. Where real economic activity is not moved from its original jurisdiction, which can be characterized as tax competition, taxing rights are effectively transferred by one means or another. This may take advantage of genuine legal differences (for example, the distinction between tax liabilities of corporate headquarters and those of real activity loci), of the absence of coordinated international tax policy (for example, exploiting differences between two or more jurisdictions' calculation of domestic and foreign tax liabilities) or of asymmetric information between jurisdictions (for example, the hiding of facts about ownership of assets and/or income streams and the associated tax liabilities).

Another frequently used term is 'offshore finance centre' (OFC). This term is preferred, for example, by the International Monetary Fund, whose mandate is more closely aligned to issues of international financial regulatory oversight and stability than of tax. Palan (1998) explores some of the difficulties of consistent definition: 'In financial literature, [offshore is used] to describe unregulated international finance ... Rather confusingly, however, the International Monetary Fund and the Bank for International Settlements consider only tax havens as OFCs, though the City of London, which does not qualify as a tax haven, is considered the hub of global offshore finance.' Palan goes on to distinguish between 'spontaneous' OFCs, which have grown up as entrepôts over time, such as the City of London and Hong Kong, and more recently created international banking facilities such as New York and Singapore.

An important IMF working paper by Ahmed Zoromé (2007) discusses the definitional issues in some detail and proposes new criteria (discussed in the following sub-section). After surveying most of the key references, Zoromé concludes that: 'Three distinctive and recurrent characteristics of OFCs have emerged from these definitions: (i) the primary orientation of business toward non-residents; (ii) the favourable regulatory environment (low supervisory requirements and minimal information disclosure); and (iii) the low- or zero-taxation schemes' (2007, p. 4).

This shifts the focus on to specific actions taken by jurisdictions, where 'tax haven' definitions tend to emphasize specific results. Zoromé's subsequent application of the criteria derived offers one solution to Palan's point about the City of London – the UK is categorized as an OFC.

The third main term used, and increasingly so since the contribution of Murphy (2008), is 'secrecy jurisdiction'. The focus remains on actions taken, but is more explicit in emphasizing the legal steps taken. In this, it follows the logic of Palan (2002), who discusses the 'commercialization of sovereignty' – the decision by certain jurisdictions to obtain economic advantage by allowing certain political decisions (over, for example, taxation of non-residents) to be dictated by likely users (for example, financial, legal and accounting practitioners). 'Jurisdiction' is used, rather than, for example, 'centre' or some other less specific term, because it is precisely the legal system which is the locus of actions taken.

The emphasis on 'secrecy' is necessary, Murphy argues, so that non-residents can take advantage of favourable changes in the jurisdiction's own legal framework, with confidence that they will not fall foul of the legal system where they reside. There are therefore two key characteristics that define a secrecy jurisdiction:

- 'that the secrecy jurisdiction creates regulation that they know is primarily of benefit and use to those not resident in their geographical domain'; and
- 'the creation of a deliberate, and legally backed, veil of secrecy that ensures that those from outside the jurisdiction making use of its regulation cannot be identified to be doing so' (2009, p. 6).

The second criterion can be seen as related to that which the OECD's 'Towards a Level Playing Field' initiative is intended to measure, by performing consistent assessment of jurisdictions on a range of aspects of their legal and regulatory frameworks (see, for example, OECD, 2006).

By focusing on what makes them attractive, this definition therefore relies, above all, on an assessment of the comparative advantage of the jurisdictions in question. Their route to attracting (the declaration of) foreign economic or financial activity is by providing relatively favourable terms to users. In effect, this indicates a reliance on regulatory arbitrage (potentially but not necessarily including tax regulation).

Given the multitude of competing definitions and the lack in most cases of clear, objectively quantifiable criteria, it is unsurprising that attempts to define jurisdictions of concern have been largely unconvincing. To consider how such criteria might be created and applied, it is useful to start with Zoromé (2007). Having established key characteristics of OFCs, he proposes the following definition: 'An OFC is a country or jurisdiction that provides financial services to nonresidents on a scale that is incommensurate with the size and the financing of its domestic economy' (2007, p. 7).

This he proposes to capture by examining the ratio of net financial services exports to GDP (from IMF balance of payments data) and looking at jurisdictions with especially high values. In practice, limited data availability on these flows requires it to be supplemented with data interpolated from stock variables, using proxy indicators created from data on variables reflecting cross-border holdings of portfolio investment assets (the IMF's Coordinated Portfolio Investment Survey, CPIS) and international investment position (using data from the IMF's International Financial Statistics).

Comparing the IMF's list with Zoromé's findings, we see that most of the definitions coincide (for those jurisdictions for which Zoromé had data), but an important addition to the latter's list is the UK. While there are some issues with the proxy indicators and the interpolation from stock to flow data, the approach illustrates clearly the value of using objective criteria – that a level playing field (including politically 'uncomfortable' findings) may be more likely to emerge.

In keeping with the emphasis of an OFC discourse, Zoromé (2007) relies on the relative intensity of financial services provision to non-residents by scaling for jurisdiction GDP. Alternative criteria include:

- openness to international trade in financial services (that is, taking the sum of exports and imports as a ratio to GDP), which might capture more about jurisdictions' role as conduits;
- net exports of financial services (exports minus imports as a ratio to GDP), as an indicator of specialization;
- 'netted' trade in financial services (the lower of exports and imports, as an indicator only of the extent to which the jurisdiction acts as a conduit);
- the *absolute* contribution to the global provision of financial services to non-residents (that is, Zoromé's criterion, but taken as a ratio to the global total rather than to the jurisdiction's own GDP).

If we are looking for a measure to capture the importance of jurisdictions, in order to consider policy against the global phenomenon, then the last criterion proposed here may be appropriate. Table 3.1 compares the results of using the relative approach of Zoromé and the absolute approach, showing the top five jurisdictions identified by each. Taking global contribution rather than relative intensity, in the provision of financial services to non-residents, leads to a quite different picture.

Finally, however, we may consider the implications of the 'secrecy jurisdiction' approach. While the relative or absolute approach to offshore specialization may capture something about the success of jurisdictions in following this path, it has nothing directly to say about the secrecy or otherwise with which this was achieved.

The ideal objective criteria for secrecy jurisdictions might therefore contain two

Table 3.1   A comparison of the absolute contribution and relative intensity approaches

Top jurisdictions	Relative intensity	Global scale
1	Cayman Islands	United States
2	Luxembourg	United Kingdom
3	Guernsey	Luxembourg
4	Cyprus	Switzerland
5	Jersey	Germany

Source: Calculations for Financial Secrecy Index 2011.

separate components – one reflecting each jurisdiction's importance in the global provision of financial services to non-residents, the 'absolute' approach here, and one reflecting the jurisdiction's (objectively measurable) performance against one or more key indicators of secrecy.

A final advantage of such an approach is that it would allow users to step away from the 'list' approach, which by necessity dictates that a given jurisdiction either does or does not meet certain criteria. More powerful, both for policy making and for research, might be a measure which falls on a sliding scale. A more nuanced method of measuring progress than a blacklist may eventually produce more positive responses (see, for example, Kudrle, 2008, on the limitations of blacklisting: 'the evidence does not suggest that blacklisting made an important systematic difference' (p. 16).

A new index, jointly produced by Christian Aid and the Tax Justice Network, reflects this analysis. The Financial Secrecy Index, launched in 2009 and updated in 2011, combines a secrecy score, based on objectively measurable criteria that reflect the secrecy or otherwise of the jurisdiction in key areas (for example, banking secrecy or tax information exchange), with a quantitative measure of absolute contribution as discussed above (here labelled the 'global scale weight').

By combining measures of jurisdictions' secrecy and relative importance to global 'offshore' finance, the index presents a different picture from that commonly envisaged. First, many of the 'usual suspects' do not feature as highly as their profile in policy discussions. For example, the Bahamas does not feature in the top 10, while Monaco ranks only 64th. Among developing countries, many oft-named Caribbean jurisdictions also rank low; for example, Antigua and Barbuda, and Grenada rank 58th and 61st respectively. Ghana and Botswana are a little more transparent, but rank 44th and 49th respectively owing to their somewhat greater role in (recorded) cross-border flows.

At the same time, many of the 'usual suspects' do feature at the top of the index; for example, Switzerland, the Cayman Islands and Luxembourg occupy the top places in that order. However, the USA also features in the top five, despite powerful statements from government about the damage done by financial opacity. The UK's position of 13th reflects its relative transparency, despite its global importance, although a hypothetical combined jurisdiction of 'UK influence' (to include the network of crown dependencies and overseas territories that feed funds to the City of London) would rank much more highly.

Table 3.2   Financial Secrecy Index 2011: top 20 jurisdictions

Rank	Secrecy jurisdiction	FSI 2011 value	Secrecy score	Global scale weight
1	Switzerland	1879.2	78	0.061
2	Cayman Islands	1646.7	77	0.046
3	Luxembourg	1621.2	68	0.131
4	Hong Kong	1370.7	73	0.042
5	USA	1160.1	58	0.208
6	Singapore	1118.0	71	0.031
7	Jersey	750.1	78	0.004
8	Japan	693.6	64	0.018
9	Germany	669.8	57	0.046
10	Bahrain	660.3	78	0.003
11	British Virgin Islands	617.9	81	0.002
12	Bermuda	539.9	85	0.001
13	United Kingdom	516.5	45	0.200
14	Panama	471.5	77	0.001
15	Belgium	467.2	59	0.012
16	Marshall Islands	457.0	90	0.000
17	Austria	453.5	66	0.004
18	United Arab Emirates (Dubai)	439.6	79	0.001
19	Bahamas	431.1	83	0.000
20	Cyprus	406.5	58	0.010

Responses

As their main attraction, secrecy jurisdictions allow multinational companies and powerful individuals to 'free-ride' on public services provided by taxpayers elsewhere. Since secrecy jurisdictions facilitate the outflow of capital and the avoidance and evasion of tax in countries where productive economic activity occurs, free-riding undermines the capacity of states to raise revenue. This liberates capital from its social responsibility and frees it from paying a good portion of the tax otherwise owed to national governments. This, in turn, affects tax morale (Brautigam, 2008).

In effect, secrecy jurisdictions use the attribute of sovereignty – the right to make laws – for commercial gain, drawing rent surpluses from income that would otherwise accrue in larger states (Fabri and Baldacchino, 1999). Individuals and companies pay millions of dollars to lawyers and accountants so they can appear to reside somewhere else. Thus, alongside the 'real' state, offshore financial centres create space for virtual citizenship. This commercialization of sovereignty allows those who do not see taxation as a moral or civic duty, reflecting the desire to participate in a social group, simply to opt out (Palan, 2003).

Of course, the undermining of one state by another is nothing new. Yet, by providing secrecy and hosting assets and companies with 'no questions asked', secrecy jurisdictions can facilitate corrupt practices, criminality and irresponsible financial behaviour. This contributes to systemic risk within the financial system.

Such processes as the 2002 UN Financing for Development (FfD) conference and its 2008 review shifted the emphasis of development policy making towards mobilizing domestic resources. The Monterrey Consensus, a product of the 2002 FfD meetings, also recognizes the need for international tax cooperation to ensure countries can benefit from the profits generated within their economies.

In addition, in the wake of the global financial crisis that erupted in 2008, tax cooperation and transparency have shot up the international policy agenda. Developed countries, keen to find new revenue streams to fill huge deficits, have heralded – perhaps somewhat prematurely – the 'beginning of the end of tax havens' (Mathiason, 2009). Meanwhile, in April 2009, the G20 threatened sanctions against secrecy jurisdictions that do not commit to signing a minimum of 12 bilateral agreements for sharing tax information based on the OECD model tax information exchange agreements (TIEAs). The G20, however, has relied on the OECD for technical support to develop information exchange standards, and to assess compliance with the standard. This is problematic for two reasons.

First, the OECD's benchmark for a cooperative jurisdiction – negotiating 12 bilateral information-sharing agreements – necessarily excludes the countries not party to these agreements. In reality, secrecy jurisdictions have signed agreements only under the threat of sanctions. But, since many developing countries do not have the economic or political influence to impose effective sanctions, they have been excluded from the benefits of these agreements. In 2007, for example, Chile requested negotiations for information exchange agreements with a number of secrecy jurisdictions and did not receive one positive response.

Second, to prevent 'fishing expeditions', authorities must set out their case for an information request in a lengthy legal document. In effect, they must already have much of the information they are seeking before their request is granted. What's more, legal technicalities provide ample opportunities to hinder and block requests for information. Ironically, information sharing is intended to provide revenue authorities with evidence of tax evasion or avoidance, thereby creating a deterrent. If companies and individuals know that information is unlikely to be exchanged, there is no deterrent.

The key international regulatory change that would provide a significant deterrent effect to those seeking to evade or avoid tax via secrecy jurisdictions is a multilateral agreement requiring the automatic exchange of tax information. A multilateral deal is needed, rather than the more than 30,000 bilateral deals that would be needed between UN member states alone; and, to be effective, it must include a measure of automatic exchange. As tax authorities around the world can testify, automatic exchange (for example, between an employer and the state) has enormous deterrent power that 'on request' exchange cannot approach.

Combined with the country-by-country reporting of multinational companies set out above, these measures would equip revenue authorities with the information needed to identify cases worthy of further investigation in a timely way, and ensure they had the power to do so.

4.   TRANSFER PRICING AND TAXING RIGHTS

The compliance burden faced by MNCs operating in numerous tax jurisdictions can be onerous. This is perhaps most significant in the area of international transfer pricing, the means by which companies allocate profits, and therefore taxing rights, between jurisdictions. This issue, widely recognized as the most complex issue in international taxation, is also one of the most important tax issues faced by MNCs (UNCTAD, 1999) and was recently highlighted by the head of the US Inland Revenue Service (IRS) as 'one of [its] most significant challenges'.

It is this complexity which can lead to intractable disputes over taxing rights and also enables unscrupulous businesses to shift profits from countries where the capacity to monitor and challenge such behaviour is limited. Of course, many MNCs seek to play a positive role through job creation, investment in infrastructure, the innovation of new technologies, and their corporate social responsibility actions. However, tax is also becoming an important part of corporate social responsibility approaches as MNC tax behaviour faces previously unknown levels of external scrutiny (Scheiwiller and Symons, 2010).

In addition to the problem of corporate behaviour that undermines revenue collection in the weakest states, the systemic impact of power imbalances *between* states is likely also to be substantial. An imbalance of power is created when the tax administration in one country has more or better information, more dedicated resources and more political power than the other. Thus the disparity in transfer pricing expertise and capacity between the revenue authorities of developing countries and those of developed countries and emerging economies can result in companies apportioning greater profits to developed countries to avoid the risk of transfer pricing disputes with an aggressive and politically powerful revenue authority.

Transfer Pricing

Transfer pricing is defined by the OECD as 'a price, adopted for book-keeping purposes, which is used to value transactions between affiliated enterprises integrated under the same management at artificially high or low levels in order to effect an unspecified income payment or capital transfer between those enterprises'. Transfer pricing is therefore a system of determining the 'correct' price of a transaction which occurs across borders but between companies or legal entities which are related (often companies which are owned by the same group) (OECD, 2003).

Intra-group transactions are not exposed to the same market forces as transactions between independent enterprises. As such they are referred to as 'controlled transactions'. Where these transactions occur across borders, they may be artificially lowered (Silbertztein, 2010). This has implications for the tax base of both tax jurisdictions and for the taxpayer.

To address this problem, the determination of an appropriate price is governed by the 'arm's length principle' (ALP), that is, the price at which a transaction would take place if the buying and selling entities were not related. The aim of this principle is the allocation of tax bases of MNCs among the countries in which they operate while avoiding double taxation (a situation in which the same profits are taxed in more than one jurisdiction).

The ALP has become an international norm for governing related transactions and is applied by all OECD countries and a number of non-OECD countries. Further, many double-tax treaties contain provisions for the resolution of transfer pricing disputes on the basis of the ALP.

Trade among MNC affiliates is so significant in the global economy because of the vertical integration of their production processes. Motivation for transfer pricing can be classified into four categories:

- managerial;
- market;
- government policy;
- taxation.

A multinational company structure can be arranged to take advantage of the business environment within a jurisdiction. This may include internal business functions such as the skill set of the workforce. Cash flow issues within an MNC may motivate non-arm's length transfer pricing. For example, an MNC may supply goods and services to a newly established subsidiary at below normal cost. Transfer pricing also has implications for the distribution of ownership shares within joint ventures (OECD, 2009).

Non-arm's length pricing may also be motivated by factors external to the MNC, for example enterprises being subject to conflicting governmental pressures relating to customs valuations, anti-dumping duties, exchange or price controls, exchange rate risks, asset capitalization policies, anti-monopoly charges and concerns about political and policy stability.

In addition to the business rationale for transfer pricing, on an internal level there may be conflicts of interest which have an impact on internal pricing, for example if managers act in their personal interests rather than in those of the shareholders, or if there is asymmetric information within the company. Such a situation has the potential to occur 'in any situation involving cooperative effort' and may exist 'in all organisations . . . at every level of management in firms' (McNair, Dottey and Cobham, 2010, p. 6).

If an MNC makes use of a secrecy jurisdiction this may be motivated by tax rates and regulation.[2] Reducing tax rates is attractive to corporations, as it can boost shareholder value, post-tax earnings and returns to shareholders. As company dividends and executive rewards are linked to reported earnings, individuals within a company may also have a personal motivation to limit effective tax rates.

Differentials in corporate tax rates can motivate MNCs to use transfer pricing to shift income from a high tax to a low tax jurisdiction. For example, jurisdictions can give tax credit for foreign tax paid by foreign subsidiaries when assessing global income. Some jurisdictions exempt MNCs from paying tax on foreign source income until the profits are remitted to the host country. MNCs can use transfer pricing to minimize customs duties. By lowering the value of imports into a country where customs duty is high, an MNC lowers duty payments.

Proponents of the arm's length principle argue that it is the most appropriate and efficient way of allocating profits between jurisdictions. However, as we have noted above, the practical implementation of this system is fraught with difficulties.

Durst (2010) and Avi-Yonah (2009) identify a range of theoretical and practical problems with its implementation. On a conceptual level, Durst argues that the entire system is based on the assumption that the tax results of multinational groups can be evaluated as if they were aggregations of unrelated independent companies transacting with each other at arm's length. This is problematic, because commonly controlled multinational groups frequently exist precisely because there are some transactions that do not occur on an economically efficient basis between unrelated parties.

For example, the exploitation of intellectual property in the pharmaceutical industry is too complex to be accomplished by unaffiliated groups of companies transacting with one another independently. As a result, establishing an appropriate arm's length price is conceptually difficult. Secondly, in treating related entities as if they were unrelated, the arm's length principle respects the results of contracts between related entities that have no real economic effects (Durst, 2010).

As a result, the multinational can restructure the business in a way that allocates risk and value to minimize tax liability. For example, valuable intellectual property can be transferred to low tax jurisdictions or subsidiaries in low tax jurisdictions can be designated 'entrepreneurs', meaning that these subsidiaries bear a disproportionate level of risk, thereby gaining the right to a disproportionate share of the income (Durst, 2010).

On a practical level, Durst argues that a whole industry of accountants, lawyers and economists has built up around gathering evidence to ensure that different parts of a multinational company which are, by definition, commonly controlled act as if they weren't related at all. Similarly, tax authorities engage their own accountants, economists and lawyers to ensure that companies have complied with these regulations.

Increasingly, academic analysis has shown evidence of large-scale and systematic abuses of transfer pricing. Germany is estimated to lose more than 10 per cent of its tax base to profit-shifting of various sorts (Huizinga and Laeven, 2008), while a more specific finding (Clausing, 2009) is that the US loses an estimated $60 billion of revenue a year to transfer pricing abuses. Azémar and Corcos (2010) find evidence that 'abusive transfer pricing' is in fact 'one of the determinants of FDI activity'.

Challenges to Developing Countries

An exploration of the complexity of transfer pricing, which is problematic for well-resourced revenue authorities, is one example of a system emerging from a northern perspective which creates systemic disadvantage to developing countries.

The UN Committee of Experts on International Cooperation in Tax Matters (2009) recognized the tension for developing countries in 'enforcing their legitimate taxing rights while ensuring an open, transparent, investment-friendly and fair environment for investors. The skills and informational gaps in many developing countries exacerbate . . . these difficulties.'

The challenges can be categorized as a lack of effective transfer pricing legislation and a lack of capacity to implement legislation and monitor transfer pricing issues.

For one former revenue official and former employee of KPMG in Mozambique the challenges were clear: 'There is no adequate legislation governing transfer pricing in Mozambique – what exists is extremely short and weak. When there is a request for transfer pricing placed with the tax authorities, nobody knows how to deal with the request', he explained. 'It is therefore easy for multinationals to take advantage to exploit the weak capacity of tax authorities, and the lack of regulation governing transfer pricing', he said.[3] Indeed, an analysis of transfer pricing legislation across the globe shows that, in 2008, only 6.9 per cent of low income countries and only 14.5 per cent of lower middle income countries had transfer pricing legislation (McNair, Dottey and Cobham, 2010).

At the heart of the challenge facing tax administrators in developing countries is the lack of capacity to follow, implement and monitor transfer pricing mechanisms occurring within MNCs that operate in their jurisdictions. Tax administrators in many developing countries lack the resources needed to monitor trade between related enterprises in a way that will let them know what is going wrong. On the other hand, MNCs have the resources to carry out complicated global transactions and procedures which tax administrators in developing countries may find difficult to trace. 'There is no capacity – government audits just check invoices – there is no capacity for deep analysis of transfer pricing arrangements. It is almost impossible for them to find examples of transfer pricing abuse' (Former revenue official and former employee of KPMG in Mozambique). This point is corroborated by a senior revenue official from Sierra Leone. When asked about transfer pricing issues he said, 'No, we don't deal with that.' This official spoke with pride of Sierra Leone's audit capacity, which had increased from one auditor in 2003 to 18 in 2010 (McNair et al., 2010). This lies in stark contrast to the US IRS, which reportedly recruited 1,200 additional staff in 2009 and planned to recruit a further 800 in 2010 to scrutinize transfer prices (Stuart, 2009).

Prospects for Change?

The fact that the BRIC countries (Brazil, Russia, India and China) now have a seat at the table at the G20, the 'premier forum for our international economic cooperation', marks a watershed in the traditional powerbase behind the global economy. This expanded forum presents both an opportunity and a challenge for progress in international co-operation. China, for example, has been taking G20 summits seriously, mobilizing large teams and undertaking considerable preparation (Martinez-Diaz and Woods, 2009).

Some analysts have suggested that the G20 may further marginalize both the interests of the poorest developing countries and the UN as a forum for discussion of economic issues. The emerging economies are unlikely to represent the interests of the poorest countries, and the onus of representing them has fallen to the secretary-general of the UN, the president of the World Bank and the managing director of the IMF, some of the fiercest proponents of the Washington Consensus (Martinez-Diaz and Woods, 2009). Indeed, the fact that tax havens are used by many in positions of power for their own personal gain makes agreement even within nation states difficult (Lesage, McNair and Vermeiren, 2010).

Yet, despite these challenges, there is considerable room for optimism. The progress made in 2009 with regard to tax haven secrecy was greater than that which occurred in the preceding decade. Developing countries are increasingly discussing the role of taxation in development and the need to redress the imbalances which globalization, accompanied by financial opacity, has created, and international policy discussions in the lead-up to the Millennium Development Goals review summit recognized the need to look at the outflows as well as addressing aid commitments.

Meanwhile a movement is building in civil society across the globe through organizations like the Tax Justice Network, which now has active chapters in Africa and Europe, with a movement building in Latin America. These groups no longer see development aid as a solution to poverty, but want to see developing countries stand on their own by raising their own revenue.

The financial crisis has shown us that financial integrity internationally is crucial to long-term development goals, as macro-economic shocks have the heaviest impact on the poorest. In this regard, the accountancy profession has a significant role to play in pursuing ethical standards with regard to providing a 'true and fair' view of a company's affairs. Given the importance of taxation in the development and democratization process, such an ethical standard would consider the implications of exploiting loopholes to minimize a company's tax burden – to the extent to which developing countries are deprived of revenues for spending on health and education.

Yet accountability is also crucial: a movement within the accountancy profession which calls for the kinds of international transparency standards which would build accountability would go a long way in contributing to long-term economic and social development in the world's poorest countries.

NOTES

*   The authors wrote this chapter while employed by UK NGO, Christian Aid. While they are now employed by Save the Children UK, they write in a personal capacity.
1.   http://www.frc.org.uk/images/uploaded/documents/220605%20-%20True%20and%20Fair%20Opinion.pdf
2.   There is evidence for tax-motivated transfer pricing in the pricing of commodities (Demirguc and Huizunga, 1998; Clausing, 2003). Bernard, Jensen and Schott (2006) find that prices for intra-firm transactions of US MNCs are significantly lower than prices for the same goods sent to an arm's length customer or non-affiliate. Using point of export customs documents between 1993 and 2000, Bernard et al. examined and compared intra-company sales to arm's length sales using the same products, exported to the same country in the same month using the same mode for transport. They found that transactions with arm's length customers were on average 43 per cent higher than intra-company trades. The difference between arm's length and intra-company trades was found to be negatively associated with destination country corporate tax rates and positively associated with destination country import tariffs – to the extent that, for a percentage point reduction in the corporate tax rate, a 0.56–0.66 price difference was observed.
3.   Interview with former revenue official and former employee of KPMG in Mozambique.

BIBLIOGRAPHY

ASSC (1975). *The Corporate Report*. London: Accounting Standards Steering Committee. (Online courtesy of ICAEW), accessed 14 May 2010, http://www.ion.icaew.com/ClientFiles/6f45ef7e-1eff-41ff-909e-24eeb6e9ed15//The%20Corporate%20Report2.pdf).
Avi-Yonah, R. (2000). Globalization, tax competition, and the fiscal crisis of the welfare state. *Harvard Law Review*, 113, pp. 1573–1676.
Avi-Yonah, R.S. (2009). Between formulary apportionment and the OECD guidelines: a proposal for reconciliation, John M. Olin Center for Law and Economics Working Paper Series, University of Michigan Law School.
Avi-Yonah, R., and K. Clausing (2008). Art. 7, business profits. In *Source versus Residence: Problems Arising from the Allocation of Taxing Rights in Tax Treaty Law and Possible Alternatives*, ed. M. Lang, P. Pistone, J. Schuch and C. Staringer. Alphen aan den Rijn: Kluwer Law International.
Azémar, C., and G. Corcos (2010). Multinational firms' heterogeneity in tax responsiveness: the role of transfer pricing. *World Economy*, 32(9), pp. 1291–1318.
Baker, R.W. (2005). *Capitalism's Achilles Heel: Dirty Money and How to Renew the Free-Market System*. Hoboken, NJ: Wiley.
Bernard, A., J.B. Jensen and P. Schott (2006). Transfer pricing by U.S.-based multi-nationals, mimeo.
Bhat, G. (2009) *Transfer Pricing, Tax Havens and Global Governance*, Discussion Paper. Bonn: Deutsches Institut für Entwicklungspolitik.
Bird, R., J. Martinez-Vasquez and B. Torgler (2006). Societal institutions and tax effort in developing coun-

tries. In *The Challenge of Tax Reform in the Global Economy*, ed. J. Alm and J. Martinez-Vazquez. Germany: Springer-Verlag.

Bosco, L., and L. Mittone (1997). Tax evasion and moral constraints: some experimental evidence. *Kyklos*, 50, pp. 297–324.

Brautigam, D. (2008). Introduction: taxation and state-building in developing countries. In *Taxation and State-Building in Developing Countries: Capacity and Consent*, ed. D. Brautigam, O. Fjeldstad and M. Moore. Cambridge: Cambridge University Press.

Christian Aid (2008). *Death and Taxes: The True Toll of Tax Dodging*. London: Christian Aid.

Christian Aid (2009). *False Profits: Robbing the Poor to Keep the Rich Tax Free*. London: Christian Aid.

Clausing, K. (2003). Tax-motivated transfer pricing and US intrafirm trade prices. *Journal of Public Economics*, 87, pp. 2207–23.

Clausing, K. (2009). Multinational firm tax avoidance and tax policy. *National Tax Journal*, December.

Cobham, A. (2005). The tax consensus has failed! Policy Recommendation No. 8. Oxford Council on Good Governance.

Cobham, A. (2012). Tax havens, illicit flows and developing countries. In *Draining Development*. Washington, DC: World Bank.

Cobham, A., A. Hogg and R. Baird (2008). *The Morning after the Night Before*. London: Christian Aid, http://www.christianaid.org.uk/Images/The-morning-after-the-night-before.pdf.

Demirguc-Kunt, A., and H. Huizinga (1998). *Determinants of Commercial Bank Interest Margins and Profitability: Some International Evidence*, Policy Research Working Paper Series 1900. Washington, DC: World Bank.

Durst, M. (2010). It's not just academic: the OECD should reevaluate transfer pricing laws. *Tax Analysts*, 18 January, pp. 247–56.

Eden, L., and R. Kudrle (2005). Tax havens: renegade states in the international tax regime? *Law and Policy*, 27(1), pp. 100–127.

Everest-Phillips, M. (2008). Business tax as state-building in developing countries: applying governance principles in private sector development. *International Journal of Regulation and Governance*, 8(2), pp. 123–54.

Fabri, D., and G. Baldacchino (1999). The Malta Financial Services Center: a study in microstate dependency management? In *Offshore Financial Centres and Tax Havens*, ed. Mark Hampton and Jason Abbott, pp. 140–66. London: Macmillan.

Financial Times (2009). Hurdles remain for G20 pact, 7 September, htttp://www.ft.com/cms/s/0/ec6fc87a-9b44-11de-a3a1-00144feabdc0.html.

Friedman, J., and N. Schnady (2009). How many more infants are likely to die in Africa as a result of the global financial crisis? Policy Research Working Paper WPS5023.

Geithner, T. (2008). Speech to the Economic Club of New York, 9 June, http://www.newyorkfed.org/news events/speeches/2008/tfg080609.html.

Gemmell, N., and O. Morrissey (2005). Distribution and poverty impacts of tax structure reform in developing countries: how little we know. *Development Policy Review*, 23(2), pp. 131–44.

Global Financial Integrity (2009). *Illicit Financial Flows from Developing Countries: 2002–2006*. Washington, DC: Global Financial Integrity.

Global Witness (2009). *Undue Diligence: How Banks Do Business with Corrupt Regimes*. London: Global Witness.

Gordon, R. (1981). *Tax Havens and Their Use by US Taxpayers: An Overview* (The Gordon Report). Washington, DC: Inland Revenue Service.

Gurría, A. (2008). Speech at the International Conference on Financing for Development, Doha, 29 November 2008, accessed 10 September 2009, http://www.oecd.org/document/35/0,3343 ,en_2649_37413_41765091_1_1_1_,00.html.

Hampton, M.P., and J. Christensen (2002). Offshore pariahs? Small island economies, tax havens, and the re-configuration of global finance. *World Development*, 30(9), pp. 1657–73.

Hendrix, C. (2007). *Leviathan in the Tropics? Environment, State Capacity, and Civil Conflict in the Developing World*. San Diego: University of California.

Hines, J.R., and E.M. Rice (1994). Fiscal paradise: foreign tax havens and American business. *Quarterly Journal of Economics*, 109, pp. 149–82.

Huizinga, H. and L. Laeven (2008). International profit shifting within multinationals: a multi-country perspective. *Journal of Public Economics*, 92(5–6), pp. 1164–82.

IAS Plus (2010). IFAC, http://www.iasplus.com/ifac/ifac.htm. (Online, accessed 26 April 2010.)

IASB (2010). IAS 1, http://eifrs.iasb.org/eifrs/bnstandards/en/ias1.pdf. (Online, accessed 26 April 2010.)

ILO (2009). *Key Indicators in the Labour Market*, 6th edn. Geneva: International Labour Organization.

IMF (2000). *Offshore Financial Centres*, Background paper prepared by the Monetary and Exchange Affairs Department, http://www.imf.org/external/np/maw/oshore/2000/eng/back.htm.

Kudrle, R. (2008). Did blacklisting hurt the tax havens? Research Paper no. 2008-23, Paolo Baffi Centre, Milan.

Kudrle, R., and L. Eden (2003). The campaign against tax havens: Will it last? Will it work? *Stanford Journal of Law, Business, and Finance*, 9, pp. 37–68.

Lane, P., and G. Milesi-Ferretti (2010). Cross-border investment in small international financial centers, IMF Working Paper WP/10/38.

Lesage, D., D. McNair and M. Vermeiren (2010). From Monterrey to Doha: taxation and financing for development. *Development Policy Review*, 28(2), pp. 155–72.

McNair, D., R. Dottey and A. Cobham (2010). Transfer pricing and the taxing rights of developing countries, Paper presented to the Tax Justice Network Africa Conference, Nairobi, April.

Mahon, J. (2005). Liberal states and fiscal contracts: aspects of the political economy of public finance, Paper presented at the annual meeting of the American Political Science Association.

Martinez-Diaz, L., and N. Woods (2009). The G20: the perils and opportunities of network governance for developing countries, Global Economic Governance Programme Briefing Paper, November.

Mathiason, N. (2009). Beginning of the end for tax havens. *Guardian*. Online, accessed 26 April 2010, http://www.guardian.co.uk/business/2009/mar/13/switzerland-tax-evasion-fight.

Mittone, L. (2006). Dynamic behaviour in tax evasion: an experimental approach. *Journal of Socio-Economics*, 35(5), pp. 813–35.

Murphy, R. (2008). Tax havens: creating turmoil. Evidence submitted to the Treasury Committee of the House of Commons by the Tax Justice Network UK, www.taxresearch.org.uk/Documents/CreatingTurmoil.pdf. (Online, accessed 6 March 2012.)

Murphy, R. (2009). Louder than words – and seriously missing the point. *Tax Research* blog, accessed 14 May 2010, http://www.taxresearch.org.uk/Blog/2009/06/05/louder-than-words-and-seriously-missing-the-point/.

Ndikumana, L. and J.K. Boyce (2008). New estimates of capital flight from Sub Saharan African countries: linkages with external borrowing and policy options, Working Paper Series No. 166, Political Economy Research Institute, University of Massachusetts.

Neilsen, S., P. Raimondos-Moller and G. Schjelderup (2001). *Tax Spillovers under Separate Accounting and Formula Apportionment*, Discussion Paper. London: Centre for Economic Policy and Research, www.cepr.org/pubs/dps/DP2831.aps, accessed 1 October 2009.

OECD (1998). *Harmful Tax Competition: An Emerging Global Issue*. Paris: OECD.

OECD (2003). Transfer price. *OECD Glossary of Statistical Terms*, http://stats.oecd.org/glossary/detail.asp?ID=2757. (Online, accessed 26 April 2010.)

OECD (2006). *Towards a Level Playing Field: 2006 Assessment by the Global Forum on Taxation*. Paris: Organisation for Economic Co-operation and Development.

OECD (2009). *Transfer Pricing Guidelines for Multinational Enterprises and Tax Administrations*. Paris: OECD.

Oxfam (2000). Tax havens: releasing the hidden billions for poverty eradication, Oxfam Policy Papers, http://www.oxfam.org.uk/policy/papers/taxhvn/tax.htm.

Palan, R. (1998). The emergence of an offshore economy. *Futures*, 30(1), pp. 63–73.

Palan, R. (2002). Tax havens and the commercialization of state sovereignty. *International Organization*, 56, pp. 151–76.

Palan, R. (2003). *The Offshore World: Sovereign Markets, Virtual Places, and Nomad Millionaires*. Ithaca, NY: Cornell University Press.

Ross, M.L. (2007). Does taxation lead to representation? UCLA Department of Political Science.

Scheiwiller, T. and S. Symons (2010). Corporate responsibility and paying tax. *OECD Observer: Tax and Development Special Supplement*, January.

Silbertztein, C. (2010). Transfer pricing: a challenge for developing countries. *OECD Observer: Tax and Development Special Supplement*, January.

Stewart, J. (2008). Shadow regulation and the shadow banking system. *Tax Justice Focus*, Research Edition, July, pp. 1–3, http://www.taxjustice.net/cms/upload/pdf/TJF_4-2_AABA_-_Research.pdf.

Stuart, A. (2009). Transfer pricing: a world of pain. *CFO Magazine*, 1 September, accessed 18 September 2009, www.cfo.com/article.cfm/14292573?f=most_read.

Tax Justice Network (2005). *Tax Us If You Can*. London: Tax Justice Network.

Torvik, R. (2009). *Tax Havens and Development: Status, Analyses and Measures*, Report from the Government Commission on Capital Flight from Poor Countries, Appointed by Norwegian Royal Decree of 27 June 2008. Oslo: Government Commission on Capital Flight from Poor Countries.

UN Committee of Experts on International Cooperation in Tax Matters (2009). Discussion of substantive issues related to international cooperation in tax matters: transfer pricing, including a manual and checklist for developing countries, E/C.18/2009/5, Fifth session, Geneva, 19–23 October.

UNCTAD (United Nations Conference on Trade and Development) (1999). *Transfer Pricing*, UNCTAD Series on Issues in International Investment Agreements. Geneva: UNCTAD.

UNCTAD (2008). *Guidance on Corporate Responsibility Indicators in Annual Reports*. Geneva: UNCTAD. (Online, accessed 14 May 2010, http://www.unctad.org/en/docs/iteteb20076_en.pdf.)

Williamson, J. and M. Mahar (1998). A survey of financial liberalization, Princeton Essays in International Finance.

World Bank (2009a). Protecting progress: the challenge facing low-income countries in the global recession, http://siteresources.worldbank.org/NEWS/Resources/WorldBankG20PaperonLICsSept2009.pdf.

World Bank (2009b). *Global Development Finance 2009: Charting a Global Recovery*. Washington, DC: World Bank.

World Bank (2010). Migration and Development Brief 12, http://siteresources.worldbank.org/INTPROS PECTS/Resources/334934-1110315015165/MigrationAndDevelopmentBrief12.pdf.

Zoromé, A. (2007). Concept of offshore financial centres: in search of an operational definition, IMF Working Paper WP/07/87.

4 The role of transnational institutions in framing accounting in the global south
Cameron Graham and Marcia Annisette

INTRODUCTION

Economic development does not happen naturally. It is a heavily politicized, highly structured, conflictual process. It pits institution against institution, government against government, and often race against race. It happens through coercion and seduction as much as through logic and analysis. In this chapter, we examine the parallel processes of high-level suasion and low-level insinuation by which transnational institutions frame accounting in the global south[1], shaping and influencing practices and regulations in order to fashion a tool fit for their purposes.

Of course, an alternative start to this chapter might read something like the following: Economic development cannot happen without the pre-existence of institutionalized processes that facilitate the transfer of information, the transparent management of funding arrangements, and the safeguarding of vital private sector investments. Transnational institutions like the World Bank, the International Monetary Fund (IMF), the World Trade Organization (WTO) and even the United Nations are working hard to ensure that all countries can compete on a level playing field.

Which of these perspectives is more helpful in understanding how transnational institutions influence accounting practices in the global south? The answer, we would argue, depends largely on one's level of analysis. At the level of policy, the creation of consistent standards for disclosing what entities have done with the money they have been given, whether by governments, aid organizations or private investors, helps grease the wheels of development, reducing the risks associated with funding arrangements between parties who are at considerable geographic and cultural distances. At the level of practice, however, one can often perceive the (un)intended consequences of these institutionalized arrangements: the undermining of traditional social norms, the cross-pollination of social practices, the rationalization of convivial work relationships, and the hybridization of prescribed arrangements into new and unexpected forms. Hence, in our discussion of the activities of transnational institutions in the global south, we will draw on studies of both policy and practice.

TRANSNATIONAL INSTITUTIONS AND PUBLIC SECTOR REFORM

The processes for establishing international financial accounting standards have received a lot of attention from accounting researchers, but accounting standards setting is just one small piece in the puzzle of the wholesale financial sector reform being attempted in the global south. For many reasons, the goals and aspirations of domestic leaders among them, countries of the global south are being refashioned to integrate them with the global economy. These efforts are being spearheaded by transnational institutions like the World Bank and the IMF. If we want fully to appreciate what is happening to accounting in the global south, we must come to grips with the activities of these non-accounting transnational institutions.

Transnational institutions consider public sector reform a key to economic development. They intervene in the global south not only to create financial markets, but also to reshape legal systems and privatize government services. The World Bank and the IMF seek to establish in poorer countries all the conditions for Western-style economic activity. This includes changes to the structure and organization of national governments, the creation of legal systems to enforce property rights, and the development of a financial sector capable of supporting emerging enterprises. The framework for this expounded by the World Bank is shown in Figure 4.1.

It is fascinating to look closely at this framework. It seems to assume that the developing country will have a weak government staffed by uneducated and corrupt government officials, yet it asserts that developing countries themselves identify with this diagnosis. It also puts individual rights and property rights at the heart of its reforms, suggesting that the World Bank will not acknowledge indigenous forms of government or community-based forms of property ownership. These are the sorts of implicit values that lead some researchers to take a more critical stance towards transnational institutions. Although the framework seems simple and unidirectional, its end point is equivocal. Does it produce Western-style countries that take part as equal players in the global economy, or client countries reshaped to reduce the risks associated with Western economic expansion?

Like all schematic diagrams, the World Bank's framework suffers from oversimplification. In contrast to the linearity suggested by the diagram, the actual process of public sector reform involves many simultaneous efforts with multiple path dependencies. A large number of transnational institutions besides the World Bank are involved at any given moment in reshaping the governments, legal systems and financial systems of countries in the global south. Looking only at financial sector reform, Table 4.1 lists many of the activities involved, along with the standards and the institutions that have been accorded responsibility for them.[2] In addition to the major players, there are many niche organizations listed. These cover banking supervision (BCBS), payment and settlement systems (CPSS), money laundering (FATF), insurance (IAIS), accountants (IFAC), securities commissions (IOSCO) and, of course, accounting standards (IASB). All of these operate in parallel, with changes in one organization often dependent on changes in another. The organizations are interconnected, sometimes through ex officio appointments and sometimes through shared members drawn from the pool of people with the requisite expertise and experience to serve on these boards. For example, a Brazilian central banker serving on the accounting task force of the BCBS is now a member of the IASB (see IASB, 2010), and a World Bank representative serves on the IASB's Standards Advisory Council (World Bank, 2005, p. 22).

Institutions like the World Bank and the IMF have been intensely involved in debates over accounting standards at least since the financial crises of the late 1990s; moments of crisis create the opportunity for these institutions to intervene in countries of the global

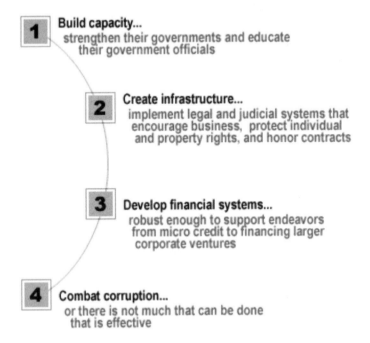

Developing countries have determined themselves that for their economies to grow and to attract business and jobs they must:

1 **Build capacity...**
strengthen their governments and educate their government officials

2 **Create infrastructure...**
implement legal and judicial systems that encourage business, protect individual and property rights, and honor contracts

3 **Develop financial systems...**
robust enough to support endeavors from micro credit to financing larger corporate ventures

4 **Combat corruption...**
or there is not much that can be done that is effective

Source: World Bank (2010).

Figure 4.1   Conceptual framework for economic development used by the World Bank

south. The World Bank and the IMF have been instrumental in crafting a framework called the International Financial Architecture (World Bank, 2001, 2005). The assumption behind these efforts appears, at first glance, to be that economic development and poverty reduction flow automatically from 'market and financial stability' (World Bank, 2005, p. 3). But in fact nothing is automatic: the World Bank pays close attention to the impact of financial crises on the poor, and attempts to ensure that mechanisms are in place to protect income, savings deposits, and access to micro-credit (World Bank, 2005, pp. 19–20), suggesting that financial crisis and subsequent reform efforts can be co-opted at the expense of the poor if not attended to carefully.

The attention of transnational institutions puts countries of the global south under a lens, revealing the state of their domestic affairs and the degree to which they conform to international economic and political expectations. The auditing and invigilation of global south countries by these institutions are now highly standardized, through repeated practice and the desire to produce comparative data. An example of these standardized efforts is the series of *Reports on the Observance of Standards and Codes*, a key joint initiative of the World Bank and the IMF. As of June 2005, observance reports had been issued on over 120 countries to assess their conformance with international

Table 4.1   Division of responsibilities for financial sector reform amongst transnational institutions

Area	Standard	Issuing body
Macroeconomic policy and data transparency		
Monetary and financial policy transparency	Code of Good Practices on Transparency in Monetary and Financial Policies	IMF
Fiscal policy transparency	Code of Good Practices on Fiscal Transparency	IMF
Data dissemination	Special Data Dissemination Standard/ General Data Dissemination System 1	IMF
Institutional and market infrastructure		
Insolvency	Insolvency and Creditor Rights	World Bank
Corporate governance	Principles of Governance	OECD
Accounting	International Accounting Standards (IAS)	IASB
Auditing	International Standards on Auditing (ISA)	IFAC
Payment and settlement	Core Principles for Systemically Important Payment Systems	CPSS
	Recommendations for Securities Settlement Systems	CPSS/IOSCO
Market integrity	The Forty Recommendations of the Financial Action Task Force	FATF
	Special Recommendations against Terrorist Financing	
Financial regulation and supervision		
Banking supervision	Core Principles for Effective Banking Supervision	BCBS
Securities regulation	Objectives and Principles of Securities Regulation	IOSCO
Insurance supervision	Insurance Core Principles	IAIS

Source: Financial Stability Board (2010).

financial standards, their transparency in various fiscal categories, and their capability in key areas like banking, insurance and securities (World Bank, 2005, p. 3).

The World Bank's part in these country-specific investigations covers accounting and auditing. The Bank's efforts have produced lists of what the Bank refers to as 'lessons and key issues going forward' (Hegarty, Gielen and Hirata Barros, 2004; World Bank, 2005, pp. 24–5) for the reform of accounting regulation and practice. These include the importance of government incentives and disincentives to reinforce the market incentives for compliance with accounting and auditing standards, the need for practical guidance on the exercise of effective regulation, the need for a modified set of accounting standards for small and medium-sized enterprises, the need for better human and financial resources for implementing standards, the need for adaptable mechanisms for public oversight of auditing in developing countries, and the priority of sound accounting and auditing practices as a foundation for banking, insurance and securities reform. On the whole, then, the World Bank and the IMF seem to pay attention to the practical aspects of accounting and auditing reform, rather than the technical content of the standards themselves.

ACCOUNTING RESEARCH ON TRANSNATIONAL INSTITUTIONS

Regulatory Networks

Accounting research on transnational institutions has examined how they structure the field of accounting standards setting. Richardson (2009) has documented the network of regulatory and institutional bodies that influence accounting standards setting, using Canada as his example. Richardson suggests that nation states are ceding governance responsibility to transnational institutions, even as they create more and more government watchdog agencies in response to financial scandals. This is part of a process of transformation from the welfare state to the regulatory state, says Richardson, wherein the state arranges the incentives and regulations that steer non-state entities in the provision of services, rather than providing the services directly through government agencies. Richardson demonstrates that the World Bank, in conjunction with the International Organization of Securities Commissions (IOSCO), plays a key role in standards setting through its ability to nominate or approve members on other key standards-related committees, such as the Basel Committee on Banking Supervision. Richardson (2009, p. 583) argues that the tighter interconnections between international organizations compared to those that exist between domestic organizations create an asymmetry of power and influence that favours the international institutions.[3] In particular, the Basel Committee emerges as a key player in the network, brokering the influence of both the World Bank and IOSCO (Richardson, 2009, p. 584).

The Role of Accountants and Accounting Firms

Similarly, Loft, Humphrey and Turley (2006) look at the role of the International Federation of Accountants (IFAC), which deals with global auditing standards.[4] Of particular interest is their discussion of the steps towards credibility that IFAC has gone through, climaxing with their recognition by the WTO as a standard setter in 1996 (Loft et al., 2006, p. 431). Their analysis helps us to recognize the rich political process by which standards bodies are formed. Like Richardson, Loft et al. examine the way that membership is determined on the boards and committees of transnational institutions. However, Loft et al. (2006, pp. 436–8) stress the importance of technical expertise, rather than institutional representation, in making up membership. They note that the Big Four accounting firms are increasingly being represented directly in international accounting institutions, rather than appearing indirectly as representatives of their country-level accounting institutions. They raise the question of conflict of interest, as the representatives of Big Four accounting firms are being asked to create standards for work that is carried out primarily by their own firms.

Accounting and Trade Liberalization

Another transnational institution which has had a profound impact on accounting in the global south is the WTO. As Arnold (2005) shows, the globalization of accounting as a service industry is highly political and structured by fiercely negotiated general treaties and country-specific agreements. The WTO's General Agreement on Trade in Services (GATS) lays the groundwork for this by establishing the WTO's authority to discipline the domestic regulation of professional services. Countries that try to protect their own accounting industry will have their legal and regulatory barriers dismantled by the WTO, involving where necessary the international courts. This removes the obstacles faced by major international accounting firms when trying to set up shop in developing countries. Arnold rejects the argument that the market's need for transparency and accountability leads naturally to the globalization of accounting. She argues instead that the market is served by transnational institutions with their own agenda of deregulation and privatization, which create the conditions for this globalization. This is a steadily escalating process of liberalization, because the GATS itself provides for successive renegotiations of its terms with the express intent of increasing transborder flows of services and the profits therefrom. Arnold (2005, pp. 307–08) demonstrates the asymmetry of the GATS even amongst developed countries, where the European Union pushes the US to use international accounting standards and the US pushes the rest of the world to allow its accounting firms greater and greater access to their professional services markets.

Arnold's observations are important. The present era of liberalized trade depends on and insists upon the free flow of capital and profits. This covers resource industries, the manufacturing of products, the sale of products, and the provision of services. In order to ensure that developing countries cannot stand in the way of progress towards these hegemonic goals, organizations like the World Bank make their aid contingent on cooperation with liberal trade agendas, and those like the IMF and the WTO insist that developing countries embark upon economic restructuring at the expense of the pursuit of their own social development. These conditions are not simply the product of democratically elected governments in the developing world. Private organizations have significant and direct influence on the agenda of transnational institutions, banding together into powerful lobby groups. In the realm of accounting, this can be seen by the membership of Deloitte & Touche and the American Institute of Certified Public Accountants in the USCSI (see Coalition of Service Industries, 2010), which lobbies the US government on trade issues; and the membership of Deloitte LLP, Grant Thornton LLP, KPMG and PricewaterhouseCoopers, along with all the major UK accounting institutes, in the IFSL (see International Financial Services London, 2010), which represents the UK financial services industry in trade negotiations.[5] Arnold documents the direct role of major UK and US accounting firms in international meetings and negotiations on trade liberalization. She also documents how multilateral agreements prevent developing countries from protecting their accounting industries from large UK and US firms: countries cannot impose residency requirements on the professional certification process, nor can they insist upon specific forms of organization or regulatory compliance that would effectively require international firms to take extraordinary compliance measures (Arnold, 2005, pp. 312–14).

The implications of the WTO's multilateral agreements must not to be oversimplified.

Arnold argues that any reading that suggests the WTO agreements are a mere extension of previous colonial patterns, or a straightforward exercise in hegemony by powerful developed nations, underestimates the impact of these agreements on nations like the United States. Even the Sarbanes–Oxley Act, with its government supervision of auditing and conflict-of-interest prohibitions, is open to challenge under the General Agreement on Trade in Services. This arises because of the requirement in WTO agreements that trade-restrictive measures cannot be used when less restrictive measures would achieve the same policy objective (Arnold, 2005, pp. 321–2). Arnold (p. 325) also argues that one cannot ignore the power differences between the elite partners of major accounting firms, who exercise their voice in international debate, and the vast lower echelons of the accounting industry, who have no effective voice. The impact on accounting of the WTO and other transnational institutions is therefore complex and nuanced. Indeed it is important to recognize here as well that impacts are not unidirectional. Extant research has also shown how accounting has served to advance the agendas of the WTO (Moerman and van der Laan, 2006), the World Bank (Catchpowle and Cooper, 1999; Rahaman and Lawrence, 2001; Annisette, 2004; Rahaman, Lawrence and Roper, 2004) and other transnational institutions, but it is not this particular aspect of the relationship that is explored in this chapter. Instead, as mentioned earlier, our concern is to highlight the varying ways in which these institutions have come to affect accounting in the global south. Whilst the foregoing has served to highlight their policy-level impacts, in what is to follow we consider how those policy-level impacts have been translated into practice.

ACCOUNTING RESEARCH ON SPECIFIC COUNTRIES IN THE GLOBAL SOUTH

Accounting Standardization in Bangladesh

So what effect do these institutional processes have on specific countries? For an example, we turn to Mir and Rahaman (2005), who studied the adoption of accounting standards in Bangladesh. They argue that an implicit assumption of the global standards setting process is that accounting is unbiased and culturally independent. They dispute this assumption, and also the contention that international accounting standards promote economic development. They cite evidence that countries which do not adopt international standards, or which adapt the standards to local needs, experience economic growth similar to or better than that of countries that adopt the standards unchanged: 'the role and relevance of the IASs in the developing world depend largely on the processes through which these standards are adopted' (Mir and Rahaman, 2005, p. 820). This study of Bangladesh reveals the messy processes of adoption. Standards adoption processes are initiated by grants from transnational institutions rather than national institutes (p. 826). National institutes have trouble convincing members of the usefulness of the standards and achieve only sporadic compliance (p. 830). The authors argue that national institutes use the adoption of international standards in part as ceremonial activities that increase their own legitimacy in the national context of accountants and accounting institutes.

Accounting and Government Legitimacy in Romania

In addition to legitimizing and privileging elites in developing countries (see also Annisette, 2000), international accounting standards can also act as a symbolic resource to governments seeking external and internal legitimacy. King et al. (2001, p.158) observed that during Romania's immediate post-reform era, given the country's political instability, decisions affecting the economy (such as the appropriate accounting model) were seen by the Romanian state to be of little importance. However, as politicians became aware of the preference of the World Bank, IMF and European Union for international accounting standards, there was a swift rise of accounting to the political agenda. The state quickly endorsed international accounting standards for fear that failure to adopt this model would jeopardize Romania's accession to the European Union, as well as its ability to attract IMF and World Bank funding.

Accounting Labour in China

Studies such as these indicate that the dependence of developing countries' national governments on transnational institutions for both funding and legitimacy spurs the adoption of international accounting standards. Yet transnational institutions influence more than just the regulation of accounting. They take a keen interest as well in the development of accounting labour, and are therefore involved in the professionalization of accounting as the economies of poor countries become liberalized. The circumstances surrounding the professionalization of accounting differ from country to country, particularly with respect to colonial history (Annisette, 1999). However, increasingly during the latter part of the twentieth century, the steering hand of transnational institutions has been evident, either though moral suasion[6] or more directly by providing funding and other resources to promote the profession. Yapa and Hao (2007), for example, describe how professional accounting was initiated in 1978 by the Chinese state with the assistance of the World Bank. The World Bank provided practical support not just for the development of Chinese accounting standards but also for the training of up to 25,000 accounting professionals per year at a continuing education facility in Beijing (Yapa and Hao, 2007, p.34).

Problems Created by Public Sector Reform in Bangladesh and Ghana

Transnational institutions nevertheless have the capacity to exert strong influences on accounting in client countries. This is accomplished not by threat or brute force but by carefully rationalized administrative requirements. Seemingly value-neutral terms like 'efficiency', 'transparency' and 'accountability' are employed, with significant implications for accounting and auditing in the client country. For an illustration, consider the studies by Uddin and Hopper (2001, 2003) of the privatization of a state-owned soap company in Bangladesh, conducted at the urging of the World Bank. It was argued by World Bank officials that the public sector in Bangladesh was inefficient and suffered from a lack of transparency stemming from weak accounting controls. The World Bank expected privatization to bring efficiency, productivity and profitability owing to the 'discipline of the market'. Similarly, Uddin and Tsamenyi (2005) document how the IMF and the World Bank promoted a series of public sector reforms in Ghana with similar expectations. In both these cases, Bangladesh and Ghana, the process of public sector reform left many of the identified 'problems' unresolved. Instead of creating ideal free-market conditions with renewed investment and fair competition, these reform efforts were exploited by opportunistic local actors, resulting in what Uddin and Hopper (2001, *passim*) refer to as 'new despotic regimes'. The intended benefits of privatization were never attained. Despite the introduction of new accounting regimes, budgeting and accountability remained problematic because local actors were able to ally with each other to avoid required procedures and circumvent prescribed lines of accountability.

ACCOUNTING AND THE MONITORING OF ECONOMIC DEVELOPMENT PROJECTS

While advocacy for international financial accounting standards arises in transnational institutions almost as a by-product of the work they do, other accounting initiatives arise directly from their core activities. Transnational institutions seek to monitor the flows of money through development and aid projects that they fund. The agreements for these projects therefore often require the recipients to adopt specific managerial accounting policies and practices. The rational argument for such requirements is usually grounded in terms of accountability: those who stump up the cash for a venture want to ensure that it is being used for the intended purposes. This is the widely accepted principal–agent perspective on accounting. Alternative perspectives are sometimes helpful, however, and are often provocative. Is formal accounting used as window-dressing to obscure a lack of oversight? Are accounting reports provided merely to ensure the continuing flow of funds from donor countries? Or are the problematic effects of development initiatives simply unintended consequences brought about by the manifest complexity of the projects and the bounded rationality of the participants?

Case Studies

Case studies of development initiatives provide some useful insights to help answer such questions. Problematic outcomes are observed even when seemingly enlightened interventions in developing countries are made by transnational institutions. For example, efforts to reform education and improve the ability of local populations to contribute to economic development, and benefit from it, achieved only mixed results in Latin America (Neu et al., 2006). While the World Bank was able to use management accounting routines to extend its reach and reinforce the legitimacy of its expertise, local actors were able to work around formal requirements to achieve their own goals. The geographical and social distance between World Bank officials and local workers mitigated the quality of the information in accounting reports. The construction of information about local activities through accounting techniques depended on poorly trained workers striving to satisfy symbolic goals. The 'act of accounting' was shown in this study to be somewhat cobbled together and sometimes ceremonial, often geared to the requirements of the system rather than the intended social goals. This does not mean that the development programmes were necessarily ineffective, simply that the accounting routines were sometimes only loosely connected to the goals.

The World Bank operates both through direct contact with client nations and through indirect funding mechanisms. Hence, accounting systems for development projects play a significant role in structuring the field of agents within the client country and connecting it to the broader field of international development efforts and transnational institutions. What happens during and as a result of any given project depends on the particular configuration of institutional forces in and around the project. Neu, Silva and Ocampo Gomez (2008) compare the World Bank's efforts to improve higher education in Guatemala and Mexico. In the case of Guatemala, despite the government's reliance on World Bank funding and accounting technologies to develop and manage lower levels of education, the field of higher education remained relatively insulated from World Bank influence. Similarities between the financial systems in place at Guatemala's university and those of World Bank projects were attributed to the university's exposure to practices at universities in other countries rather than to the direct influence of the World Bank. In the case of Mexico, however, contingent funding mechanisms and institutionalized planning processes were used to align the efforts of university administrators and faculty members with the priorities of government. Discourse around financial measures and practices in Mexican higher education came to mimic the World Bank's approach to funding. Hence, according to this study, development efforts should not be regarded as unilateral or monotonic. They depend on the social capitals of client governments, the decisions those governments make, and the unique contextual features of each project, not just on the expertise and funding of the transnational institution.

Variability in Institutional Reform Projects

Neu, Everett and Rahaman (2009) emphasize that the configuration of unique features in a project is highly dynamic. It is always becoming a different configuration, always changing shape, always growing and shrinking as new actors, technologies and vocabularies are added and taken away. They examine the way that El Salvador has been inundated with the initiatives, projects and agents of multiple transnational institutions. They looked at the activities of multilateral development banks like the World Bank, international organizations like UNICEF, quasi-governmental organizations like USAID, and non-governmental organizations like the Red Cross. Through interviews with government officials, they were able to track the Inter-American Development Bank (IDB) as it interacted with various government departments and other transnational development institutions. Differences in how the IDB located itself in the client country and in how accounting systems were used to provide surveillance on IDB projects led to different potential new organizational configurations and accounting technologies. Various modes of coordination were used in attempts to establish transparency and accountability in government activities like procurement. Accounting systems were particularly influential in enabling the use of common vocabularies, while at the same time inhibiting consistent practices, because of the unique embeddedness of particular accounting systems in particular organizations. Hence, accounting itself becomes entangled in the complex field that transnational institutions attempt to influence through development projects.

Given the inherent and constant dynamism of these configurations, how can we characterize the overall impact of transnational institutions on accounting in developing countries? The above studies suggest that the World Bank, the IMF and other such institutions do much more than simply execute development projects. They are involved in transforming developing countries to create in them the necessary conditions for accountability. They do this by mandating a variety of basic practices and training local people to perform them: the keeping of accounting records, the creation of financial information systems, and the use of performance indicators, along with various auditing and monitoring activities (Neu and Ocampo, 2007). This transformation is inherently rational, yet so complex that it is neither predictable nor inevitable.

INSIGHTS INTO THE COMPLEXITY OF TRANSNATIONAL INSTITUTIONS

This is true not simply because of the unique complexities of each national field in which a development project takes place. We must recognize, in addition, that each transnational institution is itself a complex political beast. There is no univocal World Bank, but rather a vast network of offices and agents working on multiple simultaneous initiatives, often with somewhat conflicting goals and interests. This is clearly demonstrated by Rahman (1998), who shows how the United Nations' attempt to regulate transnational companies was attenuated by political coalitions amongst member nations. This occurred entirely within the UN, even before the practical complications of implementation might be encountered. The same observation can be made about the governments of client countries, which are large and internally conflicted organizations.

This is not to say that all actors involved have similar ability (or inability) to influence the proceedings. The studies we have cited repeatedly document the imbalance of power between transnational institutions, with their backing from developed countries, and impoverished client nations. They reveal that the language of neutrality and transparency surrounding accounting technologies serves as a guise for the politics of development, in which major corporations and large accounting firms play a lead role. Although this chapter has focused its attention on transnational institutions, other actors exert an influence that must not be ignored. Critically, amongst them are international accounting firms and entrepreneurial professional accountancy institutes such as the UK-based Association of Chartered Certified Accountants (ACCA). Indeed it can be argued that accounting firms and organizations have been crucial in laying down the infrastructure for the rapid accounting harmonization processes currently taking place in the global south; for through their early diffusion processes they served to create the conditions for the high degree of path dependency towards harmonization around the Anglo-American accounting model.

In instigating public sector reform and economic development programmes in the global south, transnational institutions such as the World Bank, the WTO and the IMF espouse discourses of 'development' and more recently 'globalization' as justifications for reforming the accounting infrastructure of target nations. 'Development' on the one hand is portrayed as a self-evident, moral goal whose virtue as an end state is never questioned but is proposed as natural and incontestable. 'Globalization' on the other hand is depicted as an inexorable process, sweeping over borders and transforming the world in ways beyond the power of individual nations to resist. The global south is thus encouraged to position itself for the 'modernizing' and even 'liberating' effects of globalization, which like 'development' is linked with progress.

Underlying both justificatory discourses is a particular vision of the enabling role of accounting in achieving pre-given ends. These include improved decision making, increased transparency, and efficiency, which in turn contribute to 'development' or facilitate 'globalization'. Paradoxically, however, within the very institutions that advance the cause of an enabling accounting, the limits of accounting so conceived have been repeatedly revealed by accounting scholars. Saravanamuthu (2004) is a case in point. Focusing on the Word Bank's dismal score card in meeting its much touted social and environmental agenda, she attributes the Bank's failure in these areas to the financial bias imposed on the Bank by the accounting standards that it employs. She argues that accounting's inherent bias to privilege economic interests creates contradictions for businesses that are expected to behave in a socially responsible manner (2004, p. 297). Thus, she suggests, the World Bank's stated goals of poverty reduction in an environmentally sustainable way are constantly trumped by its financially oriented lending standards. Yet, she says, nowhere in its financial reports is this dismal failure in the social and environmental realms evident.

Annisette (2004) goes even further. Through an examination of two of the World Bank's internal reports, she demonstrates that, even from the standpoint of achieving pre-given economic ends, accounting has grimly failed within the World Bank. Rather than being used to inform decision makers about the viability of loans to support projects in the global south, both internal reports reveal that accounting came to be used in ritualistic and ceremonial ways to support a deeply embedded loan approval culture within the Bank (2004, pp. 319–21). More significantly, however, Annisette aims to expose the ideological nature of the World Bank's developmental agenda by highlighting its New Right neo-liberalist underpinnings. She disagrees with Saravanamuthu's diagnosis of the Bank's dismal social-environmental score card. She argues instead that the Bank's failure to live up to its social and environmental mission has less to do with its accounting practices and more to do with the fundamental contradiction between the nature of the neo-liberal capitalist development project and the twin objectives of poverty reduction and sustainable development (2004, p. 316).

For Murphy (2008), however, even this is an incomplete rendering of the Bank's current position within the contemporary political economy. In his view, both accounts ignore the complexities of contemporary globalization processes: the new actors which they produce, the role of institutions like the IMF and the World Bank in supporting their expansionary missions, and the manner in which accounting is deployed by them to support such. Drawing on Hardt and Negri's decentred empire thesis, Murphy's focus is on the role of international financial institutions in facilitating the emergence of a new global elite constituted by 'footloose transnationals' (2008, p. 737), corporations that are not bound to a hegemonic nation state and that often have roots outside core capitalist states (pp. 714–15). In Murphy's analysis of Mittal Steel's voracious acquisition of state-owned steel plants throughout the world, the IMF and the World Bank are presented as willing to relax their much touted values of corporate transparency, accountability, ethics and democracy, in order to support the projects of those elites it deems suitable to join the ranks of this global managerial cohort. Murphy goes on to argue that, in the case of Mittal's acquisition of state-owned steel plants in Algeria and Trinidad, the IMF and the World Bank acted as external auditors, management consultants and lenders, and in the auditor role produced an overly pessimistic view of the nations' financial balance sheets so as to justify the sale of state assets to Mittal Steel (pp. 721–2). These are pretty serious charges. They open up a space for accounting research to go beyond 'testing the World Bank's claims' (Uddin and Hopper, 2003) and instead focus attention on how the World Bank, the WTO and the IMF enact and flout these accounting-related values in their dealings with client nations in the global south.

SUMMING THINGS UP

In summing up, then, what clear insights can we make about the role of transnational institutions in accounting developments in the global south? For one, whilst contemporary research has no doubt indicated that these institutions are active players in the accounting transformations taking place in the global south, it is important to note that they come on the heels of earlier actors such as international accounting firms, imperial professional bodies and multinational firms, which have laid the groundwork for the rapid accounting harmonization processes taking place today. It is for this reason that the countries of the global south have long led the way in adopting international accounting standards as national standards (Annisette, 2004, p. 317).

At the level of financial accounting policy, the aggressive involvement of transnational institutions in contemporary public sector reform projects therefore does not necessarily involve a fundamental change in accounting orientation. Rather, these institutions promote the implementation of tighter monitoring and enforcement mechanisms in local sites. It is thus at the level of accounting practice, where accountability mechanisms are installed in grassroots organizations, that the impact of transnational institutions is most profoundly felt. In both policy and practice, accounting reforms are insisted upon in the blind faith that 'development' depends on accounting 'improvements': better accounting promotes economic development or, alternatively, poor accounting systems impede economic development. Either way, accounting's developmental role is taken as an article of faith. Yet, as has been shown, there is increasing discomfort amongst accounting researchers not only with the unproblematic relationship between accounting and development but indeed with the concept of development itself.

NOTES

1. We use the term 'global south' in an attempt to avoid the assumptions of other terms like the 'developing countries'. The orientalist underpinnings of development discourse (Said, 1979) and its role in the making of the so-called Third World (Escobar, 1995) are of concern to many accounting researchers.
2. While Table 4.1 suggests neat divisions, in reality these are messy processes that overlap considerably, and are the subject of much wrangling over whose work stops where. It is not hard to imagine that the table would look different if drawn up by some other institution than the World Bank, and that any consensus this table represents was hard won.
3. Soederberg (2003) argues that an asymmetry also exists along the public–private dimension. In her analysis of the work of the IMF on international standards for corporate governance, she says that 'the intricate

webs of governance seem to (falsely) convey a pluralistic arrangement, involving both private and public organisations, and thereby containing built-in checks and balances. Yet . . . the private sector has been granted more power over policy formation in both states and markets in the South' (p. 13). Soederberg concludes that the promotion by transnational institutions of the particular forms of corporate governance favoured in wealthy countries is a deliberate strategy to extend the influence of these countries over the global south, in service of the material interests of the wealthy.

4. IFAC is one of the organizations that promotes the notion of an unproblematic relationship between accounting reform and economic growth (International Federation of Accountants, 2007).
5. It is worth noting that the slogan of the IFSL is 'Promoting UK financial services throughout the world' (International Financial Services London, 2010). There is nothing hidden about this agenda, yet the myth of invisible market forces leading towards one global economy persists.
6. An example of the kinds of moral suasion is statements directly linking economic development with professional development; for example, 'an appropriately qualified and experienced profession is one of the keys to sustained economic development' (Althea Rose, in *Certified Accountant*, March 1991).

REFERENCES

Annisette, M. (1999). Importing accounting: the case of Trinidad and Tobago. *Accounting, Business and Financial History*, 9(1), pp. 103–33.

Annisette, M. (2000). Imperialism and the professions: the education and certification of accountants in Trinidad and Tobago. *Accounting, Organizations and Society*, 25(7), pp. 631–59.

Annisette, M. (2004). The true nature of the World Bank. *Critical Perspectives on Accounting*, 15(3), pp. 303–23.

Arnold, P.J. (2005). Disciplining domestic regulation: the World Trade Organization and the market for professional services. *Accounting, Organizations and Society*, 30(4), pp. 299–330.

Catchpowle, L., and C. Cooper (1999). No escaping the financial: the economic referent in South Africa. *Critical Perspectives on Accounting*, 10(6), pp. 711–46.

Coalition of Service Industries (2010). *CSI Members*, http://www.uscsi.org/members/current.htm, downloaded 4 March 2010.

Escobar, A (1995) *Encountering Development: The Making and Unmaking of the Third World*. Princeton, NJ: Princeton University Press.

Financial Stability Board (2010). *12 Key Standards for Sound Financial Systems*, http://www.financialstability-board.org/cos/key_standards.htm, downloaded 8 February 2010.

Hegarty, J., F. Gielen and A.C. Hirata Barros (2004). *Implementation of International Accounting and Auditing Standards: Lessons Learned from the World Bank's Accounting and Auditing ROSC Program*, http://www.worldbank.org/ifa/LessonsLearned_ROSC_AA.pdf, downloaded 4 February 2010.

IASB (2010). *Members of the IASB*, http://www.iasb.org/The+organisation/Members+of+the+IASB/Amaro+Luiz+de+Oliveira+Gomes.htm.

International Federation of Accountants (2007). *IFAC Global Survey Recognizes Profession's Role in Contributing to Economic Growth and Highlights Need for More Accounting Talent: World Accountancy Week Begins*, http://www.ifac.org/MediaCenter/?q=node/view/525, downloaded 12 April 2010.

International Financial Services London (2010). *Member Directory*, http://www.ifsl.org.uk/output/MemberDirectory-1.aspx, downloaded 4 March 2010.

King, N., A. Beattie, A.-M. Cristescu and P. Weetman (2001). Developing accounting and audit in a transition economy: the Romanian experience. *European Accounting Review*, 10(1), pp. 149–71.

Loft, A., C. Humphrey and S. Turley (2006). In pursuit of global regulation: changing governance and accountability structures at the International Federation of Accountants (IFAC). *Accounting, Auditing and Accountability Journal*, 19(3), pp. 428–51.

Mir, M.Z., and A.S. Rahaman (2005). The adoption of international accounting standards in Bangladesh: an exploration of rationale and process. *Accounting, Auditing and Accountability Journal*, 18(6), pp. 816–41.

Moerman, L., and S. van der Laan (2006). TRIPS and the pharmaceutical industry: prescription for profit? *Critical Perspectives in Accounting*, 17(8), pp. 1089–1106.

Murphy, J. (2008). International financial institutions and the new global managerial order. *Critical Perspectives in Accounting*, 19, pp. 714–40.

Neu, D., J. Everett and A.S. Rahaman (2009). Accounting assemblages, desire, and the body without organs: a case study of international development lending in Latin America. *Accounting, Auditing and Accountability Journal*, 22(3), pp. 319–50.

Neu, D., and E. Ocampo (2007). Doing missionary work: the World Bank and the diffusion of financial practices. *Critical Perspectives in Accounting*, 18, pp. 363–89.

Neu, D., E. Ocampo, C. Graham and M. Heincke (2006). 'Informing' technologies and the World Bank. *Accounting, Organizations and Society*, 31(7), pp. 635–62.

Neu, D., L. Silva and E. Ocampo Gomez (2008). Diffusing financial practices in Latin American higher education: understanding the intersection between global influence and the local context. *Accounting, Auditing and Accountability Journal*, 21(1), pp. 49–77.

Rahaman, A.S., and S. Lawrence (2001). A negotiated order perspective on public sector accounting and financial control. *Accounting, Auditing and Accountability Journal*, 14(2), pp. 147–65.

Rahaman, A.S., S. Lawrence and J. Roper (2004). Social and environmental reporting at the VRA: institutionalised legitimacy or legitimation crisis? *Critical Perspectives on Accounting*, 15(1), pp. 35–56.

Rahman, S.F. (1998). International accounting regulation by the United Nations: a power perspective. *Accounting, Auditing and Accountability Journal*, 11(5), pp. 593–623.

Richardson, A.J. (2009). Regulatory networks for accounting and auditing standards: a social network analysis of Canadian and international standard-setting. *Accounting, Organizations and Society*, 34, pp. 571–88.

Said, E. (1979). *Orientalism*. New York: Vintage Books.

Saravanamuthu, K. (2004). What is measured counts: harmonized corporate reporting and sustainable economic development. *Critical Perspectives on Accounting*, 15(3), pp. 295–302.

Soederberg, S. (2003). The promotion of 'Anglo-American' corporate governance in the south: who benefits from the new international standard? *Third World Quarterly*, 24(1), pp. 7–27.

Uddin, S., and T. Hopper (2001). A Bangladesh soap opera: privatisation, accounting, and regimes of control in a less developed country. *Accounting, Organizations and Society*, 26(7–8), pp. 643–72.

Uddin, S., and T. Hopper (2003). Accounting for privatisation in Bangladesh: testing World Bank claims. *Critical Perspectives on Accounting*, 14(7), pp. 739–74.

Uddin, S., and M. Tsamenyi (2005). Public sector reforms and the public interest: a case study in accounting control changes and performance monitoring in a Ghanaian state-owned enterprise. *Accounting, Auditing and Accountability Journal*, 18(5), pp. 648–74.

World Bank (2001). *International Financial Architecture: An Update on World Bank Group Activities*, http://www.worldbank.org/ifa/LessonsLearned_ROSC_AA.pdf, downloaded 4 February 2010.

World Bank (2005). *International Financial Architecture: A Progress Report*, http://www.worldbank.org/ifa/IFA%20progress%20report%202005.pdf, downloaded 12 February 2010.

World Bank (2010). *About Us: Challenge*, http://web.worldbank.org/WBSITE/EXTERNAL/EXTABOUTUS/0,,contentMDK:20040565~menuPK:1696892~pagePK:51123644~piPK:329829~theSitePK:29708,00.html, downloaded 8 February 2010.

Yapa, P.W.S., and Z.P. Hao (2007). An analysis of current trends in accounting professional development in People's Republic of China. *Asian Review of Accounting*, 15(1), pp. 25–44.

5 Accounting professionalization in developing countries
Chris Poullaos and Chibuike U. Uche

INTRODUCTION

Over 35 years ago Terry Johnson (1973) wondered whether professional occupations 'armed only with the authority of expertise' could or would contribute to a democratic and prosperous future for third world countries (p. 281). Would they, accountancy included, contribute to economic growth and political development and act as a bulwark against political elites in one-party states 'despite the fact that they may share a common status and occupational background' (p. 282)? Johnson thought not, in part because he doubted that professionalism was a cultural universal capable of being transmitted from a single metropolitan source (Britain) to 'a wide variety of receiving cultures' (p. 284). Today the International Federation of Accountants (IFAC), the Association of Chartered Certified Accountants (ACCA) and the international accounting/professional services firms – cross-border entities networked with transnational institutions such as the WTO – are among those operating as though a universal professionalism exists, or can and should be made to exist, across the world.

In particular IFAC's current efforts to establish 'global' professional educational/ accreditation standards (along with standards on ethics, assurance, management accounting and the public sector) to complement the financial reporting standards produced by the International Accounting Standards Board (IASB) suggest that Johnson's broad issue remains live. Just as the relevance to developing countries of the IASB's international financial reporting standards (IFRS) and 'Western' accounting practices more broadly have long been questioned,[1] so may the associated efforts to influence the organization, education and training of practitioners in developing nations. If one believes 'that the accounting systems of a developing country should be relevant to the country's needs rather than parody another country's system' (Wallace, 1990, p. 6) then one might also worry if a developing country were to mimic or be otherwise influenced by the professionalization processes of a developed nation, in whole or in part.

But why, exactly, given that the processes of producing and organizing embodied practitioners cannot be read off in a simple fashion from the ensemble of accounting standards and practices per se? The aim of this chapter is to answer this question using some of the (English-language) accounting professionalization literature that deals with developing countries. That literature is limited, so our remarks are tentative. We hope that future research will extend and correct the analysis presented here. Nevertheless, the work done to date identifies various ways in which developed nation professionalization processes have, *in conjunction with local dynamics*, had an impact upon developing nations through their impact upon the organization of accountants locally.

The broad accounting professionalization literature of the last 25 years has explored themes such as: how accountancy has been turned into an elite occupation (with relatively high wealth, status and power over its work compared to 'trades' such as plumbing and carpentry); how its elite status has been used to gain a privileged position in the markets for expert services; its relationship with significant institutions and social actors such as the state, markets (capital markets especially), social elites, the universities and other occupations (among others); and segmentation and rivalry within it.[2] While acknowledging that accountants have provided socially valued services, scholars have not been prepared to regard the achievement by (at least some) accountants of elite status as a simple by-product of their functional contribution. Instead they have highlighted the embeddedness of professionalization within broader social, economic and political contexts. Nor do scholars claim that either professionalization (as a process of occupational enhancement) or professionalism (as a way of producing and organizing accountants and their work) is uniform across space and time. Furthermore, their concerns overlap with parts of the literature on accounting in less developed and emerging economies. For all these reasons the professionalization literature provides a relevant vantage point for addressing our research question, although, as the reader may anticipate, it supports Johnson's scepticism.

In broad terms our argument is that there are both historical and contemporary links between professionalization in the developing and in the developed world. As a result professionalization in developing countries is a hybrid that is both idiosyncratic (incorporating both local specificities and offshore exemplars) and problematic (it does not function as Johnson's development theorists had hoped or predicted). A particular form of hybrid found in the Philippines, parts of Africa and possibly elsewhere is the combination of rational-legal logic introduced by colonizers (assuming more or less autonomous individuals engaging in individual social exchanges, with their individual interests in mind but constrained by the rule of law) and a local patrimonial logic based upon group solidarity centred upon a patron whose duty, ideal-typically, is to protect the group, the members of which, in turn, offer the patron their primary allegiance. The respective dynamics involved are contradictory.

Before exploring this argument further we sketch the contemporary legacies of formal empire as reflected in the organization of accountancy in a selection of former British colonies, with the situation in Nigeria, Ghana and Sierra Leone highlighted in particular. We offer some tentative, constructive suggestions that may help to move the profession forward in those locales. Turning then to the case of the Philippines (a formal colony of the USA for a time), we return to the issue of how tensions between rational-legal and patrimonial logics are problematic for professionalism in developing countries, before offering our final thoughts.

THE DEVELOPED–DEVELOPING COUNTRY PROFESSIONALIZATION NEXUS

Today few if any developing countries have before them an open slate when it comes to choosing whether or not to adopt the professionalization processes and modes of professionalism of developed nations.[3] In part this is because traces of past contact remain.

Historical Legacies of Empire

The legacies of formal empire are significant. Those pertaining to the British Empire have received the most attention to date, although even in that case the research is not so extensive, systematic and consciously comparative that we can generalize the points made below to all the former British colonies now regarded as 'developing'. Nevertheless, they are suggestive. As noted by Sian (2010, p. 217), within 'the imperial network, the professionalization of accountancy became yet another vehicle for the dissemination of British institutions and practices'.

Our approach here is to present a scenario that applies reasonably well to parts of Africa (Nigeria, Uganda, Ghana and Kenya), the Caribbean (Trinidad and Tobago, and Jamaica) and Asia (Malaysia, Sri Lanka and India). It is based on the country studies of Annisette (1999, 2000, 2003, 2010), Bakre (2005, 2006, 2010), Sian (2006, 2007, 2010), Susela (1999, 2010), Uche (2002, 2007, 2010), Verma (2010), Verma and Gray (2006), Wallace (1992) and Yapa (2006, 2010); and also Johnson and Caygill (1971), Parker (1989, 2005), Briston and Kedslie (1997) and Poullaos and Sian (2010).[4] We acknowledge that Trinidad and Tobago was (as at July 2009) classified by the World Bank as a 'high' income country, while Malaysia and Jamaica were categorized as 'upper middle'. Nevertheless they were, like the other countries mentioned, subject to British economic domination for a considerable time and experienced broadly similar professionalization histories. We speculate that some of the issues they face(d) are comparable to those faced by 'low' income countries today. We note also that Singh and Newberry (2008, p. 504) classify Jamaica and Malaysia as 'developing', while Annisette analyses Trinidad and Tobago as a 'third world' country (see below). It is in any case debatable whether classifications based on income are a sensible index of 'development', especially if income distribution and the distribution of education, medical services, clean air and water, freedom from violence and intimidation, affordable transport and so on are not allowed for.

Pre-independence

The commercial activity on which accountants thrived and to which they contributed was dominated by British firms, fuelled by British capital, organized on British lines (for example, laws based on British exemplars) and served British interests. 'Reporting back' to Britain was one source of accounting work. Local companies legislation or ordinances requiring audits for companies and specifying who could do them were another. However, the expanding local 'accounting space' so created was populated by British accountants, who brought with them their notions of professionalism and a strong sense of who fitted where in the professional status hierarchy. Barriers of race, language, education, cultural unfamiliarity (with the mores and conventions underlying British commercial practice) and local socio-economic stratification (sometimes hardened rather than softened by colonialism) meant that very few locals had access to high-level training, or credentials valued in the marketplace (for example, 'chartered accountant') and, therefore, the relatively lucrative and prestigious work in the upper echelons of the business sector. Qualification with the British chartered bodies required them to spend time in Britain, where they were not greatly welcome in any case (Poullaos, 2009b; Uche, 2010, p. 81). In such circumstances British accountants barely needed to organize themselves locally to achieve or maintain their dominance, and the locals had very little opportunity to challenge them. Opportunities for colonial accountants to partake of accountancy professionalism and take charge of local professionalization projects came only just before or after the end of formal empire. Those emerging as leaders were British-trained.

'Post-independence' – after formal empire

Thus when formal independence was achieved – by India and Sri Lanka in the late 1940s, Malaysia and Ghana in the late 1950s, and the other nations in our group in the 1960s – there did not exist a mature, locally controlled profession ready to take on the accountancy demands of emergent nationhood. That is, there did not exist large numbers of locally born practitioners, organized, trained through a locally controlled professional body and locally controlled accounting firms oriented towards locally determined national political and economic agendas, and inculcated in their working lives into a professional ethos which reflected local community norms. (India is a possible exception in regard to some of these elements.) Annisette's remarks (2010, p. 169) about Trinidad and Tobago are broadly applicable to other countries in our group:

> In contrast to the elite-inspired movements in the UK and the 'Old-Commonwealth', the source of professionalization in T&T [Trinidad and Tobago] was the state. In spear-heading the Institute of Chartered Accountants of Trinidad and Tobago (ICATT), the post-independence T&T state sought to open up the practice of accountancy, which until then had been the pre-serve of British expatriates, to locals. I therefore linked professionalization movements in these sites to nation-building (Annisette 1999), and argued that profession formation in accountancy should be considered part and parcel of the making of the post-colonial 'Third World' state.

Typically, state-sponsored national professional bodies were not established till after independence, by legislation, and after intense negotiation and debate, both within the occupation and with state agents, about such things as who (of those already working as accountants) were to be included as members, the training programmes and entry rules for new entrants (including those trained outside the country), the designations to be used and the work to which members of the body would be granted exclusive access. In at least some places the rights of lower-tier or 'unqualified' accountants to continue practising (legally) were protected by the creation of a lower-tier 'registered accountant' grade of membership, potentially protecting their clients from having to pay for more expensive 'chartered accountants' (or 'CPAs'). Generally speaking, British qualifications (and, in some cases, qualifications from other Commonwealth countries) continued to be recognized locally after independence. Nevertheless the early independence period was one of strong support for a localized profession on the part of nationalist governments, with British-born accountants relatively marginalized and in some cases driven back to Britain. It was at this time that the prospects for a genuinely 'indigenous' or 'local' profession to emerge seemed brightest.

Arguably, however, they have not been realized.[5] Trinidad and Tobago remained dependent on British capital and subsequently came to rely on American capital as that country emerged as the neo-imperial hegemon of the late twentieth century. This development undercut what is arguably a necessary condition for the development of a truly local profession: economic and financial independence from 'outside' influence.

We suspect that this point applies to other countries in our group and to other developing countries, especially those in sufficiently dire straits to need the support of the IMF, World Bank and similar transnational agencies. We suspect also that an associated factor operating at the occupation level identified by Annisette is also broadly applicable, namely:

> the subjugation of minds (Nandy 1983; Fanon 1967). For them [colonialism/imperialism] is also a mental/psychological/cognitive process. To the extent that in 1995 T&T was 'as dependent on metropolitan actors for guidance, inspiration and solutions to local accounting matters as it was during the period of formal British colonialism' (Annisette 2000, 654), then from a cognitive standpoint in 1995, some 33 years after the country's independence from Great Britain, very little had changed. (Annisette, 2010, p. 188)[6]

In Ghana British influence was felt through ongoing metropolitan tutelage:

> The Institute of Chartered Accountants of England and Wales . . . gave every help in the conduct of examinations. An arrangement was agreed such that, for every examination subject where the English Institute appointed an Examiner, the Ghana Institute would appoint a Moderator and vice versa, so that every examination paper was scrutinized by an Examiner and by a Moderator. We were bent on keeping our examination standards equal to, if not better than the English Institute's. This went on with all examinations of the Ghana Institute from 1968 to 1978 when the English Institute of Chartered Accountants, gave our Institute its independence, satisfied that we could carry on on our own. (Amegashie, 2003, p. 70)

The situation was similar in Nigeria, where the local institute also started its professional examination in 1968. To operationalize this examination, the Institute of Chartered Accountants of Nigeria (ICAN) had to sign a technical agreement with the Overseas Accountancy Examinations Advisory Board (OAEAB). This was a sub-committee of the Joint Standing Committee of the three institutes of chartered accountants (Ireland, England and Wales, and Scotland), whose remit was to develop and conduct professional examination and certification schemes.[7] With respect to Malaysia, the then (1980) president of the Malaysian Association of Certified Practising Accountants (MACPA) wrote: 'We consider that help [from OAEAB] important because we wanted to be sure that right from the start our professional examinations were of the highest standards. That was of the utmost import[ance]; we wanted to ensure that our professional qualifications would be recognized and respected by the government, the private sector and the community generally' (cited in Susela, 2010, p. 104).

With respect to Kenya, Sian (2010, p. 234) observes that, 'with the dominant presence of so many British qualified accountants for so long, it was inevitable that British ideals and concepts of professionalism would also be transferred and engrained within the professionalization process in Kenya'. Similarly, one of Yapa's (2010, p. 132) Sri Lankan interviewees remarked: 'As far as I know the comments of the British moderators gave the Institute . . . valuable guide lines to prepare examination papers and in the conduct of examinations. As a result the Institute developed the capacity to maintain British standards.'

In Sri Lanka the British connection both penetrated into and emanated from the local social structure. Yapa notes (2010, p. 133) that up to 1977 those wanting to follow a professional course of study had to do their examinations in English, 'secure an articled clerkship, pay a premium to the principal and successfully complete five years of study without a salary for non-graduates (three years for graduates). [This suited] ... those from privileged backgrounds with an English-language education, namely the children of the British-educated elite with plantation and business interests.' That is, the Institute of Chartered Accountants of Sri Lanka (ICASL) 'seemingly intended to attract the children of the Sri Lankan elite who had working relations with former colonial administrators and capitalists; sharing their essentially British outlook, politics and lifestyles' (2010, p. 133).

In India, the accountants leading the post-independence professional project lobbied vigorously to gain access to the British 'chartered accountant' (CA) designation, conscious of its value in the Indian market for accountancy services, even while fending off protests from some amongst their own number (CAs themselves) who had trained in Britain and would lose the benefit of an elite British credential if all members of the new Indian institute could call themselves CAs. This was but one of a number of ways in which the notion that 'British is best' (Verma, 2010, p. 201) persisted after independence.

In Jamaica:

> in the period leading up to independence, the virtual exclusion of indigenous Jamaican accountants by the foreign firms became a cause for concern. In response, the small number of indigenous Jamaican accountants grouped together to consider ways of professionalizing and indigenizing accountancy in Jamaica, ultimately proposing the establishment of a national professional body ... Paradoxically, when some of the local accountants began to assert themselves, they were doing so as members of UK professional bodies. Such actions were to some extent, therefore, constrained. (Bakre, 2010, pp. 149–50)

Bakre goes on to note that the experience of cultural identity-conflict was present throughout Jamaican society as well as in accountancy circles. He distinguishes between a '"local" capitalist elite ... [which seemed determined] to break with the colonial past' and a '"global/international" capitalist class ... [whose "nationalism" was tempered by the belief that] Jamaica could successfully build a miniature Britain, America or Europe' (2010, p. 153). Even the former 'did not wish to entirely sever their colonial and transnational capitalist ties' (p. 153). The accountancy community was divided along similar lines, and in Bakre's view the latter group has predominated, both within accountancy and more broadly, leaving the 'independent' accountancy terrain open for (re)colonization by the ACCA. Bakre also observes that Jamaica became an offshore theatre for a broader struggle between British accountancy bodies and their members – a tendency not limited to Jamaica by any means.[8] As one of Susela's Malaysian interviewees put it: '[For] a long time, the accountancy profession here was indirectly controlled by the UK base [a reference to the control of MACPA by locals trained as CAs in the UK]. Of course, the war in UK has been transferred here also. There the CAs looked down on the ACCAs and the ACCAs say I am better than you etc.' (Susela, 2010, p. 106). Indeed, post-independence arrangements in Nigeria and Kenya (and elsewhere) reflected concerted efforts to avoid the duplication of accountancy bodies based upon the experience of squabbling between local accountants with different British qualifications.

Annisette (2010) has highlighted a further factor restricting the capacity of local accountants and governments to create a coherent and autonomous profession: the ongoing influence of international accounting firms (originally British, then Anglo-American) on local accountancy arenas as the 'former' colonies continued to rely upon international capital. In Trinidad and Tobago the pioneer British firms that 'became localised in terms of ownership' became incorporated 'into . . . mega US-based multi-national practices' (2010, p.178). Simultaneously, pressures were in train 'to socially reconstruct accountancy as a single worldwide international profession with an increasingly standardized knowledge base' (p.182). Although applied locally it was developed elsewhere. Annisette (pp.186–7) relates a poignant story of a two prominent Trinidad and Tobago accountants, one a white British expatriate, the other an Afro-Trinidadian CA trained in Scotland, 'a nationalist at heart' (p.186), involved in the formation of ICATT, who did not envisage it as 'being a Colonial Institute' (p.186). Despite their contrasting backgrounds both 'converged on the view that surrendering some degree of control of their local practices to US-based MAFs [multinational accounting firms] provided them access to what they saw as highly valued accountancy knowledge products centred around standardization' (pp.186–7).

What have been some of the worrying consequences of the above legacies (keeping in mind that local actors and factors have also figured prominently)? First, the early nationalist governments in Sri Lanka and Nigeria (and probably elsewhere) apparently thought they were authorizing their new national accountancy bodies to train accountants for all areas of accounting that might foster national development. However, in Sri Lanka (and probably elsewhere) the mimicking by those bodies of the elite British associations whose iconic figure was the public practitioner servicing the 'big end of town' led to a neglect of specialist 'management' and 'public sector' accountancy functions (see also Wallace and Briston, 1993, p.216). Second, while opening up access to accountancy to those with the potential to attain 'the authority of expertise' would have been desirable in a development context, closure was often the reality. Those 'high British standards' and the commercial and social milieux associated with them acted as barriers to entry, particularly in public practice. In Sri Lanka, for example, British training models 'discouraged the entry of Sri Lankans from the lower strata of society', while 'those that did sit for the ICASL examinations modelled on those of the ICAEW were subjected to high failure rates and arduous practice requirements' (Yapa, 2010, p.141). In addition, the ICASL elite marginalized both the local 'registered accountants' and university graduates. According to one of Yapa's interviewees, 'Chartered accountants were . . . more concerned with personal gain than with the growth of the national economy' (p.135). In Sri Lanka, Kenya and elsewhere, schemes to establish lower-tier grades of accountants were taken on only reluctantly and under pressure. In Kenya, Trinidad and Tobago, and Malaysia (at least), even barriers based upon race did not immediately disappear, in public practice particularly.

Third, and related directly to the previous point, the result has been an at times chronic shortage of accountants. In Sri Lanka, Nigeria and elsewhere, the elite response to constant complaints from excluded accountants and annoyed state agents about the small number of accountants being produced by the national professional body was to keep pressing the quality argument – but 'quality' here was derived from exemplars from the outside: first from the agents of formal empire and then from the representatives of informal empire. That is, the shortage of accountants in developing countries isn't just a reflection of poverty, or poor educational facilities, or the inherent difficulty of accounting. It is likely to be also (partly) a function of the professionalization strategies of elite local accountants practising exclusion. Fourth, a consequence of the previous points (at least in some places) is evident in the case of Nigeria, where the ICAN has been unable to hold the line against its critics inside and outside the profession: within 40 years the 'national' profession has disintegrated into a combative and divided occupation 'wasting' its energy and resources on internal disputation. The division in the Jamaican accountancy community has already been noted. Fifth, post-independence openness to foreign capital, professional models, knowledge-generation processes and accountants, the preference of local accountants for internationally recognized (rather than purely local) qualifications, and the disinterest (or inability) of the British chartered bodies and the American Institute of Certified Public Accountants (AICPA) to expand offshore have all combined to provide the ACCA with a tremendous opportunity to expand into developing and transitioning nations. In Jamaica and Trinidad and Tobago the ACCA has taken advantage of such circumstances to marginalize the University of the West Indies (UWI) and to dominate the training programmes of ICATT and ICAJ. As Annisette puts it (2000, p.647), the ICATT has become the ACCA's 'local agents'; while Bakre (2005, p.996) argues that the ACCA was the 'caretaker' of the Jamaican profession before independence and the 'landlord' afterwards.

Sixth, Annisette has recently made the insightful argument with respect to Trinidad and Tobago (probably applicable elsewhere) that the engagement of local accounting firms with MAFs actively complemented the privileging of the ACCA as a provider of basic accounting training or education. Both the firms and ICATT struggled to cope on their own in a world of increasing standardization. ICATT's decision to 'cede control of professional accountancy education and training . . . to the expansionary UK-based ACCA . . . is consistent with the mindset [within the firms] which accepted the idea of accounting standardization around the Anglo-American (private enterprise) accounting model' (2010, p.187). Seventh, the cascading of standardization noted here, taken in conjunction with the sidestepping of the UWI as a possible source of context-sensitive education and accounting knowledge generation, probably makes it harder to resist the contentious standardization of financial reporting inherent in the promotion and adoption of international financial reporting standards across the planet.[9] Eighth, all this standardization probably contributes to the growing influence of international accountancy and professional services firms in twenty-first-century transnational 'regulation' (Arnold, 2005; Cooper and Robson, 2006; Suddaby, Cooper and Greenwood, 2007).

We now briefly discuss the situation in Nigeria, Ghana and Sierra Leone to show how a combination of at least some of the above dynamics and effects can combine to produce a ninth consequence: the emergence of professionalization processes and forms of professionalism that do not support small and medium enterprises – a significant issue in developing countries. In all three countries, accounting bodies were formed prior to independence. In pre-independence Ghana (Gold Coast), for instance, the Association of Accountants in the Gold Coast was formed not with the intention of aiding African development but to coordinate the lobbying efforts of accountants, who found it necessary to speak with one voice in their dealings and interactions with the various government agencies at a time of rapid change in the Gold Coast economy. According to one of the founding fathers of the Association, James Barnes of Deloitte, Haskins and Sells:

> When I first came to the Gold Coast in 1939 there were very few qualified Accountants in the country. Most organizations only produced local returns, which were forwarded to their overseas bodies to be incorporated into final accounts. With the introduction of Income Tax in 1943, the production of accounts for tax purposes increased the demand for accountancy services both internally in organizations and externally as auditors and after the war . . . [the number of accountants] increased in professional practice, the commercial firms, the mines, Government and Income Tax and the need for an Association whereby we could meet, discuss common problems and have a unified body to make representations to Government . . . grew . . . The Association was formed in 1954 and was based on a similar Association, which had been formed in East Africa previously. (Barnes, 1981, p. 6)

The Association was essentially formed to service the needs of foreign companies then operating in the territory. Very little thought was given to the small and medium-scale businesses which have dominated the economy since then.

As independence approached and the formation of local bodies under government-sponsored legislation loomed, the issue arose as to what would become of local accountants whose skills and training were limited but who made a living servicing the basic accounting needs of small businesses. As occurred elsewhere, the category of 'registered accountant' was adopted to provide a space for them. In Sierra Leone the president of the Association of Accountants of Sierra Leone wrote to the finance minister suggesting a provision in the accountancy legislation then under consideration to the effect that:

> Persons entitled to be admitted to the Institute as Registered Accountants shall be persons who apply in that behalf within six months of the coming into force of the proposed Act and who satisfy the Council of the proposed Institute that for the three years next preceding the commencement of this Act, they have as their main source of livelihood been in continuous active public practice on their own account in Sierra Leone as Accountants, or in partnership with other Accountants and are otherwise fit persons to be registered as Registered Accountants. The thinking behind this provision is that subject to the public interest no citizen should be deprived of his main source of livelihood on which he has in the past depended and is a concession to unqualified and partly qualified persons who have in the past engaged in some aspects of accountancy in public practice on their own account. (Quoted in Uche, 2007, p. 78)

This was also the case in Nigeria and Ghana. However, rather than seeing such provisions as part of a coordinated and considered strategy of ensuring that accountancy services would be available to all businesses needing them, irrespective of size, the promoters of the Western-styled accounting profession simply saw this as a compromise they could live with until such time as the registered accountants would be phased out.[10] The fact that their constituency remained strong was of little consequence in the promoters' calculations.[11]

Unsurprisingly, then, even with Africans dominating indigenous accounting bodies, very little was done to assist small and medium-scale businesses. This was partly because most of the founding members of these emergent indigenous institutions were already affiliated with British professional bodies. Their training therefore did not prepare them for the socio-economic terrain of the West African region. Rather than reinvent themselves in the context of their local terrain, the African pioneer accountants were content with seeing themselves as either competitors or alternatives to the foreign accountants whose influence (they thought) was bound to diminish with the achievement of independence. While Africans who joined foreign firms waited in the wings to replace their foreign masters, those who set up indigenous accounting firms either employed nationalist sentiments or partnered with foreign firms in their attempt to increase their share of the audit market (cf. Anibaba, 1990, p. 11; Inanga, 1992, p. 18; and Aborisade, 1994, pp. 11–13). The need to provide accountancy services to small and medium-scale businesses so as to promote the economic development of the region was of little consequence in the calculations of either indigenous or foreign accounting firms. It is also unsurprising that the design of accounting education by the emergent indigenous accounting bodies mimicked closely that in the United Kingdom.

Perhaps the problem of relying on foreign experts in the design and examination of the accounting syllabuses in developing countries is best brought out in the case of Sierra Leone. In 1992, the ACCA and the British Council, at the request of the Institute of Chartered Accountants of Sierra Leone (ICA Sierra Leone), commissioned a study on accountancy development in Sierra Leone.[12] The resulting report argued that ICA Sierra Leone needed to be identified with a credible examination process in order to enhance its overall standing. The report also talked down the possibility of ICA Sierra Leone running its own examinations:

> The Institute has prepared an outline examination syllabus. While this is not in a form which enables us to assess the depths at which subjects would be covered, it appears to be closely modelled on the ACCA syllabus. Four papers do however have new syllabuses; these deal with the subjects of Information Technology, Taxation (two papers) and Law. The Institute recognizes however the resources and security problems of running its own examination scheme and that this is not a realistic option for the foreseeable future. Setting, marking and monitoring professional examinations is a costly process. The Institute's current income is limited to the small number of members and practising firms on which it can call. It would, in our opinion be sensible to broaden the membership base before attempting to launch a full fledged examination programme . . . Although it has excellent links with the professional bodies in Ghana and Nigeria, it does not feel that they could (or would wish to) provide an appropriate examination service. It also takes the view that now that there is an ACCA Course in place at IPAM [Institute of Public Administration and Management], and students are familiar with the ACCA Programme, it would not be sensible to seek to go down a different route. Many people we spoke to confirmed this preference of students for an internationally recognized accountancy qualification. (ACCA, 1992, p. 13)

As occurred in Jamaica and Trinidad and Tobago, the ACCA was given the authority to pass judgement on alternatives to its own offerings. While the problems identified with the Sierra Leone institute running its own examinations may have been real ones, the proposed solution played further into the hands of the offshore body, and dragged Sierra Leone further into the world of standardization described above. The opportunity to develop a distinctively local solution in the longer term was passed up in favour of addressing immediate concerns.

The ACCA report advised a three-phased approach for the introduction of examinations by the ICA Sierra Leone. The first phase was the setting up of a joint examination between ACCA and the Institute whereby the names of both bodies were printed on the ACCA examination question papers and related stationery. On successful completion of the examination and experience requirements, students would become members of both bodies. This practice was then supposed to metamorphose into a second phase, which would involve the substitution of local tax and law papers for the UK papers. However, the promise of reciprocal membership and local control was pushed into the future:

> If the students are to achieve membership of the ACCA as well as the local body, the tax and law must be of equivalent complexity to that in the UK. The Institute accepts that this phase will only be possible when economic and legislative change can provide an adequate underpinning for local tax and law papers; it will not be possible to model suitable examination papers on the equivalent of the 1929 Companies Act and in the absence of national authoritative regulations and modern tax legislation. We note that the Commissioner of Taxes is a member of the Institute's Council and we hope that he may be prepared to take the lead in helping in the area of taxation. (ACCA, 1992, p. 14)

That is, there will be no reciprocation unless and until Sierra Leone undertakes tax reform – or at least introduces complexity into its taxation system. In the meantime, local students would continue to grapple with the complexities of the UK tax system if they wanted an 'international' credential, irrespective of how useless the resulting knowledge might be locally. The second phase was expected to metamorphose into the third and final stage within five years. It would involve ICA Sierra Leone putting in place its own examination scheme and perhaps taking some papers from ACCA on a service basis. The third phase is yet to commence. Subsequent to the report, the Institute and the ACCA signed an agreement under which the Institute could, with the ACCA's agreement, use and modify ACCA materials for local use.

In our view the report's recommendations are unlikely to lead to any meaningful development in the emergence of an accounting syllabus and local case studies that can be adapted to the social and economic specificities of Sierra Leone. For a start, foreign accountancy bodies have very limited understanding of indigenous accounting terrain, so they are unlikely to produce appropriate materials (Pujeh, 1996, p. 4). Also, the recommendation that Sierra Leone revise its tax and business laws to be in line with that in the United Kingdom will, if followed, further widen the gap between regulation and the business environment such regulation is supposed to facilitate. Furthermore, once entrenched, it is difficult to displace Western accounting traditions for the training of accountants, especially if the remarks above about the local appeal of international credentials and standardization and the domination of international capital (including intellectual capital) are correct. Nevertheless the ICA Sierra Leone still prefers the ACCA as a partner to any of the two established accounting bodies in West Africa: the Institute of Chartered Accountants of Ghana (ICAG) and ICAN, notwithstanding that these two bodies are much closer to Sierra Leone, at least in terms of social and economic attributes, than they are to the UK. On the face of it, it makes more sense for ICA Sierra Leone to forge closer ties with these West African bodies than the ACCA. On closer inspection, however, the issue is more complicated. The so-called local bodies in West Africa have extensively been mimicking the practices of UK accounting bodies rather than trying to adapt to the socio-economic conditions of their local terrains. In real terms, therefore, there is very little difference between cooperating with local West African accounting bodies and cooperating with British bodies, but the latter course is preferred. For example, although the African bodies recognize UK (and American) professional qualifications on a non-reciprocal basis, for a long time they did not recognize each other's qualifications in the same way. ICAG and ICAN have only recently entered into a reciprocal recognition arrangement.

A WAY FORWARD?

At the level of training accounting technicians, however, ICA Sierra Leone is today more accommodating towards the emerging regional initiative by the Accountancy Bodies of West Africa (ABWA). An 'accounting technician' has been defined as a person who has the capabilities at a technical level in specific spheres of accounting, without necessarily the sum of knowledge and ability to handle problems of a more complex nature at a professional level (Obe, 1989, p. 6)[13] ICAN introduced an Accounting Technicians Scheme (ATS) in 1989 aimed at producing a second tier of accounting professionals 'that is so much needed in industry, commerce and the public sector' and removing 'the frustration of students . . . unable to satisfy the registration requirements of ICAN' (Olukoya, 1990, p. 20; see also Nwankwo, 1999, pp. 1–2). ICAG introduced its own Ghana Accounting Technicians Scheme shortly afterwards. The Nigerian and Ghanaian schemes have now been collapsed into a West African ATS. In Sierra Leone the ICA has adopted the Certified Accounting Technicians Scheme organized by the ACCA. Nevertheless, the Institute is sympathetic towards the development of a West African region-wide accounting technicians scheme to exist side by side with the existing Certified Accounting Technicians Scheme (see Institute of Chartered Accountants of Sierra Leone, 2003, p. 4).

While it would make more sense for the three bodies to collaborate with each other, rather than with or through the ACCA, the development of accounting technicians schemes in developing countries is welcome. They can function as a major pivot to aid the economic growth and development of such territories by helping small and medium-scale enterprises to grow. Pursuance of such an objective by ICAN, ICAG and ICA Sierra Leone as *a*, or *the*, major plank of their professionalization projects has the potential to turn them into strong, virile and effective bodies attuned to their local context, in contrast to the poor cousins of the ACCA, IFAC and so on that they seem to be now. If they can fulfil such an objective, on their own terms, they will contribute to development locally and, in the longer term, enhance the value of local qualifications as the local market recognizes their contribution to value creation. To undertake accounting technicians schemes under the auspices of ACCA (or IFAC) runs the serious risk of having the most local of local specificities colonized, commodified and swallowed up in the vortex of sameness.

For the above strategy to have any chance at succeeding, company law must be changed in at least some countries. In several jurisdictions, company law has had the effect of outlawing small indigenous businesses. Complex company law requirements are sometimes imposed upon small indigenous companies that are clearly not in any position to operationalize them. In Nigeria, for instance, every limited liability company is required by law to have its accounts audited by a chartered accountant. This makes little sense. Aside from the enormous costs such requirements impose on small businesses, the country does not have enough chartered accountants to undertake such tasks. There is therefore a need to reform the Companies Act to exempt small and medium-scale businesses from audit – as, ironically, occurs in the UK. There is, for instance, no justifiable reason for owner manager businesses that have no agency issues to be compulsorily required to have their accounts audited. This does not in any way prevent third parties like potential creditors from requesting such audits on a case-by-case basis. If there were a plausible rationale for requiring all limited liability companies to be audited then accounting technicians should be trained and legally validated to audit simple businesses, rather than envisaged as being on a remedial pathway to a true professionalism as represented, in ideal-typical terms, by today's international accounting and professional services firms. Allowing the technicians to operate in this space would also help sustain them financially while they teach their clients the importance of accounting and financial structures. Perhaps more importantly, it might help to shift small businesses from the informal realm to that of the formal, thereby further facilitating (potentially) economic development and planning in developing countries.

In a country like Sierra Leone which is officially recorded as one of the poorest in the world, change must also start with the redesign of the macroeconomic framework under which businesses operate. Calls for the business and tax laws of the country to be further revised to bring them to the same level of complexity as those in the UK must be ignored. What Sierra Leone needs is a very simple business law that applies to the majority of the informal businesses in operation. Such a law, for instance, can encourage itinerant traders to belong to market unions organized and run by their members. It is such unions that will interface with government and serve as an appropriate proxy for business registration and submission of basic returns. It will also provide the structural framework for studying and understanding the accounting and economic needs of such small businesses. Once this is done, then the accounting profession will be in a better position to develop an appropriate training structure for the servicing of the needs of such businesses.

To get into and take advantage of such a position, however, the accountancy community and relevant state agents in developing countries must rethink their attitude to standard-setting. In our view there is little in the history, structure or operation of either the IASB or the transnational institutions that push the adoption of IFRS on to developing countries to suggest that they have any great empathy with the latter's situation. The assumption that the IASB will have adequately responded to the concerns of developing countries if it produces an SME reporting standard is a case in point. Singh and Newberry (2008, p. 512) come to the disquieting conclusion that:

> There is little evidence that the IASB sought to deal with specific issues facing developing countries . . . [Rather, it] . . . offered [a] pre-existing policy solution for SMEs, possibly regarding that as a partial solution for developing countries.
>   The history of this issue suggests that an acceptable policy solution for developing countries is yet to be devised. Whether the IASB possesses the knowledge and resources required to address financial reporting matters that go beyond a capital market is not clear.

This conclusion is grist for our mill. While multinationals operating in developing countries might be required to comply with IFRS for the time being, local professional bodies, state agents and universities might focus on the accounting problems faced by the numerous small and medium-scale businesses that dominate their economic terrain. This has various dimensions:

- a knowledge-generation dimension – finding out about those problems and developing solutions;
- a training and education dimension – getting that knowledge on to training and educational agendas;
- a social-validation dimension – one which professionalization projects elsewhere typically address – creating rewards (material and other) and supportive organizational vehicles to support practitioners who contribute to small and medium-scale business. This is a major problem: imagine the accounting technician as hero (rather than the local partner of a Big Four firm). The market is unlikely to solve it in the short term but may make a contribution over time.

To date the track record of local accountancy elites along those dimensions has been poor. Are they up to the job or should someone else step in? The state, for example? That option is itself problematic, at least in some places, as the next section suggests.

PATRIMONIALISM AND PROFESSIONALISM: A DANGEROUS LIAISON

Accountancy professionalization in the Philippines is also an outcome of formal empire – American not British. Unlike the British cases discussed above, the initiative was taken by a non-Anglo-Saxon local community, well before formal independence – not by local (or British or American) practitioners, but by local legislators inspired by a bruising encounter with an American governor-general who had used American CPAs to uncover the extent to which they and their elite allies had looted the new national bank into which taxation revenue had been deposited. It seems that that the formation of the Philippine Institute of Certified Public Accountants (PICPA) in 1923 was an attempt by local elites, organized along traditional lines as patrimonial 'families', to set up a profession that looked American whilst allowing them to colonize the role of the public accountant. There is some evidence that the PICPA leadership was behaving in a manner consistent with this view in the late twentieth century.[14]

Following Weber (1978), patrimonial family groupings involve a 'patron' (head) to whom other members owe a primary allegiance; reciprocally, the patron's ideal-typical role is to protect other family members ('clients') so that a form of accountability operates between patron and client. In this arrangement the patron (ideal-typically) appropriates economic and political opportunities available to family members, including non-blood relatives accepted into the family, on condition that the patron's leadership is accepted and loyalty to the group is demonstrated (thus the term 'clientelism'). As modern national polities are constructed, 'patrons' compete with each other to share the spoils of power or form alliances to share it. The Filipino lending officers who disobeyed bank rules when making loans were consciously following patrimonial logic rather than the rational/legal logic introduced by the Americans, which assume a social world consisting of atomized (socially distant) individuals contracting with each other subject to the rule of law in a world where market, state and community are reasonably autonomous from each other. This is the world that Anglo-American professionalism both assumes and ostensibly contributes to. The importation or imposition of that professionalism into locations where patrimonial relationships are prevalent is yet another source of problems for accountants in developing nations, as the case of the Philippines illustrates.

The analyses of Wallace (1992, pp. 44–6) and Okike (2004) of the travails of indigenous professional accountants in Nigeria suggest a rather more hostile environment for accountants than the Philippines. Wallace claims that 'there is little that the internal and/ or external auditor can do to correct [widespread corruption] without risking the loss of his or her life' (pp. 44-5). As Okike (2004, p. 709) puts it:

> Although it is possible to argue that since corruption is rife in Nigeria, as in most developing countries, audits would be ineffective, a counter-argument is that it is because of this potential for ineffectiveness that highly corrupt countries are mostly in need of tight control and greater investment to develop systems capable of coping with their corrupt environment. Instead, most developing countries like Nigeria have adopted accounting and audit practices suited to the developed (and often less corrupt) countries.

They might need to refine their model of professionalism as well as their technical practices. Prior to articulating this point, we note that defining the problem as simply one of corruption (or culture, broadly defined) understates its socio-political roots. The pessimistic analyses by historians and social scientists of Africa since independence have identified (neo)patrimonialism, the patrimonial state in particular, as an important (dysfunctional) factor.[15] Van de Walle's (2001, pp. 51–2) analysis suggests that the situation in many parts of Africa resonates with that in the Philippines. He argues that:

> political authority in Africa is based on the giving and granting of favors, in an endless series of dyadic exchanges that go from the village level to the highest reaches of the central state. Under this general rubric of clientelism can be placed a wide variety of practices involving the giving and receiving of favours, almost invariably based on corruption. Clientelism can be associated with corruption simply because the former relies on privileged access to public resources and some kind of conflict of interest . . . Outwardly the state has all the trappings of a Weberian rational-legal system with a clear distinction between the public and private realm, with written laws and a constitutional order. However, this official order is constantly subverted by a patrimonial logic, in which office-holders almost systematically appropriate public resources for their own uses and political authority is largely based on clientelist practices.

This presidential 'style of rule . . . combined the authoritarian legacy of the colonial administration and village traditions of patrimonialism' (van de Walle, 2001, p. 116) in such a way that 'clientelism moved in the direction of large-scale corruption and fraud' (p. 120).[16] Van de Walle analyses how patrimonial arrangements have to date contributed to, been affected by and survived financial and economic volatility, political repression and poor economic performance, waste and pillaging of national resources, war and civil unrest, ethnic, religious and regional cleavages, weak civil societies, the disintegration of public services and infrastructure, geopolitical competition, aid donors and transnational institutions, neoliberalism, and democratization movements.

Significantly, van de Walle observes that even in the most egregious cases of neopatrimonialism 'there are rational legal pockets attempting to assert themselves' (p. 128). Some accountants may see themselves as fitting into those pockets. The problem for them is that 'no state in Africa can claim to have entirely avoided neopatrimonial tendencies at its apex. The two tendencies coexist, overlap, and struggle for control of the state in most cases' (p. 128). The result is a struggle to balance reasonable life chances with ostensibly desirable professional values ('independence', 'objectivity', 'integrity' and so on) that is perhaps more raw and visceral in Lagos than it is in London or New York. As far as we are aware, IFAC offers little in the way of resources to help solve this problem, as one of either professionalism (how is professional work to be organized to protect accountants and stakeholders in their work from the dysfunctional or dangerous aspects of patrimonialism?) or professionalization (once a position on professionalism is devised, how is it to be institutionalized?). Signing on to the IFAC agenda[17] without an effective strategy for dealing with these questions may amount to a form of auto-entrapment (setting oneself up to fail) rather than a means of garnering useful outside support. Devising an 'effective strategy' is itself a task of considerable magnitude, extending way beyond the world of accountancy. In the limit, it may require incorporation into an effective strategy for the reordering of the socio-political arena by the citizens of developing countries themselves.

CONCLUDING REMARKS

We doubt that the organization of accountancy in developing countries in the mode of Anglo-American professionalism has contributed to economic growth and political development to the degree that either the modernization theorists of Johnson's era or the early nationalist governments of newly independent developing nations either anticipated or hoped for. Partly this reflects the nature of that professionalism and the way it was enacted; partly it reflects the circumstances faced by developing nations.

To answer our research question: we believe that developing country professionalization processes based upon those in developed countries have tended not to produce 'enough', or a sufficient variety of, accountants, or served the needs of small and medium businesses. We suspect also that (in some places at least) they have fostered division within the accounting community and facilitated the domination of local accountancy arenas by the ACCA and international accounting firms, thereby fostering training geared to 'outside' needs and inhibiting the generation of valuable context-specific accounting knowledge. We acknowledge, however, that accountants in developing countries face great difficulties in developing a form of professionalism that responds 'appropriately' to the demands of outsiders while offering some respite from the intense pressures of local circumstances.

Those responsible for devising such a form (or forms) of professionalism (which might well vary from place to place) might seriously consider the suggestions in our 'A way forward?' section. They might also consider how to manage the production and organization of different types and grades of accountants so that professionalization does not generate resource-wasting rivalry. Promoting the vision of 'professionalism for development' as *a*, if not *the*, major priority might help a little. Supporting the teaching of accounting and commerce as distinct subjects in commercial and trade schools at the post-primary school level might also generate a range of entrants who might usefully match or complement the range of accountants needed for development, while development of regional accounting bodies (such as the ABWA) might allow accountants to learn from their neighbours. A particularly awkward challenge is the extent to which, and the way in which, the professionalization process might interact with broader processes of reform. A cultivated veneer of apolitical expertise and separation from politics may not be feasible in dangerous times.

NOTES

1. See, for example, Wallace (1990); Wallace and Briston (1993); Briston and Kedslie (1997); Hooper and Morris (2004); Singh and Newberry (2008); and Chapter 6 of this volume.
2. For recent reviews see Cooper and Robson (2006) and Poullaos (2009a).
3. Even in China, which (i) has never been formally colonized by Western powers, (ii) has a long tradition of compliance with the official ideologies of a powerful state apparatus which (iii) has effectively directed the pattern of accountancy professionalization (post-1978), and (iv) is already a major economic power, the issue of integrating local priorities and specificities with models of professionalism familiar to Western investors is an ongoing work in progress. See, for example, Hao (1999), Xu and Xu (2003), Yapa and Hao (2007), Shafer (2008, 2009), Yee (2009) and Yee and West (2010). Even in the extreme case of Cambodia, where French influence was ostensibly obliterated along with the social class from which accountants came and a post-Khmer Rouge regime is keen to protect local accountants from foreign domination, Yapa, Jacobs and Huot (2010, p. 19) wonder whether the dream of a local accountancy project will 'be washed away by the flood of international capital'.
4. Readers interested in country specificities are strongly advised to consult the cited works.
5. In the discussion that follows we relate stories pertaining to particular countries without being confident of whether they apply to all countries in our group or to developing countries more generally.
6. Bakre (2010), Susela (2010) and Verma (2010) make a similar point in respect of Jamaica, Malaysia and India respectively.
7. The OAEAB advised a number of the countries in our group on the conduct of professional accounting examinations. At times it also assisted with the implementation of examinations. The general understanding was that over a period of time, generally within six or seven years, the local institute should be able to take charge of such examinations (Wallace, 1989, pp. 43–4).
8. See, for example, Johnson and Caygill (1971), Parker (1989), Briston and Kedslie (1997), Chua and Poullaos (2002) and Poullaos (2010).
9. In a recent interview with *Business Day* (Nigeria) Alistair Impey (n.d.), a partner of PricewaterhouseCoopers in Nigeria, asserted: 'We, PricewaterhouseCoopers network of firms, have been long proponents of a single set of high quality, global accounting standards – for one simple reason – our markets are global and it is important for those markets to operate under a single, principle-based language.'
10. In Ghana, for example, it was noted that: 'The nucleus of the new Institute of Chartered Accountants will be formed by the existing members of the Association of Accountants in Ghana and the Society of Ghanaian Practising Accountants. It has been necessary to have the thirteen members of the Society . . . admitted into the Institute even though some of them have no recognized accountancy qualifications in order to avoid hardship to persons who have had long standing practice in Accountancy in this country. Upon the coming into effect of this Act, subsequent membership of the Institute shall be limited to persons properly trained in accounting' (Government of Ghana, 1963, Ghana Parliamentary Debates, 19 March 1963, Columns 428–9). See also Coker (1990).
11. Dev and Inanga (1978, p. 128), for instance, have noted that: 'There are numerous small businesses in Nigeria, many of which are run by people with little or no education, and the small firms see no need for accounting services nor managerial services. Generally, the standard of financial management is deficient, and the lack of financial management and control has been largely responsible for the failure of many firms in Nigeria. Accounts are often kept carelessly. This indicates a need not only for qualified accountants but also for a substantial number of skilled accounting technicians to assist small businesses.'
12. This study had the following terms of reference: to review the training arrangements for professional accountants operated through the Institute of Public Administration and Management (IPAM) and also the university accountancy courses to assess their adequacy or otherwise; to advise on the desirability of the Institute conducting its own examinations, taking account of the available resources and the possibility of conducting exams through ACCA and the relative costs; to advise on the optimum method and approach to be adopted for an ICA Sierra Leone training programme to be operated through IPAM; appraisal of the structure and organization of ICA Sierra Leone with regard to providing the full range of services to members and to meeting its responsibilities on examination and training standards; the provision of technical and secretarial support by ICA Sierra Leone, particularly in the setting up and maintaining of an up-to-date reference library and for identification and procurement of suitable equipment; the

setting up of recruitment and training programmes amongst major employers in order to secure and train suitable students; and to identify possible sources of financial and technical assistance to meet with the desired objectives.

13. ABWA was founded by ICAN and ICAG in 1982. Sierra Leone joined it in 1986. Its objectives are: to develop and enhance the accountancy profession in West Africa; to promote the development of professional ethics and standards in member bodies; to act as a centre for the dissemination of information concerning accountancy standards and the development of accountancy thoughts and practices in West Africa; to develop a forum for the professional development of member bodies through seminars, symposia, conferences and interchange of ideas and experiences; and to provide advice on and participate in the programme of work of IFAC and to adopt as appropriate and publish to its members IFAC's guidelines, statements and studies (ABWA, 1982, Constitution, paragraph 5).

14. See Dyball, Chua and Poullaos (2006), Dyball, Poullaos and Chua (2007) and Dyball and Valcarcel (1999).

15. See, for example, Herbst (1996), van de Walle (2001), Arnold (2006), Meredith (2006) and Bates (2008). For additional references see van de Walle (2001, p. 51, n. 80). The brief account here relies mostly on van de Walle (2001). Note that the cited works identify a depressingly long list of contributing factors, geopolitical competition amongst outside powers for influence in Africa (and access to African resources) included. See Arnold (2006, especially ch. 39).

16. On the desirable side of 'traditional' norms and practices see Ndiweni (2008). See also van de Walle's caution (2001, p. 127) against simply treating such outcomes as instances of traditional African practices undermining already-existing modern states.

17. That is, joining IFAC's Membership Compliance Program and accepting its Statements of Membership Obligations (see http://www.ifac.org/ComplianceAssessment/published.php). Professional bodies from all countries discussed in this chapter have signed up.

REFERENCES

Aborisade, P.A. (1994). *BDO Balogun, Badejo and Co.: The History of the Firm.* Lagos: BDO Balogun, Badejo and Co.

Amegashie, R. (2003). Dr. Amegashie shares his thoughts on the 40th anniversary: the genesis of ICA Ghana. *Professional Accountant*, 40th Anniversary Special, pp. 69–70.

Anibaba, M.O. (1990). *A Short History of the Accounting Profession in Nigeria.* Lagos: West African Book Publishers.

Annisette, M. (1999). Importing accounting: the case of Trinidad and Tobago. *Accounting, Business and Financial History*, 9(1), pp. 103–33.

Annisette, M. (2000). Imperialism and the professions: the education and certification of accountants in Trinidad and Tobago. *Accounting, Organizations and Society*, 25(7), pp. 631–59.

Annisette, M. (2003). The colour of accountancy: examining the salience of race in a professionalisation project. *Accounting, Organizations and Society*, 28(7/8), pp. 639–74.

Annisette, M. (2010). Maintaining empire: the practice link in Trinidad and Tobago. In *Accountancy and Empire: The British Legacy of Professional Organization*, ed. C. Poullaos and S. Sian, pp. 168–91. New York and London: Routledge.

Arnold, G. (2006). *Africa: A Modern History.* London: Atlantic Books.

Arnold, P.J. (2005). Disciplining domestic regulation: the World Trade Organization and the market for professional services. *Accounting, Organizations and Society*, 30(4), pp. 299–330.

Association of Accountancy Bodies in West Africa (ABWA) (1982). *Constitution and Bye-Laws.* Negro Ind. Press Nigeria.

Bakre, O.M. (2005). First attempt at localising imperial accountancy: the case of the Institute of Chartered Accountants of Jamaica (ICAJ) (1950s–1970s). *Critical Perspectives on Accounting*, 16(8), pp. 995–1018.

Bakre, O.M. (2006). Second attempt at localising imperial accountancy: the case of the Institute of Chartered Accountants of Jamaica (ICAJ) (1970s–1980s). *Critical Perspectives on Accounting*, 17(1), pp. 1–28.

Bakre, O.M. (2010). Imperialism and professionalization: the case of accountancy in Jamaica. In *Accountancy and Empire: The British Legacy of Professional Organization*, ed. C. Poullaos and S. Sian, pp. 144–67. New York and London: Routledge.

Barnes, J.D. (1981). Interview for the *Professional Accountant. Professional Accountant*, April to September, pp. 6–9.

Bates, R.H. (2008). *When Things Fell Apart: State Failure in Late-Century Africa.* New York: Cambridge University Press.

Briston, R.J., and M.J.M. Kedslie (1997). The internationalization of British professional accounting: the role of the examination exporting bodies. *Accounting, Business and Financial History*, 7(2), pp. 175–94.

Chartered Association of Certified Accountants (ACCA) (1992). *Consultants Report: Accountancy Development in Sierra Leone*. London: ACCA.

Chua, W.F., and C. Poullaos (2002). The Empire strikes back? An exploration of centre–periphery interaction between the ICAEW and accounting associations in the self-governing colonies of Australia, Canada and South Africa, 1880–1907. *Accounting, Organizations and Society*, 27(4/5), pp. 409–45.

Coker, F.C.O. (1990). How it all started. *Nigerian Accountant*, 23, pp. 23–4.

Cooper, D.J., and K. Robson (2006). Accounting, professions and regulation: locating the sites of profession-alisation. *Accounting, Organizations and Society*, 31(4/5), pp. 415–44.

Dev, S., and E. Inanga (1978). Educating accountants in Nigeria. *Accountancy*, April, pp. 127–9.

Dyball, M., W.F. Chua and C. Poullaos (2006). Mediating between colonizer and colonized in the American empire: accounting for government monies in the Philippines. *Accounting, Auditing and Accountability Journal*, 19(1), pp. 47–81.

Dyball, M., C. Poullaos and W.F. Chua (2007). Accounting and empire: professionalization as resistance – the case of the Philippines. *Critical Perspectives on Accounting*, 18(4), pp. 415–49.

Dyball, M.C., and L.J. Valcarcel (1999). The 'rational' and 'traditional': the regulation of accounting in the Philippines. *Accounting, Auditing and Accountability Journal*, 12(3), pp. 303–27.

Fanon, F. (1967). *Black Skin, White Masks*, trans. C.L. Markham. New York: Grove Press.

Government of Ghana (1963). *National Assembly Parliamentary Debates: Official Report*. Accra: Government Printing Department.

Hao, Z.P. (1999). Regulation and organization of accountants in China. *Accounting, Auditing and Accountability Journal*, 12(3), pp. 286–302.

Herbst, J. (1996). Is Nigeria a viable state? *Washington Quarterly*, 19(2), pp. 151–72.

Hooper, V. and R.D. Morris (2004). Washington consensus, emerging economies and company financial reporting: an appraisal. In *Research in Accounting in Emerging Economies*, Supplement 2: *Accounting and Accountability in Emerging and Transition Economies*, ed. T. Hopper and Z. Hoque, pp. 93–116. Oxford: JAI Press.

Impey, A. (n.d.). Interview with *Business Day*, hppt://www.pwc.com/nig/en/publications/understanding ifrs, downloaded 20 October 2009.

Inanga, E.I. (1992). *A History of Akintola Williams and Co.* Lagos: West African Book Publishers.

Institute of Chartered Accountants of Sierra Leone (2003). President's Report to the Annual General Meeting, Unpublished.

Johnson, T.J. (1973). Imperialism and the professions: notes on the development of professional occupations in Britain's colonies and the new states. In *Professions and Social Change*, Sociological Review Monograph 20, ed. P. Halmos, pp. 281–309. Keele: University of Keele.

Johnson, T.J., and M. Caygill (1971). The development of accountancy links in the Commonwealth. *Accountancy and Business Research*, 11, Spring, pp. 155–73.

Meredith, M. (2006). *The State of Africa: A History of Fifty Years of Independence*, London: Free Press.

Nandy, A. (1983). *The Intimate Enemy: Loss and Recovery of Self under Colonialism*. New Delhi: Oxford University Press.

Ndiweni, E. (2008). Towards a theoretical framework of corporate governance: perspectives from Southern Africa. In *Research in Accounting in Emerging Economies*, vol. 8: *Corporate Governance in Less Developed and Emerging Economies*, ed. M. Tsamenyi and S. Uddin, pp. 335–58. Bingley: JAI Press.

Nwankwo, U.S. (1999). The professional accountant: middle level manpower development, Paper presented at the 5th Congress of the Association of Accountancy Bodies in West Africa, Abuja, Nigeria, 6 May.

Obe, F. (1989). Accounting technicians scheme comes alive. *Nigerian Accountant*, April/June, pp. 6–7.

Olukoya, S.M. (1990). 25 years of ICAN. *Nigerian Accountant*, July/September, pp. 18–22.

Okike, E. (2004). Management of crisis: the response of the auditing profession in Nigeria to the challenge to its legitimacy. *Accounting, Auditing and Accountability Journal*, 17(5), pp. 705–30.

Parker, R.H. (1989). Importing and exporting accounting: the British experience. In *International Pressures for Accounting Change*, ed. A. Hopwood, pp. 7–29. Hemel Hempstead: Prentice-Hall International and ICAEW.

Parker, R.H. (2005). Naming and branding: accountants and accountancy bodies in the British Empire and Commonwealth, 1853–2003. *Accounting History*, NS 10(1), pp. 7–46.

Poullaos, C. (2009a). Professionalisation. In *Routledge Companion to Accounting History*, ed. R. Edwards and S. Walker, pp. 247–73. London and New York: Routledge.

Poullaos, C. (2009b). Profession, race and empire: keeping the centre pure, 1921–1927. *Accounting, Auditing and Accountability Journal*, 22(3), pp. 429–68.

Poullaos, C. (2010). The self-governing dominions of South Africa, Australia and Canada and the evo-lution of the imperial accountancy arena during the 1920s. In *Accountancy and Empire: The British*

Legacy of Professional Organization, ed. C. Poullaos and S. Sian, pp. 10–52. New York and London: Routledge.

Poullaos, C. and S. Sian (2010). Accountancy and empire: connexions, patterns and suggestions. In *Accountancy and Empire: The British Legacy of Professional Organization*, ed. C. Poullaos and S. Sian, pp. 238–50. New York and London: Routledge.

Pujeh, M. (1996). Keynote address by the deputy minister of finance to the Fourth Congress of the Association of Accountancy Bodies in West Africa, Freetown, 10–14 June.

Shafer, W.E. (2008). Ethical climate in Chinese CPA firms. *Accounting, Organizations and Society*, 33, pp. 825–35.

Shafer, W.E. (2009). Ethical climate, organizational–professional conflict and organizational commitment. *Accounting, Auditing and Accountability Journal*, 22(7), pp. 1087–1110.

Sian, S. (2006). Inclusion, exclusion and control: the case of the Kenyan accounting professionalisation project. *Accounting, Organizations and Society*, 31(3), pp. 295–322.

Sian, S. (2007). Patterns of prejudice: social exclusion and racial demarcation in professional accountancy in Kenya. *Accounting Historians Journal*, 34(1), pp. 1–42.

Sian, S. (2010). Between the lines: the professionalization of accountancy in Kenya. In *Accountancy and Empire: The British Legacy of Professional Organization*, ed. C. Poullaos and S. Sian, pp. 215–37. New York and London: Routledge.

Singh, R., and S. Newberry (2008). Corporate governance and international financial reporting standards (IFRS): the case of developing countries. In *Research in Accounting in Emerging Economies*, vol. 8: *Corporate Governance in Less Developed and Emerging Economies*, ed. M. Tsamenyi and S. Uddin, pp. 483–518. Bingley: JAI Press.

Suddaby, R., D.J. Cooper and R. Greenwood (2007). Transnational regulation of professional services: governance dynamics of field level organizational change. *Accounting, Organizations and Society*, 32(4–5), pp. 333–62.

Susela, D.S. (1999). 'Interests' and accounting standard setting in Malaysia. *Accounting, Auditing and Accountability Journal*, 12(3), pp. 358–87.

Susela, D.S. (2010). The Malaysian accountancy profession and its imperial legacy (1957–1995). In *Accountancy and Empire: The British Legacy of Professional Organization*, ed. C. Poullaos and S. Sian, pp. 99–123. New York and London: Routledge.

Uche, C.U. (2002). Professional accounting development in Nigeria: threats from the inside and outside. *Accounting, Organizations and Society*, 27(4/5), pp. 471–96.

Uche, C.U. (2007). *The Accounting Profession in British West Africa*. Edinburgh: Institute of Chartered Accountants of Scotland.

Uche, C.U. (2010). Colonial heritage and the accounting profession in Nigeria. In *Accountancy and Empire: The British Legacy of Professional Organization*, ed. C. Poullaos and S. Sian, pp. 77–98. New York and London: Routledge.

Verma, S. (2010). The influence of empire on the establishment of the Institute of Chartered Accountants of India after independence. In *Accountancy and Empire: The British Legacy of Professional Organization*, ed. C. Poullaos and S. Sian, pp. 192–214. New York and London: Routledge.

Verma, S., and S.J. Gray (2006). The creation of the Institute of Chartered Accountants of India: the first steps in the development of an indigenous accounting profession post-independence. *Accounting Historians Journal*, 33(2), pp. 131–56.

Wallace, R.S.O. (1989). *Accounting and Financial Reporting in Nigeria*. London: Institute of Chartered Accountants in England and Wales.

Wallace, R.S.O. (1990). Accounting in developing countries: a review of the literature. In *Research in Third World Accounting*, ed. R.S.O. Wallace, vol. 1, pp. 3–54. Oxford: JAI Press.

Wallace, R.S.O. (1992). Growing pains of an indigenous accountancy profession: the Nigerian experience. *Accounting, Business and Financial History*, 2(1), pp. 25–53.

Wallace, R.S.O., and R. Briston (1993). Improving the accounting infrastructure in developing countries. In *Research in Third World Accounting*, ed. R.S.O. Wallace, vol. 2, pp. 201–24. London and Greenwich, CT: JAI Press.

Walle, N. van de (2001). *African Economies and the Politics of Permanent Crisis, 1979–1999*. Cambridge: Cambridge University Press.

Weber, M. (1978). *Economy and Society: An Outline of Interpretive Sociology*, ed. G. Roth and C. Wittich. Los Angeles and London: University of California Press.

Xu, X. and Xu, X. (2003). Becoming professional: Chinese accountants in early 20th century China. *Accounting Historians Journal*, 30(1), pp. 129–53.

Yapa, P.W.S. (2006). Cross-border competition and the professionalisation of accounting: the case of Sri Lanka. *Accounting History*, NS 11(4), pp. 447–73.

Yapa, P.W.S. (2010). The imperial roots of accounting closure: the case of Sri Lanka. In *Accountancy and*

Empire: The British Legacy of Professional Organization, ed. C. Poullaos and S. Sian, pp. 124–43. New York and London: Routledge.

Yapa, P.W.S., and Z.P. Hao (2007). An analysis of current trends in accounting professional development in People's Republic of China. *Asian Review of Accounting*, 15(1), pp. 25–44.

Yapa, P.W.S., K. Jacobs and C.B. Huot (2010). Revolution and the accountant: the practice and profession of accounting in Cambodia, Paper presented at the 6th Asia-Pacific Interdisciplinary Perspectives on Accounting Conference, Sydney, Australia, July.

Yee, H. (2009). The re-emergence of the public accounting profession in China: a hegemonic analysis. *Critical Perspectives on Accounting*, 20, pp. 71–92.

Yee, H., and B. West (2010). Accounting professionalisation and occupation context: the role of the public accounting profession in China, Paper presented at the 6th Asia-Pacific Interdisciplinary Perspectives on Accounting Conference, Sydney, Australia, July.

6 Adoption of international financial reporting standards in developing countries

Hector Perera

1. INTRODUCTION

The accounting systems of most developing countries (DCs) are largely extensions of those of industrialized countries, mainly Anglo-American (AA), imposed either through colonial influence or by powerful investors, multinational corporations, and international accounting firms and organizations. Perhaps the International Accounting Standards Board (IASB) has been one of the most effective vehicles that has extended AA accounting technology to DCs in recent years. The key role of the International Accounting Standards Committee (IASC), the predecessor to the IASB, was to develop and establish a uniform set of accounting standards (international accounting standards – IASs) harmonizing financial reporting across the world. The change of name of the IASC to IASB in 2001 was accompanied by a shift in focus from accounting harmonization to accounting convergence. For example, the objective of the IASB is 'to bring about convergence of national accounting standards and international financial reporting standards to high quality solutions' (http://www.iasb.org).

Similar to harmonization, convergence is a process that takes place over a period of time. However, unlike harmonization, convergence implies the adoption of one set of financial reporting standards internationally. It means reducing international differences in financial reporting standards by developing a set of high-quality standards in partnership with national standard setters. According to *IAS Plus* (http://iasplus.com), currently over 100 countries, including many DCs such as Fiji, Iraq, Kenya, Mongolia, Nepal, Tanzania and the West Bank/Gaza, have adopted the international financial reporting standards (IFRSs) issued by the IASB for their domestic listed companies. Of these, 90 countries require the use of IFRSs for all listed companies, and in nearly all of them the audit report refers to conformity with IFRSs.

The efforts of the IASB (and IASC) have been associated with AA accounting, a term used to describe the accounting systems prevalent in the United States, the United Kingdom, Canada, Australia and New Zealand. For example, the IASB's Conceptual Framework for Accounting and Financial Reporting is largely based on that of the US FASB. Some even criticize the IASB for attempting to promote AA accounting throughout the world; in particular there are some serious concerns with regard to the adoption of IFRSs in DCs. Further, the recent global financial crisis has raised a few questions about AA accounting. For example, the concept of fair value, defined as the price determined by an exchange between two willing parties and promoted in IFRSs, has been described as a root cause of the global financial crisis. A report issued in the United States in early March 2010 lays out how Lehman Brothers used what amounted to financial engineering to shuffle US$50 billion off its books in the months before its collapse in September 2008 to conceal its dependence on leverage, or borrowed money.[1] These events have further strengthened the concerns about adopting IFRSs in DCs.

The purpose of this chapter is to examine the issues related to the adoption of IFRSs in DCs. The chapter is organized into six sections. Section 2 describes the major harmonization efforts of the IASC. Section 3 explains the establishment, objectives and institutional arrangements of the IASB. Section 4 explains the nature and significance of IFRSs. Section 5 discusses the challenges facing the DCs in adopting IFRSs. Section 6, the last section, provides concluding remarks, which include some suggestions for the way forward.

2.   MAJOR HARMONIZATION EFFORTS OF THE IASC

The IASC was established in 1973 by an agreement of the leading professional accounting bodies in 10 countries (Australia, Canada, France, Germany, Ireland, Japan, Mexico, the Netherlands, the United Kingdom and the United States) with the broad objective of formulating 'international accounting standards'. Prior to its dissolution, the IASC consisted of 156 professional accountancy bodies in 114 countries, representing over 2 million accountants in public practice, education, government service, industry and commerce. The IASC was funded by contributions from member bodies, multinational companies, financial institutions, accounting firms, and the sale of IASC publications. The IASC issued a total of 41 IASs during the period 1973–2001.

The IASC's harmonization efforts evolved in three phases. In the initial phase, covering the first 15 years, the IASC's main activity was the issuance of 26 generic IASs, many of which allowed multiple options. The IASC's approach to standard setting during this phase can be described as a 'lowest-common-denominator' approach, as the standards reflected an effort to accommodate existing accounting practices in various countries. For example, IAS 11, 'Construction contracts', as originally written in 1979, allowed companies to choose between the percentage of completion method and the completed contract method in accounting for long-term construction contracts, effectively sanctioning the two major methods used internationally. Given the lowest-common-denominator approach adopted by the IASC, it was obvious that IASC standards existing in 1988 introduced little if any comparability of financial statements across countries.

In the second phase, two significant activities took place from 1989 to 1993. The first was the 1989 publication of the *Framework for the Preparation and Presentation of Financial Statements*, which set out the objectives of financial statements, the qualitative characteristics of financial information, definitions of the elements of financial statements, and the criteria for recognition of financial statement elements. The second activity was the Comparability of Financial Statements Project, the purpose of which was 'to eliminate most of the choices of accounting treatment currently permitted under International Accounting Standards'. As a result of this project, 10 revised IASs were approved in 1993 and became effective in 1995. As an example of the changes brought about by the Comparability Project, IAS 11 was revised to require the use of the percentage of completion method when certain criteria were met, thereby removing the option to avoid the use of this method altogether.

This phase was supported by the International Organization of Securities Commissions (IOSCO) and the International Federation of Accountants (IFAC). IOSCO is the leading organization for securities regulators around the world, with about 177 ordinary, associate and affiliate members (including the US Securities and Exchange Commission – SEC) from about 100 countries. IOSCO aims, among other things, to ensure a better regulation of the markets on both the domestic and the international level. It provides assistance to ensure the integrity of the markets by a rigorous application of the standards and by effective enforcement.

IOSCO works to facilitate cross-border securities offerings and listings by multi-national issuers. It has consistently advocated the adoption of a set of high-quality accounting standards for cross-border listings. For example, a 1989 IOSCO report entitled 'International equity offers' noted that cross-border offerings would be greatly facilitated by the development of internationally accepted accounting standards. To this end, IOSCO supported the efforts of the IASC in developing IASs that foreign issuers could use in lieu of local accounting standards when entering capital markets outside their home country.

The IFAC was established in October 1977 at the 11th World Congress of Accountants in Munich, with 63 founding members representing 51 countries. It is now a global organization of 158 member bodies and associates in 123 countries, representing over 2.5 million accountants employed in public practice, industry and commerce, government and academia. Its mission is to serve the public interest and to strengthen the worldwide accountancy profession and contribute to the development of strong international economies by establishing and promoting adherence to high-quality professional standards on auditing, ethics, education and training. In June 1999, IFAC launched the International Forum on Accountancy Development (IFAD) in response to a criticism from the World Bank (following the Asian financial crisis) that the accounting profession was not doing enough to enhance accounting's capacity and capabilities in developing and emerging nations. IFAD's membership includes the international financial institutions (such as the World Bank, International Monetary Fund and Asian Development Bank), other key international organizations (such as IOSCO, IASB and SEC) and the large accountancy firms. The primary aim of this forum is to promote transparent financial reporting, duly audited to high standards by a strong accounting and auditing profession. In May 2000, IFAC and the large international accounting firms established the Forum of Firms, also aimed at raising standards of financial reporting and auditing globally in order to protect the interests of cross-border investors and promote international flows of capital. The forum works alongside IFAD in achieving common objectives.

The third and final phase in the work of the IASC began with the IOSCO agreement in 1993 and ended with the creation of the IASB in 2001. The main activity during this phase was the development of a core set of IASs that was endorsed by IOSCO for cross-listing purposes. IOSCO became a member of the IASC's Consultative Group in 1987 and supported the IASC's Comparability Project. In 1995, the IASC and IOSCO agreed on a work programme for the IASC to develop the set of 30 core international standards, and IOSCO agreed to evaluate the standards for possible endorsement for cross-border security offering and listing purposes upon their completion. With the publication of IAS 39,

'Financial instruments: recognition and measurement', in December 1998, the IASC completed its work programme to develop the set of 30 core standards. In May 2000, IOSCO's Technical Committee recommended that securities regulators permit foreign issuers to use the core IASC standards to gain access to a country's capital market as an alternative to using local standards. The Technical Committee consisted of securities regulators representing the 14 largest and most developed capital markets, including Australia, France, Germany, Japan, the United Kingdom and the United States. IOSCO's endorsement of IASC standards was an important step in the harmonization process.

Compliance with International Accounting Standards

Several studies investigated the extent of compliance by those firms that claimed to follow IASs. These studies found various levels of non-compliance with IASs (for example, Street, Gray and Bryant, 1999). Former IASC secretary-general David Cairns referred to the use of IASs with exceptions as 'IAS-lite'. In response to the use of 'IAS-lite', IAS 1 was revised in 1997 to preclude firms from claiming to be in compliance with IASs unless they complied with all the requirements (including the disclosure requirements) of each standard and each applicable interpretation.

3. THE ESTABLISHMENT, OBJECTIVES AND INSTITUTIONAL ARRANGEMENTS OF THE IASB

The IASC faced problems of legitimacy with regard to constituent support, independence, and technical expertise. For example, some interested parties perceived the fact that IASC board members worked at international standard setting only part time and were not necessarily selected because of their technical expertise as an indication of the lack of commitment on the part of the IASC to develop the highest-quality standards possible. Responding to these concerns, the IASC appointed a Strategy Working Party in 1996, which issued a discussion document in December 1998 entitled 'Shaping IASC for the future'. This document proposed a vastly different structure and process for the development of IASs.

The final recommendations of the IASC Strategy Working Party were approved at its Venice meeting in November 1999. These recommendations, designed to deal with the issue of legitimacy, attempted to balance calls for a structure based on geographic representativeness and those based on technical competence and independence. Accordingly, it was decided that representativeness would be provided by the geographic distribution of the trustees, who would be essential to ensuring the effectiveness and independence of the board, but that board members would be selected based on their expertise. On 1 April 2001, the newly created IASB took over from the IASC as the creator of international accounting standards, which were to be called IFRSs. The formation of the IASB in 2001, with a change in focus from harmonization to global standard setting, marked the beginning of a new era in international financial reporting. In addition to the IASB itself, the other main components of the new international standard-setting structure include the IFRS Foundation and its trustees, the IFRS Interpretation Committee and the IFRS Advisory Council.

The standard-setting work of the IASB is funded by the IFRS Foundation, whose revised constitution, effective from 1 March 2010, describes its objective as follows:

a. To develop, in the public interest, a single set of high-quality, understandable, enforceable and globally accepted financial reporting standards based upon clearly articulated principles. These standards should require high-quality, transparent and comparable information in financial statements and other financial reporting to help investors, other participants in the world's capital markets and other users of financial information make economic decisions.
b. To promote the use and rigorous application of those standards.
c. In fulfilling the objectives associated with (a) and (b) to take account of, as appropriate, the needs of a range of sizes and types of entities in diverse economic settings.
d. To promote and facilitate adoption of international financial reporting standards (IFRSs), being the standards and interpretations issued by the IASB, through the convergence of national accounting standards and IFRSs.

Currently, a majority of the membership of the trustees are from Europe and North America (12 out of 22), and the majority of the IASB's members are from Europe and North America (8 out of 14). The IASB follows a due process procedure and adopts a principles-based approach in developing IFRSs. These are briefly discussed here:

- *The Board.* The IFRS Foundation's constitution provides that the trustees select members of the IASB so that it will comprise a group of people representing, within that group, the best available combination of technical skills and background experience of relevant international business and market conditions in order to contribute to the development of high-quality, global accounting standards. All full-time members (12) are required to sever their employment relationships with former employers and are not allowed to hold any position that gives rise to perceived economic incentives that might call their independence into question. Sir David Tweedie, former chairman of the United Kingdom's Accounting Standards Board, continues to be the chairman of the IASB. Clearly, there is a very strong Anglo-American influence on the board. The IASB has sole responsibility for establishing IFRSs.
- *IASC Foundation trustees.* The governance of the IASC Foundation rests with the trustees. The revised constitution of 2010 has created a Monitoring Board mainly to develop a charter that sets out its organizational, operating and decision-making procedures for the trustees. The trustees are from diverse functional backgrounds. The Foundation trustees publish draft interpretations for public comment and report final interpretations to the Board for approval.
- *IFRS Interpretation Committee* develops interpretations on financial reporting issues not specifically addressed in an IAS or IFRS.
- *IFRS Advisory Council* provides a forum for participation by organizations and individuals, with an interest in international financial reporting.

4. THE NATURE AND SIGNIFICANCE OF INTERNATIONAL FINANCIAL REPORTING STANDARDS

The IASC had issued 41 IASs, and of those 11 IASs have been superseded or withdrawn. Most of the 30 remaining standards have been revised one or more times. Since 2001, the IASB has issued eight IFRSs. The term IFRS is used to describe broadly the following:

● IASB international financial reporting standards;
● IASC international accounting standards;
● interpretations originated by the IFRS Interpretations Committee.

The IASB uses a principles-based approach in developing IFRSs. Principles-based standards focus on establishing general principles derived from the IASB Conceptual Framework, providing recognition, measurement, and reporting requirements for specific transactions. This approach results in a limited amount of guidance for applying the general principles to typical transactions. It encourages professional judgement in applying the general principles to transactions. Sir David Tweedie, the IASB chairman, explained the principles-based approach taken by the IASB as follows:

> The IASB concluded that a body of detailed guidance (sometimes referred to as *bright lines*) encourages a rule-based mentality of 'where does it say I can't do this?' We take the view that this is counter-productive and helps those who are intent on finding ways around standards more than it helps those seeking to apply standards in a way that gives useful information. Put simply, adding the detailed guidance may obscure, rather than highlight, the underlying principles. The emphasis tends to be on compliance with the letter of the rule rather than on the spirit of the accounting standard.
>
> We prefer an approach that requires the company and its auditors to take a step back and consider with the underlying principles. This is not a soft option. Our approach requires both companies and their auditors to exercise professional judgement in the public interest. Our approach requires a strong commitment from preparers to financial statements that provide a faithful representation of all transactions and strong commitment from auditors to resist client pressures. It will not work without those commitments. There will be more individual transactions and situations that are not explicitly addressed. We hope that a clear statement of the underlying principles will allow companies and auditors to deal with those situations without resorting to detailed rules. (Tweedie, 2002)

Since IFRSs provide accountants only with guidelines which require the application of professional judgement, it is crucial to understand the rationale behind the principles espoused in particular standards.

In addition to broad principles, IFRSs also contain uncertainty expressions such as 'probable', 'significant influence', 'control' and 'substantial', which are accounting terms and concepts that are used to guide judgements made by professional accountants. These uncertainty expressions are used to denote levels of probability in prescribing recognition, measurement and disclosure thresholds involving considerable judgement. For example, in IAS 27, 'Consolidated and separate financial statements', the rules-based quantitative criterion of over 50 per cent shares in entities has now been replaced with a qualitative criterion of 'control' which required the exercise of professional judgement in identifying an entity for which consolidated accounts may be prepared. Similarly, in IAS

17, 'Leases', and IAS 28, 'Investments in associates', rules-based quantitative criteria have been replaced with qualitative principles. In addition, IAS 18, 'Revenue', states that it is *probable* that the economic benefits associated with the sale will flow to the seller; and IAS 16, 'Property, plant, and equipment', specifies a condition that costs related to property, plant and equipment should be recognized as an asset when it is *probable* that future economic benefits will flow to the enterprise.

The interpretation of uncertainty expressions contained in accounting standards has always been one of the most difficult problems facing professional accountants. Researchers have pointed out that professional accountants from a highly conservative country will tend to assign a higher numerical probability to uncertainty expressions that determine the threshold for the recognition of items that increase income, and vice versa (for example, Doupnik and Riccio, 2006).

The accounting profession and standard setters have been under pressure from multinational companies, stock exchanges, securities regulators, and international lending institutions, such as the World Bank, International Monetary Fund (IMF), Organisation for Economic Co-operation and Development (OECD), IFAC, IOSCO, World Trade Organization (WTO), Asian Development Bank (ADB), and Association of South East Asian Nations (ASEAN), to reduce diversity in financial reporting. They all promote the idea of creating business structures which will facilitate international trade and commerce. There is an expectation within the international capital market that, since accounting is an important source of business information, it should transcend national boundaries, and practices should converge. Accounting convergence has become an essential, albeit implicit, component of the globalization process. The forces of globalization and political expediency are forcing an increased number of countries to adopt IFRSs. Further, joint ventures, the most common way for foreign investors to invest in DCs, also create a need for adopting internationally acceptable accounting standards in those countries.

It has been pointed out that accounting convergence would enhance the international acceptance of a country's accounting system and generally improve the image of the country as a member of the international business community. Some DCs would adopt IFRSs to gain instant international respectability or to serve as a politically correct substitute for their own accounting standards. Some DCs would also like to signal to the world that they are joining the drive for convergence towards IFRSs to facilitate international investment. It would also provide DCs with the opportunity to improve their accounting systems with a minimum cost in terms of both funds and expertise required.

5.   THE CHALLENGES FACING THE DCS IN ADOPTING INTERNATIONAL FINANCIAL REPORTING STANDARDS

The challenges facing DCs in adopting IFRSs can be divided into two categories, namely challenges common to the idea of convergence in general and challenges that are specific to DCs. Focusing on the former, the greatest obstacle to convergence is the magnitude of the differences that exist between countries and the fact that the political cost of eliminating those differences would be enormous. As stated by Dennis Beresford, former chairman of the Financial Accounting Standards Board (FASB), 'high on almost everybody's list of obstacles is nationalism. Whether out of deep-seated tradition, indifference born of economic power, or resistance to intrusion of foreign influence, some say that national entities will not bow to any international body' (Beresford, 1988). Arriving at principles that satisfy all of the parties involved throughout the world seems an almost impossible task.

Second, not only is convergence difficult to achieve, but the need for such standards is not universally accepted. Convergence is probably neither practical nor truly valuable. For example, a well-developed global capital market exists already, and it has evolved without uniform accounting standards. Further, it may be unnecessary to force all companies worldwide to follow a common set of rules, as this would lead to a situation of standards overload as a result of requiring some enterprises to comply with a set of standards that are not relevant to them. In any case, the international capital market will force those companies that can benefit from accessing the market to provide the required accounting information without convergence.

Third, because of different environmental influences, differences in financial reporting across countries might be appropriate and necessary. For example, countries that are at different stages of economic development or that rely on different sources of financing perhaps should have differently oriented accounting systems. Frederick Choi refers to this as the dilemma of global harmonization: 'The thesis of environmentally stimulated and justified differences in accounting runs directly counter to efforts at the worldwide harmonization of accounting. Hence, the dilemma' (Choi, 1981).

Fourth, in the drive towards convergence there is an implicit assumption that international adoption of IFRSs will automatically lead to comparability in financial reporting. However, it is important to recognize that there is a difference between adoption and implementation of financial reporting standards. In other words, apart from adopting a single set of standards, comparability in financial reporting, which is the ultimate objective of convergence, requires consistent interpretation and application of standards across countries. Prior studies have provided evidence that adoption of international standards alone may not necessarily result in consistency in practices across countries, as accounting practices are a product of the accounting environment of a country, and a particular environment is unique to its time and locality (for example, Rahman, Perera and Ganesh, 2002).

Finally, several cross-cultural studies have shown that national culture can affect the numerical probability that professional accountants assign to uncertainty expressions used in IFRSs (Doupnik and Richter, 2003, 2004; Doupnik and Riccio, 2006). Differences in the interpretation of uncertainty expressions might lead to differences in the application of the recognition criteria in which those terms are used, resulting in different recognition decisions being made.

While these are potential challenges that countries in general, including DCs, are likely to face in adopting IFRSs, there are other challenges which are specific to DCs, as the objectives of the IASB are not congruent with the needs and aspirations of those countries. They are described below.

First, IFRSs developed in an AA environment emphasize the importance of professional judgement, which requires a capacity to understand professional rules and professional self-regulation. For example, as stated earlier, IFRSs use 'uncertainty expressions', which are required to be interpreted in making professional judgements. Further, IFRSs represent a principles-based or 'substance over form' approach, in contrast to a legalistic approach. The goal of principles-based standards is to provide the flexibility to deal with different situations, where professional accountants have to assume more responsibility for making judgements. Therefore, to be able to apply these standards consistently it is necessary to be able to interpret uncertainty expressions and apply them in making professional judgements and understand the rationale behind the principles espoused in particular standards. However, it is doubtful that the accountants in many DCs would have the capacity to do these as required (Chand and White, 2005).

Some DCs may not have an adequate supply of qualified and experienced accountants or a well-established accounting profession and regulators to interpret and adequately enforce the IFRSs. In some DCs, accounting has been recognized as a profession relatively recently. The low level of professionalism in many DCs is mainly due to the lack of professional education and training and strong incentives for manipulating accounting information. Poorly educated accountants would find it difficult to exercise professional judgement following the guidelines provided in IFRSs in their routine work.

The second challenge relates to the economic development needs of DCs. In DCs, there is a need to achieve rapid economic development within the shortest possible time. It seems to be generally accepted in these countries that the public interest is best served if business enterprise accounting interrelates with national economic policies, emphasizing the significant role accounting could play in achieving these purposes. For example, accounting could be used to ensure that macroeconomic policies and broad national economic goals are harmoniously interrelated. But, although financial reporting and capital market activity in AA countries are closely related, an accounting system focused on efficient functioning of the capital market may not be suitable for DCs. Thus DCs could adopt organizations of accounting which would consist of adaptations of modern ways to the special conditions of their countries.

DCs are compelled to design domestic policies which will achieve the maximum possible efficiency in the utilization of available resources. As a necessity, the government has to take the initiative in this process. The self-regulatory competitive market system cannot be depended upon as a mechanism for efficient allocation of scarce economic resources, since this mechanism is unreliable and unpredictable in its effect. It can also be very slow in its progress. In the case of DCs the accounting profession is already weak and relatively small, and it is exactly for this reason that government intervention in accounting regulation becomes necessary to safeguard the public interest. One can argue that an active role of governments in developing accounting principles and providing legal authority is likely to result in a higher reliability of published financial information, as the public sector is more likely to be insulated from private pressures (for example, practising accountants, business firms and statement users) and can therefore be more objective in setting up norms and procedures.

The conditions under which accounting operates in DCs suggest that the reliability of financial disclosures is not likely to reach any significant level unless legal disclosure standards are set. Therefore, in order to be able to provide much needed professional services, the development of accounting may have to be promoted through appropriate laws and regulations rather than depend on professional self-regulation.

In earlier, less complex times, it was assumed, in the countries with a common-law heritage such as the UK and the US, that accounting should be developed by accountants, independent of legal direction or government interference. However, in most DCs it is highly unlikely that an accounting profession will evolve as it did in the UK and the US, without strong government involvement. Accounting information is important not only to make decisions with regard to a single firm, but also to make comparisons between firms. Further, it is well known that the receivers of accounting information in DCs are generally unsophisticated and their capacity to interpret and use information is limited. If each enterprise were to explain the methods it has adopted in its financial statements, such users are likely to be overwhelmed and confused by the information provided by different firms.

Political priorities in economic activities are not a totally new idea, because non-AA accounting development patterns, particularly in Japan, Germany, France and the Scandinavian countries, clearly demonstrate political priorities and influences. Further, in the 2007–08 crisis, many financial institutions in AA countries were saved only by state interventions. Governments around the world acted in unison to prevent the collapse of the entire global banking system, recapitalizing banks, slashing interest rates, boosting government spending and printing money.

It is doubtful if the economic advancement of today's DCs will follow the path taken by the AA countries when they were developing. The requirements of capital markets have been a major factor for increased disclosure in financial statements in AA countries. The accounting principles and practices developed in those countries are appropriate for an environment with a large private sector and a well-developed capital market.

The third challenge relates to the approach to accounting regulation. Establishing the credibility of accounting reports in the eyes of the public is particularly important in DCs. Flexible accounting methods are at least partly responsible for the failure of financial statements to command a high level of public credibility in DCs. Some even argue that flexible accounting was at least partly responsible for the global financial crisis in 2007–08. Flexibility may compromise comparability, as it is possible for two companies in the same industry to follow entirely different accounting principles and both get 'true and fair' view audit reports. The situation in many DCs is that financial statements neither comply with standards nor disclose. Therefore, one can argue that compliance with law as the main objective of accounting has some merit in the case of DCs. Legislative control over accounting could reduce the number of alternatives available to individual enterprises. Whatever the shortcomings which are usually attributed to a mandatory system at the more sophisticated level of accounting, it may be possible to improve the overall usefulness of accounting as a source of information for economic decision making through a mandatory system in DCs.

Further, if the accounting profession is not effective in its sphere of operation, government interference to safeguard the public interest is the most natural outcome that can be expected in any country. In DCs the government becomes an important, or in many cases the most important, user of accounting information, in addition to its role as the regulator of the economy.[2]

The legal systems in many DCs, compared to those of AA countries, are much younger and underdeveloped. While it is common for shareholders in AA countries to resort to legal protection, it may not be so in DCs. The accounting profession in DCs is unable to gain much support from the legal system and has to rely heavily on government administration, as social control or regulation is achieved more through administrative powers and machinery than through the legal system. Courts in many DCs lack independence and expertise, and the judiciary is heavily influenced by the government. In particular, the legal system provides little protection to shareholders.[3]

Fourth, the business environments in many DCs are likely to create difficulties in adopting certain IFRSs. For example, according to IAS 24, 'Related party disclosures', transactions between related parties must be disclosed in the notes to financial statements. Parties are related if one party has the ability to control or exert significant influence over the other party. Related parties can include parent companies, subsidiaries, equity method associates, individual owners and key management personnel. In many DCs, given the existing social structures which permeate organizations, social practices associated with 'relationship building' considered important in business, and family ownership of business, identifying related parties can be a highly complicated matter.

IAS 32 and IAS 39, 'Financial instruments', require financial assets and liabilities to be measured and reported at fair value. The definition of fair value in IAS 16 indicates that it is the amount at which an asset could be exchanged between knowledgeable, willing parties in an arm's length transaction. The fair values of land and buildings, and plant and equipment are usually determined through appraisals conducted by professionally qualified valuers. Implementing these ideas in DCs can be problematic, as there may not be knowledgeable and willing parties to exchange transactions.

Fifth, the adoption of IFRSs in some DCs would require a conceptual shift. Some of the concepts which are integral to AA accounting may not be relevant to, or understandable or acceptable in, some DCs. For example, the concept of conservatism, which is fundamental to AA accounting, had been regarded in China as a tool of capitalist exploitation and may not be easily accepted in that country. Further, the independent professional judgement emphasized in IFRSs may be a new concept in some DCs.

Sixth, although ethical standards are important in professional accounting work, ethical issues can be local and contextual, as professional ethics reside in the form of a contract between a professional group and the community within which that professional group operates. Therefore the notion of a universal or global set of ethical norms that is embedded in IFRSs can be challenged, as the notion of an 'international community' reflects the aspirations of AA culture. For example, some of the accepted methods of relationship building generally accepted in Chinese society (known as *guanxi*) may be considered bribery and corruption in an AA culture. It can be argued that a more communitarian view of professional ethics is needed.

Seventh, there seem to be identifiable differences between AA countries and DCs in terms of their cultural orientations. According to Hofstede (1980), individualism stands for a preference for a loosely knit social framework in society wherein individuals are supposed to take care of themselves and their immediate families only, and collectivism stands for a preference for a tightly knit social framework in which individuals can expect their relatives or other in-group to look after them in exchange for unquestioning loyalty. Hofstede (1980) concludes that the degree of individualism in a country is statistically related to that country's wealth. Accordingly, wealthy countries tend to be more individualistic, whereas poor countries tend to be more collectivistic. This would mean that, unlike the people in the industrialized countries, the people in DCs tend to identify their own interests with the interests of the society, indicating a greater acceptability of uniformity. Further, some of the cultural characteristics of DCs tend to represent a preference for secrecy in providing information to outsiders instead of being transparent. This will have a direct effect on information disclosure through financial reports.

To the extent that accounting skills and attitudes are culturally specific, there will be additional problems of relevance, because the societal values which influence the attitudes towards accounting in DCs, such as disclosure, tend to be significantly different from those of AA countries. It is hard to transfer some values of one culture on to another.

Finally, it may be necessary for DCs to invent new methods to increase the serviceability of accounting information in the absence of a developed capital market. The accounting standards developed in an AA environment may be not only irrelevant but also positively harmful to DCs, as they tend to become accepted norms and thereby pre-empt any possibility of evolving standards which are better suited to DCs' specific needs.[4]

6.   CONCLUDING REMARKS

This chapter proposed to examine the issues related to the adoption of IFRSs in DCs. The chapter pointed out that a common feature shared by most DCs is that their accounting systems are extensions of those of industrialized countries imposed without any serious consideration for the local needs. The discussion in the chapter also highlights that the objective of international convergence of financial reporting standards, where every country uses IFRSs the way they are used in Anglo-American countries, is likely to be unachievable. In this respect DCs are facing many challenges. On the one hand, DCs need to adopt internationally acceptable financial reporting standards in order to be recognized as good citizens of the world and able to attract foreign aid and investment. Given the rapid rate of globalization of markets, no country is able to consider domestic issues, including accounting issues, in isolation. On the other hand, there are serious issues related to capacity, relevance and usefulness in adopting IFRSs in DCs. In meeting these challenges, while there are issues common to all countries including DCs, there are other issues that are unique to individual countries depending on their particular circumstances. The discussion in this chapter shows that there should be a level of flexibility which allows for making amendments to suit local contexts in the drive towards convergence of IFRSs, as 'one size does not fit all'. The implication is that, as mentioned earlier, without such flexibility IFRSs may also be positively harmful to DCs, as they tend to become accepted norms and thereby pre-empt any possibility of evolving standards which are better suited to DCs' specific needs.

Suggestions for the Way Forward

1.   A selective approach for adoption of IFRSs may be appropriate for DCs that do not have the resources to support the full adoption of the IFRSs, where some of the IFRSs may not be relevant, where some of the IFRSs may be culturally insensitive.
2.   In determining appropriate financial reporting standards for DCs, consideration should be given to the needs and aspirations of these countries.
3.   Professional accountants need to be well trained and extensively exposed to principles-based standards before they are expected to be able to interpret and apply these standards.

4. There should be a coordinated effort among the international bodies, particularly IFAD, and governments and accounting organizations of DCs to ensure financial reporting standards are suitable for DCs, and to improve enforcement mechanisms for accounting standards.

NOTES

1. Securities and Exchange Commission, Lehman Brothers Holding Inc., Form 8-K, Washington, DC, 15 March 2010.
2. Even in the US, the Securities and Exchange Commission (SEC), with legislative authority over accounting practices, was created by Congress at a time when doubts were expressed about the ability of the US accounting profession to control financial reporting.
3. UK auditors enjoyed a better legislative and judicial environment during the early stages of development. The auditors were backed by both legal sanctions and those imposed by the professional societies, which strengthened their position of independence. On the other hand, UK auditors could maintain audit quality because UK professional accounting bodies emphasized professional education, training and examinations.
4. The adoption of IAS 39 met with considerable resistance in the European Union. The European Commission ultimately decided in 2004 to endorse IAS 39, but with exceptions. The Commission modified the version of IAS 39 to be applied by publicly traded companies in the EU with respect to certain provisions on the use of a full fair value option and on hedge accounting.

REFERENCES

Beresford, D.R. (1988). Accounting for international operations. *CPA Journal*, October, pp. 79–80.

Chand, P., and M. White (2005). Can Fiji accountants handle IASs? *Fiji Accountant*, April, pp. 9–14.

Choi, F.D.S. (1981). A cluster approach to harmonisation. *Management Accounting*, August, pp. 27–31.

Doupnik, T.S., and E.L. Riccio (2006). The influence of conservatism and secrecy on the interpretation of verbal probability expressions in the Anglo and Latin cultural areas. *International Journal of Accounting*, 41, pp. 237–61.

Doupnik, T.S., and M. Richter (2003). Interpretation of uncertainty expressions: a cross-national study. *Accounting, Organizations and Society*, 28, pp. 15–35.

Doupnik, T.S., and M. Richter (2004). Impact of culture on the interpretation of 'in context' verbal probability expressions. *Journal of International Accounting Research*, 3(1), pp. 1–20.

Hofstede, G. (1980). *Culture's Consequences: International Differences of Work Related Values*. Beverly Hills, CA: Sage Publications.

Rahman, A., H. Perera and S. Ganesh (2002). Accounting practice harmony, accounting regulation and firm characteristics. *Abacus*, 38(1), pp. 46–77.

Street, D.L., S.J. Gray and S.M. Bryant (1999). Acceptance and observance of international accounting standards: an empirical study of companies claiming to comply with IASs. *International Journal of Accounting*, 34(1), pp. 11–48.

Tweedie, D. (2002). Speech delivered before the Committee on Banking, Housing and Urban Affairs of the United States Senate, Washington, DC, 14 February.

7 Audit markets in less developed economies: caveats for globalization?
Javed Siddiqui

1. INTRODUCTION

Although the serious effects of cultural, political, historical, religious and other contextual differences on accounting practices have been stressed extensively in the accounting literature, there have been consistent calls for harmonization of accounting and auditing practices throughout the globe. In the area of auditing, significant harmonization attempts have been initiated by the International Federation of Accountants (IFAC). The ongoing rapid economic and political globalization has led to the emergence of the IFAC as a global authority in auditing (Loft and Humphrey, 2006). The mission of IFAC, as stated in the organization's much-publicized website, is 'the worldwide development of an accountancy profession with harmonized standards, able to provide services of consistently high quality in the public interest'.[1] In 2006, IFAC issued seven 'statements of membership obligations' (SMOs) to assist 'high quality performance by professional accountants' (IFAC, 2006). The member bodies of IFAC, which includes national accountancy bodies from most of the countries in the world, are required to make their best efforts to comply with the SMOs, and failure to do so without satisfactory explanations would result in suspension or removal of membership. IFAC's globalization attempts are supported by donor agencies such as the World Bank and the International Monetary Fund (IMF), which, as part of their Review of Standards and Codes (ROSC) programme, assess whether national auditing standards and institutional environments are consistent with international standards on auditing (ISAs) and other IFAC SMOs such as the code of ethics.

Prior literature has questioned the appropriateness of Western-styled accounting, auditing and corporate governance mechanisms in the context of developing economies (see, for example, King et al., 2000; Lance, Ferfila and Herzog, 2000; Haniffa and Hudaib, 2007; Alawattage and Wickramasinghe, 2008; Siddiqui, 2010a). It is argued that these mechanisms, developed in the context of developed economies, would only work under assumptions of an efficient capital market, higher investor sophistication, and the presence of effective second-order institutions (such as efficient regulators, judiciary and so on) that would complement such governance schemes. However, despite this, attempts to harmonize accounting and auditing practices have continued, and such efforts have been supported by international donor agencies such as the World Bank and the IMF, which have sometimes prescribed adoption of such standards in member states as a condition for receiving loans. This sets the context for this chapter.

Based on an extensive review of existing literature, the chapter attempts to identify some unique characteristics of the audit markets in less developed countries (LDCs) with a view to understanding whether such socio-political and cultural traits may actually act as deterrents to the globalization attempts initiated by the IFAC and World Bank. For the purpose of this chapter, Bangladesh is used as an example to highlight the distinctive characteristics of audit markets in LDCs. Like many other LDCs, Bangladesh is financially reliant on international donors or lending institutions such as the World Bank and the IMF, and instances of donor influence in government policy making have been documented (Sobhan, 2002). Siddiqui (2010a) reports that, as with many other LDCs, donor agencies attached conditions of financial sector reforms for advancing loans to the Bangladesh government for various projects. As part of the financial sector reforms, Bangladesh adopted the international standards of accounting (ISAs) and auditing (IASs). Mir and Rahaman (2005), investigating adoption of ISAs in Bangladesh, concluded that such adoption may have been due to a number of institutional pressures rather than reasons of efficiency, as these standards do not appear to be entirely suitable for the socio-economic conditions prevailing in Bangladesh. This is consistent with Siddiqui (2010a), who reports similar institutional pressures for the adoption of the apparently incompatible Anglo-American model of corporate governance in Bangladesh.

The remainder of this chapter is organized as follows. Section 2 discusses the auditing harmonization attempts initiated by the IFAC and the World Bank. Section 3 then presents some distinctive attributes of audit markets in LDCs, using Bangladesh as a case. Section 4 attempts to assess the potential effects of such characteristics on the globalization efforts. Section 5 then summarizes the findings in line with the research questions.

2. GLOBALIZATION OF AUDITING STANDARDS

Although there is a vast literature relating to harmonization of accounting standards, harmonization of auditing practices has received relatively little attention. The few studies that have looked at harmonization of auditing standards have largely concentrated on the area of audit reports.[2] Gangolly et al. (2002), investigating harmonization of auditing reports, state that such attempts have been relatively new and have mostly been spearheaded by the IFAC. Such attempts have been supported by the World Bank and the IMF, which, as part of their ROSC programme, have suggested adoption of a number of SMOs proposed by the IFAC in developing countries. This chapter will now discuss the IFAC and World Bank efforts to initiate and disseminate one global set of auditing standards in further detail.

2.1 The IFAC Compliance Programme

The IFAC was established in 1977, headquartered in New York, with a view to issuing international standards covering the areas of ethics, auditing and assurance, education and public sector accounting (IFAC website). The objective of IFAC is to provide globally homogeneous standards that will yield higher coordination in the international accounting profession by developing ISAs. IFAC was successful in gaining global recognition as the standard setter for auditing, and its position was further strengthened when the European Commission announced its intention to mandate all the countries included in the European Union to adopt the ISAs under the condition that the ISAs as well as the governance of the IFAC itself had to promote the public interest (Loft, Humphrey and Turley, 2006). At present, the number of IFAC members has reached 159 in 124 member countries, representing 2.5 million accountants worldwide.

In 2006, IFAC issued seven statements of membership obligations (SMOs) to assist 'high quality performance by professional accountants' (IFAC, 2006). The member bodies of IFAC, which include national accountancy bodies from most of the countries in the world, are required to make their best efforts to abide by the SMOs, and failure to do so without satisfactory explanations will result in suspension or removal of membership. The seven SMOs issued by the IFAC cover areas such as audit quality, audit education, code of ethics for professional auditors, disciplinary procedures to be adopted by national auditing bodies, adoption of ISAs and international financial reporting standards (IFRSs), and accountability and auditing in the public sector.

SMO 1 is concerned with ensuring that member bodies subject their audit firms to quality review programmes. At the least, audit firms that undertake audit and assurance engagements of listed companies should be reviewed for quality purposes. The IAASB is responsible for developing standards concerning audit quality (IFAC, 2006). SMO 2 dictates the education requirements that are supposed to be followed by IFAC member bodies. According to SMO 3, members of IFAC are required to comply with the standards that are issued in terms of quality control, auditing and assurance. SMO 4 is concerned with the IFAC Code of Ethics for Professional Accountants and pronouncements by the International Ethics Standards Board for Accountants (IESBA). Public sector auditing and accountability are incorporated in SMO 5. SMO 6 is related to investigations of cases of misconduct such as cases of breaching any codes or standards. The IFAC does recognize that each country has its own legal systems. Consequently, the IFAC has set minimum requirements which could enable member firms to comply with this obligation. SMO 7 relates to the adoption of IFRSs and ISAs in member countries. The IFRSs are issued by IASB, and this SMO relates to member bodies complying with this obligation.

2.2 World Bank and IMF Joint ROSC Programme

The ROSC programme was jointly launched by the World Bank and the IMF in 1999 with a view to 'promote greater financial stability, at both the domestic and international levels, through the development, dissemination, adoption, and implementation of international standards and codes' (IMF, 2005, p. 5). ROSC covers a set of 12 internationally recognized 'modules' consisting of core standards and codes relevant to economic stability and private and financial sector development of member countries.[3] The accounting and auditing module is led by the World Bank. A 2004 report by the World Bank, presenting an overview of the ROSC accounting and auditing module, mentions that the module has twofold objectives: first, to assess the comparability of national accounting and auditing standards with IASs and ISAs respectively, and the degree to which corporate entities comply with established accounting and auditing standards in the country; second, to assist the country in developing and implementing a country action plan for improving the institutional framework which underpins the corporate financial reporting regime in the country (World Bank, 2004, p. 2). Under the project, an evaluation exercise is conducted to compare the national auditing standards with the ISAs. The current strengths and weaknesses of the accounting and auditing profession in a member state are also evaluated. The ultimate outcome of the ROSC programme is the production of a country action plan for each member state, which 'if requested by country authorities' can result in the design of loans to be financed by the World Bank (World Bank, 2004, p. 6).

This section has presented a brief overview of the auditing harmonization and globalization attempts initiated by the IFAC and disseminated by donor agencies such as the World Bank and the IMF. Section 3 will now discuss some characteristics of the audit market in an LDC, using the case of Bangladesh.

3.   THE AUDIT MARKET IN BANGLADESH

The audit environment in Bangladesh is characterized by the presence of a relatively small number of publicly traded companies, many of which are owned and managed by families, a poor perception regarding the skill and competence of auditors, and the absence of appropriate monitoring. Prior literature has identified a number of socio-political characteristics of the environment within which auditors in Bangladesh operate, namely ownership concentration and family domination in public limited companies (Farooque et al., 2007; Khan, Hossain and Siddiqui, 2011), poor incentives for companies to go public (Sobhan and Werner, 2003), poor perception regarding the skill and competence of auditors (World Bank, 2003; Siddiqui, 2010b), and the absence of 'second-order' institutions (Siddiqui, 2010a). These factors will now be discussed in detail.

3.1   Ownership Concentration and Family Domination in the Corporate Sector

As in many other developing countries, most companies in Bangladesh are either family owned or controlled by substantial shareholders (a corporate group or government). Farooque et al. (2007) report that, on average, the top five stockholders hold more than 50 per cent of a firm's outstanding stocks. They state that managements in many companies are effectively just extensions of the dominant owners. The companies are closely held small and medium-sized firms where corporate boards are owner driven. Consequently, most of the companies have executive directors, a CEO and a chairman from the controlling family. A survey conducted by Sobhan and Werner (2003) found that an overwhelming majority (73 per cent) of the boards of non-bank listed companies were heavily dominated by sponsor shareholders 'who generally belong to a single family – the father as the chairman and the son as the managing director is the norm' (Sobhan and Werner, 2003, p. 34). Imam and Malik (2007) analyse the ownership patterns of 219 companies from 12 different industries listed on the Dhaka Stock Exchange, the major stock exchange in the country. It is reported that, on average, 32.33 per cent of the shares are held by the top three shareholders, the results being even higher for the real estate, fuel and power, engineering, textile and pharmaceutical sectors. In a recent paper, Muttakin, Khan and Siddiqui (2011) point out that, unlike the case in many developed economies, the family firm is the most dominant form of publicly listed company in Bangladesh.

3.2   Easy Access to Bank Credit

The capital market in Bangladesh is still in a primitive stage. The country has two stock exchanges: the Dhaka Stock Exchange (DSE) and the Chittagong Stock Exchange (CSE). Although DSE was set up in the early 1950s, the capital market in Bangladesh has not flourished in comparison with its South Asian counterparts, and has already experienced two major collapses, one in 1996 and another very recently in 2011. The market capitalization to GDP ratio for Bangladesh is only 7.5 per cent, which is significantly lower compared to other South Asian countries. Sobhan and Werner (2003) report that the capital market does not seem to offer adequate incentives for companies to go public:

> Bank financing is readily available as result of excess liquidity and extensive competition in the banking sector due to the fact that new private bank licenses had been issued mostly on a political basis; banks therefore are reluctant to enforce additional requirements or strict conditions in lending. This phenomenon is substantiated by our survey which revealed that equity requirement had been the prime motivator for only 10% of the public companies interviewed – the remaining companies had cited reasons like tax advantages and legal compulsion, for going public. (Sobhan and Werner, 2003)

Siddiqui (2010a) mentions that bank loans are easily available as a result of excessive liquidity. Competition in the banking sector also has resulted in lenient conditions for credit. Sobhan (2002) reports that the banking sector and the capital market are heavily affected by the existence of a 'default culture', where a class of entrepreneurs find it more convenient to obtain credit from the bank, and then take the opportunity of weak bank regulations, ineffective law enforcement, and political patronage to resort to malpractices of not repaying the credit. Khan (2003) points out that the sponsors, promoters and beneficiaries of this 'default culture' all belong to a particular class of society with connections with the government, and subsequently they protect each other.

Easy access to bank credit and the scope for adopting malpractices for not repaying bank loans through the exercise of political influence have contributed to the development of a culture where companies prefer debt financing to raising capital through the capital market. The ADB quarterly economic update on Bangladesh (ADB, 2006) identifies the poor quality of auditing and corporate governance, the lack of quality shares, and inadequate and irregular participation of the institutional shareholders as major reasons for the stagnant capital market.

3.3   Skill, Competence and Independence of Auditors

Despite having a very large population, the number of auditors in Bangladesh is surprisingly low, even compared with its neighbours. The World Bank (2003) suggests that the auditing profession does not attract the best-quality students, and the job does not really differentiate between an MBA and a professional auditor. Karim and Moizer (1996) identified that audit fees in Bangladesh were significantly low. Sobhan and Werner (2003) conducted a survey on the state of corporate governance in Bangladesh. The study reported that the majority of respondents did not believe that audit reports reflected a true and fair view of the affairs of the company. There was also a perception that, except for a very few reputed audit firms, the auditors generally did not understand or apply relevant auditing standards. Based on this, the study commented on the dismal state of the auditing profession in Bangladesh: 'The auditing function would seem to represent a vicious circle; auditors are not perceived as independent, and do not provide quality audits, therefore, companies and shareholders are not willing to pay high fees for an audit. The low fee structure, in turn, does not provide an incentive to provide quality personnel and audits' (Sobhan and Werner, 2003, p. 62).

Siddiqui (2010b) also questions the independence, skill and competence of the auditors. He states that the level of accountancy education offered at the undergraduate and professional stages affects the skill and proficiency of auditors. Also, because of the absence of most of the Big Four firms in Bangladesh, auditors are deprived of the training schemes offered by these reputed firms. The skill, competence and independence were also highlighted recently after the share market collapse of 2011, as the share market manipulation probe committee identified auditors as one of the major parties involved in the collusion that resulted in the market collapse.[4]

3.4   Absence of 'Second-Order' Institutions

Unlike the case in many developed economies, second-tier accountancy bodies (such as the ACCA) are absent in Bangladesh. This, along with the very small number of qualified chartered accountants, implies that the vast majority of accountants working in the corporate sector do not possess any accounting qualifications. In addition to this, the other second-order institutions, such as the regulatory bodies and the judiciary, suffer from lack of skills and proper training, especially in dealing with corporate cases (Sobhan and Werner, 2003). Bangladesh is a former British colony, and has inherited the common legal system. The Companies Act 1994 (revised after 81 years from the Companies Act 1913, when Bangladesh was part of British India) defines the structure of the firms, including the composition of the board of directors, appointment of the CEO, appointment and remuneration of the auditors and so on. However, the problem with the legal environment has always been its poor implementation (Sobhan and Werner, 2003). Uddin and Hopper (2001), examining the success of privatization of state-owned companies in Bangladesh, also identified the lack of legal enforcement as a major problem. A World Bank study on the state of financial accountability and governance in Bangladesh identified that the sharing of responsibility by a number of government agencies complicated the enforceability of corporate regulations: 'Responsibility for enforcement is shared among the Registrar of Joint Stock Companies, the Securities and Exchange Commission, the professional accountancy bodies, and the judiciary. The involvement of several bodies in corporate accountability complicates enforcement and reduces overall effectiveness' (World Bank, 2002, p. 83).

Siddiqui (2010a) reports that market regulators, such as the Securities and Exchange Commission of Bangladesh (SEC) and the Bangladesh Bank, are also constrained by severe shortage of human resources, and are seldom blamed for their failure to stop share market manipulations. The association of the SEC has been reported in successive share market enquiry reports, resulting in a decline of investor confidence in market regulators.

4.   CAVEATS FOR HARMONIZATION?

From the above discussion, it appears that the audit markets in LDCs such as Bangladesh possess some distinctive attributes that would not exist in developed economies. Therefore, it is likely that Western-styled governance and auditing schemes, based on notions such as efficient capital markets, may not entirely be suitable for such countries. This might have important implications for the IFAC initiative to globalize auditing practices. As mentioned before, the IFAC SMOs mainly concentrate on areas such as audit quality, audit education, skill and competence, code of ethics, self-regulation and other disciplinary procedures taken by national auditing bodies, adoption of international auditing standards, and public sector auditing. Each of these areas has the potential to be significantly affected, individually or collectively, by the socio-political characteristics prevailing in Bangladesh as identified above.

Figure 7.1 summarizes the audit market in Bangladesh. Three factors seem to contribute to the significantly low level of audit fees prevailing in Bangladesh at the moment: firstly, ownership structure and family dominance in the corporate sector; secondly, the ability of companies to secure funds elsewhere than the capital market; and thirdly, the shortage of skilled auditors. In a recent study, Khan et al. (2011) reported audit fees in Bangladesh to be significantly negatively correlated with ownership concentration in the corporate sector. Muttakin et al. (2011) concluded that family dominance in the corporate sector in Bangladesh has led to the development of a corporate culture where the role of auditing as a governance mechanism is not generally appreciated. They found that family-dominated firms, constituting more than 60 per cent of the companies listed on the DSE, paid significantly lower amounts of audit fees and were less inclined to employ better-quality auditors. Poor incentives for companies to be listed on the capital markets, together with easy access to bank credit, have resulted in the reluctance of companies to be listed on the capital market. As demand for audited financial statements for companies not listed with the stock exchanges tends to be low, audit fees in these companies have also suffered. The World Bank, in a report on the observance of standards and codes in Bangladesh (ROSC), has identified poor levels of education and training as one of the major problems for the development of the auditing profession in Bangladesh (World Bank, 2002). Sobhan and Werner (2003) report that investors in Bangladesh perceive auditors not to be sufficiently skilled. This negative image of auditors in the minds of investors will be reflected in the audit fees. Auditing literature has long identified the audit fee premium as an indication of audit quality. It is argued that better-quality auditors will charge significantly higher levels of audit fees as a premium for the quality of their services. This implies that audit quality has a cost. Therefore it can be argued that, because of the low levels of audit fees prevailing in Bangladesh, auditors cannot afford to provide quality audit services.

Audit quality, or the lack of it, has been associated with auditors' ability, firstly, to detect misstatements and, secondly, to report such incidents to the investors. The first attribute, therefore, relates more to the education and training received by the auditors, whereas the second feature refers to auditor independence and the ability of the profession to regulate its members. The main problems with education and training for professional accountants in Bangladesh, as identified by a World Bank report (2002), includes the failure of the profession to attract good-quality students, the poor quality

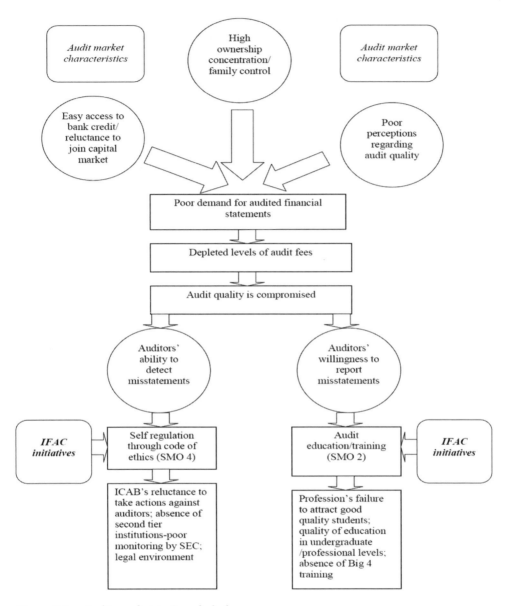

Figure 7.1   Audit market in Bangladesh

of accounting and auditing education offered at the undergraduate levels, and the inadequate training programmes offered by the ICAB. The World Bank (2002) reported a number of weaknesses in the education and training programmes offered by the ICAB. These include the lack of updated training materials, the lack of knowledge of the instructors, and a poor pass rate. The report mentioned that the ICAB pre-qualification curricula did not include the code of professional ethics, and sufficient depth in teaching functional business management, and communication skills. Poor pass rates are also identified as one of the major problems in the accountancy profession. The World Bank (2002) reports that, between 1972 and the end of June 2003, 11 026 students enrolled with the ICAB as trainee accountants. However, the current number of members in the ICAB is less than a thousand, indicating the poor pass rate and a high percentage of dropouts. The quality of accounting education at the undergraduate level has been the cause of major concern for the development of professional accounting education in Bangladesh. The World Bank ROSC report summarized this as follows:

> The quality of higher education suffers from the lack of modern curriculum and skilled instruction. Accounting courses in the bachelor's degree program do not include practical application of national and/or international accounting and auditing standards. Many accounting teachers lack the experience and adequate knowledge to teach either the theoretical or practical aspects of IAS and ISA. Undergraduate-level teaching in accounting and auditing mainly focuses on elementary topics and application of some basic standards. The outdated curriculum and lack of appropriate literature leaves students without an applicable background for modern accounting and auditing. The academic programs do not challenge students to improve critical thinking. (World Bank, 2002, p. 5)

The medium of instruction in the undergraduate programmes was another cause of concern. In Bangladesh, many universities still conduct their undergraduate programmes in Bengali, the national language. However, the professional accountancy courses run by the ICAB is in English. This creates difficulties for the students. The absence of Big Four audit firms implies that audit professionals in Bangladesh are not exposed to the superior levels of training offered by these internationally renowned firms.

The perceived independence of the auditors in Bangladesh has been questioned by a number of studies (for example, Sobhan and Werner, 2003; Siddiqui, 2010b). Bangladesh adopted the IFAC code of ethics in 2006. However, although it seems that the ICAB has a sound disciplinary process in place to tackle possible breaches of the code of professional ethics by its members, there is a widespread perception that the ICAB is reluctant to take action against its members (World Bank, 2002; Sobhan and Werner, 2003). The World Bank (2003) mentioned that the investigation and disciplinary committee of the ICAB 'is not proactive with respect to disciplining errant public practitioners' (World Bank, 2003). Also, the regulatory bodies such as the SEC are not deemed to be effective enough to monitor the quality of audited financial statements. A number of research reports also support the notion that the SEC in Bangladesh lacks the required technical expertise and resources. Sobhan and Werner (2003) identified a number of constraints:

> Right from the beginning, the SEC suffered from a lack of an adequate number of staff properly trained in capital market affairs. That lack still continues. The SEC does not have a full time Corporate Accountant in place. The current Chairman and members are not from a capital market background, and neither have most past chairmen and members been so; Commission members are usually retired public servants. (Sobhan and Werner, 2003)

Siddiqui (2010b) reports that the shortage of skilled human and other resources also affects the judicial procedures, where court litigation takes a very long time to be resolved, and acts as a potential deterrent for actions to be taken against ICAB members.

The ICAB, in response to IFAC's compliance programme questionnaire, has developed an action plan to demonstrate progress towards compliance with the IFAC SMOs (ICAB, 2009). It is mentioned that, in response to IFAC's compliance project, the ICAB has made significant progress in terms of adoption of the IFAC code of professional ethics (SMO 4). A new policy on investigation and discipline is being launched in line with the IFAC SMO 6. In response to SMO 7, ICAB is in the process of adopting the IFRS and making the Bangladesh standards on auditing consistent with the ISAs. Also, the education and training requirements for auditors are being revised to make these consistent with SMO 2. Overall, a reading of ICAB's response to IFAC's questionnaire related to the compliance programme would suggest notable progress towards harmonization of auditing and accounting practices. However, as this chapter suggests, the ground reality of the audit market in Bangladesh may be too different from that of the developed world for these SMOs to be effectively applied.

ICAB's unwillingness to regulate its members, together with the legal environment, may make the adoption of the IFAC code of professional ethics largely ceremonial. It is hard to see why the IFAC code of professional ethics would work where a number of similar codes issued and adopted by the ICAB earlier have not made much difference to the ethical behaviour of its members. Also, given that there is no second-tier accountancy body in Bangladesh and the corporate sector mostly recruits accountants who do not possess any professional accountancy qualification, it would be difficult to implement SMOs such as the adoption of IFRSs in the context of Bangladesh. In addition, there is a severe shortage of qualified financial analysts. As a result, general investors tend to lack a basic understanding of financial statements. Sobhan and Werner (2003) point out that the deficiency of investor sophistication leads to lack of shareholder activism in Bangladesh. The adoption of the IFAC SMO relating to accountancy education is unlikely to have an effect on the skill and competence of auditors, given the quality of accountancy education offered at the undergraduate level in universities and then by the ICAB. The absence of Big Four firms also has an effect on the quality of training received by auditors in Bangladesh.

5.   CONCLUSION

The chapter investigates the harmonization efforts initiated by the IFAC in the context of the audit market in an LDC, namely Bangladesh. The chapter identifies the ownership structure and family dominance, easy access to bank credit, the perceived deficiency in skill of auditors, and the absence of second-tier institutions supplementing the audit market as major obstacles for implementing the IFAC statement of membership obligations. However, despite this, countries such as Bangladesh, under pressure from the donor agencies, have been keen to demonstrate compliance with the IFAC harmonization efforts, ignoring the fact that the socio-economic characteristics prevailing in Bangladesh may not necessitate such wholesale adoption.

It is important to note that the characteristics of the Bangladesh audit market as identified in the chapter are not unique. Rather, audit markets in many other LDCs have demonstrated similar traits. However, because of the 'checklist' approach adopted by the IFAC, it may seem that the globalization efforts are being largely successful, especially in developing countries, which, under pressure from the World Bank and the IMF, attempt to demonstrate such compliance even though the ground realities of these countries may be completely different.

NOTES

1. IFAC website, www.ifac.org, accessed July 2011.
2. For example, Hussein, Bavishi and Gangolly (1986) investigate differences and similarities in the audit reports issued in 27 countries, Archer, McLeay and Dufour (1989) compared the audit reports of European countries, and Jones and Karbhari (1996) compared the audit reports of France, Germany, Japan, the Netherlands, the UK and the USA.
3. The 12 standards are data dissemination, fiscal transparency, transparency in monetary and financial policies, banking supervision, securities market regulation, insurance supervision, payments and settlements, anti-money laundering, corporate governance, accounting, auditing, and insolvency and creditor rights (World Bank, 2004).
4. The probe committee report mentioned that systematic failure had allowed massive manipulation of stock markets in Bangladesh in 2011, and identified the SEC, the Dhaka Stock Exchange, the Investment Corporation of Bangladesh, issuers, valuers and auditors as those who had colluded in 'turning the market volatile' (*Yahoo News*, 7 April 2011).

REFERENCES

ADB (2006). *Bangladesh Quarterly Economic Update*, December. Dhaka: Asian Development Bank.
Alawattage, C., and D. Wickramasinghe (2008). Appearance of accounting in a political hegemony. *Critical Perspectives on Accounting*, 19(3), pp. 293–339.
Archer, S., S. McLeay and J. Dufour (1989). *Audit Reports on Financial Statements of European Multinational Companies: A Comparative Study*. London: Institute of Chartered Accountants in England and Wales.
Farooque, O.A., T.V. Zijl, K. Dunstan and A.K.M.W. Karim (2007). Corporate governance in Bangladesh: link between ownership concentration and financial performance. *Corporate Governance: An International Review*, 15(6), pp. 1453–68.
Gangolly, J., M. Hussein, G. Seow and K. Tam (2002). Harmonization of the auditor's report. *International Journal of Accounting*, 37(3), pp. 327–46.
Haniffa, R., and M. Hudaib (2007). Locating audit expectations gap within a cultural context: the case of Saudi Arabia. *Journal of International Accounting, Auditing and Taxation*, 16(2), pp. 179–206.
Hussein, M.E., V. Bavishi and J.S. Gangolly (1986). International similarities and differences in the auditor's report. *Auditing: A Journal of Practice and Theory*, 15(2), pp. 124–33.
ICAB (2009). Action plan developed by the Institute of Chartered Accountants of Bangladesh. Available at www.ifac.org.
IFAC (2006). Statements of membership obligations, 1–7. (Revised; originally issued in 2004.)
Imam, M.O., and M. Malik (2007). Firm performance and corporate governance through ownership structure: evidence from Bangladesh stock market. *International Review of Business Research Papers*, 3(4), pp. 88–110.
IMF (2005). *The Standards and Codes Initiative: Is It Effective? And How Can It Be Improved?* Public information notice no. 15/106. Washington, DC: International Monetary Fund.
Jones, M.J., and Y. Karbhari (1996). Auditors' reports: a six country comparison. *Advances in International Accounting*, 9, pp. 129–55.
Karim, A.K.M.W., and P. Moizer (1996). Determinants of audit fees in Bangladesh. *International Journal of Accounting*, 31(4), pp. 497–509.
Khan, A., D.M. Hossain and J. Siddiqui (2011). Corporate ownership concentration and audit fees: the case of an emerging economy. *Advances in International Accounting*, 27(1), pp. 125–31.
Khan, M.M. (2003). State of governance in Bangladesh. *Round Table: Commonwealth Journal of International Affairs*, 92(370), pp. 391–405.
King, N., A. Beattie, A.-M. Cristescu and P. Weetman (2000). Developing accounting and audit in a transition economy: the Romanian experience. *European Accounting Review*, 10(1), pp. 149–71.
Lance, T.L., B. Ferfila and C. Herzog (2000). Budgeting in Slovenia during the democratic transition. *Public Budgeting and Finance*, 20(3), pp. 51–79.
Loft, A., and C. Humphrey (2006). IFAC.ORG: organizing the world of auditing with the help of a website.

In *Digital Governance: Networked Societies*, ed. H.K. Hansen and J. Hoff. Copenhagen: Samfundslitteratur Press.

Loft, A., C. Humphrey and S. Turley (2006). In pursuit of global regulation: changing governance and accountability structures at the International Federation of Accountants (IFAC). *Accounting, Auditing and Accountability Journal*, 19(3), pp. 428–51.

Mir, M. and A. Rahaman (2005). The adoption of international accounting standards in Bangladesh: an exploration of rationale and process. *Accounting, Auditing and Accountability Journal*, 18(6), pp. 816–41.

Muttakin, M.B., A.R. Khan and J. Siddiqui (2011). Audit fees and auditor choice in a family-firm dominated economy. Working paper, Deakin University, Australia.

Siddiqui, J. (2010a). Development of corporate governance regulations: the case of an emerging economy. *Journal of Business Ethics*, 91(2), pp. 253–74.

Siddiqui, J. (2010b). The existence of auditing as a profession: the case of an emerging economy. 3rd BAA ALDEE workshop, University of Birmingham.

Sobhan, F. and W. Werner (2003). Diagnostic study of existing corporate governance scenario in Bangladesh. In *A Comparative Analysis of Corporate Governance in South Asia*, ed. F. Sobhan and W. Werner. Dhaka: Bangladesh Enterprise Institute.

Sobhan, R. (2002). *The Political Economy of the State and the Market in Bangladesh*. Dhaka: Centre for Policy Dialogue.

Uddin, S., and T. Hopper (2001). A Bangladesh soap opera: privatisation, accounting, and regimes of control in a less developed country. *Accounting, Organizations and Society*, 26(7–8), pp. 643–72.

World Bank (2002). *Bangladesh: Financial Accountability for Good Governance*. Washington, DC: World Bank.

World Bank (2003). *Bangladesh: Accounting and Auditing: Report on the Observance of Standards and Codes (ROSC)*. Washington, DC: World Bank.

World Bank (2004). *Overview of the ROSC Accounting and Auditing Programme*. Washington, DC: World Bank.

8 Accounting standards and capital market development

Mahmud Hossain, Monirul Hossain and Kunal Sen

1. INTRODUCTION

Financial development, broadly defined to include not just financial sector deepening but also improvements in the efficiency of the financial sector,[1] is vital for pro-poor growth (Mavrotas, 2009). Financial development enhances domestic resource mobilization and also allows these resources the most productive uses. The cross-country literature on the relationship between financial development and economic growth is vast – and most studies show that financial development unambiguously and positively impacts on economic growth (Aghion and Bolton, 1997; Levine, 1997; Athukorala and Sen, 2002). While the effects of financial development on economic growth are well understood, it is less clear how financial development may affect poverty, and whether financial development can bring about a reduction in poverty directly, and not just by an indirect route through economic growth. Nor is it clear what are the determinants of financial development and, in particular, the role of accounting standards. In this chapter, we assess the theoretical arguments on the relationship between sound accounting standards and financial development, and between financial development and economic development, including poverty reduction. We also examine the cross-country evidence on the relationship between accounting standards and financial development, with particular reference to the South Asian experience. The rest of the chapter is in four sections. In Section 2, we examine the relationship between financial development and economic development. In Section 3, we discuss why accounting standards matter for financial development. In Section 4, we present evidence on the cross-country relationship between accounting standards and financial development and summarize the South Asian experience with the development of sound accounting standards. Section 5 concludes.

2. WHY FINANCIAL DEVELOPMENT MATTERS FOR ECONOMIC DEVELOPMENT

Since the work of the economic historian Raymond Goldsmith (1969), who found that a 'rough parallelism can be observed between economic and financial development if periods of several decades are considered' (p. 48), it has been widely recognized that a well-functioning financial system is crucial to economic growth (McKinnon, 1973; Shaw, 1973). Financial development can lead to economic growth in the following five ways: i) by facilitating the trading, hedging, diversifying and pooling of risk; ii) by allocating resources to the most productive uses; iii) by monitoring managers and exerting corporate control; iv) by mobilizing savings; and v) by facilitating the exchange of goods and services (Levine, 1997).

The theoretical mechanisms by which financial development leads to economic growth is best captured by Figure 8.1. The figure shows schematically how financial markets and intermediaries can be linked to growth by means of their five main functions. In fulfilling those five functions to overcome market frictions such as information costs and transaction costs, financial markets and intermediaries actually affect saving and allocation decisions in ways that influence growth. Levine (1997) identifies two channels through which each financial function may affect growth: capital accumulation and technological innovation (Barro and Sala-i-Martin, 1995; Barro, 1997). The financial system affects resource allocation either by altering the savings rate or by reallocating savings among different capital producing technologies. With respect to technological innovation, the functions performed by the financial system affect economic growth by altering the rate of technological innovation.

Therefore the degree of financial development can have a positive effect on economic growth by increasing both the volume of investment and its efficiency (Khan and Senhadji, 2000). Financial development can increase the volume of investment by the greater mobilization of investible resources in the economy (Bandiera, Honohan and Schiantarelli, 2000). With respect to the efficiency of investment, the financial sector can improve the allocation of investible funds in four ways. Firstly, the financial sector improves the screening of fund-seekers and the monitoring of the recipients of funds, which improves the allocation of resources. Secondly, in the presence of information and transactions costs, the financial system eases the trading, hedging and pooling of risk. Thirdly, financial markets and intermediaries mitigate the information acquisition and enforcement costs of monitoring managers of firms and exerting corporate control. Finally, financial systems spur technological innovation by encouraging specialization

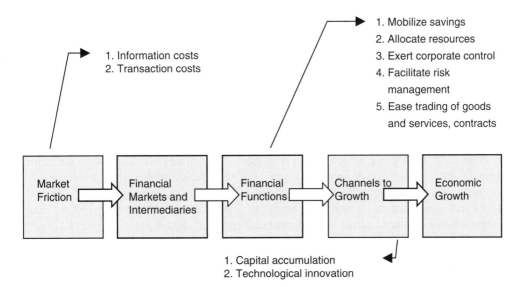

Figure 8.1   Understanding the finance–growth nexus

in the economy via the lowering of transactions costs. There is persuasive empirical evidence both across countries and for individual countries that countries with better-developed financial systems tend to grow faster, controlling for all other determinants of economic growth.[2]

However, while financial development can lead to higher economic growth, it is not obvious that it will lead to higher poverty reduction (Holden and Prokopenko, 2001). This is for two reasons. Firstly, the effect of financial development on poverty reduction is itself dependent on the level of income or asset inequality in the country. For countries with high levels of inequality, the effect of growth on poverty and, therefore, of finance on poverty will be less than for countries with low levels of inequality (Ahluwalia, 1976). Secondly and more importantly, financial development may itself exacerbate inequality in the country. Thus, as banks and other financial intermediaries grow in size and number, they may choose to lend only to those who have collateral and who can borrow against such collateral. This may be high net worth households and medium and large firms in the country. Poorer households or small and micro-enterprises that do not have access to collateral may be rationed out of financial markets (Armendariz de Aghion and Morduch, 2005). Stock markets as they emerge – another crucial indicator of financial development – may list only companies that are medium or large in size, and the richer households will be less risk averse in investing in shares with uncertain income streams than poorer households, which will be more risk averse (Demirguc-Kunt and Levine, 1996; Levine and Zervos, 1998; Demirguc-Kunt, 2006).

A high level of inequality may not only reduce the poverty reducing impact of economic growth, but itself contribute to reducing the impact of financial development on economic growth (Clarke, 1995; Partridge, 1997; Aghion, Caroli and Garcia-Penalosa, 1999; Banerjee and Duflo, 2000). The reason why income distribution is likely to exert an influence on economic efficiency is that productive opportunities might vary along the wealth distribution (Banerjee and Newman, 1993; Blanchflower and Oswald, 1998; Parker, 2000). Where information is costly and imperfect, equilibrium credit rationing will arise, that is, agents will be able to obtain credit only if they own assets that can be used as collateral (Stiglitz and Weiss, 1981). A more unequal distribution of assets would then imply that, for any given level of per capita income, a greater number of people are credit constrained (Deininger and Olinto, 2000). In an economy where individuals make indivisible investments – in schooling, for example – that have to be financed through borrowing, this would imply lower physical and human capital formation and hence aggregate growth (King and Levine, 1993a, 1993b; Deininger and Squire, 1998).

The fact that the effect of finance on growth is conditional on the level of inequality is clear from Figure 8.2, which shows the effect of financial development on economic growth at different levels of income inequality. The figure shows that the greater the level of inequality (as measured by the Gini coefficient), the lower the magnitude of the positive effect of finance on growth. The impact of finance on growth is more than six times larger when a country has a Gini coefficient of 10 per cent as compared to when a country has a Gini coefficient of 90 per cent.

The inter-relationships between financial development, economic growth and income inequality are depicted in Figure 8.3. Financial development can reduce poverty by increasing economic growth. However, financial development can exacerbate income inequality and thus can lead to higher poverty for the same economic growth. Higher

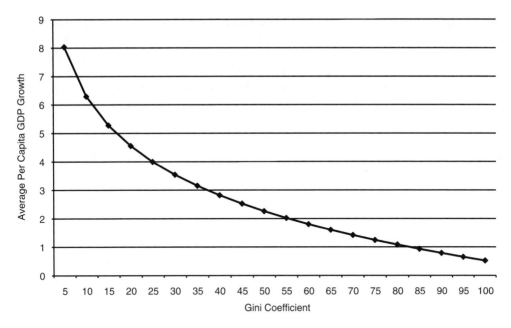

Source: Ozer and Sen (2009).

Figure 8.2 *The net effect of finance on growth at different levels of inequality*

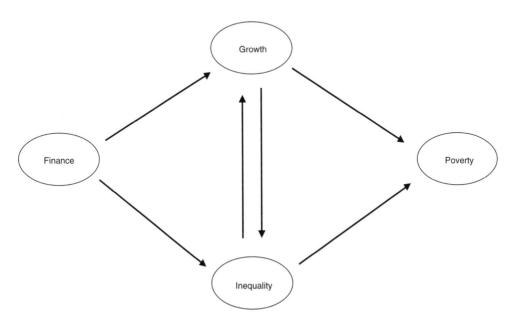

Figure 8.3 *The inter-relationships between financial development, economic growth, income inequality and poverty*

income inequality can have a negative impact on economic growth and thus bring about a decrease in the rate of economic growth. Economic growth also may widen disparities between individuals and groups in the economy and, by increasing inequality, reduce the impact of financial development on poverty reduction. This suggests that the relationship between financial development and poverty reduction is complex and depends on whether financial development increases inequality and whether this increased inequality is large enough to dwarf the positive effect of financial development on poverty reduction via higher economic growth. It also depends on whether economic growth and income inequality mutually reinforce each other such that higher inequality leads to lower growth and higher growth leads to higher inequality. The overall conclusion of this section is that, for financial development to have an unambiguous positive effect on poverty reduction, it must lead to both an increase in economic growth and a decrease in income inequality.

3.   WHY ACCOUNTING STANDARDS MATTER FOR FINANCIAL DEVELOPMENT

A major challenge in wealth creation in an economy is the efficiency with which scarce resources are allocated for potential investments. Countries that allocate scarce resources efficiently can take new business ideas and create wealth at a rapid pace. In contrast, economies that allocate resources poorly tend to waste their opportunities and fail to create economic growth (Palepu and Healy, 2008). Savings (scarce resources) in an economy are distributed across numerous individuals and institutions. There are usually many new entrepreneurs and existing companies that would like to attract the savings of numerous investors for their large-scale capital investments. While capital markets facilitate allocating scarce resources from investors to entrepreneurs, matching funds to potential investment opportunities is complicated by imperfect information and moral hazard problems (Healy and Palepu, 2001). First, entrepreneurs have superior information to outsiders (savers) about the future prospects of their firms. Second, the communication of entrepreneurs to potential investors (savers) is not completely credible, since savers know entrepreneurs have incentives to distort reported information. For instance, entrepreneurs seeking to raise capital may present a very optimistic profit forecast in their prospectus. Third, these small savers lack necessary expertise to analyse financial statements and differentiate between alternative investment opportunities. These information and other market imperfections may create situations where low-quality firms can crowd out good firms and erode investors' confidence in the market (Healy and Palepu, 2001). Financial economists indicate that strong corporate governance and related institutions such as financial accounting (reporting) systems can contribute to improve the economic performance (efficient capital allocation). The relation between financial accounting (reporting) systems and economic performance is discussed below.

Financial Reporting Systems and Economic Performance

The objectives of financial reporting in a market-based economy are to provide useful information to stakeholders for (1) firm valuation, (2) performance measurement and (3) control or stewardship. Investors searching for opportunities to invest their money are likely to invest in companies that disclose reliable value-relevant information. Levine, Loayza and Beck (2000), as cited in Habib (2007), discuss 'information about corporations for identifying best investments. Accounting standards that simplify the interpretability and comparability of information across corporations will simplify financial contracting. Furthermore, financial contracts that use accounting measures to trigger particular actions can only be enforced if accounting measures are sufficiently clear' (p. 5). La Porta et al. (1998) suggest:

> Accounting plays a potentially crucial role in corporate governance. For investors to know anything about the company they invest in, basic accounting standards are needed to render company disclosures interpretable. Even more important, contracts between managers and investors typically rely on verifiability in courts of some measures of firms' income or assets. If a bond covenant stipulates immediate repayment when income falls below a certain level, this level of income must be verifiable for the bond contract to be enforceable even in court in principle. Accounting standards might then be necessary for financial contracting, especially if investors' rights are weak. (p. 1140)

Bushman and Smith (2001, pp. 294, 306) show a relation between financial accounting information and economic performance. They show how a financial accounting regime is affected by legal and other institutional variables. In their model they show the link between a financial accounting regime and economic performance through three channels whereby this could happen. According to Bushman and Smith, a financial accounting system can affect economic performance at least via three channels. First, financial accounting information assists managers and investors to identify positive net present value projects. Moreover, financial accounting information, prepared in accordance with generally accepted accounting standards, indirectly affects economic performance by helping the stock market to evaluate accounting earnings and impound that information into stock prices. Second, accounting information is useful, in the corporate governance process, in contracts aimed at limiting agency problems in the firm (for example, managers' opportunistic actions). For example, managerial compensation contracts tied to accounting numbers and stock prices may motivate managers to create value for shareholders. Third, financial accounting information influences economic performance by reducing information asymmetry and estimation risk. Greater disclosure reduces investors' estimation risk and lowers a firm's cost of capital. Lambert, Leuz and Verrecchia (2007) show that informative financial reports will reduce estimation risk. Hence the possibility of reducing investor risk by more informative reporting is of interest to managers making voluntary disclosures. Well-developed capital markets are expected to increase economic growth by attracting more funds into the market and reduce risks faced by the investors, and the accounting regime provides support for this capital allocation function of markets. However, a high-quality financial reporting (standards) regime does not evolve by itself; instead, it is shaped by a variety of institutional factors. Indeed, the variations in financial reporting regimes across countries reflect the differences in institutional factors around the world. Section 3.2 discusses the role of institutions in financial accounting quality.

Role of Legal Institutions

History, economic, legal and political environments, and culture differ from country to country. These differences result in different legal environments, corporate governance, ownership structure and accounting regulations. Of the country level variables, the legal environment is important, since it determines the level and enforcement of shareholders' rights and protection (for example, voting rights, the duty of management to shareholders, and protection from insider trading). The nature and enforcement of accounting regulations (for example, financial reporting standards) affect investors' ability to figure out the true financial condition of a firm and assess the performance of management.

Around the world two main legal systems have evolved. This difference stems from the development of law in England and France in the twelfth and thirteenth centuries. Common law is defined as 'Body of law based on custom and general principles and that, embodied in case law, serves as precedent or is applied to situations not covered by statute. Under the common-law system, when a court decides and reports its decision concerning a particular case, the case becomes part of the body of law and can be used in similar cases involving similar matters.' Civil law is a body of law based on statute, not custom. It is 'characterized by fact-finding by state employed judges, automatic superior review of decisions and later the reliance on procedural and substantive codes rather than judicial discretion' (Djankov et al., 2002). It is widely believed that accounting information produced in common law countries is of higher quality compared to that in civil law countries. Common law countries operate on the 'shareholder equity' governance model, where information asymmetry between managers and outside capital providers is mitigated predominantly through public release of accounting and other information (Ball et al., 2000).

By contrast, civil law countries develop close relationships with major stakeholders. Compared to common law countries where there is a strong equity market as a source of finance, civil law countries develop a relationship (for example, banking) finance system. Therefore demand for publicly disclosed information is greater in common law countries than in civil law countries. From an economic standpoint, the costs and benefits associated with supply of information, public financial reporting is viewed as an efficient means to reduce information asymmetry between corporate insiders and outside stakeholders. Public disclosure can provide economies of scale, while private disclosure with a large number of shareholders may result in high information dissemination costs. By contrast, private disclosure of information in civil law countries is an efficient way to alleviate information asymmetry between managers and a small number of stakeholders. A related strand of this law and finance literature (that relies on shareholders' right indices instead of a simple dichotomy between common and civil law) has documented the role of legal protection of shareholders and extra-legal institutions such as laws regarding competition, press coverage and tax compliance in reducing the agency problems arising from consumption of private control benefits by insiders (Dyck and Zingales, 2004; Haw et al., 2004). The potential for private control benefits provides an incentive to insiders to distort the financial reports and thereby decrease their credibility (Leuz, Nanda and Wysocki, 2003). By reducing the private control benefits, the legal and extra-legal institution factors play a role in improving the credibility of financial statements. While the intermediaries such as auditors and analysts focus on improving the quality of financial information of individual clients, the institutional variables such as the legal environment affect the overall reporting environment in which the financial statements are prepared and disseminated.

Relation between legal environment and auditing

Auditing of the financial statements could be viewed as an enforcement mechanism of financial accounting standards. Srinidhi, Lim and Hossain (2009) discussed four possible linkages of legal variables to auditing. First, the extant literature suggests that legal variables such as the rule of law index and judicial efficiency reduce the extraction of private control benefits by controlling shareholders and thereby reduce the agency problem between insiders and outsiders. Consequently, the need for insiders to 'hide' their transactions by earnings management is reduced. If there is less opportunistic earnings management, investors will find greater assurance in the reported numbers, and therefore the incremental assurance value of auditors is reduced. Second, in countries where the legal systems are strong, the risk faced by managers both to their reputation and in terms of the expected cost of litigation for not promptly revealing value-relevant bad information will be high. Therefore we should expect a speedier disclosure of any information that might adversely affect the current or future performance of the firm. From the investor's viewpoint, the cost of undisclosed bad news is typically higher than the cost of unrealized good news. The conservatism in reporting that this environment brings about is shown to reduce verification costs (Roychowdhury and Watts, 2007) by compensating for potential overstatement of positive news by managers. In effect, the incremental value added by auditing and financial analysts' monitoring in this situation is correspondingly reduced. Third, legal regimes that give more rights to investors promote shareholder activism and support constraints placed on financing by creditors. These limitations constrain managers in their accrual estimates, mitigating the need for additional assurance on the veracity of reported earnings by high-quality auditors (Srinidhi et al., 2009). Fourth, strong legal regimes encourage strong markets for corporate control which also limit managers from deviating much from shareholder interest (Monga, 2006). This also improves the value relevance of financial accounting information and reduces the incremental demand for assurance by external auditors. These four linkages between legal variables and financial reporting all suggest a negative (substitutive) association between them.

The above arguments can be driven by arguments for both the demand and the supply of information. In so far as the demand for assurance by an average auditor is driven by the litigation cost imposed by the legal environment, the incremental demand for additional assurance by specialist auditors is reduced. Further, a strong legal environment might increase firm-specific disclosures and reduce the marginal cost of additional assurance by a specialist auditor. In this scenario, even though the specialist auditors might be willing to supply more assurance, the specialist audit fee premium will be lower. However, these arguments ignore the effect of the environment on the competence and knowledge of the auditors. In a strong legal environment with higher levels of disclosure, the additional knowledge that the specialist brings to bear on the audit might become more valuable. The result could be an increased specialist fee premium to compensate for the more valuable incremental specialist knowledge. It is therefore essentially an empirical issue as to whether the substitutive or the complementary relationship dominates.

Relationship between legal environment and analysts

Analysts are intermediaries between a firm and the capital market. They contribute to information environment by searching for and disseminating information about a firm. Analysts' decisions to follow a company provide value to the company by increasing market visibility. Extant studies (see Armstrong et al., 2010 for a review of the literature) indicate that greater analyst following is related to an improvement of information flowing to the market.

Countries with strong legal institutions generally have higher-quality transparent financial reporting systems. On the other hand, countries with a weak legal environment have a reduced demand for earnings information.

Countries with high-quality accounting standards for financial reporting should have greater analyst following, since they have more reliable information with which to make predictions. But an alternative viewpoint is that, in jurisdictions where required disclosure is poor, the pay-off from private information acquisition is likely to be greater and could attract analyst following. This is consistent with the complementary relation between the two. On the other hand, a higher-level disclosure could substitute the demand for analyst services (activity), since it reduces the need for analysts uncovering information if it competes with, rather than complements, company information. Thus higher-level disclosures lessen the competition amongst analysts and the incentive to cover a company.

4.   ACCOUNTING STANDARDS AND FINANCIAL MARKET DEVELOPMENT: CROSS-COUNTRY EVIDENCE

Issues concerning emerging economies in relation to financial accounting have generated considerable interest among accounting scholars and practitioners in developed and emerging economies, and authors have examined them from different standpoints (Ali, 2005). In recent years, research work has been undertaken relating to emerging economies which deals with the accounting and reporting practices of South Asian countries (Ali, Ahmed and Henry, 2004). It has been argued that most of the emerging economies' industrialization, political institutions and cultures are largely influenced by the socio-political traditions (Perera, 1989). These systems are imposed either through colonial influence or by powerful investor or multinational companies (Perera, 1980; Belkaoui, 1985; Hove, 1986). Hove (1986) identified that (1) colonial rule, (2) operations of transnational corporations, (3) professional accounting institutions and (4) the special conditions in foreign aid agreements are the vehicles by which accounting technology was imposed by developed countries on the emerging economies.

The accounting systems of developed countries have been claimed to be unsuitable to meet the needs of developing economies; 'it is likely that inappropriate external financial reporting systems result from historical ties with developed countries' (Ali, 2005). There are several reasons for this. For example, in many emerging economies the accounting system and system of professional accounting education were the legacy of the former colonial power and were not developed indigenously; and many of the emerging economies were members of the International Accounting Standards Committee (IASC) and adopted the IASs and IFRSs with or without modifications. Despite these criticisms, several arrangements have been made over the last decade to harmonize the accounting practices of emerging economies with those of developed countries. The main argument in favour of harmonization, either at regional or international level, of financial reporting is that it will remove diversity in financial reporting and facilitate economic integration by removing barriers to the international movement of goods, services and capital (Saudagaran and Diga, 1997).

Development of Accounting Systems and Standards in Emerging Economies

Although the international accounting literature has recognized for at least 40 years that accounting practices differ based on legal systems, empirical research has recently started rigorously to examine this proposition (Ali, 2005; Habib, 2007). It has been argued by Fohlin (2005) that 'neither formal theoretical research nor cogent empirical research has rationalized the endogenous development of distinct financial system designs and their persistence in the absence of regulation . . . Neither political nor legal structure is clearly independent of economic backwardness, and the three factors may be mutually enhancing, rather than mutually exclusive' (p. 9).

There are studies dealing with many different dimensions of financial reporting and corporate information disclosure in the Western capitalist market economics. There is a constant review of the financial reporting practices followed by these industrialized countries leading to regular promulgation of legislation dealing with corporate disclosure and reporting practices.[3] But there is a dearth of research dealing with the financial practices of the developing countries in general and the adequacy and reliability of published financial reports in particular. Not many studies can be found that deal specifically with the question of whether the available financial information of financial reports in developing countries or emerging economies is able to meet the user's needs (Ali, Ahmed and Eddie, 2009).

It is very difficult for a developing country to have its own indigenously determined accounting system. The corporate legislation, including financial disclosure requirements, of many developing countries is based on the British companies acts of 1948 or earlier, and often such countries adopted British legislation as their own companies acts with few or no modifications. India, Pakistan and Bangladesh are examples of former British colonies which followed the British accounting system without taking into consideration their domestic social, cultural and environmental factors. In many developing countries corporate legislation remained unchanged over many years, although the United Kingdom has had several amendments to the original acts to respond to changing requirements in the corporate environment (Hove, 1986, pp. 82–3). It is very interesting to see that even the Companies Act 1913 was replaced by the Companies Act 1994 in Bangladesh, the Indian Companies Act 1956 and the Pakistani Companies Ordinance 1984 in line with the British Companies Act.

Many international and regional organizations (for example, the IASC, the IFAC, the United Nations and the OECD) are engaged in the problem of national and international harmonization of financial reporting, and they need to consider the above-mentioned issues in designing uniform accounting practices for emerging economies. There are many emerging economies whose accountancy professions are members of the IASC. As noted, many of the emerging economies adopt IASs with or without modifications. For example, in 1986 the government of Pakistan issued an ordinance requiring compliance with IASC standards.

The IASC (now IASB) was formed in 1973 to bring about harmonization in the accounting and reporting practices of individual countries. The IASB has issued a number of IASs and IFRSs covering the most important accounting issues.

There are researchers who favour the adoption of IASs and IFRSs by emerging economies. Emerging economies which are unable to mount their own standard setting process can adopt IASs at a negligible cost (Saudagaran and Diga, 1997). Hossain, Cooper and Islam (2006) argued that, if the enterprises within IASB member countries do not comply with the promulgated accounting or financial reporting standards, global harmonization would not be achieved. However, the adoption of IASs by emerging economies may have no impact on the accounting system of the developing country unless it is mandatory. The IFRSs were developed in advanced economies, but are increasingly being applied in emergent economies, potentially ignoring considerations of whether IFRSs are appropriate or relevant to such economies (Tyrrall, Woodward and Rakhimbekova, 2007). Some researchers are opposed to the adoption for IASs by emerging economies. For example, Ball et al. (2003) opined that the adoption of high-quality accounting standards does not improve earnings quality in Asian countries unless their legal enforcement and other institutional factors also improve. It can be argued here that some empirical studies show that the developing countries have not adopted the IASs with enthusiasm. There is evidence from some empirical studies like Ahmed and Nicholls (1994), Owusu-Ansah (2000), Joshi and Ramadhan (2002), Abd-Elalam and Weetman (2003), Akhtaruddin (2005), Hossain et al. (2006), Dahawy and Conover (2007) and Samaha and Stapleton (2008) that companies in several developing countries are not following the mandatory accounting standards while preparing their financial reports or statements (Hossain, 2007). Chamisa (2000), while examining the extent of compliance with IASC/IFRS standards by a sample of Zimbabwe listed companies, found that listed companies in Zimbabwe voluntarily and significantly complied with certain provisions of IASs, which provides indirect evidence that IASs are relevant in Zimbabwe. On the other hand, Owusu-Ansah (2000) believed that the mechanism for monitoring and enforcing corporate mandatory disclosure requirements in Zimbabwe was not stringent. Akhtaruddin (2005) reports the results of an empirical investigation of the extent of mandatory disclosure by 94 listed companies in Bangladesh. His study showed that the sample companies, on average, disclose only 44 per cent of the items of necessary information, which suggests that prevailing regulations are ineffective monitors of disclosure compliance by companies (Akhtaruddin, 2005). The study of Hossain et al. (2006) reports that the average disclosure level as per two sample accounting standards of the sample companies is 69.05 per cent, with a minimum and maximum level of 35.85 per cent and 94.34 per cent respectively, which is not very encouraging. Further, Islam (2006) empirically investigated compliance with disclosure requirements from a sample of the annual reports of 10 companies from the manufacturing sector of each of Bangladesh, India, Pakistan and Sri Lanka. Based on the disclosure index of 124 information-item requirements from 21 mandatory accounting standards, respective companies acts and listing rules of the stock exchanges, Islam (2006) showed that the compliance levels for Bangladeshi, Indian, Pakistani and Sri Lankan companies were 71.68 per cent, 68.05 per cent, 72.79 per cent and 89.83 per cent respectively.

5.   THE INSTITUTIONAL FACTORS INFLUENCING FINANCIAL REPORTING IN INDIA, PAKISTAN AND BANGLADESH

This section focuses on how the legal requirements have influenced company financial reporting, which in turn may explain possible divergence of disclosure made by the companies in their corporate annual reports in these three countries.

The Legal Environmental Influence

The legal bases of financial reporting in India, Pakistan and Bangladesh for companies are the respective companies acts for each country. However, in Pakistan and Bangladesh, listed companies are required to follow their respective securities and exchange rules, which provide certain requirements in the preparation of financial statements. However, in India, there are no such securities and exchange rules for listed companies.

India
In India, the Indian accounting standards issued by the ICAI have legal recognition through the Companies Act 1956, whereby every company is required to comply with the accounting standards and the statutory auditors of every company are required to report whether the accounting standards have been complied with or not. The Securities and Exchange Board of India (SEBI) and the Reserve Bank of India also require compliance with the accounting standards issued by the ICAI from time to time.

Pakistan
Pakistan adopted the Indian Companies Act 1913, amended in 1936. This was the source of financial reporting in Pakistan until it was replaced by the Companies Ordinance 1984. The Companies Ordinance 1984 was enforced on 8 December 1984, and it is still in force. Comprehensive provisions governing accounts and financial reports are contained in sections 203 to 247, which require informative disclosure in corporate financial reports through various schedules annexed to the ordinance.

Bangladesh
The accounting and financial reporting system in Bangladesh is greatly influenced by the history of colonial rule. Bangladesh was a part of Pakistan until 1971, and had adopted the Indian Companies Act 1913. Subsequently, Bangladesh has replaced its Companies Act 1913 by the Companies Act 1994. Consequently, the Companies Act 1994 becomes the main basis for the corporate disclosure requirements in Bangladesh. In Bangladesh, there are the Securities and Exchange Rules 1987 for listed companies, which have more

disclosure requirements than the provisions laid down in the Companies Act 1994. Since 1983, Bangladesh has been trying to adopt the international accounting standards (IASs and IFRSs). These became mandatory from 2000 for listed companies, driving preparation and auditing of financial statements.

Further, the Securities Exchange Commission (SEC) of Bangladesh passed Corporate Governance Guidelines in February 2006 to try to increase the level of disclosure made by listed companies in Bangladesh. The Companies Act 1994 is the most important regulation for company financial reporting in Bangladesh. The main provisions with regard to financial reporting and disclosure are set out below.

Securities Market Rules

Development of financial reporting is related to the industrial and stock market growth levels of emerging economies. It has been said that high standards of financial reporting are one of the important characteristics of developed market economies and there is a strong correlation between the level of disclosure and well-developed securities markets (Gray, McSweeney and Shaw, 1984). This section will focus on how developed the stock exchanges of India, Pakistan and Bangladesh are and whether there is any influence from the stock exchanges on corporate financial reporting in these three countries.

India

The Indian stock exchanges started in the eighteenth century when the Indian Companies Act introduced limited liability. The Bombay Stock Exchange (BSE) can be referred to as the oldest stock exchange in Asia. The BSE was formed on 9 July 1875, the Calcutta Stock Exchange (CSE) was formed in June 1908, and other stock exchanges were formed in Madras, Kanpur, Nagpur and Delhi in the 1920s. In 1925 a Securities Control Act was passed by the then colonial government, which specified that a stock exchange deal must be made according to the government-approved rules. There was a crash on the BSE in 1929 and also in 1946 just after the Second World War. After independence, in 1956, the government of India prepared a draft bill for stock exchange regulation, and as a result the Securities Contracts (Regulation) Act 1956 was passed. With the promulgation of this act, the government acquired the authority to regulate the working of the stock exchanges. Stock exchanges were granted permanent recognition under the act. Currently, there are 21 national stock exchanges in India. However, at present, the BSE is the premier stock exchange, accounting for more than two-thirds of the trading volume, with more than 70 per cent of the listed capital in the country.

The Indian government has consistently offered foreign enterprises a number of incentives, which include: depreciation allowances, tax holidays and tax exemptions; priority access to credit, foreign exchange, imports and equipment; and subsidies. Since late 1992, the government of India has introduced new economic reforms, which include increased participation by foreign companies operating in India. The new policy encourages foreign investment in India, and large international firms such as IBM, BMW, Kellogg's, General Motors, General Electric, Coca-Cola, Motorola and Suzuki have been granted approval for foreign collaborations. From 1991 to 1995 the total direct investment committed and approved was $12 billion in terms of foreign equity. Stock exchanges frequently require disclosures beyond mandatory information required by law. However, as noted above, Indian stock exchanges do not require listed companies to disclose any more than the Companies Act requires.

According to the Securities Contract (Regulation) Rules 1957, a company must comply with guidelines issued by the Securities and Exchange Board of India (SEBI) and exchange rules, by-laws and regulations, to get its shares listed on any recognized stock exchange in India. The basic listing requirements of the BSE are as follows:

1. The memorandum and articles of association must not contain any provisions that restrict free transfer of shares.
2. The company must offer for public subscription at least 25 per cent of its issued capital.
3. The minimum issued capital of the company should be at least Rs. 3 crores.
4. Application should be invited in denominations of market's units of trading.
5. No previous track record is necessary.

In India, the stock exchanges do not enforce compliance with the adopted accounting standards as listing requirements. The reason for this may include unawareness of such factors by the investor group, the additional cost of producing such information, and the difficulty of enforcement.

Pakistan

The largest stock exchange in Pakistan, the Karachi Stock Exchange (KSE), was established on 18 September 1947. Lahore Stock Exchange (LSE) was formed in 1971, and prior to this Dhaka Stock Exchange was established. The Islamabad Stock Exchange was established in 1991. Until the 1950s, the capital market of Pakistan made unremarkable progress. With the subsequent growth in the economy, the KSE made significant improvement and experienced a boom.

However, by 1991 the KSE had become a key institution in the financial sector of Pakistan, and the total number of listed companies on the KSE was 653, with a paid-up capital of Rs. 69 466 million. There are two other national stock exchanges, in Lahore and Islamabad. During the early 1970s, the government of Pakistan began to nationalize key companies, and by 1974 it was estimated that almost 70 per cent of the country's economy was under state control. In 1977, martial law was declared, and no substantial policy guide was available until 1985. Stock exchanges suffered a setback in the post-nationalization period, when the investment climate scared away both private sector capital and investors. Major changes in government policy were made in 1991, permitting the opening up of the market to investors, and privatization of public sector companies, and allowing commercial banks in the private sector. These policy measures were mainly responsible for the accelerated economic activities on the capital market. With Pakistan opened to large-scale foreign investment, foreigners now own an estimated 5 to 7 per cent of equities, although its attraction to foreign investors is limited by political instability. The KSE is now an emerging stock market, which has grown rapidly since 1986. The listing rules of the KSE enforce a minimum paid-up capital of Rs. 5 million. Most Pakistani companies tend to be tightly held, family-managed concerns, because of the fear of dilution of control (Khan, 1993). The estimated ownership structure of the KSE companies is 60 to 70 per cent with sponsors, families or associates; 20 to 30 per cent with institutions like the Investment Corporation of Pakistan (ICP) and the National Investment Trust (NIT); and 5 to 10 per cent with the general public (Baring Securities, 1993). In Pakistan it was estimated that total investors numbered 700,000 and the larger companies had fewer than 250 investors (Euromoney, 1992).

The listing requirements of the KSE regarding disclosure in all prospectuses and offers for selling shares stipulate:[4]

3   (i)   No financial statements shall be incorporated in the prospectus/offer for sale which is not audited and certified by the auditors and which is not accompanied by the accounting policies.
   (ii) The Audited accounts incorporated in the prospectus/offer for sale shall not be older than 6 months before the application of Listing is made to the Exchange.
   (iii) Disclosure of financial and governance information
   (iv) Any other disclosure which the Exchange may require for the benefit of the investors.

For companies listed on stock exchanges in Pakistan, the Companies Ordinance 1984, the Securities and Exchange Ordinance and the Securities and Exchange Rules 1971 are the major pieces of legislation governing the preparation of corporate annual reports. The stock exchanges are administered by the Securities and Exchange Ordinance 1969 and rules framed thereunder in 1971. However, in context of the present requirements it can be argued that it is necessary that this legislation be reviewed, particularly the Companies Ordinance 1984 for administering corporate activities and reporting. There is room for improvement in the requirements governing disclosure in financial reports as part of the listing requirements.

Bangladesh
After independence, all major companies were nationalized and there was no stock exchange in Bangladesh till 1976. Before independence, a stock exchange had been established in Dhaka, the Dhaka Stock Exchange (DSE), in 1954 as a corporate body under the Companies Act 1913. However, it operated on a very small scale in the first 25 years of its existence. After the emergence of Bangladesh in 1971, the DSE market ceased to exist because of the government policy of nationalizing all the major industries of the country.

In 1992, the number of listed companies increased to 145 with paid-up capital of Taka 6020.34 million. The listing rules of the DSE enforce a minimum paid-up capital of 1 million taka ($25,000). The DSE, although small in terms of market capitalization, has received some attention from international investors because of its rapid increase in market value and high dividend returns, and because of the liberalization and reform measures adopted in Bangladesh since 1991. These measures include full convertibility of taka, lifting of all restrictions and limits on foreign participation in securities and of repatriation of gains and profits, non-taxability of capital gains, the formation of the Investment Corporation of Bangladesh (ICB), and deregulation and privatization policies.

The stock market in Bangladesh is underdeveloped and cannot be said to be an 'emerging market'. The market capitalization and trading volume relative to capitalization are both low. The comments of Chaudhury and Miyan (1990, p. 74) can be noted in this respect:

The economies of Taiwan, Korea, India and Malaysia are roughly 2.4, 5.1, 14.0 and 1.9 times the economy of Bangladesh. However, their stock market capitalizations are approximately 272, 184, 133 and 104 times that of Bangladesh. One obvious factor is the degree of industrialization. For example, with about the same percentage of the labour force, the Indian industrial sector's relative contribution to GDP is almost three times that of Bangladesh. However, that is a lot more than the low degree of industrialization as indicated by the trading volume relative to capitalization.

One of the features of the capital market in Bangladesh is the concentration of share ownership – a few shareholders account for a substantial part of total shareholder value. At present, the capital market in Bangladesh consists mainly of the DSE, three government development financial institutions (DFIs), namely the Bangladesh Shilpa Rin Sangstha (BSRS), the Bangladesh Shilpa Bank (BSB) and the Investment Corporation of Bangladesh (ICB), and a few newly created private investment banks (Nicholls and Ahmed, 1995).

The Companies Act 1994 and the Securities and Exchange Rules 1987 are the most important laws which regulate financial reports. The Security and Exchange Rules 1987 contain the detailed provisions regarding the contents of the balance sheet, profit and loss accounts, and auditors' report. The security and exchange rules have increased the disclosure requirements of the listed companies in Bangladesh.

In Bangladesh, listing does not prescribe any additional disclosure requirements in financial reports beyond the legal disclosure requirements, that is, the Companies Act 1994 and the Securities and Exchange Rules 1987. According to the Listing Rules of the DSE, all companies listed and quoted on the exchange shall:

(a) forward to the Exchange copies of Statutory and Annual Reports and Audited Accounts, as soon as issued;
(b) forward to the Exchange copies of all notices before they are published or sent to the shareholders.

Development of Financial Reporting and Capital Markets – Role of International Financial Reporting Standards (IFRSs)

India
Since its birth, the Institute of Chartered Accountants of India (ICAI) has become one of the largest accountancy professions in the world (Bose, 1988). Another accountancy professional body, the Institute of Cost and Works Accountants in India (ICWAI), was established in 1959. The ICAI and ICWAI are members of the Confederation of Asian and Pacific Accountants (CAPA), and the South Asian Federation of Accountants (SAFA). India has made considerable progress in the development of accounting standards. In 1977, the ICAI formed the Accounting Standards Board (ASB). Soon after, the ASB adopted 15 IASs taking into consideration the applicable laws, customs, usages and business environment of India, and draft standards were formulated by the ASB (Hossain, 1999). It is worth emphasizing that the issuance of the accounting standards in India by the ASB is based on the framework of IASs of the IASC/IASB. Accounting standards are formulated on the basis of the international financial reporting standards (IFRSs) and international accounting standards (IASs) issued by the IASB. Among the

41 IASs issued by the IASB, the ASB made 29 IASs mandatory, and issued eight IFRSs according to the IASB.

Pakistan
Over the last 20 years, Pakistan has made an ongoing effort to converge with IFRSs. Pakistan has been adopting international standards promulgated by the IASB, and the Pakistani authorities have made continuous efforts to adopt IFRSs fully. The ICAP, in association with the regulatory authorities, has worked to ensure that Pakistani generally accepted accounting practices (GAAP), required for listed companies, are fully compliant with IFRSs. Currently, the ICAP has not adopted the Pakistani equivalents of IFRS 1 and IFRS 4, and the SECP – the governmental body that must approve standards after ICAP adoption – has not yet approved the Pakistani equivalents of IAS 29, IFRS 7 and IFRS 8. According to the November 2007 ICAP report on the adoption status of IFRSs in Pakistan, IAS 41 is effective for annual periods beginning on or after 1 January 2007. However, Ashraf and Ghani (2005) observed that weak enforcement mechanisms are more critical for explaining the state of financial reporting in the country, and they have opined that Pakistan's adoption of IFRSs as national standards has not led to improvement in the quality of financial reporting.

Bangladesh
In 1983, ICAB became a member of IASC. The accounting standards issued by the ICAB have been mandatory for the SEC of Bangladesh since 2000. As a result, the accounting standards greatly influenced financial reporting practices in Bangladesh. The laws of Bangladesh set minimum legal requirements for the disclosure of accounting information in corporate annual reports. In such a situation, accounting standards, having legal backing, are likely strongly to influence the financial reporting systems in Bangladesh. The Securities and Exchange Commission by a notification dated 29 December 1997 requires all listed companies to abide by the Bangladeshi accounting standards adopted by the ICAB and, hence, accounting standards are mandatory only for companies listed on the stock market. At present 26 IASs are mandatory and three IASs are under consideration by the SEC of Bangladesh, while eight IFRSs are mandatory. As a result, the accounting standards are likely to a have greater influence on the financial statements of listed companies in Bangladesh.

Empirical Evidence on the Impact of IFRS Adoption in the Development of Financial Reporting Practice and Capital Market Development

Compliance with accounting or financial reporting standards promulgated by the International Accounting Standards Board (previously the IASC) has become a crucial issue after a series of corporate debacles over a decade. Regulators, professional bodies and researchers around the globe have expressed their concerns about the need for improved accounting and audit pronouncements and compliance to provide better information than previously required for the preparation and presentation of corporate financial statements. To this end, major South Asian countries such as India, Pakistan and Bangladesh have adopted IFRSs as a way of improving financial reporting standards and to attract international investors to invest in their countries. In an exploratory study, Hossain et al. (2006) found that the listed non-financial Bangladeshi companies significantly complied with certain IFRSs. The regression result also revealed that the net profit margins of local companies and subsidiaries of multinational companies were significantly related to the extent of mandatory disclosure of IFRSs. Hossain et al. (2006) also observed that the attempt made by the ICAB in developing accounting standards in the light of the IASs is encouraging and may be viewed as a 'revolution' for the development of capital market and corporate financial reporting practice in Bangladesh.

However, some studies report that the aggregate levels of compliance in these countries are quite low and public companies within these countries do not provide more than the minimum information required. For example, Ali, Ahmed and Henry (2006) examined the degree of harmonization in selected accounting measurement practices in India, Pakistan and Bangladesh. They developed an index to measure the degree of harmonization. Their results were mixed. They found a high degree of harmonization in areas of plant property and equipment, foreign currency translation, and long-term investment, and lower levels of harmonization in relation to reporting practices of inventories, amortization and leases. The results of Ali et al. (2006) suggest that regulators and policy-makers need to concentrate on the reporting policies of firms if the goals of regional and international harmonization are to be achieved.

In addition, there are some studies which investigated the association between compliance with IAS-based national standards and corporate characteristics in emerging economies. For example, Ali et al. (2004) analysed the level of compliance with disclosure requirements mandated by 14 IAS-based local standards for a large sample of companies from India, Pakistan and Bangladesh and examined firm characteristics that affected the degree of compliance with these standards. The results revealed significant variation in total disclosure compliance levels across the three South Asian countries and different national accounting standards. Compliance levels were found to be positively related to the following firm characteristics – firm size, profitability and multinational status.

In a related study Ali et al. (2009) examined the extent of adoption of IFRSs in India, Pakistan and Bangladesh. The authors found that overall adoption of IFRSs regarding measurement and disclosure practices was higher in Pakistan relative to India and Bangladesh. The authors concluded that the adoption of IFRSs was not satisfactory in several areas of measurement and disclosure for companies in each country. These findings indicate that regulators and standard setters need to monitor and implement IFRSs more strictly in these countries.

As a follow-up to these preliminary studies, future research could examine whether harmonization of national IASs or adoption of IFRSs in emerging economies has significantly improved firms' stock price informativeness (less synchronous stock price) and liquidity of the capital market. Future research in South Asian countries could address the following questions. Does compliance with IFRSs reduce firms' cost of capital and improve earnings quality? Do investors find IFRS-based accounting information value-relevant? Does IFRS-based accounting information improve analysts' information environment?

6. CONCLUSIONS

Deepening and widening the financial sector so that it increases in both size and scope is an essential pre-condition for economic development. For this to occur, policy-makers must encourage the development of strong accounting standards and the appropriate legal infrastructure. This chapter discussed the theoretical arguments for the propositions that strong accounting standards are essential for financial development and financial development is essential for economic development. It then discussed the experiences of developing countries on the relationship between accountancy standards and financial development, using case studies from three South Asian countries – India, Pakistan and Bangladesh. It noted the varied experience of three South Asian countries, namely India, Pakistan and Bangladesh, in setting up sound accounting standards and the requisite financial regulatory framework. Influenced by British colonial rule, similarities in financial reporting in terms of company law requirements, securities law and standard setting mechanisms place the three countries in a unique situation for the harmonization of financial reporting practices. As the South Asian economies, particularly India, gradually industrialize, and as foreign investors diversify their portfolio in these emerging markets, pressure for strong legal protection of shareholders' rights and high-quality accounting information will minimize the differences in financial reporting practices in the region.

As is clear from the discussion, the South Asian emerging economies have begun to create or adopt IFRSs for financial development, though much remains to be done in this regard. Some differences have been detected by researchers in the way that IASs or IFRSs are adopted and enforced (Ali and Ahmed, 2007). We have argued that the differences in accounting practices caused by the socio-economic conditions of the South Asian countries cannot be removed immediately. Therefore there will always be differences in the level of compliance across jurisdictions even when IFRSs are adopted and implemented.

NOTES

1. This refers to efficiency of capital allocation. Economic theories posit that formal financial markets and associated institutions (for example, financial reporting systems) improve the capital allocation process (see Wurgler, 2000).
2. See Demetriades and Hussein (1996), Arestis and Demetriades (1997), Sen and Vaidya (1997); Choe and Moosa (1999), Khalifa (1999), Beck, Levine and Loayza (2000a, 2000b), Amable and Chatelain (2001), Beck and Levine (2001), Cetorelli (2002), Christopoulosa and Tsionas (2004), Rioja and Valev (2004); Abu-Bader and Abu-Qarn (2006), Acaravci, Ozturk and Acaravci (2007), Levine and Demirguc-Kunt (2008) and Cole (2009).
3. This is evident from the host of amendments in British company law (in the UK), the Securities and Exchange Commission (SEC) promulgation in the USA, IAFC releases, new IASs and IFRSs, new FASB statements and SSAPs, FRSs and so on.
4. Criteria/guidelines for listing of companies on the exchange, Karachi Stock Exchange (Guaranteed) Limited, p. 11.

REFERENCES

Abd-Elalam, O.H., and P. Weetman (2003). Introducing international accounting standards to an emerging capital market: relative familiarity and language effect in Egypt. *Journal of International Accounting, Auditing and Taxation*, 12, pp. 63–84.

Abu-Bader, S., and A.S. Abu-Qarn (2006). *Financial Development and Economic Growth Nexus: Time Series Evidence from Middle Eastern and North African Countries*, Discussion Paper No. 06-09. Beer Sheva: Monaster Center for Economic Research.

Acaravci, Ali, Ilhan Ozturk and Songul Kakilli Acaravci (2007). Finance–growth nexus: evidence from Turkey. *International Research Journal of Finance and Economics*, 11.

Aghion, P., and P. Bolton (1997). A theory of trickle-down growth and development. *Review of Economic Studies*, 64(2), pp. 151–72.

Aghion, Philippe, Eve Caroli and Cecilia Garcia-Penalosa (1999). Inequality and economic growth: the perspective of the new growth theories. *Journal of Economic Literature*, 37, pp. 1615–60.

Ahluwalia, M. (1976). Inequality, poverty and development. *Journal of Development Economics*, 3, pp. 307–42.

Ahmed, K., and D. Nicholls (1994). The impact of non-financial company characteristics on mandatory compliance in developing countries: the case of Bangladesh. *International Journal of Accounting*, 29(1), pp. 60–77.

Akhtaruddin, M. (2005). Corporate mandatory disclosure practices in Bangladesh. *International Journal of Accounting*, 40(4), pp. 399–422.

Ali, M.J. (2005). A synthesis of empirical research on international accounting harmonization and compliance with international financial reporting standards. *Journal of Accounting Literature*, 24, pp. 1–51.

Ali, M.J., and K. Ahmed (2007). The legal and institutional framework for corporate financial reporting in South Asia. *Research in Accounting Regulation*, 19, pp. 175–205.

Ali, M.J., K. Ahmed and I.A. Eddie (2009). The adoption of international financial reporting standards (IFRS) in emerging economies: the case of South Asia. *Research in Accounting in Emerging Economies*, 9, pp. 1–30.

Ali, M.J., K. Ahmed and D. Henry (2004). Compliance with national accounting standards by listed companies in South Asia. *Accounting and Business Research*, 34, pp. 183–99.

Ali, M.J., K. Ahmed and D. Henry (2006). Harmonization of accounting practices in South Asia. *Advances in International Accounting*, 19, pp. 25–58.

Amable, Bruno, and Jean-Bernard Chatelain (2001). Can financial infrastructures foster economic development? *Journal of Development Economics*, 64, pp. 481–98.

Arestis, Philip, and Panicos Demetriades (1997). Financial development and economic growth: assessing the evidence. *Economic Journal*, 107, pp. 783–99.

Armendariz de Aghion, B., and J. Morduch (2005). *The Economics of Microfinance*. Cambridge, MA: MIT Press.

Armstrong, C.S., W.R. Guay and J.P. Weber (2010). The role of information and financial reporting in corporate governance and debt contracting. *Journal of Accounting and Economics*, 50(2–3), pp. 179–234.

Ashraf, J., and W. Ghani (2005). Accounting development in Pakistan. *International Journal of Accounting*, 40(2), pp. 175–89.

Athukorala, P., and K. Sen (2002). *Saving, Investment and Growth in India*, pp. xiii, 181. Delhi: Oxford University Press.

Ball, R., S.P. Kothari and A. Robin (2000). The effect of international institutional factors on properties of accounting earnings. *Journal of Accounting and Economics*, 29(1), pp. 1–51.

Ball, R., A. Robin and J.S. Wu (2003). Incentives versus standards: properties of accounting income in four East Asian countries. *Journal of Accounting and Economics*, 36(1–3), pp. 235–70.

Bandiera, Oriana, Patrick Honohan and Fabio Schiantarelli (2000). Does financial reform raise or reduce savings? *Review of Economics of Statistics*, 82, pp. 239–63.

Banerjee, A.V. and Esther Duflo (2000). Inequality and growth: what can the data say? NBER Working Paper No. 7793.

Banerjee, Abhijit V., and Andrew F. Newman (1993). Occupational choice and the process of development. *Journal of Political Economy*, 101, pp. 274–98.

Baring Securities (1993). Pakistan stock market review. Pakistan research, July, Bangkok.

Barro, R.J. (1997). *Determinants of Economic Growth: A Cross Country Empirical Study*. London and Cambridge, MA: MIT Press.

Barro, R.J., and Xavier Sala-i-Martin (1995). *Economic Growth*. New York: McGraw-Hill.

Beck, Thorsten and Ross Levine (2002). Industry growth and capital allocation: does having market- or bank-based system matter? *Journal of Financial Economics*, 64, pp. 147–80.

Beck, T., Ross Levine and Norman Loayza (2000a). Finance and the sources of growth. *Journal of Financial Economics*, 58, pp. 261–300.

Beck, T., Ross Levine and Norman Loayza (2000b). Financial intermediation and growth: causality and causes. *Journal of Monetary Economics*, 46, pp. 31–77.

Belkaoui, A. (1985). *International Accounting: Issues and Solutions*. Westport, CT: Greenwood Press.

Blanchflower, D.G., and A.J. Oswald (1998). What makes an entrepreneur? Evidence on inheritance and capital constraints. *Journal of Labor Economics*, 16(1), pp. 26–60.

Bose, A. (1988). The Indian accountancy profession: its origins and current status. In *Recent Accounting and Economic Developments in the Far East*, ed. V.K. Zimmerman, pp. 149–62. Urbana-Champaign: Center for International Education and Research in Accounting, Department of Accountancy, University of Illinois.

Bushman, R.M., and A.J. Smith (2001). Financial accounting information and corporate governance. *Journal of Accounting and Economics*, 32, pp. 237–333.

Cetorelli, Nicole (2002). The role of financial services in economic growth. *Chicago Fed Letter*, 173.

Chamisa, E. (2000). The relevance and observance of the IASC standards in developing countries and the particular case of Zimbabwe. *International Journal of Accounting*, 35(2), pp. 267–86.

Chaudhury, M.M., and M.A. Miyan (1990). Developments of capital markets in Bangladesh. *Journal of Business Administration*, 16(1–2), pp. 70–90.

Choe, Chongwoo and Imad A. Moosa (1999). Financial system and economic growth: the Korean experience. *World Development*, 27(6), pp. 1069–82.

Christopoulosa, Dimitris K., and Efthymios G. Tsionas (2004). Financial development and economic growth: evidence from panel unit root and cointegration tests. *Journal of Development Economics*, 73, pp. 55–74.

Clarke, G.R.G. (1995). More evidence on income distribution and growth. *Journal of Development Economics*, 47, pp. 403–27.

Cole, S. (2009). Financial development, bank ownership and growth: or, does quantity imply quality? *Review of Economics and Statistics*, 91(1), pp. 33–51.

Dahawy, K., and T. Conover (2007). Accounting disclosure in companies listed on the Egyptian stock exchange. *Middle Eastern Finance and Economics*, 1, pp. 5–20.

Deininger, Klaus, and Pedro Olinto (2000). Asset distribution, inequality and growth. World Bank Development Research Group, Working Paper 2375.

Deininger, Klaus, and Lyn Squire (1998). New ways of looking at old issues: inequality and growth. *Journal of Development Economics*, 57, pp. 259–87.

Demetriades, P.O., and K.A. Hussein (1996). Does financial development cause economic growth? Time series evidence from 16 countries. *Journal of Development Economics*, 51, pp. 387–411.

Demirguc-Kunt, Asli (2006). Finance and economic development: policy choices for developing countries. Policy Research Working Paper Series 3955, World Bank.

Demirguc-Kunt, Asli, and Ross Levine (1996). Stock market development and financial intermediaries: stylized facts. *World Bank Economic Review*, 10(2), pp. 291–322.

Djankov, S., R. La Porta, F. Lopez-De-Silanes and A. Shleifer (2002). The regulation of entry. *Quarterly Journal of Economics*, 117(1), pp. 1–37.

Dyck, A., and L. Zingales (2004). Private benefits of control: an international comparison. *Journal of Finance*, 59(2), p. 537.

Euromoney (1992). *GT Guide to World Equity Markets*. London: Euromoney.

Fohlin, C. (2005). The history of corporate ownership and control in Germany. In *A History of Corporate Governance around the World: Family Business Groups to Professional Managers*, ed. R.J.C. Morck, pp. 223–77. Cambridge, MA: NBER Books.

Goldsmith, R.W. (1969). *Financial Structure and Development*. New Haven, CT and London: Yale University Press.

Gray, S.J., L.B. McSweeney and J.C. Shaw (1984). *Information Disclosure and the Multinational Corporation*. Chichester: John Wiley & Sons.

Habib, A. (2007). Legal environment, accounting information, auditing and information intermediaries: survey of the empirical literature. *Journal of Accounting Literature*, 26, pp. 1–75.

Haw, I.-M., B. Hu, L.-S. Hwang and W. Wu (2004). Ultimate ownership, income management, and legal and extra-legal institutions. *Journal of Accounting Research*, 42(2), p. 423.

Healy, P., and K.G. Palepu (2001). Information asymmetry, corporate disclosure, and capital market: a review of the empirical disclosure literature. *Journal of Accounting and Economics*, 31, pp. 405–40.

Holden, P., and V. Prokopenko (2001). Financial development and poverty alleviation: issues and policy implications for developing and transition countries. IMF Working Paper, WP/01/160.

Hossain, M.A. (1999). Disclosure of Information in developing countries: a comparative study of non-financial companies in India, Pakistan and Bangladesh. Unpublished Ph.D. thesis, University of Manchester.

Hossain, M.A. (2007). Enforcement and compliance of accounting standards in Bangladesh: a framework. Paper presented at the Nineteenth Asian-Pacific Conference on International Accounting Issues, Kuala Lumpur, 11–14 November.

Hossain, M.A., K. Cooper and K.S. Islam (2006). Compliance with IASs: the case of Bangladesh. Paper presented at the Seventh Asian Accounting Association Conference, Sydney, 17–19 September.

Hove, M.R. (1986). Accounting practices in developing countries: colonialism's legacy of inappropriate technologies. *International Journal of Accounting Education and Research*, 22, Fall, pp. 81–100.

Islam, M. (2006). Compliance with disclosure requirements by four SAARC countries – Bangladesh, India, Pakistan and Sri Lanka. *Journal of American Academy of Business*, 10(1), pp. 348–56.

Joshi, P.L., and S. Ramadhan (2002). The adoption of international accounting standards by small and closely held companies: evidence from Bahrain. *International Journal of Accounting*, 37(4), pp. 429–40.

Khalifa, H.G. (1999). Financial development and economic growth: the Tunisian experience. *Review of Development Economics*, 3(3), pp. 310–22.

Khan, B.A. (1993). The trading and the stock market in Pakistan. Management Research Papers, Templeton College (Oxford Centre for Management Studies), Oxford.

Khan, M.S., and A.S. Senhadji (2000). Financial development and economic growth: an overview. IMF Working Paper WP/00/209.

King, R.G., and R. Levine. (1993a). Finance and growth: Schumpeter might be right. *Quarterly Journal of Economics*, 108(3).

King, R.G., and R. Levine. (1993b). Finance, entrepreneurship and growth: theory and evidence. *Journal of Monetary Economics*, 32, pp. 513–42.

La Porta, Rafael, Florencio Lopez-de-Silanes, Andrei Shleifer and Robert Vishny (1998). Law and finance. *Journal of Political Economy*, 106, December, pp. 1133–55.

Lambert, R.A., C. Leuz and R.E. Verrecchia (2007). Accounting information disclosure, and the cost of capital. *Journal of Accounting Research*, May, pp. 385–420.

Levine, Ross, and Asli Demirguc-Kunt (2008). Finance, financial sector policies, and long-run growth. Policy Research Working Paper Series 4469, World Bank.

Leuz, C., D. Nanda and P.D. Wysocki (2003). Earnings management and investor protection: an international comparison. *Journal of Financial Economics*, 69(3), p. 505.

Levine, Ross (1997). Financial development and economic growth: views and agenda. *Journal of Economic Literature*, 35(2), pp. 688–726.

Levine, Ross, Norman Loayza and Thorsten Beck (2000). Financial intermediation and growth: causality and causes. *Journal of Monetary Economics*, 46, pp. 31–77.

Levine, Ross, and S. Zervos (1998). Stock markets, banks, and economic growth. *American Economic Review*, 88(3), pp. 537–58.

McKinnon, R.I. (1973). *Money and Capital in Economic Development*. Washington, DC: Brookings Institution.

Mavrotas, G. (2009). Domestic resource mobilization and financial development: looking at the MDGs from a different angle? *UNU-WIDER Angle Newsletter*.

Monga, A. (2006). Using derivatives to manipulate the market for corporate control. *Stanford Journal of Law, Business and Finance*, 12(1), p. 186.

Nicholls, D., and K. Ahmed (1995). Disclosure quality in corporate annual reports of non-financial companies in Bangladesh. *Research in Accounting in Emerging Economics*, 3, pp. 149–70.

Owusu-Ansah, S. (2000). Noncompliance with corporate annual report disclosure requirements in Zimbabwe. *Research in Accounting in Emerging Economics*, 4, pp. 289–305.

Ozer, U., and S. Sen (2009). Does inequality matter in the finance–growth nexus? *Trade and Development Review*, 2(1), pp. 9–27.

Palepu, K., and P. Healy (2008). *Business Analysis and Valuation Using Financial Statements*, 4th edn. Mason, OH: Thomson South-Western.

Parker, S.C. (2000). Saving to overcome borrowing constraints: implications for small business entry and exit. *Small Business Economics*, 15, pp. 223–32.

Partridge, M.D. (1997). Is inequality harmful for growth? *American Economic Review*, 87, pp. 1019–37.

Perera, M.H.B. (1980). *Accounting for State Industrial and Commercial Enterprises in a Developing Country*. New York: Arno Press.

Perera, M.H.B. (1989). Accounting in developing countries: a case for localised uniformity. *British Accounting Review*, 21(2), pp. 141–57.

Rioja, Felix, and Neven Valev (2004). Does one size fit all? A re-examination of the finance and growth relationship. *Journal of Development Economics*, 74, pp. 429–47.

Roychowdhury, S., and R.L. Watts. (2007). Asymmetric timeliness of earnings, market-to-book and conservatism in financial reporting. *Journal of Accounting and Economics*, 44(1/2), p. 2.

Samaha, K., and P. Stapleton (2008). Compliance with international accounting standards in a national context: some empirical evidence from the Cairo and Alexandria stock exchanges. *Afro-Asian Journal of Finance and Accounting*, 1(1), pp. 22–41.

Saudagaran, S.M., and J.G. Diga (1997). Accounting regulation in ASEAN: a choice between the global and regional paradigm of harmonization. *Journal of International Financial Management and Accounting*, 8, pp. 1–32.

Sen, K., and R.R. Vaidya (1997). *The Process of Financial Liberalization in India*. Delhi: Oxford University Press.

Shaw, E.S. (1973). *Financial Deepening in Economic Development*. New York: Oxford University Press.

Srinidhi, B., M. Hossain and C.-Y. Lim (2010). Auditor concentration and audit fee: international evidence from Arthur Andersen's demise. Working paper, City University of Hong Kong and Curtin University.

Srinidhi, B., C.-Y. Lim and M. Hossain (2009). Effects of country-level legal, extra-legal and political institutions on auditing: a cross-country analysis of the auditor specialization premium. *Journal of Contemporary Accounting and Economics*, 5, pp. 34–46.

Stiglitz, J., and A. Weiss (1981). Credit rationing in markets with imperfect information. *American Economic Review*, 71, pp. 393–410.

Tyrrall, D., D. Woodward and A. Rakhimbekova (2007). The relevance of international financial reporting standards to a developing country: evidence from Kazakhstan. *International Journal of Accounting*, 42(1), pp. 82–110.

Wurgler, J. (2000). Financial markets and the allocation of capital. *Journal of Financial Economics*, 58(1/2), pp. 187–214.

9 Accounting and accountability for NGOs
Jeffrey Unerman and Brendan O'Dwyer

INTRODUCTION

The topic covered in this chapter is accounting and accountability for and by non-governmental organizations (NGOs), exploring whether their accounting and accountability systems are and should be different from those used by other forms of organization. The chapter specifically focuses on the role and potential of accounting and accountability processes in those NGOs that are concerned with delivering poverty reduction programmes in developing countries, such as welfare aid, education and development programmes.

A prerequisite for exploring these issues is defining what a non-governmental organization is. In practice, it can be difficult precisely to define an NGO because the definitions are rather blurred at the boundaries (Gray, Bebbington and Collison, 2006; Unerman and O'Dwyer, 2006). In some ways it is easier to start by defining what an NGO is not: in broad terms, an NGO is an organization that is neither a private commercial sector organization nor a public sector organization. Nor is it an organization that is managed directly by either national or local government, and the core purpose of an NGO is not to make commercial gain. Within this broad 'definition-by-exclusion', some organizations are very clearly NGOs. However, there are a number of organizations that are widely regarded as NGOs that do engage in some non-core commercial-type activities (such as charity shops run by Oxfam, and income-generating conferences). A number of NGOs also carry out some activities that might be more traditionally regarded as functions of the public sector (such as the provision of health care, education and welfare services). Overall, NGOs cover many different activities, from welfare activities to development activities and all the way through to education, research and advocacy. Some NGOs focus almost exclusively on advocacy, for example campaigning NGOs like Amnesty International and many other NGOs that lobby for particular issues (often these NGOs are based in developed nations). Other NGOs focus more on education, welfare and/ or development activities, where the larger of such NGOs (for example Oxfam or ActionAid) often combine these activities with advocacy on behalf of the beneficiaries that are the focus of their education, welfare and/or development activities (Unerman and O'Dwyer, 2006).

NGOs operate at a range of different levels. Some are very small, sometimes one-person, NGOs that operate just at a local grassroots level. These NGOs will receive funding and other resources from various sources, including directly or indirectly from larger international NGOs (INGOs), where the INGOs themselves do not necessarily directly provide on the ground all of the education, welfare and/or development projects that they fund, but use local grassroots NGOs with local knowledge and expertise as intermediary partners in delivering effective and efficient aid solutions (Oller, 2006). Depending upon how the boundaries of what constitutes an NGO are drawn, in addition to these local NGOs there are other NGOs that operate at the national level in developing countries (acting as an additional intermediary level between international donors, including governments and some INGOs, and the local grassroots NGOs), some NGOs are global, and some operate at the inter-government level. Several INGOs have operations at a variety of these levels, for example raising funds in developed nations and channelling these funds to their own national and local branches in developing nations, as well as to third-party local grassroots partner NGOs.

In terms of numbers, there are several tens of thousands of NGOs in the world. Statistics from the Union of International Associations (UIA) put the number of NGOs that are 'international' at 53 815 in 2006 (Union of International Associations, 2007, vol. 5, p. 3, fig. 0.1). However, Gray et al. (2006, pp. 326–7) caution that 'there is doubt about the comprehensive nature of the UIA [statistics] and there is a considerable (largely inestimable) number of nationally-orientated NGOs which do not qualify for inclusion in [the UIA] figures'. Therefore the true number of NGOs is likely to be considerably higher than the UIA estimate, with a large number of very small local grassroots NGOs. Other NGOs (which almost certainly will be in the UIA statistics) are very large INGOs such as ActionAid, Oxfam, the Red Cross and Save the Children: organizations that each channel significant amounts of aid directly and indirectly from developed to developing nations.

This chapter will focus on issues of accountability within local and national NGOs and INGOS that provide welfare, development and/or education aid. The different forms of accountability within these NGOs that will be covered in the chapter are identity accountability and relational accountability. Identity accountability is a form of accountability where the people running the NGO feel accountable for their identity as ethical beings, and which will be discussed very briefly in this chapter, as it is not a major form of accountability in NGOs other than some NGOs that are largely advocacy NGOs. Relational accountability is a form of accountability in the sense that accountants would often understand the concept: it is a requirement for the NGO to provide an account to somebody to whom the NGO has responsibilities. In broader terms, the idea here is that, if a person or an organization (A) has a responsibility to behave or refrain from behaving in a certain way towards another person or organization (B), then person or organization A also has a duty to provide person or organization B with an account of how A has behaved in relation to, and has discharged, its responsibility owed to B. Relational accountability therefore covers situations where an individual or organization is required or expected to take responsibility for its actions (and the impacts of these actions) and to provide an account in relation to these actions and impacts. This chapter will focus on the forms of relational accountability prevalent within, and relevant for, NGOs: upward accountability, downward accountability and holistic accountability.

Before addressing these forms of accountability, the next section of this chapter explains the context of NGOs as a focus for accounting and accountability studies by establishing why and how NGO activities are significant for both governments and populations within developing countries. With the context for the exploration of the roles, issues and challenges of NGO accounting and accountability in developing country contexts established, the subsequent section explains characteristics of the main different forms of NGO accountability outlined above. It then explores these different accountability mechanisms in more depth, focusing particularly on how downward accountability mechanisms can help in improving the effectiveness of aid delivery in the context of an approach to aid termed the 'rights-based approach to development'. The chapter then concludes by looking at some of the problems of realizing, in practice, downward and more holistic forms of accountability. Even though such forms of accountability are an ideal, there is a variety of problems in realizing this ideal in practice.

CONTEXT TO NGO ACCOUNTING AND ACCOUNTABILITY – THE SIGNIFICANCE OF THE NGO SECTOR

Statistics regarding the amount of aid funding deployed by NGOs in developing nations are somewhat opaque. Figures are available from the OECD that show the total amount of aid funding (termed official development assistance, ODA) flowing from OECD member country governments to developing nations. At the time of writing this chapter, the latest figures available covered years up to and including 2008. These figures show the amount of ODA flowing from the 22 countries that constitute the OECD's Development Assistance Committee (DAC), which together represented about 90 per cent of total worldwide ODA flows in 2007 (OECD, 2007, p. 2). The OECD describes these ODA statistics as 'the only reliable source of internationally comparable data on foreign aid' (OECD, 2007, p. 7).

The OECD statistics show that total ODA provided by DAC member governments in 2008 amounted to US$121.5 billion (OECD, 2009c). Of this, US$86.5 billion was provided on a bilateral basis from DAC donor governments to developing nations through a variety of funding routes (including funding provided directly to a selection of NGOs). The remaining US$35.0 billion was provided by DAC member governments to multilateral agencies, for the multilateral agencies then to use to fund development assistance. These multilateral agency recipients of funding provided by DAC member governments include: various agencies, funds and commissions of the United Nations (total US$5.8 billion in 2008); the European Commission (US$13.0 billion); the International Development Association (US$8.1 billion); regional development banks (US$3.1 billion); and a variety of other multilateral agencies.

Of the 2008 US$86.5 billion of bilateral aid, only US$2.5 billion is shown in the OECD statistical tables as direct government funding provided to a selection of INGOs. There is a list of 55 INGOs in Annex 2 of the DAC Statistical Reporting Directives, contributions to which can be 'reported as bilateral aid' (OECD, 2009a, pp. 6–7). While this list does include several INGOs that are well known for their aid and development activities (such as the International Committee of the Red Cross) there are many INGOs that are active in aid delivery that are not on this list of 55 INGOs – such as ActionAid, Oxfam and Save the Children. So it would appear that ODA-funded work that is delivered to grassroots beneficiaries, possibly indirectly, via these aid NGOs is not classified within the 'funding to NGOs' heading in the OECD figures.

However, several of the other ODA headings in the table appear to be of a nature in which these INGOs, along with many national and local NGOs, would be involved in distribution of aid – possibly more as grassroots recipients of funding to deliver aid at the local level than as direct recipients of bilateral aid at OECD–government level. These include funding for: project and programme aid (US$32.9 billion); technical cooperation (US$17.0 billion); development food aid (US$1.4 billion); humanitarian aid (US$8.8 billion); refugees in donor countries (US$2.5 billion) and other grants (US$4.5 billion). Other ODA headings would appear to cover funding for types of aid activities in which NGOS may be expected to play no, or an insignificant, role in aid delivery, such as debt forgiveness (US$11.1 billion) and administrative costs (US$5.4 billion).

Table 18 of the 2008 OECD ODA statistics indicates that 6.5 per cent of total bilateral ODA was deployed to or through NGOs (OECD, 2009d), and this would amount to US$5.6 billion based on total bilateral aid of US$86.5 billion indicated above. However, this table indicates, for example, that none of the bilateral ODA provided by the USA in 2008 was deployed to or through NGOs. In 2008 bilateral aid from the USA amounted to a total of US$23.9 billion (Table 13 of the 2008 OECD ODA statistics), or 27.6 per cent of total DAC bilateral aid. An impression given by the ODA figures that none of this was deployed via NGOs appears implausible, as INGOs do receive funding, either directly or indirectly, from the US government. For example, taking one US branch of an INGO at random, the financial accounts for Save the Children's US member organization for the year ended 30 September 2008 show that US$108.7 million of incoming resources came from 'U.S. Government Grants and Contracts', out of a total of US$446.9 million incoming resources (Save the Children USA, 2009, p. 31).

Thus, while clearly showing the significant amount of total aid flowing from OECD DAC member country governments, it is apparent that the OECD statistics do not provide a particularly clear or full picture of how much of this ODA is deployed directly and indirectly via INGOs, national NGOs and local grassroots NGOs. Indeed, Agg (2006, p. 15) notes that within the OECD ODA statistics 'any data illustrating NGO activity is notoriously unreliable'. Other academic literature on NGO funding also indicates the complex and opaque nature of funding flowing from donor governments and multilateral agencies, through INGOs and national NGOs, to grassroots NGO aid delivery (see, for example, Morena, 2006; Oller, 2006; Sadoun, 2006).

Our own ad hoc observations whilst conducting research indicate that a number of projects and programmes that are delivered by NGOs locally are funded by multilateral agencies. In corroboration of the information given above regarding Save the Children USA, it also appeared to us while working among local grassroots NGOs that a proportion of bilateral funding for education, development and welfare projects was ultimately channelled through, or used in partnership with, NGOs at the grassroots level.

Looking to the future (and on-going) significance of ODA funding for developing nations, governments of OECD countries have long-standing commitments to increase ODA to a level of 0.7 per cent of their gross national income (GNI) by 2015. In 2008, ODA represented only 0.3 per cent of OECD member countries' GNI (OECD, 2009b), so ODA has to more than double to reach the 2015 target. However, in the context of the recent global financial and economic crisis, there is pressure to reduce levels of government expenditure in many developed nations. Although many OECD governments have pledged to maintain their commitments to increased ODA, and to protect ODA from general cuts in government expenditure, if GNI reduces because of the economic crisis then the absolute level of aid provided by a given percentage of GNI will also fall.

In addition to the amount of funding that aid delivery NGOs receive both directly and indirectly from governmental sources, they also raise substantial sums from private donations – from charitable trusts, public donations and corporate giving. As is the case with total government aid funding delivered via NGOs, the total amount of private donations across the NGO sector is also rather opaque. However, some academic literature indicates the potential size of private donations to development aid NGOs. For example, O'Dwyer and Unerman (2010) indicate that in Ireland, while some 20 per cent of ODA funding from the Irish government was channelled directly to NGOs in the early to mid-2000s, some 70 per cent of the income of Irish development INGOs was raised through public donations. Similarly, Atkinson et al. (2008) analyse UK data that indicate that in 2004/05 'The largest [UK] charities focusing on overseas development and emergency relief received nearly £1 billion [from private giving] . . . equal to about a quarter of the figure for [UK] ODA in that year' (p. 2).

Therefore, while it is problematic to obtain precise figures that indicate the amount of development aid funding deployed by and/or through NGOs in developing nations, it is reasonable to infer from the available data that many billions of dollars are channelled to ultimate grassroots beneficiaries through NGOs. As many of these beneficiaries are living on very low levels of income, it is also reasonable to infer that the quantum of aid funding deployed through NGOs is important and significant to many hundreds of millions of people in terms of the proportion of the overall resources available to them.

Much aid is intended to provide resources to help the poorest in society. The World Bank defines someone in poverty as a person with an income of less than US$1.25 per day (World Bank, 2008), and estimates put the number of people living below this poverty line as approximately 1.4 billion (in 2005) (Chen and Ravallion, 2008; World Bank, 2008). Development aid tends to be targeted both at those living below the World Bank poverty line and at large numbers of people living in need but whose incomes are above those of the 1.4 billion living below the poverty line (Collier, 2008). For someone who is living on an income below or marginally above US$1.25 per day, a relatively small per capita quantum (by Western standards) of aid funding has the potential to make a significant impact on their life experiences, and raise their standard of living.

Overall, therefore, the picture developed in this section of the chapter is that NGOs are responsible for channelling, both directly and indirectly, substantial amounts of governmental and private aid funding to those living in poverty in developing nations. The sums of aid involved can represent a relatively sizeable amount in proportion to the incomes of the recipients of the development aid, and thus can have the potential to make a real contribution to improving the life experiences, and alleviating the suffering, of these aid recipient citizens in developing countries. NGO activities are thus significant both for governments and for populations within these developing countries.

However, it is not only the quantum of aid funding that is important in its potential to alleviate the suffering of many in developed nations. It is also important to ensure that this funding is spent in the most efficient and effective manner (Herfkens and Bains, 2008), to obtain the greatest possible alleviation of suffering for every dollar, pound or euro of aid spending. This need to obtain the greatest impacts for aid funding has been exacerbated by the recent economic and financial crisis, which may result in pressures on the level of aid funding (as discussed earlier); it has also been widely argued that a global economic downturn is likely to have a disproportionately negative impact on the economies of developing nations – and thus the already low levels of per capita incomes in these nations. For example, in the background briefing note for a 2009 United Nations conference on the world financial and economic crisis and its impact on development, it was stated that:

> The situation in the world's developing countries – which contributed least to the crisis and are most severely affected – has led some economists to warn of 'lost decades for development' which could have catastrophic consequences for rich and poor countries alike.
>
> After struggling with high prices for food, fuel and fertilisers as well as the effects of climate change, these countries face rapidly shrinking trade and export–import credits. Private capital flows to emerging economies this year are projected to be down by 82 per cent from the boom year of 2007, the Institute of International Finance says. The World Bank, which has described the crisis as a 'development emergency', projected a finance gap of up to $700 billion in these countries, and the possibility of a 'lost generation,' with added deaths of 1.5 to 2.8 million infants by 2015. Over 100 million people are expected to be tipped into extreme poverty each year for the duration of the crisis.
>
> UN Secretary-General Ban Ki-moon recently warned that the international community 'should not lose sight of the challenges and plight of hundreds and hundreds of millions of the poorest people of the developing countries who have been impacted by this crisis.' (United Nations, 2009, p. 1)

It is in the area of maximizing the efficiency and effectiveness of the deployment of aid that accounting and accountability mechanisms have the potential to help (or, indeed, to hinder) in ensuring that aid funding is used in the most efficient and effective manner – thus helping the maximum possible number of the increasing proportion of the world's population likely to be living in poverty. The next section of this chapter will discuss common forms of NGO accounting and accountability mechanisms, and explain how these can have an impact upon the efficiency and effectiveness with which aid funding is deployed. This explanation will draw, in particular, on an approach currently considered to be among the best practices in aid delivery – the rights-based approach to development.

ROLES, ISSUES AND CHALLENGES OF NGO ACCOUNTING AND ACCOUNTABILITY IN DEVELOPING COUNTRY CONTEXTS

The previous section highlighted that the large and increasing quantum of aid funding to developing nations, coupled with the efficiency and effectiveness with which this aid funding is deployed directly and indirectly via NGOs, has the potential to alleviate considerable human suffering. The proposition in this section of the chapter is that mechanisms of NGO accounting and accountability can do a considerable amount to help improve the efficiency and effectiveness with which aid is delivered and thus can have a very real impact on the quality of many hundreds of millions of peoples' lives in developing nations.

Identity Accountability

Before turning to the relational NGO accounting and accountability processes and practices that can affect the efficiency and effectiveness of aid delivery, we will briefly (for the
sake of completeness) deal with a different form of NGO accountability mentioned in the
introduction to this chapter: identity accountability. This form of NGO accountability
occurs in situations where the people running an NGO (the NGO's officers and activists) feel accountable only to what they themselves believe is the right thing to do. In the
purest form of identity accountability, an NGO will not have any mechanisms to consult
externally on what those affected by the NGO's activities consider the NGO's duties to
be, or how the NGO affects the lives of these stakeholders. In other words, those running
the NGO consider that they know what their responsibilities are; they know that they
(and their NGO) are doing right. So long as they are happy that they are doing the right
thing, that the identity of the NGO remains pure to their 'cause', then that is as far as the
accountability needs to go under identity forms of accountability.

Where it is practised (either fully or in part), this form of NGO accountability tends to
be found among some advocacy NGOs where there are activists with very strong views
about the issues their NGO campaigns upon, and who do not believe that they should
be answerable to anybody but themselves for maintaining the specific identity of their
NGO. However (as noted in the introduction to this chapter), identity accountability is
not common within development NGOs. This is partially because development NGOs
usually need to raise substantial amounts of funding externally, for example from government funding agencies, and government funding agencies tend not to provide funds
unless an NGO provides some form of account – which we will return to below when
discussing upward accountability mechanisms.

As an analogy with corporate accountability, NGO identity accountability is akin to
a board of directors of a corporation refusing to be accountable to anybody (investors
or other stakeholders) for any of their actions, policies, practices or activities. Given that
identity accountability does not tend to be found within development aid NGOs, we will
now move on to look at issues of upward accountability.

Upward Accounting and Accountability Mechanisms

There are several terms used within the academic and practitioner literature to refer to
the form of accounting and accountability that we term *upward accountability*, including
hierarchical accountability and functional accountability. This form of NGO accountability is broadly similar to a traditional financial accounting relationship. Where a
donor provides funding, the NGO has to provide that donor with an account of how
it has utilized this funding. This is almost always predominantly a quantified (but not
solely financial) account that explains how the NGO has spent the resources provided
by the donor, focusing on outputs in terms of the objectives that the donor set when it
provided the NGO with the funding (Fowler, 1996; Edwards and Hulme, 2002a, 2002b;
Dillon, 2004; Agyemang et al., 2009). Normally the upward account has to be provided
in a fixed, rigid format specified by each donor, and the information flows in one direction – upward from the grassroots NGO workers or officers through local and national
NGOs (or branches of NGOs) to the INGO and then to the donor or funder – with

the information in the fixed format becoming aggregated, or consolidated, with other accounts at each level. Implicit in the requirement to provide this type of fixed format quantitative account is a message from the donor or funder that the donor is providing the funding to enable the NGO to acquire resources to provide a particular type of aid, and the donor or funder just wants to know how much of this particular type of aid has been brought to bear with the resources that it has provided. It is a very narrow form of account, usually with little or no scope for reporting other matters, so it provides little or no opportunity for feedback on broader issues.

Ebrahim (2003) explains that the upward accountability process involves collation and provision of information from grassroots levels in the form of disclosure statements, disclosure reports and performance assessments and evaluations. Agyemang et al. (2009) provide a summary of the focus of some of these upward accountability processes as they are enacted in practice at the start of the upward accountability process – information provided in a fixed format by grassroots NGO officers. This summary is shown in Table 9.1.

As can be seen from Table 9.1, each form of report in upward accounting or accountability provides scope for provision of some narrative commentary. However, Agyemang et al. (2009) found in their empirical study that there was a widespread perception among NGO officers they interviewed that, because the information in these standard form (for each donor or funder) upward accountability reports is aggregated with reports from other projects, the narrative information would either not be communicated higher up the accountability process so would not reach donors, or not be taken into account or acted upon by donors. There was also a widespread perception that most donors were not interested in any information beyond the narrow information asked for in their standard form reports and, in particular, did not use the accountability process as an opportunity to learn from the grassroots officers (or the beneficiaries) about what aspects of a project implementation were particularly successful or problematic.

Overall, the focus of hierarchical, upward accountability is to help ensure that donors' funds are spent efficiently in terms specifically of the purpose for which that donor specifies that its funds should be spent. So, if a donor specifies that it wants to spend €1 million on educating female children between the ages of 5 and 10, a form of upward accountability would report back to the donor: this is how many girls we educated through the projects that you funded between those ages and how much we spent in doing so. Agyemang et al. (2009) provide examples of various types of such upward accountability reports. The one reproduced in Table 9.2 is a financial summary interim report.

In terms of a narrative commentary provided in conjunction with such interim reports, Agyemang et al. (2009) give the example shown in Table 9.3, and note that 'The commentary tended to be brief and in many instances took the form of bullet points' (p. 15).

Although such reports can communicate to donors or funders aspects of whether their funding has been spent efficiently in terms of the quantity or volume of a particular type of service delivered for the money provided, what such predominately quantitative reports cannot convey is the effectiveness with which the funding has been deployed. For example, in the case of education projects, in the absence of any accountability dialogue with the beneficiaries, with the parents, with the local teachers and so on it will not be readily apparent whether the funding is being spent effectively. The fact that a project may have funded a number of children who are sitting in a classroom and being educated

Table 9.1 Characteristics of upward accountability mechanisms

Accountability mechanism	Financial information	Narrative	Quantitative performance indicators	Written or oral	Frequency	Stakeholder focus
Disclosure statements and reports						
Annual reports	Yes	Yes	Yes	Written	Once a year	Range of stakeholders
Interim reports	Yes	Yes	Yes	Written	Monthly, quarterly and half-yearly	Donors
Performance assessment and evaluations						
Assessment reports	Yes	Yes	Yes	Written	Continuous	Donors and internal stakeholders
Evaluation/final project report	Yes	Yes	Yes	Written	At end of project	Donors

Source: Agyemang et al. (2009, p. 13).

Table 9.2   Financial summary interim report

Activity items	Objectives	Output achieved	Remarks	Budget for this quarter	Actual expenditure	Percentage of total budget spent
Monitor activities of clients	Visit all 150 clients	Only 103 clients visited (69% visited)	Late receipt of funding	£350	£250	71%
Overheads, administration costs, staff costs, equipment costs				£30	£50	160%

Source: Agyemang et al. (2009, p.14).

Table 9.3   Example of commentary in an interim report

Instructions for completing the form: Please keep as brief as possible. Provide key information that may have a bearing on NGO work.

Sub-heading	Commentary
Activity	Capacity building workshop: assertiveness training
Objective	To build the capacity of 100 women in a selected community
Target group	Women groups
Challenges	Late disbursement of funds
Outputs	Number of women trained
Indicators	Photographic evidence

Source: Agyemang et al. (2009, p. 15).

does not necessarily mean that these children are being educated with the types of know-ledge and skills that are needed in their communities, or that they are being educated in the most effective manner. Where funding is specified for education of girls only, upward accountability processes do not usually provide scope to communicate the longer-term impacts on community sustainability of any lack of funding for the education of boys.

To provide this type of information requires feedback mechanisms. And a key point here is that donors sitting in Brussels or London or Dublin or Washington are very remote from the facts on the ground – they do not and cannot know what works in every local community to which they ultimately provide aid funding. However, if they were able and willing to draw on the experience and the knowledge of people at the grassroots level (both NGO officers and the beneficiaries themselves), they would be more likely to be able to adapt their provision so that the education, in this example, would be delivered in the most effective way for each community. In this context, it is also important to be willing to learn from past mistakes and adapt future provision.

The foregoing discussion highlights the difference, and potential tension, between the efficiency and the effectiveness of aid spending.

Efficiency versus Effectiveness of Aid Spending and the Rights-Based Approach to Development Aid

Drawing upon the above discussion, in this chapter we define *efficiency* of aid spending to mean how much of a particular form of aid product or service (such as a particular type of technology provided in infrastructure projects, or a particular type of education or health service) as specified by donors has been provided for every pound, dollar or euro of funding provided. In general, the greater the volume of specified aid product or service provided for a given amount of funding, the greater the efficiency of aid spend-ing is considered to be. In contrast, we define *effectiveness* of aid spending to mean the extent to which the outcome of the aid spending achieves its broader overall aim of alleviating as much suffering of those in need as possible. Clearly, in situations where a narrowly defined form of aid provision as specified by a donor is the best way of alleviat-ing the suffering of a particular grassroots community, then maximizing efficiency and maximizing effectiveness will result in the same outcome. However, as indicated in the discussion above, in many situations and contexts, the narrowly defined form of aid provision specified by a donor may not be the best way of alleviating suffering in a particular community, in which case maximizing efficiency will not deliver maximum effectiveness in deployment of aid.

One argument for focusing on effectiveness (rather than just efficiency) of aid spending rests on a moral reason for giving aid. Many donors give aid because they recognize that they have a moral responsibility to alleviate the suffering of ultimate beneficiaries – either in the short term by providing resources that can be used today and/or by providing longer-term development of intellectual and physical infrastructure. Where donors recognize that they have a moral responsibility to the beneficiaries, do they not have an equal moral responsibility to ensure that the aid they give is deployed in the most effective manner to provide the maximum possible alleviation of suffering?

This perspective links to a perspective on aid that is increasingly common: the rights-based approach (RBA) to development aid. More traditionally, development aid work was regarded as a gift from the donors to the beneficiaries. From this perspective, donors would identify a development need and out of their generosity would provide funds or other resources to help impoverished people improve their lives. The RBA reverses this traditional perspective and regards every human as having basic inalienable human rights, such as rights to a certain level of food, water, shelter and education. Where people are born into, and/or live in, situations where lack or resources make it near impossible for them to realize or enjoy their basic human rights, under the RBA they are regarded as having a right to claim the resources needed to enjoy these rights from those who have the ability to provide such resources – with the latter having a moral obligation to ensure that the former's basic human rights are respected and delivered. Thus, in contrast to the traditional view that development is need and development work is a gift, the RBA regards a minimum level of development as a right, and development work as a duty that people in developed nations have to help impoverished people achieve their basic human rights.

In order to achieve this, the RBA focuses on empowering beneficiaries: empowering the people who need the aid, who have the basic human rights that are not being met. It focuses on empowering them to articulate and claim their rights from people and nations that have money and power. Within the RBA, the complementary concepts of accountability, empowerment and participation are absolutely central features, with accountability generally regarded as one of the core mechanisms to help effectively deliver the RBA. The forms of accountability that are needed to do this involve dialogue between donors, NGOs and beneficiaries, seeking to empower beneficiaries to claim their rights. Such dialogical forms of accountability, taking into account the views, experiences and expertise of local beneficiary communities, and seeking to redress (as far as is practically possible) power imbalances between donors, NGOs and impoverished beneficiaries, are generally known as downward and holistic forms of accountability. Furthermore, we argue that, by making deployment of aid sensitive and responsive to local variations in the circumstances in which the aid is delivered, such downward and holistic accountability mechanisms not only help deliver rights-based approaches to aid, but also can directly improve the effectiveness of aid delivery irrespective of whether or not a particular donor subscribes to the rights-based approach to aid.

Downward Accounting and Accountability Mechanisms

A key aspect of downward accountability, especially when used in conjunction with the RBA, is that it seeks to improve the effectiveness of NGO delivery of aid by encouraging the NGO and its aid delivery partners to become learning organizations. This is facilitated by the NGO and its partners (both donors and aid delivery partners) engaging in a variety of accountability dialogues. As dialogues, and in contrast to hierarchical upward accountability processes, these do not involve the flow of information in just one direction. Rather, they involve an accountability dialogue between donors, the NGO, the grassroots officers and the beneficiaries, with an aim of learning what is the most effective way of delivering aid in each individual situation and local context.

For NGOs to implement downward accountability effectively requires flexibility in approaches to aid delivery by both the NGO and its donors. They need to be prepared to adapt specific aspects of their provision of aid to meet the real needs of beneficiaries, with these needs being identified through the downward accountability dialogue mechanisms that enrol the views and experiences of the beneficiaries and grassroots officers. The key point here is that downward accountability mechanisms, through engaging in dialogue with the beneficiaries, have the potential to identify more effective ways of deploying the aid funding and the aid resources, and this more effective deployment can then result in a 'bigger bang for your buck'.

When identifying various different forms of downward accountability mechanisms, Ebrahim (2003) explains that the downward accountability process can involve a variety of participatory, self-assessment and social auditing practices. Agyemang et al. (2009) provide a summary (shown in Table 9.4) of the focus of some of these downward accountability processes that they found to be used in practice in a study of accountability at the grassroots level in Ghana.

Although many donor governments, and the fund-raising arms of INGOs in donor countries, along with many local NGOs, recognize the potential benefits of the RBA in terms of improving the effectiveness of aid delivery, and also recognize the importance of downward accountability in delivering an effective RBA, O'Dwyer and Unerman (2010) found in practice that there were impediments and resistance to implementing the downward accountability mechanisms that are an essential part of an effective RBA. The difficulties in practice are now considered.

Where downward accountability is imposed because donor governments require downward accountability as part of the RBA, it could well be imposed in a fairly inappropriate and dysfunctional manner. It might be imposed by using mechanisms that just don't work for that particular local community. It would be rather paradoxical if donor governments, by promoting the RBA, recognized that there was no single fixed, rigid way of effectively delivering aid to every single community, because they recognized that it is important to adapt aid provision to the needs of every individual community, and then required rigid application of downward accountability mechanisms that were not flexible or adapted to the needs of each community. So any attempt at imposing a rigid form of downward accountability might not work.

Other significant practical problems with implementing downward accountability are issues with differential power and deference. This can be summed up in the phrase and belief among some that 'you don't bite the hand that feeds you'. It is perhaps

Table 9.4   *Characteristics of downward accountability mechanisms*

Accountability mechanism	Financial information	Narrative	Quantitative performance indicators	Written or oral	Frequency	Stakeholder focus
Participation and beneficiary involvement						
Community, consultations and dialogues	Not always	Yes	Yes	Oral	Varies	Beneficiaries
Participatory review reports	Not always	Yes	Yes	Oral and written	Varies	Range of stakeholders
Informal reporting	Not always	Yes	Yes	Oral	Continuous	Beneficiaries
Social auditing						
Accountability notice boards	Yes	Yes	Yes	Written	Quarterly	Range of stakeholders
Newsletters	Yes	Yes	Yes	Written	Monthly, quarterly	Range of stakeholders
Self-regulation						
Networks and NGO membership organizations	Not always	Yes	Yes	Written and oral	Varies	Sector and regional NGOs

Source: Agyemang et al. (2009, p. 13).

understandable that people living on less than \$1.25 a day will feel that, despite the rhetoric in the RBA, they do not have a great deal of power in relation to those providing them with aid. In this context it may be considered by aid recipients to be an unacceptable risk to risk upsetting somebody who is providing them with aid. They may therefore not be particularly vociferous in expressing their true views and concerns in any RBA accountability dialogue. There are also associated problems of their ability or capacity to articulate their needs and participate in accountability dialogues, because a lot of people in deeply impoverished communities have not benefited from high standards of education.

The more effective dialogue that is a characteristic of downward accountability requires a variety of effective partnership relationships between donors, INGOs, local NGOs, grassroots NGO officers and beneficiaries that are not hierarchical and not dictatorial. It is therefore important to try to minimize as far as possible power differentials between the people who need the aid and the people who have the resources, by establishing partnership arrangements where all parties involved can genuinely participate. In practice this is difficult to achieve.

This participative downward accountability dialogue should involve beneficiaries in all aspects of the design and implementation of projects. However, in a recent study O'Dwyer and Unerman (2010) found some resistance in practice from some of the INGOs they studied to putting into place the practical mechanisms that would enable these INGOs to engage in effective downward accountability with and between their local grassroots partner NGOs. In particular they found there was a lack of attention to donor oversight of downward accountability in local NGOs, so the Western donors who have skills to be able to show the local partners what can be achieved through downward accountability tended to ignore these possibilities. The INGOs studied were also somewhat resistant to transferring influence to their local partner NGOs and, clearly, if they are unwilling themselves to transfer influence, maintaining their dominant position in the relationship, that does not lead to effective participatory partnerships. O'Dwyer and Unerman (2010) also found perceived problems related to the control of some local NGOs by local educated elites who could speak English and thereby who could communicate with the donors. There was a feeling among some that these local elites might be distant from the beneficiaries, although O'Dwyer and Unerman (2010) argue that just because people are educated does not mean they cannot empathize with the situation in which beneficiaries find themselves. O'Dwyer and Unerman also found a perception among their interviewees that there was a lack of demand from local NGOs and from grassroots communities for downward accountability; this is possibly quite understandable because for beneficiaries to engage in dialogue with an NGO requires them to take time away, for example, from working in the fields growing the crops that will feed their family that day.

Overall, and taking into account these issues and problems of fully realizing downward accountability in practice, a key aim of downward accountability is to empower beneficiaries: to empower them so that they can demand more effective deployment of aid in the realization of their basic human rights.

However, there is also a moral argument that donors and NGOs, in recognizing the need to deliver solutions that enhance the realization of the human rights of their beneficiaries, should not take actions that risk infringing the rights of others who are not directly involved in either the funding or the activities of the NGO. In other words, they need to recognize moral responsibilities to all who might be affected by their actions and, as argued earlier, recognition of responsibilities brings a parallel duty to provide an account to these other stakeholders regarding how the organization has acted in relation to its responsibilities. This is akin to a corporate duty, widely recognized and theorized in both the sustainability accounting and accountability academic literature and the corporate social responsibility academic literature, that corporations have responsibilities for their actions, and are therefore accountable, to a much broader range of stakeholders than just investors, customers and employees. This raises issues of broader, more holistic forms of NGO accountability.

Holistic Accountability

Holistic accountability incorporates upward and downward accountability, but also broadens the accountability focus by recognizing that there may well be a wide range of stakeholders who are not necessarily the direct beneficiaries of a particular NGO's aims and objectives, but who nevertheless are affected by the NGO's activities. For example, there are some environmental advocacy NGOs that campaign to stop the transport of fresh food produce by air from Africa to Europe. From an ecological point of view that is a sound argument, but what also needs to be taken into consideration is the farmers and communities in African nations who may be living in deep poverty, and who are lifted slightly out of poverty by being able to supply European markets with this produce. These impoverished farmers in Africa might not be the direct object of the environmental advocacy NGOs, but holistic accountability would say that the environmental NGOs in European countries that are seeking to curtail imports of fresh African produce by air should also take into account the needs and interests of these impoverished African communities, and the impact upon them should this source of income be curtailed. In this respect, there are a number of environmental campaign groups that recognize that reducing environmental impact from air transport of fresh produce from Africa to Europe is not simply a case of stopping buying from Africa to solve the environmental problems – it is also necessary to take into account the social sustainability issues intertwined with the ecological and economic sustainability issues. Alternatives could be for these advocacy NGOs also to campaign to develop local markets and/or to develop alternative ways of growing different crops locally for different uses.

These issues move the discussion of NGO accountability towards factors that are at the core of sustainability accounting and accountability. In that field it is widely recognized not only that organizational actions have a direct impact in potentially numerous ways upon society, the natural environment and the economy, and can thus have a positive and/or negative impact on social, environmental and economic sustainability, but also that impacts in each of these spheres lead to many indirect second-order impacts on social, ecological and economic sustainability. In other words, social, environmental and economic systems (and sustainability) are deeply intertwined. Thus any strategic or operational decision can lead to many positive and negative impacts upon a broad range of stakeholders. The sustainability accounting and accountability academic literature argues that these impacts give rise to responsibilities owed by an organization taking decisions (and acting upon these decisions) to those whom these actions might directly and indirectly affect. The literature further argues that these responsibilities have associated duties of the organization to provide an account to a broad range of stakeholders regarding how it has discharged its responsibilities (Gray, Bebbington and Gray, 2010; Hopwood, Unerman and Fries, 2010). In this context, we maintain that NGOs are in substance no different from other forms of organization in having responsibilities and allied duties of accountability to those who are negatively affected by the outcomes of their actions.

CONCLUSIONS

NGOs delivering development aid play a vital role in the world today. There are an estimated 1.4 billion people living below the poverty line of US$1.25 of income per day, and many more living marginally above this level. Many of these people are living in real need with real suffering. The rights-based approach to development has been recognized as a way to improve the effectiveness with which every pound, dollar or euro of the multi-billion-dollar global aid spend is translated into alleviating the poverty and suffering of those living below or near the poverty line in a long-term sustainable manner. While upward accountability can help to improve the efficiency with which this aid funding is spent, in terms of the maximum provision of specific and often narrowly defined forms of aid set out in the objectives of a funder, downward accountability is needed to improve the effectiveness of the deployment of aid.

Upward, hierarchical NGO accountability is narrowly focused, and tends to be formal and rigid. It tends to account for resource use and immediate impact. Upward accountability does not usually incorporate mechanisms to provide donors with information regarding how to make their aid provision more effective. It does not usually enable donors to learn from past mistakes, as it discourages information about 'failure', so it is less likely to identify where and why a specific project has gone wrong, and what effective mechanisms could be used to overcome these deficiencies in future aid projects – both in the community where the narrowly specified project did not work last time and in other communities.

In contrast, downward NGO accountability tends to be more dialogical and is less formal and less rigid than upward accountability mechanisms, as it needs to be adapted to the situation of each NGO and each local context. It provides clear opportunities to learn from and with both beneficiaries and local grassroots NGO officers and workers. Thus it is also potentially an effective mechanism for enabling the beneficiaries themselves to learn what might work best within their individual community. Downward accountability is generally regarded as a key element of both maximizing the effectiveness of deployment of aid and delivering an effective rights-based approach to aid.

Holistic accountability encompasses both upward accountability and downward accountability, as it recognizes that NGOs need to be accountable both to their funders and to their beneficiaries. However, it also broadens the scope of accountability to include the many indirect accountability relationships arising from the many indirect responsibilities any organization or person, including an NGO, owes to a broad range of stakeholders whose lives might be affected by the NGO's actions. Thus it is a multi-directional form of NGO accountability.

One final point is that in all forms of NGO accountability it is essential to ensure that the accountability mechanisms employed are suited to the nature of each individual NGO or each individual grassroots community. Where inappropriate accountability mechanisms, or mechanisms that are inappropriate for any particular individual situation, are imposed or required, this could well be destructive to some of the NGOs that currently do play a very important role within many local communities in developing nations. From this perspective, appropriate accountability mechanisms will not necessarily take the form of traditional written accounts. Very often informal face-to-face engagements between NGO workers and the grassroots communities will be more appropriate and effective in helping develop the capacity of those communities to live in an economically, socially and environmentally sustainable manner in the long term.

REFERENCES

Agg, C. (2006). Winners or losers? NGOs in the current aid paradigm. *Development*, 49(2), pp. 15–21.

Agyemang, G., M. Awumbila, J. Unerman and B. O'Dwyer (2009). *NGO Accountability and Aid Delivery*, Research Report no. 110. London: ACCA.

Atkinson, A.B., J. Backus, J. Micklewright, C. Pharoah and S.V. Schnepf (2008). *Charitable Giving for Overseas Development: UK Trends over a Quarter Century*, Working Paper A08/09: Applications and Policy. Southampton: University of Southampton Statistical Sciences Research Institute.

Chen, S., and M. Ravallion (2008). *The Developing World Is Poorer than We Thought, but No Less Successful in the Fight against Poverty*, Policy Research Working Paper Series. Washington, DC: World Bank.

Collier, P. (2008). *The Bottom Billion*. Oxford: Oxford University Press.

Dillon, E. (2004). Accountabilities and power in development relationships. *Trocaire Development Review 2003/4*, pp. 105–17. Dublin: Trocaire.

Ebrahim, A. (2003). Accountability in practice: mechanisms for NGOs. *World Development*, 31(5), pp. 813–29.

Edwards, M., and D. Hulme (2002a). Beyond the magic bullet? Lessons and conclusions. In *NGO Management*, ed. M. Edwards and D. Hulme. London: Earthscan.

Edwards, M., and D. Hulme (2002b). NGO performance and accountability: introduction and overview. In *NGO Management*, ed. M. Edwards and D. Hulme. London: Earthscan.

Fowler, A. (1996). Demonstrating NGO performance: problems and possibilities. *Development in Practice*, 6, pp. 58–65.

Gray, R., J. Bebbington and D. Collison (2006). NGOs, civil society and accountability: making the people accountable to capital. *Accounting, Auditing and Accountability Journal*, 19(3), pp. 319–48.

Gray, R., J. Bebbington and S. Gray (eds) (2010). *Social and Environmental Accounting*, vols I–IV. London: Sage.

Herfkens, E., and M. Bains (2008). *Reaching Our Development Goals: Why Does Aid Effectiveness Matter?* Paris: OECD.

Hopwood, A.G., J. Unerman and J. Fries (eds) (2010). *Accounting for Sustainability: Practical Insights*. London: Earthscan.

Morena, E. (2006). Funding and the future of the global justice movement. *Development*, 49(2), pp. 29–33.

O'Dwyer, B., and J. Unerman (2010). Enhancing the role of accountability in promoting the rights of beneficiaries of development NGOs. *Accounting and Business Research*, 40(5), pp. 451–71.

OECD (2007). *OECD Development Assistance Committee: Where Governments Come Together to Make Aid Work*. Paris: Organisation for Economic Co-operation and Development.

OECD (2009a). Annex 2: list of international organisations. *DAC Statistical Reporting Directives*. Paris: Organisation for Economic Co-operation and Development.

OECD (2009b). *Development Aid at Its Highest Level Ever in 2008*. Paris: Development Co-operation Directorate, Organisation for Economic Co-operation and Development.

OECD (2009c). *OECD: StatExtracts Development ODA by Donor, DAC Countries*. Paris: Organisation for Economic Co-operation and Development.

OECD (2009d). *Statistical Annex of the 2010 Development Co-operation Report*. Paris: Organisation for Economic Co-operation and Development.

Oller, S.D. (2006). Power relations in the financial aid chain. *Development*, 49(2), pp. 34–9.

Sadoun, B. (2006). Donor policies and the financial autonomy of development NGOs. *Development*, 49(2), pp. 45–51.

Save the Children USA (2009). *Annual Report 2008*. Westport, CT: Save the Children USA.

Unerman, J., and B. O'Dwyer (2006). On James Bond and the importance of NGO accountability. *Accounting, Auditing and Accountability Journal*, 19(3), pp. 305–18.

Union of International Associations (2007). *Yearbook of International Organizations*. Munich: K.G. Saur Verlag.

United Nations (2009). *Backgrounder for United Nations Conference on the World Financial and Economic Crisis and Its Impact on Development*, DPI/2535A. New York: United Nations Department of Public Information.

World Bank (2008). *Overview: Understanding, Measuring and Overcoming Poverty*. Washington, DC: World Bank.

10 Empowering or oppressing: the case of microfinance institutions

Kerry Jacobs, Mohshin Habib, Nzilu Musyoki and Christine Jubb

INTRODUCTION

This chapter examines the origins of microfinance and the institutions which provide it, and it gives an overview of the research literature, showing the contradictory and competing objectives of microfinance institutions caught between the objective of poverty reduction and the pressures for profitability. Notions of field, capital and habitus are used to theorize the influences and impact of microfinance institutions on the poor and to explain in particular the role of accounting at the boundary and interface of different fields. The actual processes associated with microfinance are explored in three case studies of microfinance clients and three of microfinance lenders. From these cases it becomes evident that much of the accounting and controlling process is privatized to the individuals involved in the microfinance borrowing groups which monitor and control each other because they often share liability for loan repayment. While this can be empowering and supportive in some settings, it is also clear that there is potential for exploitation and abuse.

While accounting is sometimes represented as a tool of oppression or exploitation it has also been argued that it can function as a tool of social betterment (Gallhofer and Broadbent, 1997). Few other examples illustrate so clearly the balance between an empowering and an oppression role for financial models and institutions as the case of microfinance. Over the last two decades microfinance institutions have become one of the most notable responses to poverty alleviation and development, culminating in the United Nations declaring 2005 the 'International Year of Microcredit'. Microcredit refers to 'small loans', whilst microfinance refers to the provision of a wide range of financial services for the poor, often with no requirement for collateral. Microcredit and microfinance seem to promise to improve the lot of the most extremely poor in a way that is sensitive to community needs and still pose relatively little by way of financial burden on wealthy Western countries, as loans, unlike grants, generally are repaid. Given this, microfinance has been promoted as an effective way to reduce poverty and to improve development. Yet little attention has been paid to how the practices of control and visibility associated with microfinance create governable subjects and governable spaces.

According to the Credit Development Forum (CDF), the following are the characteristics of microfinance services (CDF, 2004): (1) small loans, typically for working capital; (2) informal appraisal of borrowers and investments; (3) collateral substitutes, such as group guarantees or compulsory savings; (4) access to repeat and larger loans, based on repayment performance; (5) streamlined loan disbursement and monitoring;

and (6) secure savings products. However, not all models of microfinance reflect these characteristics and not all institutions share the same commitment to development and poverty reduction.

The role of accounting in microfinance institutions is not immediately obvious, as it can be seen as an example of the absence as opposed to the presence of accounting (Choudhury, 1988; Jacobs and Kemp, 2002). This is so because these organizations operate beyond the framework circumscribed by traditional financial reporting and management control. However, this characterization is an oversimplification, as the process and practices of control associated with microfinance institutions have rendered new groups visible and calculable (Miller and O'Leary, 1994). This visibility and calculability occurs through the social and cultural process of lending to and collecting from village-based groups and organizations. It could be argued that these more direct forms of visibility through the loan collectors and more indirect forms of collective visibility and control through group registration offer a substitute to the relatively expensive (and in this context ineffective) processes of accounting measurement and control. To some extent the community arrangements associated with microfinance can be seen as a privatization of the costs of monitoring and control where these costs are transferred from the microfinance institution to the individual and the community.

There is a danger that accounting notions are used to legitimatize the reduction of poverty to a solely microfinancial or economic issue – essentially a question of access to credit. As a consequence the broader structural, social and political questions associated with poverty are ignored. Miller and O'Leary (1994) particularly emphasize how practices of account render the actions of individuals visible and discipline them in conformity with 'wider political norms'. However, the second issue relating to microfinance and accounting is the construction of governable spaces. In effect the sovereignty of the economic is extended to new areas of social and personal life (Llewellyn and Walker, 2000). Watts (2003, p. 9) highlights this link between development or poverty reduction practice and the construction of governable subjects and governable spaces.

THE COMPETING AND CONTRADICTORY OBJECTIVES OF MICROFINANCE INSTITUTIONS

It is the dual construction of the governable subject and the governable space which so characterizes the emergence of microfinance. Microfinance has been lauded as the 'Holy Grail' of development and the solution to the problem of world poverty. However, it also exists as a form of governmentality, rendering the poorest and weakest subject to new and inescapable forms of external and internal visibility. Governable spaces are created as new aspects of life, and new communities are subject to visibility and control as part of a broader objective of 'economic development'. Yet these agenda are not fully aligned, and microfinance institutions face three different competing demands. The first is that the microfinance institution is expected to contribute to the economic development of the country as a whole by promoting economic activity and growth, the second is the requirement that the institution generates sufficient profit to survive (and possibly grow) and the third is that the microfinance institution provides the poor with a way out of their poverty.

In addition to balancing these competing and contradictory objectives there is a real danger that microfinance does not lead to development or empowerment, but rather represents a new way to exploit the poor. Even in the context of the best of motivations and intentions, pressures on aid agencies and on the microfinance institutions can lead to mission drift and developmental work being abandoned in favour of more profitable activities and visible target groups. As a consequence, the poorest applicants fail to receive loans, with credit provision directed increasingly at richer and, as a consequence, 'safer' applicants. There is a real and important empirical question as to the conduct of these institutions in balancing their legitimate objectives and whether they function as a tool of oppression or empowerment. While giving loans to the poor can reduce poverty, it does not necessarily maximize economic development, which might be more effectively addressed by giving loans to the not-so-poor. In contrast the objective of profitability might be best addressed by giving loans to the not-really-poor-at-all.

MICROFINANCE – A BRIEF HISTORY

The origin of the modern microfinance movement is generally attributed to Dr Muhammad Yunus. In the late 1970s, Yunus initiated the first microfinance programme as an experiment in rural Bangladesh, which formed the basis of the Grameen Bank. Yunus was awarded the 2006 Nobel Peace Prize for his anti-poverty efforts.[1] Yunus's experiments and their success led to the wider acceptability of the notion that providing access to credit can bring about change in the socio-economic situation of the poor (Khalily, 2004). Grameen's success has also been instrumental in encouraging more than 750 non-governmental organizations (NGOs) to operate small-scale microfinance programmes in Bangladesh (ADB, 2000a).

The innovative feature of Yunus's and the Grameen Bank's approach was that they were willing to lend to the poor lacking the assets required for collateral by other loan providers. Previous attempts at subsidized credit had not reached or benefited the poor, whilst arguably they did benefit the rich and were sometimes politically motivated (Vogel, 1984). For instance, in Costa Rica, 80 per cent of the US$56 million subsidies provided to the largest bank during 1974 went to wealthy farmers (Khandker, 1998; Coleman, 2006). Moreover, monopolistic power, higher interest rates, and exploitation through undervaluation of collateral have restricted the informal financial sector's capacity to provide credit to the poor, hindering economic and social development (Ghate et al., 1992).

Yunus's idea was to target very small loans to the landless women who wanted to start a small business through buying a cow or a sewing machine. Such people did not have financial capital. The provision of credit was normally accompanied by training in both business and group dynamics. The major innovation was the notion of group lending, where groups of generally five borrowers form and, while loans are made to individuals, each member of the group is responsible for loan repayment. The group meets weekly with a bank officer and with a number of other such groups. If one member of the group defaults then all in the group are denied subsequent loans. The group structure takes advantage of local information and social capital networks associated with informal enforcement and risk sharing, and peer pressure is used generally to monitor and enforce contracts, providing an incentive for borrowers to repay and therefore reducing the risks for the microfinance institution. This social-capital-based group mechanism constitutes a powerful tool to improve the loan recovery rate and minimize costs, thereby enabling microfinance institutions to improve profitability and sustainability (Del Conte, 2000).

While microfinance had its roots in Bangladesh it has now spread to both developing and developed countries (OECD, 1995). However, not all institutions reflect the Grameen Bank approach. For instance, Banco Sol in Bolivia started as a microfinance NGO in 1987 and became a bank in 1992. It serves the 'richest of the poor', offering larger loans and focusing on banking rather than social services and training (Morduch, 1999, p.1576). Morduch (1999) reported its interest rates as high at a 48 per cent annual base rate with an up-front commission of 2.5 per cent. Clients with a performance record are offered a better deal at 45 per cent per annum (Morduch, 1999, p. 1576). The organization is a financial success, although it is questionable whether it can be regarded as an agent of poverty reduction, and the levels of interest charged open it to accusations of exploitation. Bank Rakyat Indonesia also lends to the 'better-off' poor and non-poor and provides comparatively large loans. It does not use group lending structures, requires the borrowers to provide financial collateral for their loans, and does not provide training or social services to the poor. Annualized interest rates are around 34 per cent generally, although they were reduced to 24 per cent if the loans were paid without delay (Morduch, 1999, p.1578). The repayment rates and profit from loans to the 'poor' clients exceed those on the loans to corporate clients (Morduch, 1999, p.1578). Bank Kredit Desa (BKD) in rural Indonesia is a sister organization to Bank Rakyat. It lends small amounts of money to the poorest and does not require collateral. Whilst it does not use a group lending approach, the funds are allocated through village-level management commissions under the authority of the village chief (Morduch, 1999, p.1578). The reported interest rate is 10 per cent on the weekly repayment, although this translates to a nominal annual interest rate of 52 per cent.

THE MICROFINANCE DEBATE – THE EVIDENCE

There is an extensive literature on microfinance's impact on development and poverty reduction which suggests a positive impact of microfinance on clients with regard to economic well-being and resilience. Grameen members in Bangladesh are reported to have had a significant increase in employment opportunities (Hossain, 1988), personal income (Hanifan, 1996), housing condition (Rahman and Hasnat, 1993) and nutrition (Rahman, 1986), a reduction in exposure to seasonal vulnerability, a contribution to lower volatility or smoothing of consumption, and better crisis management (Mustafa et al., 1996; Khandker, 1998; Pitt and Khandker, 1998; Khalily, 2004). Khandker (1998) found that a Grameen-type microfinance programme had an impact on both individual and household education, income, savings, expenditure, wealth accumulation and women's empowerment. Hossain (2002) shows that about 60 per cent of borrowers believe capital gained from a microfinance programme assisted them primarily in achieving a better socio-economic condition.

From the perspective of economic development, microfinance is seen as an 'inducer' in many community development activities, and an ingredient in many larger programmes, such as education and training, employment generation, empowerment of women, social responsiveness and political awareness (Alamgir, 1997; ADB, 2000a). It also promotes the growth of local enterprises and female entrepreneurs (Pitt and Khandker, 1998; Morduch, 1999; Bertaux and Crable, 2007). Grameen Bank's microfinance programme is augmented by social development programmes in maternal health, nutrition and childcare, which in themselves should provide beneficial impacts upon the poor (Pitt and Khandker, 1998; ADB, 2000a, 2000b; Mahmud, 2001; Holvoet, 2004).

Additionally, there appears to be an important symbolic impact on individual social capital arising from the effect of microfinance institutions on poverty reduction and economic development. The fact that a microfinance institution was willing to lend to a given individual is an important source of social distinction and therefore social status (Rahman, 2002a, 2000b). This lack of access to economic capital in the form of credit can directly affect social networks of individuals in settings such as rural Bangladesh. Rahman (2002b, p. 72) recounted a response from a Grameen Bank (GB) member:

> I was starving. No one bothered to give me a handful of rice. I went to so many shop-keepers. They would not trust me. They would not give me a seer of rice on credit. Now that I have joined GB and I am doing fine in terms of income earnings, everybody cares for me. If I want a mound of rice, those very shop-keepers will possible [*sic*] send it to my house without asking for a penny. What a change.

Therefore entities such as Grameen are an important source of symbolic social status and recognition (Rahman, 2002b, p. 72) and reduce feelings of social exclusion (Habib and Jubb, 2010).

Chowdhury, Ghosh and Wright (2005) studied the impact of microfinance programmes on both subjective and objective poverty in Bangladesh. The study took place in 1999 among the clients of three major Bangladeshi microfinance institutions, namely Grameen, BRAC and ASA, and found that microcredit borrowing is associated with lower poverty. It is not clear whether this was a direct effect of the symbolic and social capital effects of the increased social standing or the benefits of economic productivity arising from the microfinance loan. Chowdhury et al. (2005) also argued that short-run impacts of microfinance loans were limited and long-term arrangements of at least six years were required to have a real benefit. The danger of short-term arrangements is that when the money is spent people fall back into poverty.

Alamgir (2000) studied the 20 partner microfinance institutions of the Palli Karma Sahayak Foundation (PKSF) (Rural Employment Support Foundation) in Bangladesh. That study found that most (97.51 per cent) borrowers had an improvement in their overall quality of life, with membership in microfinance programmes bringing improvements in family income and expenditure, quantity of food, housing condition, child education, sanitation, and social awareness.

Existing studies suggest that microfinance programmes have the capacity to address socio-economic and developmental problems in the lower strata of the population (Mustafa et al., 1996; Khandker, 1998; Pitt and Khandker, 1998; Rutherford, 1998; Rahman, 1999; Mosley, 2001; Wright and Dondo, 2003). Rahman (2002a, p. 236) found a significantly lower incidence of diseases among Grameen members' children aged under nine years compared to children of non-Grameen Bank members.

Habib, Hartel and As-saber (2006) found that the Grameen approach to microfinance with a commitment to credit, training and broad-base social development has the broadest impact on the income, housing and children's education of the poor because of the broad range of social, health and business skills training it provides. However, institutions which lack delivery of the social provision and skills training have a more limited impact. The question of the nature and extent of training and social services provided is one of an important distinction between different types of microfinance provision and may be a significant factor in explaining the tension between microfinance as a form of poverty reduction and development and microfinance as an example of exploitation of the poor. Even Yunus has started to express concerns about businesses and big commercial banks that see money-making opportunities in cultivating low income borrowers. The danger is that these businesses will become too focused on the bottom line and forget the customer (Wilhelm, 2009).

While several authors and institutions extol the virtues of microfinance and its positive impact on community and individual welfare, some have raised concerns about microfinance generally and the operation of some microfinance institutions specifically. Issues such as the impact of microfinance on the very poor and especially women, the wear and tear of social trust among individuals and communities as a result of negative loan experiences, and the impacts of particular loan institutions, especially the for-profit lenders, have been debated widely.

A major issue of debate is the extent to which microfinance benefits the very poor. A cross-country study (Hulme and Mosley, 1996) revealed that microfinance loans increase income for the 'upper poor' or 'entrepreneurial poor' and non-poor participants (who are above the national poverty line). However, they found that 50 per cent of the 'poorest' or 'core poor' could not participate, while these of the 'poorest' who did participate experienced only a small and short-lived increase in income. Wright (2000) argued that Bangladesh is the only place where microfinance is considered a mature market (CDF, 2004), and elsewhere most microfinance institutions are not reaching the 'poorest of the poor'. This can be attributed to an overemphasis by microfinance institutions on credit delivery with limited consideration of the needs of the poorest (Wright and Dondo, 2003; Datta, 2004).

While participants in microfinance generally report an increase in their income, some report falls (McNelly and Dunford, 1998, 1999; Capestake, Bhalotra and Johnson, 2001; Mosley, 2001). By participating in microfinance programmes, poor households can become poorer as they fall into additional debt (Chowdhury et al., 2005). It can be argued that, for them, opportunities for productive use of loans are often limited, the requirement for weekly meetings too time consuming, and the risk of taking loans repayable on a weekly basis unacceptably high (Rutherford, 1998; Wright, 2000). It is also evident that the poorest of the poor lack the educational and social capital required for business success and are very vulnerable to a change in personal or environmental conditions (Jacobs and Kemp, 2002). Generally microfinance borrowers work in low-return activities in a saturated market and are vulnerable to various environmental (for example, flood, drought and crop failure) and socio-economic (for example, sickness, bad business ventures, unfavourable market situations, theft and violence) shocks

(Hulme, 2003), often beyond their control, causing some borrowers to encounter great difficulty in repaying their loans on time.

The operation and approach of different microfinance institutions are also the subject of debate and criticism. Grameen is the 'gold standard' approach, combining a broad programme of social development with education and microfinance loans at reasonable rates. However, not all other institutions include similar social development or educational projects, and the effective interest on loans can be as high as 50 per cent (Morduch, 1999; Ulvila and Hossain, 2002; Chowdhury et al., 2005). Yunus observed that if an institution is charging above 15 per cent on a loan it has perverted microcredit's charitable intentions and is now no longer a microcredit provider but a loan shark (Wilhelm, 2009). Thus for-profit institutions risk exploiting the very people they are claiming to help. However, non-profit institutions supported by charity and international aid funders are also criticized for becoming too focused on the needs of the donors and being distant from the needs and expectations of beneficiaries (Shobhan, 1982; Task Force, 1991, p. 379). Based on their study of a Zambian microfinance institution, Dixon, Ritchie and Siwale (2006) argue that microfinance institutions find it difficult to accommodate multiple stakeholders and that the demands for top-down vertical accountability and good governance, as articulated by official aid and development agencies, can stifle more horizontal or relational forms of accountability, thereby undermining core organizational values.

That many microfinance institutions lend primarily to women raises particular issues, as the cultural context of many developing countries (particularly in the poorest areas) has tended to be less supportive of female involvement in commercial activity. Goetz and Gupta (1996) illustrate that, in 63 per cent of the cases they studied, women reported 'partial', 'very limited' or 'no involvement' in production processes. Yet borrowers (women) are liable for making the repayments, which could potentially position them in a problematic and vulnerable situation. There are reports that pressure for repayments from microfinance institution credit officers can result in increasing physical and verbal abuse in the household (Rahman, 1999). Montgomery (1996) also claimed that members with payment difficulties can be subject to abuse and threats from credit officers and having their possessions (for example, pots and pans, and roofing iron) seized. Dixon et al. (2007, p. 63) describe the use of police officers to enforce loan repayment, which resulted in the client being imprisoned. While this reflected the use of direct force, the primary objective was to generate embarrassment and shame. Dixon, Ritchie and Siwale (2007, p. 64) also relates how loan officers harassed clients by making regular visits to defaulting families at 4.00 in the morning and again at 7.00 in the evening.

However, while external controls are used occasionally, the most powerful force was the internal pressure from other loan group members, who could become abusive and threatening to group members who were late in their repayments (Montgomery, 1996). The consequence is that, if one group member does not pay, the entire group can be denied future access to credit. Hence the very group lending structure and social capital resources which enable the microcredit loans can be a powerful and damaging force when directed against offending individuals. Hulme (2003) illustrates how far this can go, with claims that female suicides have resulted from problems in repaying loans in Bangladesh.

Concerns have also been raised about the contribution of microfinance to long-term sustainable poverty alleviation (Elahi and Danopoulos, 2004). It is argued that the microfinance short-term objective of poverty alleviation may undermine development financing in rural areas and hence distort rural financial markets (Adams, Graham and Pischke, 1984; Braverman and Guasch, 1989; Meyer and Nagarajan, 2000) and divert attention from the need for investment in social and physical infrastructure (Shaw, 2004).

In addition there are concerns about the financial viability and managerial competence of microfinance institutions. A study conducted by UNDP (1988) revealed that NGOs advocating microfinance programmes in rural Bangladesh had high cost structures and institutional limitations, while some NGO managers have been criticized for being inefficient and lacking the required competence (ADB, 1993).

THEORIZING MICROFINANCE

Llewellyn and Walker (2000, p. 447) argued that accounting is an interface activity which allows objects and artefacts to attain value (in use or exchange) across the boundaries of different domains. Llewellyn and Walker's (2000) analysis highlights the importance of the use of calculable technologies by individuals and families and the interface between different realms of existence such as the public and the private (p. 448). Instead of the notion of domains or the binary distinctions between the public and the private realm, Bourdieu (1990) used the term 'field' to describe a network of social relations – structured systems of social positions within which struggles or manoeuvres take place over resources, stakes and access.

Jacobs and Kemp (2002) used the notions of social capital to explain the relative success of micro-entrepreneurs in Bangladesh, drawing on the work of Putnam (1993), Coleman (1990) and Bourdieu (1977a, 1977b). Putnam (1993) defined social capital as 'socially accepted norms of trust or reciprocity' and illustrates it by using the example of a rotating credit association which reflects closely the group lending arrangements found in microfinance. Microfinance institutions carry new forms of visibility and calculability into areas of life, bridging the public and the private domains and rendering the private visible. That other community members are willing to be formal or informal guarantors for a loan and enforce loan repayment significantly reduces risk for financial institutions and provides an alternative to traditional asset-based security. However, Bourdieu (1986) argued that social capital associated with networks and relationships is only one of the resources available to agents and that there is also economic capital (as understood by the economics discipline and which is convertible into money) and cultural capital (embodied in long-lasting dispositions of mind and body, objectified in cultural goods and institutionalized in qualifications and titles). Bourdieu (1977a, 1977b) claimed that social status and social success were based on manipulation and transfer between generations of different forms of capital. In addition dispositions, attitudes and skills (which Bourdieu calls 'habitus') are required to use the capital resources successfully, but the same dispositions and skills are also the embodiment of social divisions and therefore the social and the cognitive are linked (Everett, 2002, p. 58).

Because Bourdieu seeks to transcend the distinction between structure and agency, the notion of field is closely aligned to the notion of habitus. In that sense what is real is not institution or structure but relationship, and thus relationships are mediated by the habitus of the respective participants. Therefore a field is where those relationships can be 'played out', respective capitals exploited, and the rules followed or rewritten to benefit one person or another. Thus particular kinds of capital might be valued more in one field than another. Further, a field reflects the subjective habitus of the participants, who incorporate into their habitus the necessary knowledge to maintain the field in order to maintain or improve their social status. In effect, legitimacy is generated by acting according to the implicit habitus embodied in a particular field.

This theoretical approach goes some way to accommodate the position of both advocates and detractors of microfinance. First the world of banking and the household or the village community can be seen as separate fields. In the former there is a relatively plentiful supply of financial capital, as all the key players in the field will have access to financial capital as a condition of their entry. The traditional requirement to demonstrate a strong asset base in order to receive a loan is evidence of this. The arrival of microfinance institutions means that financial capital is made available in the field of the village community, where there has previously been little access to credit and this form of capital has been in short supply. The control over access to financial capital places the microfinance institutions in a powerful position, with potential to perpetrate both harm and good.

Individual community members can gather status from being associated with a microfinance situation. The social networks associated with the microfinance loan can significantly enhance the social standing of an individual within his or her community and thence others' willingness to engage and to lend them further financial or physical resources. However, it is apparent that microfinance institutions play out their own status game with funders and shareholders. This is particularly problematic where microfinance institutions have a for-profit focus, because their powerful position in poor villages and communities makes them able to exploit the poor, who have relatively little recourse.

Bourdieu's notion of habitus, field and capital also explains why the impact and benefit of microfinance loans can be variable. While microfinance loans represent the possibility of access to financial capital, not everybody is equally equipped to use it. For those with the appropriate training and family background (habitus) and access to business or commercial networks, this access provides an important opportunity for economic enhancement. However, in contrast, those who lack the skills and dispositions to utilize the loan effectively are unlikely to benefit either economically or socially from the microfinance process. Business start-up research shows that entrepreneurs with access to appropriate business and social skills are more likely to succeed than those who have access just to financing (Bates, 1990; Baron and Markman, 2000; Musyoki, 2010). Therefore microfinance clients from families with a history of a particular business or with access to effective training and support from the microfinance lender are more likely to be successful. In addition, community and family networks (social capital) relevant to the particular enterprise undertaken are likely to be beneficial.

CASE STUDIES IN MICROFINANCE

This section describes six case studies purposively selected from original fieldwork based in Kenya and part of a wider project (Musyoki, 2010). Interviews were audio-recorded

and later transcribed. All names have been changed because of confidentiality requirements. The three case studies involving microfinance clients demonstrate how micro
and small enterprise owner-managers' disposition (habitus) and access to various forms
of capital, that is, social and economic, influence the chance of success in business. In
addition, the three microfinance lenders' case studies reflect variations in microfinance
operations consistent with changing microfinance institutional aims.

Microfinance Clients

Matata the fish trader

Matata is a single mother of two. She is now in her mid-forties and all she has known in
her life so far is struggle. Matata lives in the lakeside city of Kisumu in Kenya where she
grew up. Like most women living in Kisumu, Matata became interested in the fish trade.
Equipped with basic literacy skills from high-school-level education and a donation of
KES 20000 (AUD 400) from her uncle, Matata was ready to trade in fish. Initially she
had to rely on the good will of close acquaintances in the fish business to find her way
round in getting fish supplies. She reiterates that this was a good indicator of what lay
ahead. Although she has now managed fully to penetrate the supply chain, she reckons
this is still a major challenge in the fish business.

By 2000, 16 years after starting her business, Matata was in a position to sell an
average of at least 10 tonnes of fish per week, an operation mode she had established
for several years. Later that year Matata received some unexpected visitors: credit sales
executives from the local branch of a microfinance bank. They convinced Matata to
open an account with their bank, and six months later Matata secured her first loan of
KES 50000 (AUD 1000) at an interest rate of 0.5 per cent per week (which is equivalent
to 26 per cent per annum).

Matata invested three-quarters of her first loan to set up a small restaurant and the
remaining quarter to pay school fees for her children. To Matata, the restaurant was a
good opportunity to expand and add value to her business by offering fish-based dishes
to the city's working class. Matata managed to repay the loan fully within six months,
after which she applied for a second loan of KES 100000 (AUD 2000). As at the end
of 2008, Matata had borrowed more than 10 times from the same bank under similar
terms. However, Matata was getting a little worried because, although she could repay
the loans, her businesses were not doing so well. The restaurant was in rent arrears and
she had difficulty paying her three employees regularly. As for the fish trade, the daily
volume of supplies was declining because she did not have enough working capital.

Matata is determined to fight on, because the businesses are the only source of livelihood for her and her two children. She however regrets having got herself into a debt
cycle. Matata says: 'I was poor when they came, but now I am not only poor but also in
debt!'

Matata's relationship with the microfinance industry is at best ambiguous. Her business was established through the application of her educational skills, social networks
and family finances. The collective good will or social capital of the community was
essential in the establishment and success of her fish trading, and despite being a single
mother she had built her business skills and developed an effective business. The microfinance institution was visible in the form of the loan officer, who provided capital

and encouraged Matata substantially to extend her business enterprises. However, the microfinance loan provided was not clearly targeted, since only three-quarters of the money was used in the business while the other quarter was used in personal expenses. In addition there was no evidence of support or training or even the requirement for an effective business plan reflecting how the loan would be used. Matata did repay the loans, but rather than facilitating rapid development and poverty reduction it locked her into a cycle of debt and servicing the significant interest burden of the microfinance lender. In some ways her situation is similar to the relationship with the money lenders and loan sharks which existed prior to the arrival of the microfinance institutions.

Through processes of accounting, Matata's family and life have become visible and governable. From an economic development and growth perspective this would be presented as a success story. This previously insignificant single mother was converted into a significant business person but more importantly into a significant and ongoing source of profit for the microfinance lender, who was receiving 26 per cent interest. The benefit to Matata was more ambiguous. It is also evident that Matata was not the poorest of the poor, as she had some access to financial resources and networks in the fish trade and skills (habitus) and she had access to the social capital network (contacts) in the industry.

Mama Bidii the shopkeeper

In 2000, in a Kenyan town called Chongoria lived a 'Mama', who was running a small grocery shop. This Mama was a member of a local women's group. Through her group she was able to access modest business training from Ukweli, a local microfinance organization. Having been an active member of her group, Mama was enlisted to apply for her first loan of KES 15000 (AUD 300). She used the money to boost the business and she fully repaid the loan within just six months. Mama then applied for a second loan of KES 30000 (AUD 600). She again contributed it to the shop and again paid it back in six months, and then borrowed KES 45000 (AUD 900) and again repaid it within six months. Then she decided to take KES 75000 (AUD 1500) to diversify her business by opening a small butchery next to the shop. She also fully repaid the KES 75000 within six months.

Then Mama decided to go for a bigger loan of KES 120000 (AUD 2400), with which she bought a dairy cow and started also planting vegetables on a commercial basis. Then from KES 120000, she went for KES 150000 (AUD 3000) and diversified further and opened a hotel! These three businesses were running concurrently, as well as the farming one. Then from KES 150000 she took KES 250000, then KES 450000 (AUD 9000), KES 600000 (AUD 12000), and KES 900000 (AUD 18000), and managed to repay each of these loans[2] within nine months.

At this point Mama Bidii could buy more dairy cows, and she expanded the operation of her butchery, supplying meat to the neighbouring schools. As at the beginning of 2009 Mama had 10 dairy cows, was still running the shop, a hotel, and the butchery, and was doing horticultural farming! She had repaid the last instalment of the loan of KES 900000, and was asking for KES 1 million (AUD 20000) in order to buy a lorry to engage in the livestock trade on a wholesale basis. Given her impressive track record, Ukweli has used Mama Bidii to train other women in business.

Mama Bidii has created a business empire employing 22 people within 10 years, including some of her group members. For example, at the hotel there are 10 employees, at the shop she employs one person, at the butchery she employs five people, and then at home she has six people working on the farm. In every sense her story is a success. The microfinance credit provided the opportunity for Mama Bidii to develop her business, and all the money borrowed was spent on the expansion of the business. Many people in the community have benefited and been lifted from poverty because of this process.

The accounting process made Mama Bidii visible and subject to financial calculation by bridging between the field of the household and the field of the commercial. Mama Bidii was both active and keen to access financial capital through a succession of loans from Ukweli and used these loans almost entirely to build her business. There was a significant interest rate (19 per cent), but the small size of the initial loans (and associated repayments) gave Mama Bidii the opportunity to develop her business habitus and social capital networks before more substantial loans with more onerous repayment burdens were allowed. Her business skills are clear from the growth of her activities and that she is now used to train others. However, Mama Bidii was not the poorest of the poor. She was a significant local person who was well respected in the community and had considerable business experience and networks from running her shop. Ukweli, the local microfinance lender, provided her business training as the first stage, which enhanced her skills and abilities.

Ujuzi the furniture maker

In 2002, Ujuzi heard about a microfinance organization (Lengo) that had set up offices in his home town of Machakos in the eastern part of Kenya. Ujuzi had been running a furniture business for five years. Before starting his business Ujuzi was a grade three carpenter who was laid off from T-Joint Limited (a furniture company) in Nairobi, where he had worked for close to 10 years. He had not been able to access the money (financial capital) he needed to buy machines and tools to move his business to a 'take-off' stage, a dream he had always cherished. Determined to succeed, Ujuzi formed a group with his close business friends with the aim of benefiting from the financial services of Lengo. After six months of training on group dynamics and business proposal writing, the group was challenged to nominate one of its members to apply for their first loan. Ujuzi was nominated, and he still remembers that day vividly. He states: 'It was all joy for me, having struggled to raise money to expand my business for many years; it could not have come sooner!'

Ujuzi's first loan was only KES 50 000 (AUD 1000), for which he paid an interest rate of 1.75 per cent per month (equivalent to 21 per cent per annum). Ujuzi has since successfully accessed and repaid five other loans, taking nearly double the previous loan amount every time. Besides the money, Ujuzi also decided to improve his management skills by enlisting the services of a small business advisory agency (Biashara Masomo) recommended to him by his financier, Lengo. Through Biashara Masomo, Ujuzi has received one-on-one training on basic accounting, marketing and management with special reference to his business. Ujuzi recalls that, before seeking help from Lengo and Biashara Masomo, 'My business was in a deplorable condition and I could not meet the daily household needs of my family of six members – just me, my wife and four children. In addition to lacking basic tools and machinery, my business did not have decent premises where I could store and display products. Moreover because of a lack of working capital, I relied on asking customers to make deposits (when placing orders) to buy the necessary materials.'

By the end of 2008, seven years later, Ujuzi boasts of having transformed his business into a medium-sized furniture factory. He has expanded his product lines. Whereas previously he relied on household (home) sofa sales, he now offers dining sets, beds, desks, wall units, wardrobes, various types of chairs, and just about any furniture made from wood. Ujuzi has acquired a sizeable yard, which houses a workshop of more than 30 carpenters, a storage warehouse, and a front display shop which can hold close to 50 units. Ujuzi feels his future looks brighter; he says: 'My kids now go to school without much struggle. My business is growing and I can now serve markets far beyond my home town. I am building a house for my family. What more could I want in life?'

Ujuzi's case shows how access to accounting skills and to financial capital laid the foundation of the effective growth and development of his business. It was clear that he already had some business skills and a well-established business, but the lack of access to financing was a significant constraint on the development of his business. As a consequence he was willing to invest the time and resources in developing the social network associated with the microfinance loans. Ujuzi provides a virtually 'textbook' case for business development built on an existing business base combined with a steadily increasing series of loans over an eight-year period that allowed him to develop the networks, expertise and experience to manage the larger loans and the substantial interest expense (21 per cent) successfully. It is interesting to note that while the loans were not used for personal and family-related expenses it was the direct benefit to the family, their housing and their education which Ujuzi highlights as the real benefits of the microfinance loans. However, it is also clear that Ujuzi was not among the poorest, as he had access to resources, expertise and networks.

Microfinance Institutions

The microfinance institutions as lenders are the counterpart to any account of individual borrowers. Existing literature suggests that these organizations are not the same, but differ in their approach, interest rate and attitudes.

Maendeleo was an initiative of 50 street families in Nairobi, Kenya and was registered as a charitable trust in 1999. The mission of Maendeleo is to assist its clients to get out of poverty, and it is focused on building a better life for families. At the core of this mission is a belief that any family, however poor, is capable of this. Maendeleo argues that this transformation can take hold if people are willing to utilize their skills, and are determined enough to commit themselves to hard work. Maendeleo has currently more than 200 000 member clients, most of whom are street beggars, ex-street beggars, and destitute families from both the urban and the rural communities. Wanza the operations manager said: 'Nobody is too poor to become a member of Maendeleo.'

Unlike other microfinance institutions in Kenya, Maendeleo offers a savings facility and loans to poor street mothers and the less fortunate. Maendeleo also offers housing, and life and health insurance services. Besides financial services, Maendeleo microfinance trains its clients on how to run a business successfully. In addition Maendeleo clients get access to mentorship and counselling that encourage them to lead a productive, self-reliant life. It funds its operations with financial support from member savings and donor funding. Maendeleo is fully owned by its members, and therefore the issue of a gap between the profit expectations of investors and the needs of the clients does not arise. However, the provision of these services does increase costs, which together with increasing lack of access to affordable long-term finance either from government or from donor agencies means that Maendeleo is forced to charge high interest rates for its loans, which may impede long-run objectives of poverty reduction and development.

Maendeleo connected with several different areas which have the potential to alter the lives of members. First and most obviously it provides access to financial capital to its members. However, this functions through a process of social networks which build the social capital resources available to members. Access to financial capital and development of social capital are combined with extensive training in business practices, which equips members with the habitus skills to start and run businesses. However, because of the secretiveness and fluidity of the lives of the target group, informal and face-to-face approaches are taken rather than traditional formal accounting controls to gain people's trust. Thus people who would never otherwise be part of the economic system are made visible and calculable.

Kenda-Kumi microfinance had its origin in a 1983 USAID study. Today Kenda-Kumi, the financial services arm of the Kenda-Kumi Group, is registered as Kenda-Kumi Bank, whose credit terms of around 18 per cent per annum compare favourably with those of other microfinance institutions. Its management insists that the aim is not profit maximization but financial sustainability through the provision of deposit (savings) and loan facilities to its clients. The bank uses social security (peer group member guarantors) as alternative collateral, besides chattels for the low-income borrowers who form the bulk of its clientele; however, it is not involved in training or social development activities.

Given the nature of Kenda-Kumi activities it continues to receive considerable financial and institutional support from international donor agencies, for example the Danish International Development Agency (DANIDA), Plan International, and the Department for International Development (DfID). Kenda-Kumi illustrates that microfinance institutions must balance competing interests and demands. They must be economically viable to receive grants and funding from international development agencies so they can lend money to the poor at a lower interest rate, but to become economically viable they had to abandon the training and social development activities which contribute to their development and poverty reduction goals.

Mavuno transformed from a microfinance institution to a bank in 1984, and at the end of 2008 it controlled more than half of all bank accounts in Kenya. While its reputation is as the largest microfinance institution in Africa, it now functions as a 'financial supermarket' which combines banking, insurance and stock brokerage. In effect it goes where money can be made.

For the millions of Mavuno's clients, before they can access credit they need to have operated a business account (with the Bank) for a minimum of six months. Loan approvals are determined strictly by how active one's account is. The average loan amount offered by Mavuno is KES 40000 (AUD 800), with an interest rate of 18 per cent per annum on a reducing balance. The loan term is strictly one year with mostly weekly repayments.

Since its establishment the Bank has won several awards. In June 2009 it won the Emerging Markets Most Sustainable Bank of the Year in Africa and the Middle East. Later that year, Mavuno received the African Business of the Year award from the Commonwealth Business Council and was voted the best microfinance bank in Africa by the Africa Banking Awards group. However, it now functions as a commercial enterprise, with little explicit development agenda, and it targets the marginally poor and 'wealthy' who are economically active.

While some microfinance institutions such as Maendeleo have a clear link to the community and community development and poverty reduction, it is evident that others like Mavuno no longer have a development or poverty reduction focus but instead function like other profit-focused banks and financial institutions. Both of these entities have the effect of bridging the field of banking and finance with the field of the domestic and private life. However, the objective and focus of this process of bridging are different between Maendeleo and Mavuno. Maendeleo aims to shift financial capital into the domain of the poor to facilitate development and poverty reduction, while Mavuno aims to render the realm of the poor to a new field of profitability and exploitation. Within both examples the accounting systems make the borrower visible. However, the purpose and impact of that visibility differ. In effect the role of accounting in the microfinance processes is divergent and contingent.

ACCOUNTING PROCESSES AND MICROCREDIT

Llewellyn and Walker (2000) highlight the role of accounting as an interface activity, which allows objects and artefacts to attain value across the boundary of the private and the public domain. Therefore, in the language of this chapter, accounting can provide an interface between the field of the household and the field of finance and business. However, in the three cases presented this was not an interface activity. The microfinance institutions bypassed the expected processes of formal financial control and accounting-based monitoring and transferred the monitoring and control activities into the private domain of the borrowers. This is sometimes explained in terms of social capital, whereby existing networks and relationships are used to monitor and control behaviour and therefore to ensure that loans are repaid on time. Although programmes vary, generally low income people, whether in business or not, are encouraged voluntarily to form groups of between five and eight members before they borrow funds. When forming groups, emphasis is put on leveraging existing social ties. In particular, prospective microcredit borrowers are advised to form groups either with other people they have worked with previously or with neighbours where possible.

Once a group is in place, members proceed to formalize it. Initially members must nominate a chair person to lead discussions during group meetings, a secretary to take notes and a treasurer, as a minimum. The group then becomes official, in some cases by registering with the relevant government ministry (for example, in the case of Kenya) or simply by filling in formal registration documentation from the respective microfinance institution. Either way, a newly formed group generally drafts a constitution, assisted by staff from the microfinance institution, stipulating its objectives, rights and responsibilities to members. The group then opens an account (under its name) with the microfinance institution and commences compulsory weekly savings, commonly referred to as shares, which continue indefinitely. At this stage each group member has to furnish the microfinance institution with some form of official identification to help account for individual savings over time. This establishes these individuals as calculable entities in the microfinance institution's accounting system. Official member identification documents also are used to control fraud. Because identity is clearly established, a visibility is created, and the implication is that the police may be involved if necessary. Rendering borrowers visible in the accounting system also renders them controllable. The process provides an accounting identity to individuals who might otherwise escape such accounting. Rather than the creation of the governable self, it is an example of the creation of governable space. Individuals must account to each other for their financial activities in a manner similar to the processes of confession and examination observed in the Iona Community (Jacobs and Walker, 2004). In order to function within the microfinance context members must form a family-like setting.

The next step in preparing new group members involves training. Regardless of whether the members are in business or not, normally initial training focuses on managing group cohesion. These training sessions, which often last for up to six weeks, are facilitated by staff from the microfinance institution. The training is mostly interactive, and members use it to familiarize themselves with the mission of the microfinance institution and with their collective and individual roles in the microcredit delivery process. Where members of a new group are not in business, their initial training is tailored towards business idea generation, name registration, and basic ground rules on managing government regulations. Then for this category of microfinance clients, training may relate to cottage industry skills, taking into account existing talents, skills and individual member resources. However, for members with operational businesses, the focus of training is mostly basic bookkeeping, that is, maintaining a sales ledger and a cash register and other generic business development services.

After the six weeks of training, the next step is preparation for a loan application. Although practice varies across institutions, this normally entails mobilizing members' savings for a minimum of six months. The savings serve as collateral against borrowed funds, and normally members are not permitted to withdraw these funds. Although the amount saved is modest, given that group members are permitted only to borrow in turn, collective group savings are likely to provide substantial loan security. In addition, loan applicants are required to prepare a basic business plan. Whether for an entire group or an individual member's business, it provides documentation of the basis for how the loan will be used to generate funds. Upon submission, the business plans are evaluated by designated credit officers, and the member with the best plan is the first to apply for a loan, all other things considered, for example transaction history and value of pledged collateral. These individuals can now be measured, quantified, analysed and disciplined.

Once a loan application has been approved, a designated account tagged to the borrower's savings is created and credited. The field officer then notifies the group chair and respective member about the 'good news'. For the member, though, the hard work of repayment begins immediately in the following week. Like savings, microfinance loans are payable in weekly instalments. All weekly collections (savings and loan repayments) are submitted to the microfinance institution either through an appointed field officer or by the nominated group treasurer. The emergence of both internet and mobile phone banking has greatly eased the time burden on poor microfinance clients. Using modern technology, clients can now make their 'remittances' direct to their microfinance account without having to meet credit officers regularly or visit branch offices.

To minimize the risk of default and to ensure group members continue to secure credit through the schemes, members are expected to meet at least once a week and minute their deliberations. It is in these meetings that members record attendance, compare notes, and ensure the accuracy of the records of member contributions and loan repayments. In a sense, the microfinance institution enlists its members to conduct its accounting processes.

If a member confides with his or her peers about possible financial distress, a resolution can be passed to bail that person out. In the unlikely event that this does not happen, the chair must immediately notify the respective microfinance field officer about the development. Where a default is reported, the microfinance institution holds group members collectively responsible for the full amount owing. Nevertheless, all affected members are expected to recover their money by taking assets (such as household goods) belonging to the member in default. Assets can be taken by microfinance institutions where a defaulting borrower is not affiliated with a group.

CONCLUDING REMARKS

While the processes and structures of empowerment and exploitation are far from clear, the consequences are fairly obvious. The interest rates charged by some local and many international microfinance institutions are excessive and exploitative. In these cases the term 'microfinance' and the development rhetoric just legitimate this exploitation (see, for example, *Economist*, 2009). The tragedy is that many well-meaning aid and development agencies are supporting and funding these exploitative institutions. However, the story as a whole is more complex. Some microfinance institutions have worked hard to maintain their values and sustain the focus on development and poverty reduction. To achieve this they have invested in extensive training and community development. However, this commitment to training and social development is costly and likely to push up the interest rates charged. Because these institutions focus on development and poverty reduction, the institutions are not profitable and therefore are not deemed to be economically sustainable. There is evidence that international aid and development agencies are more reluctant to provide funds and support, which also increases the interest rates. As a consequence organizations with the strongest commitment to development and poverty reduction can end up charging high interest rates which disadvantage the very poor they seek to help.

In contrast, some microfinance institutions that have embraced the notion of economic sustainability have increased their emphasis on profitability. Consequently they have been diverted from the objectives and business practices embodied in their mission as microfinance institutions. They have reduced the emphasis on training and developmental activities and focused more strongly on the provision of microcredit loans. This has reduced their overhead costs, made them more appealing to external funders and aid agencies and therefore increased access to loan funds. In some cases the microfinance institutions have shifted away from the no-collateral approach which has barred the very poor from receiving loans. Hence many have already shifted from a focus on the very poor to those considered to be economically active and who have more education and access to financial or personal social capital.

From an accounting perspective, accounting makes aspects of life previously not subject to economic and financial control visible and controllable. Access to financial capital is a source of power (Bourdieu, 1986). However, financial capital needs to be combined with business networks (social capital) and accounting or business skills (habitus) to be successful.

While individuals are constructed as calculable and visible, it is evident that much of the accounting and control is privatized to the microfinance borrowing groups. These groups monitor and control each other, because they often share liability for loan repayment. Formal at-a-distance accounting shifts to mutual face-to-face accounting. While this can be empowering and supportive in some settings, there is potential for exploitation and abuse. This case does illustrate the danger that noble objectives of development and empowerment can be subverted by demands for profitability and economic sustainability, sometimes driven by the very international bodies which have the term 'development' in their name.

NOTES

1. The Nobel Peace Prize in 2006 was jointly won by the Grameen Bank and Yunus.
2. All the loans were obtained from Ukweli microfinance and were charged at a base interest rate of 1.25 per cent per month plus an additional 4 per cent per annum for administration fees. This translates to an effective annual interest rate of 19 per cent.

REFERENCES

Adams, D.W., D. Graham and V. Pischke (eds) (1984). *Undermining Rural Development with Cheap Credit.* Boulder, CO: Westview Press.

ADB (1993). *An Assessment of the Role and Impact of NGOs in Bangladesh.* Manila: Asian Development Bank.

ADB (2000a). *Finance for the Poor: Microfinance Development Strategy.* Manila: Asian Development Bank.

ADB (2000b). *The Role of Central Bank in Microfinance in Asia and the Pacific*, vol. 1. Manila: Asian Development Bank.

Alamgir, D. (1997). *Achieving Financial Viability by a Large Microfinance Institution (MFI): The Association for Social Advancement (ASA) in Bangladesh*, Case Study Series 1. Dhaka: Credit and Development Forum (CDF).

Alamgir, D. (2000). Financing the microcredit programs of non-governmental organizations (NGOs): a case study. *Journal of Developmental Entrepreneurship*, 5(2), pp. 157–68.

Baron, R., and G. Markman (2000). Beyond social capital: how social skills can enhance entrepreneurs' success. *Academy of Management Executive*, 14(1), pp. 106–15.

Bates, C. (1990). Entrepreneur human capital inputs and small business longevity. *Review of Economics and Statistics*, 72(4), pp. 551–9.

Bertaux, N., and E. Crable (2007). Learning about women, economic development, entrepreneurship and the environment in India: a case study. *Journal of Developmental Entrepreneurship*, 12(4), pp. 467–79.

Bourdieu, P. (1977a). Cultural reproduction and social reproduction. In *Power and Ideology in Education*, ed. J. Karabel and A.H. Halsey, pp. 487–511. New York: Oxford University Press.

Bourdieu, P. (1977b). *Outline of a Theory of Practice*, trans. R. Nice. Cambridge: Cambridge University Press.

Bourdieu, P. (1986). The forms of capital. In *Handbook of Theory of Research for the Sociology of Education*, ed. J. Richardson, trans. R. Nice, pp. 241–58. New York: Greenwood Press.

Bourdieu, P. (1990). *The Logic of Practice*, trans. R. Nice. Cambridge: Polity.

Braverman, A., and J. Guasch (1989). Rural credit in LDCs: issues and evidences. *Journal of Economic Development*, 14, pp. 7–34.

Capestake, J., S. Bhalotra and S. Johnson (2001). Assessing the impact of microcredit: a Zambian case study. *Journal of Development Studies*, 37(4), pp. 81–100.

CDF (2004). *Microfinance Statistics*, vol. 17. Dhaka: Credit and Development Forum.

Choudhury, N. (1988). The seeking of accounting where it is not: towards a theory of non-accounting in organizational settings. *Accounting Organizations and Society*, 13(6), pp. 549–57.

Chowdhury, J., D. Ghosh and R. Wright (2005). The impact of micro-credit on poverty: evidence from Bangladesh. *Progress in Development Studies*, 5(4), pp. 298–309.

Coleman, B. (2006). Microfinance in Northeast Thailand: who benefits and how much? *World Development*, 34(9), pp. 1612–38.

Coleman, J. (1990). *Foundations of Social Theory*. Cambridge, MA: Harvard University Press.

Datta, D. (2004). Microcredit in rural Bangladesh: is it reaching the poorest? *Journal of Microfinance*, 6(1), pp. 55–81.

Del Conte, A. (2000). *Roundtable in Micro-Insurance Services in the Informal Economy: The Role of Microfinance Institutions*. New York: UNCDF.

Dixon, R., J. Ritchie and J. Siwale (2006). Microfinance: accountability from the grassroots. *Accounting, Auditing and Accountability Journal*, 19(3), pp. 405–27.

Dixon, R., J. Ritchie and J. Siwale (2007). Loan officers and loan 'delinquency' in microfinance: a Zambian case. *Accounting Forum*, 31(1), pp. 47–71.

Economist (2009). A partial marvel: microcredit may not work wonders but it does help the entrepreneurial poor. *Economist*, 18 July 2009.

Elahi, K., and C. Danopoulos (2004). Microfinance and third world development: a critical analysis. *Journal of Political and Military Sociology*, 32(1), pp. 61–77.

Everett, J. (2002). Organizational research and the praxeology of Pierre Bourdieu. *Organizational Research Methods*, 15(1), pp. 56–80.

Gallhofer, S., and J. Broadbent (1997). Enabling accounting: the way forward (editorial). *Accounting, Auditing and Accountability Journal*, 10(3), pp. 265–75.

Ghate, P., A. Gupta, M. Lamberte, N. Poapongsakor, D. Prabowo, A. Rahman and T. Srinivasan (1992). *Informal Finance: Some Findings from Asia*. New York: Oxford University Press.

Goetz, A., and S. Gupta (1996). Who takes the credit? Gender, power and control over loan use in rural credit programs in Bangladesh. *World Development*, 24(1), pp. 45–63.

Habib, M., C. Hartel and S. As-saber (2006). Social protection and the role of micro finance programs: the case of the Philippines. *Asian Profile*, 34(6), pp. 567–75.

Habib, M., and C. Jubb (2010). Does microfinance fight social exclusion? Working Paper, Swinburne University of Technology.

Hanifan, L. (1996). The rural school community centre. *Annals of the American Academy of Political and Social Science*, 67, pp. 130–8.

Holvoet, N. (2004). Impact of microfinance programs in children's education. *Journal of Microfinance*, 6(2), pp. 27–49.

Hossain, M. (1988). *Credit for the Alleviation of Rural Poverty: The Grameen Bank in Bangladesh*, Research Report 65. Washington, DC: International Food Policy Research Institute.

Hossain, M. (2002). Credit for alleviation of rural poverty: the experience of Grameen Bank in Bangladesh. In *Early Impact of Grameen*, ed. A. Rahman, R. Rahman, M. Hossain and S.M. Hossain. Dhaka: Grameen Trust.

Hulme, D. (2003). Is microdebt good for poor people? A note on the dark side of microfinance. In *Microfinance: Evolution, Achievements and Challenges*, ed. M. Harper. London: ITDG Publishing.

Hulme, D., and P. Mosley (1996). *Finance against Poverty*, vols 1 and 2. London: Routledge.

Jacobs, K., and J. Kemp (2002). Exploring accounting presence and absence: case studies from Bangladesh. *Accounting, Auditing and Accountability Journal*, 15(2), pp. 143–61.

Jacobs, K., and S. Walker (2004). Accounting and accountability in the Iona Community. *Accounting, Auditing and Accountability Journal*, 17(3), pp. 361–81.

Khalily, B. (2004). Quantitative approach to impact analysis of microfinance programmes in Bangladesh: what have we learned? *Journal of International Development*, 16, pp. 331–52.

Khandker, S. (1998). *Fighting Poverty with Microcredit: Experience in Bangladesh*. New York: Oxford University Press.

Llewellyn, S., and S. Walker (2000). Household accounting as an interface activity: the home, the economy and gender. *Critical Perspectives on Accounting*, 11, pp. 447–78.

McNelly, B., and C. Dunford (1998). *Impact of Credit with Education on Mother and Their Young Children's Nutrition: Lower Pra Rural Credit with Education Program in Ghana*. Davis, CA: Freedom from Hunger.

McNelly, B., and C. Dunford (1999). *Impact of Credit with Education on Mother and Their Young Children's Nutrition: CRECER Credit with Education Program in Bolivia*. Davis, CA: Freedom from Hunger.

Mahmud, S. (2001). Participation of micro-credit programme and household social well-being. In *Monitoring and Evaluation of Microfinance Institutions*, ed. S. Zohir, M. Simeen, M. Asaduzzaman, J. Islam and N. Ahmed. Dhaka: PKSF-BIDS.

Meyer, R., and G. Nagarajan (2000). *Rural Financial Markets in Asia: Policies, Paradigms and Performances: A Study of Rural Asia*, vol. 3. New York: Oxford University Press.

Miller, P., and T. O'Leary (1994). Governing the calculable person. In *Accounting as Social and Institutional Practice*, ed. A. Hopwood and P. Miller, Cambridge Studies in Management 24. Cambridge: Cambridge University Press.

Montgomery, R. (1996). Disciplining or protecting the poor: avoiding the social costs of peer pressure in microcredit schemes. *Journal of International Development*, 8(2), pp. 289–305.

Morduch, J. (1999). The microfinance promise. *Journal of Economic Literature*, 37, pp. 1569–1614.

Mosley, P. (2001). Microfinance and poverty in Bolivia. *Journal of Development Studies*, 37(4), pp. 101–32.

Mustafa, S., I. Ara, A. Hossain, A. Kabir, M. Mohsin, A. Yusuf and S. Jahan (1996). *Beacon of Hope: An Impact Assessment Study of BRAC's Rural Development Programme Research and Evaluation Division*. Dhaka: BRAC.

Musyoki, N. (2010). Microfinance and business development service linkages: synergies for micro and small enterprise development in Kenya. Ph.D. thesis, Australian National University, Canberra.

OECD (1995). Self employment programmes for the unemployed, Joint US Department of Labor and OECD International Conference.

Pitt, M., and S. Khandker (1998). The impact of group-based credit program on poor household in Bangladesh: does the gender of participants matter? *Journal of Political Economy*, 106(5), pp. 958–79.

Putnam, R. (1993). *Making Democracy Work: Civic Traditions in Modern Italy*. Princeton, NJ: Princeton University Press.

Rahman, A. (1986). *Impact of Grameen Bank on the Nutritional Status of the Rural Poor*. Dhaka: Bangladesh Institute of Development Studies.

Rahman, A. (1999). Microcredit initiatives for equitable and sustainable development: who pays? *World Development*, 27(1), pp. 67–82.

Rahman, A. (2002a). Impact of Grameen Bank on the nutritional status of the rural poor. In *Early Impact of Grameen*, ed. A. Rahman, R. Rahman, M. Hossain and S. Hossain, p. 233. Dhaka: Grameen Trust.

Rahman, A. (2002b). Impact of Grameen Bank intervention on the rural power structure. In *Early Impact of Grameen*, ed. A. Rahman, R. Rahman, M. Hossain and S. Hossain. Dhaka: Grameen Trust.

Rahman, A., and B. Hasnat (1993). Housing for the rural poor: the Grameen Bank experience. In *The Grameen Bank: Poverty Relief in Bangladesh*, ed. A.N.M. Wahid. Boulder, CO: Westview Press.

Rutherford, S. (1998). The savings of the poor: improving financial services in Bangladesh. *Journal of International Development*, 10(1), pp. 1–15.

Shaw, J. (2004). Microenterprise occupation and poverty reduction in microfinance programs: evidence from Sri Lanka. *World Development*, 32(7), pp. 1247–64.

Shobhan, R. (1982). *The Crises of External Dependence: The Political Economy of Foreign Aid*. Dhaka: University Press.

Task Force (1991). NGO approach to poverty alleviation. In *Report on Bangladesh Development Strategies for the 1990s*, vol. 1: *Policies for Development*. Dhaka: University Press.

Ulvila, M., and F. Hossain (2002). Development NGOs and political participation of the poor in Bangladesh and Nepal. *Voluntas: International Journal of Voluntary and Nonprofit Organizations*, 13(2), pp. 149–63.

UNDP (1988). *Bangladesh Agriculture Sector Review*. Dhaka: UNDP and UNIFEM.

Vogel, R. (1984). The effect of subsidized agricultural credit on income distribution in Costa Rica. In *Undermining Rural Development with Cheap Credit*, ed. D. Adams, D. Graham and V. Pischke, pp. 133–45. Boulder, CO: Westview Press.

Watts, M. (2003). Development and governmentality. *Singapore Journal of Tropical Geography*, 24(1), pp. 6–34.

Wilhelm, I. (2009). Grameen Bank founder says he's 'nervous' about for-profit microcredit. *Chronicle of Philanthropy*, 24 April, http://philanthropy.com, accessed 8 February 2010.

Wright, G. (2000). *Microfinance Systems: Designing Quality Financial Services for the Poor*. Dhaka: University Press.

Wright, G., and A. Dondo (2003). 'Are you poor enough?' Client selection by microfinance institutions. In *Microfinance: Evolution, Achievements and Challenges*, ed. M. Harper. London: ITDG Publishing.

11 Government accounting in the Global South: the design, implementation and use of global solutions for local needs
Andy Wynne and Stewart Lawrence

1. INTRODUCTION

This chapter examines the impact of globalized accounting and economic reforms on the public sectors of the Global South, focusing particularly on the countries in Sub-Saharan Africa. Over the last three decades, people living in these countries have experienced debt crises, civil wars, coups and, on top of all that, externally imposed neoliberal economic reforms. Accounting has been an integral part of those imposed 'reforms'.

International creditor institutions and donor agencies have promoted new public management (NPM) reforms in all developing countries (Ayeni, 2002). The central features of NPM have been said to include: a shift in emphasis from process accountability (input controls and bureaucratic procedures, rules and standards) to accountability for results (quantifiable outcomes, measures and performance targets); and devolution of management control, coupled with the development of improved reporting, monitoring and accountability mechanisms (Awio, Lawrence and Northcott, 2007). The claimed benefits of such reforms include improvements in efficiency, effectiveness and accountability of the public sector. Universally, the reforms were expected to engender greater public service responsiveness and increased choice of providers of services, private as well as public (Olson, Guthrie and Humphrey, 1998). However, we argue that the results indicate that the global reforms have not necessarily met the needs of the local populations who have had to endure them.

After stripping away activities that could be privatized, the remaining core government services were the targets of better financial management. Two of the most frequently recommended tools of public financial management for developing countries are the medium-term expenditure framework (MTEF) and integrated financial management information systems (IFMIS). We examine the design, implementation and use of these global remedies, whose introduction we argue was based on theoretical assumptions as opposed to experience of their effects. We note the growing concern that is being expressed about the effectiveness of such interventions.

We illustrate that the reforms in accounting procedures in central government have been less successful than anticipated. The use of expensive external consultants at the expense of local experts is discussed. We conclude with some lessons for a way forward, suggesting greater reliance be placed on local expertise, which needs to be nourished.

Before solutions can be assessed we have to understand the problem and how it arose. For this reason, this chapter provides some background on the financial plight of the governments in the Global South, and argues that there may be a widespread misconception about the causal nature of their predicaments. Typically it is assumed that the poverty and lack of economic growth in these countries were the result of the poor administration and public financial practices. In our view, the causal direction may have been in the opposite direction. It is argued below that it was economic decline and poverty that caused poor administration and financial management and encouraged corruption. If this was indeed the case, the use of foreign consultants to introduce large-scale 'modern' reforms may have accentuated the problem. This approach may have further undermined the confidence of local managers and so reduced their ability to ensure that the local environment was fully considered. We argue that the reforms needed the full involvement of local public financial managers in the rebuilding of their systems and institutions, ensuring that the reforms had a good fit with associated systems and were fully owned and understood by local officials. The involvement of local officials is particularly important with accounting reforms, where the information produced has to be fully appreciated if it is to be used effectively.

2.   BACKGROUND TO THE LARGE LEVELS OF DEBT

The argument in this section is that the causal relationship runs contrary to the conventional view. Economic problems (originating from external events) led to the deterioration in the quality of governance and public financial management in many African countries. The international financial institutions and bilateral aid agencies used the crises to introduce wide-ranging public sector financial management reforms, for example the MTEF and IFMIS. They also unsuccessfully argued for the adoption of international public sector accounting standards and performance audit.

2.1   The Origins of the Global South's Debt Burden

In the first few years after independence the economies of many African countries grew significantly and so their governments could afford to expand public services dramatically, especially for health and education. With the first major oil price rises in 1973–74, funds were readily available for these countries to borrow for significant public investment programmes.

> Not surprisingly, then, many countries concentrated on Big Projects – showpiece government development projects that could be the motor for economic transformation, such as Ghana's Volta River Project, which involved construction of the Akosombo Dam in the early 1960s to form the world's largest artificial lake and building aluminium smelters to take advantage of the country's bauxite resources. (Situmbeko and Zulu, 2004, p. 16)

The experience of the US and UK in the years following the Second World War had shown that extensive government borrowing could facilitate economic growth. In the US the federal debt alone (excluding state or local government debt) reached over 120 per cent of GDP in 1946 (Office of Management and Budget, 2007) and in the UK government debt peaked at nearly 250 per cent of GDP (Clark and Dilnot, 2002) at around the same time. The sustained economic boom of the 1950s and 1960s meant that these levels of debt were sustainable, could be accommodated and were eventually repaid. In addition, inflation did not reach double figures in the UK until the mid-1970s.

However, most governments of the Global South were not so lucky. In 1979–80 further oil price rises increased the price of their imports. Around the same time, in the late 1970s and early 1980s the United States raised interest rates to nearly 20 per cent in a battle to throttle back its persistent inflation (Stiglitz, 2006). The real (inflation-adjusted) interest rates paid by the Global South increased from −4 per cent in 1975 to almost +4 per cent a decade later (Bond, 2006).

> A strategy for development, based on indebtedness . . . was suddenly transformed into an actual catastrophe by a decision emanating from a fraction of ruling classes within leading capitalist countries, with a total indifference for the hardship imposed on the third world (as well as for the rise of unemployment everywhere). (Duménil and Lévy, 2005)

The rapid increase in world interest rates in the early 1980s on top of the oil price rises led to a world recession. As a result most countries in the Global South faced a reduced demand for their exports whilst having to pay much higher interest rates on their debts. As Christian Aid (2003, p. 22) reported:

> the prices Third World countries receive for many of their traditional exports, from coffee and cocoa to rice, sugar, and cotton, continue to decline. The relative value of their exports has declined even more – for example, in 1975 a new tractor cost the equivalent of 8 metric tons of African coffee, but by 1990 the same tractor cost 40 metric tons.

The United Nations Food and Agriculture Organization (FAO, 2005) estimated that, if commodity prices had maintained the same real value as in 1980, the Global South would be earning an additional $112 billion in annual export revenues, which was double the then level of their aid receipts. Putting it another way, between 1970 and 1997 changes in the terms of trade cost non-oil-producing African states (excluding South Africa) a total of 119 per cent of their annual GDP, according to the World Bank (2000). External debt grew by 106 per cent of GDP over the same period. So all the external debt of African countries at the end of the twentieth century could be explained by falling prices for their exports and increasing prices of imports – both changes over which their governments had little or no control.

As UNCTAD (2004, p. 5) describes the result:

> From just over $11 billion in 1970, Africa had accumulated over $120 billion of external debt in the midst of the external shocks of the early 1980s. Total external debt then worsened significantly during the period of structural adjustment in the 1980s and early 1990s, reaching a peak of about $340 billion in 1995.

In the same report UNCTAD calculates that between 1970 and 2002 Sub-Saharan Africa received $294 billion in loans, and paid back $268 billion in debt service, but was left with debts of some $210 billion (2004, p. 9).

> Africa now repays more than it receives. In 1980, loan inflows of $9.6 billion were comfortably higher than the debt repayment outflow of $3.2 billion . . . by 2000, only $3.2 billion flowed in, and $9.8 billion was repaid, leaving a net financial flows deficit of $6.2 billion . . . By the early 2000s, the debt remained unbearable for at least 21 African countries at more than 300 per cent of export earnings. (Bond, 2006, p. 39)

The solution to the indebtedness envisioned by the World Bank and other international development agencies was the introduction of NPM reforms in all developing countries. The claimed benefits of such reforms included improvements in efficiency, effectiveness and accountability of the public sector.

3.   NEED FOR AND DESIGN OF 'MODERN' FINANCIAL MANAGEMENT SYSTEMS

The high and unsustainable levels of debt in many developing countries were thus due to external economic events beyond the control of their governments. However, whatever its origin, this debt forced governments to approach the IMF and the World Bank for support. The debt burden gave the World Bank and IMF the leverage needed to implement policies of deregulation and privatization through structural adjustment programmes. These almost invariably included the following elements:

- reduced government spending and greater fiscal discipline to control inflation;
- removing import controls and restrictions on capital movements;
- privatization of state enterprises;
- devaluation of the currency;
- making labour more flexible by reducing legal protection, food subsidies and minimum wages.

As Colin Leys described, the dominant view became that:

> Governments were part of the problem, not part of the solution; they were inefficient and often corrupt and hence parasitic, not stimulators of growth. The solution was to privatize the public sector, reduce the scale and scope of government spending and give up all policies, from exchange rate controls to subsidies and redistributive taxation, that altered any prices that would otherwise be set by the impersonal forces of the market. (Leys, 1996, p. 18)

As well as greater fiscal discipline, privatization of previously state-run organizations, in industries such as telecommunications, postal services, shipping, forestry and water supplies, was encouraged.

After stripping away activities that could be privatized, the remaining core government services were the targets of better financial management. Modern tools of public financial management were imported to governments of the Global South. These tools were the MTEF and IFMIS. We will examine the design rationality and claims made for each of these techniques, then their implementation using overseas consultants, and finally their limitations and outcomes.

Although MTEFs differ across countries, broadly defined the MTEF approach is a means for linking policy, planning and budgeting. The time horizon for government budgeting was to be extended from the traditional annual budget to the medium term, usually three years. Simultaneously, budgetary control was to move from agreeing resource inputs to providing the resources necessary for agreed outputs and, ideally, outcomes. An MTEF consists of a 'top-down resource envelope, a bottom-up estimation of the current and medium-term costs of existing policy and, ultimately, the matching of these costs with available resources' (World Bank, 1998, p. 48). The aim of the system was that government ministries would have increased predictability of resource flows over the next few years, and improved accountability and transparency for the level of services they provided in addition to the resources they consumed, and that this would ultimately lead to a more effective and efficient process of resource allocation towards strategic priorities within and between sectors.

The generic objectives of an MTEF are generally considered to be:

- facilitating the achievement of a balanced budget (fiscal discipline);
- enabling the shift of resources to pro-poor areas of the budget in line with agreed poverty reduction strategies.

Another major reform which the World Bank and other donors have heavily promoted across the public sectors of the Global South is the concept of an IFMIS. This is a computerized system designed to support public expenditure management goals and priorities across the whole of government. An IFMIS 'usually refers to computerization of public expenditure management processes, including budget formulation, budget execution, and accounting, with the help of a fully integrated system for financial management of the line ministries and other spending agencies' (Diamond and Khemani, 2005, p. 3).

By tracking financial events through automated financial operations, governments are expected to be able to control expenditure better and improve transparency and accountability in the budget cycle as a whole. While definitions of the key components of an IFMIS vary, proponents argue that this technology provides a set of tools that assist government in undertaking the following tasks:

- designing appropriate fiscal and monetary responses to changing macroeconomic conditions;
- ensuring accountability for the deployment and use of public resources;
- improving the effectiveness and efficiency of public expenditure programmes;
- mobilizing domestic resources and managing external resources (foreign aid and loans);
- managing civil services; and
- decentralizing operations with adequate controls.

The aim of an IFMIS is to integrate all aspects of the government's budgetary cycle and provide suitable interfaces to other systems and entities. Thus an IFMIS may be based on the generic model shown in Figure 11.1.

An integrated treasury system offers several significant benefits in managing public monies more effectively:

- Full integration of budget and budget execution data, thereby allowing greater financial control;
- Improved planning for cash as well as close and timely monitoring of the government's cash position;
- Provision of adequate management reporting at various levels of budget execution;

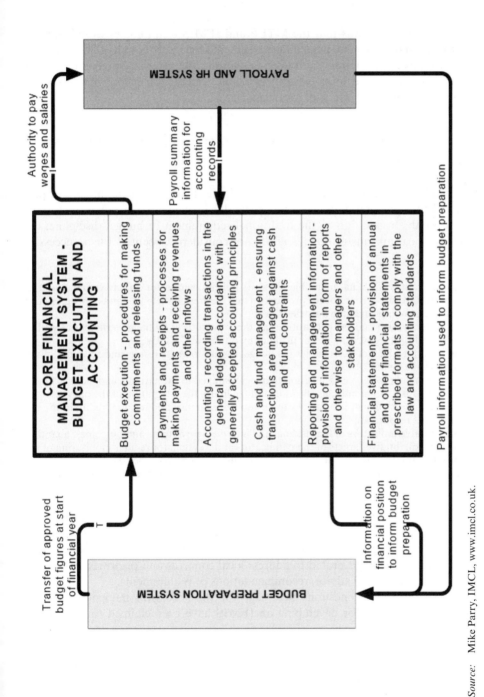

Source: Mike Parry, IMCL, www.imcl.co.uk.

Figure 11.1   Overview of IFMIS component interfaces

- Improvement of data quality for the preparation and execution of the budget; and
- Facilitation of the preparation of financial statements and other financial reports for budgeting, analysis and financial control. (Hashim and Allan, 2001)

The hope of reformers was that the MTEF and IFMIS technologies would support the modernization of public financial management and the introduction of good governance. However, as considered in the following sections, the necessary preconditions for these complex reforms were not necessarily available, and the use of foreign consultants accentuated the problem of a lack of local capacity.

4.   IMPLEMENTATION – AND THE (MISSING) NECESSARY PRECONDITIONS

The successful introduction of these new technologies is dependent upon certain preconditions. These preconditions were not generally in place in the public sectors of the Global South. In addition to the traditional requirement of budget discipline, the following technical and institutional factors are considered essential for a successful MTEF:

- a clear framework of national objectives and policies, and sector objectives and strategies
- realistic medium-term resource projections that ensures predictable flows of programmed resources to implementing agencies
- a comprehensive budget that captures all the expenditures by the government as well as on behalf of the government, for instance by donors and NGOs
- an integrated budget that enables the budget system to relate results and accountabilities to resource inputs
- a budget and program classification that can be linked to the national and sectoral objectives, that is a functional classification and facilitates the integration of the budget
- financial management institutions to ensure transparency and accountability in the use of budget resources
- monitorable indicators of inputs, final and intermediate outputs and outcomes, quantitative and qualitative targets of these indicators and a system for regular monitoring of the progress toward meeting the targets. The monitoring provides the basis to assess results and accountabilities and make adjustments in objectives, targets and budget allocations. (World Bank, 2005, p. 8)

Two questions over the implementation of the MTEF are the extent to which objectives have been formally agreed for the country concerned, and whether these have been agreed by all the major stakeholders. Questions may also be raised about whether these objectives were internally generated to address local concerns and priorities or whether they were based on external advice, recommendations or requirements.

Similarly there are preconditions necessary for the successful implementation of an IFMIS. Preconditions for developing an IFMIS have been claimed to include the following:

● *Authorities' commitment and ownership is clear*

  Clear institutional designation
  Clear authority to implement
  Active involvement, with no undue delegation to suppliers

● *Preconditions are ready for reform*

  Authorities prepared to reengineer work practices
  Environment encourages reform
  Sufficient skills and/or training available
  Users are 'sold' on the system
  Steering group is active and representative

● *Project design is sound*

  Adequate time taken on design phase
  Users fully involved in specification
  Not too ambitious in scope
  Timetable is realistic

● *Management of project is capable*

  Adequate management skills
  Managers motivated to reform
  Full-time implementation team identified
  In-house or outsourced maintenance capacity identified, in place, and properly costed

● *Adequate resources are assured*

  Sufficient funds since actual costs might exceed anticipated cost
  Resource demands caused by operating two parallel systems simultaneously
  Sufficient resources for long-term operation and maintenance of the system

(Diamond and Khemani, 2005)

4.1   Implementation Issues: Consultants and Expertise

Private sector international consultants have been called upon widely to assist with the implementation of IFMIS, MTEF and other major public financial management reforms in the Global South. The nature of these reforms means that knowledge and experience are not available locally. So, for example, almost invariably, IFMIS projects will be unique in the country concerned, at least in the public sector. Thus the use of international consultants will usually be considered essential.

However, the success of such large-scale reforms is also dependent upon a detailed understanding of the local environment, existing systems and institutions. This is only available from local public financial management officials. As a result, to be successful, such reforms require close co-operation, understanding and mutual respect between these two sets of experts, the local officials and international consultants.

However, the consultancy firms are usually major companies, and so the relationship between the client government officials and the consultants is not a relationship between equals. The budgets of consultancy firms, for example, often outstrip those of the countries in which they work. PricewaterhouseCoopers, for example, recorded a total revenue of US$26.2 billion for its 2009 financial year– a figure that far outstrips the GDP of any country in Sub-Saharan Africa with the exception of Nigeria and South Africa (www.pwc.com). In addition, the international consultancy firms have access to more information about actual successes and challenges that other governments have experienced with their MTEF and IFMIS reforms (they may also have relationships with suppliers of IT equipment or software).

As a result, the local knowledge, experience and detailed appreciation of the local government officials are not necessarily used effectively. Capacity development is often a key dimension of such large-scale projects. However, the use of international experts may have the effect of further demoralizing local officials, undermining their self-confidence and so actually reducing their capacity. As a result some research has highlighted the risk of dependency on consultants; for example, Fyson (2009), based on research into the introduction of an IFMIS in Ghana, outlined the dilemma as follows:

> Some of the literature focuses on the work of contractors as a necessary contribution to the development effort bringing both resources and expertise to assist in building local capacity ... In contrast, other scholars, have argued that the work of consultants funded by development agencies, almost by definition, will have a nefarious impact on the longer-term prospects for development (Berg 1993, Reality of Aid 1999, Easterly 2002). After all, how can private sector consultants earning many times their counterpart's salary assist the public sectors of low income and aid dependent countries (Wedel 1998, Jones 1997)? Instead expatriate consultants and advisors are perceived as a systematic destructive force which is undermining the development of capacity in Africa.

In the UK, private sector consultants are also used extensively to advise public sector officials, but the relationship between the two partners is far more equal. Despite this, the National Audit Office (UK, 2006) identified the following recommendations to ensure the more effective use of consultants:

1. Public bodies need to be much better at identifying where core skill gaps exist in relation to medium- and long-term programme requirements. This knowledge should be used to plan for recruitment, training, and using consultants. Recruitment of full-time personnel and training of existing personnel can provide better value for money than continued use of consultants.
2. Public bodies should start with the presumption that their own staff are best fitted for their requirements. While it will often be the case that they need to purchase specific expertise from consulting firms, more generalist requirements can be met more cost-effectively by internal resources.
3. Public bodies should adhere to agreed regulations on the recommended threshold levels requiring ministerial or permanent secretary approval of consultancy contracts. Approvals should be based on a robust business case. Adhering to the guidance will ensure that senior management has full sight of the larger consulting contracts, promoting better accountability for this spend.
4. Public bodies need to engage with the market earlier to explore a range of possible approaches and contracting methods. Early contact with suppliers during the procurement process improves both the supplier's and the client's understanding of the

requirement. Public bodies would get more tailored and innovative responses to their invitations to tender.

5. Public bodies should make more use of different payment mechanisms such as fixed price and incentivized contracts instead of the standard time and materials. Different payment mechanisms can help control costs and formalize the joint objectives between clients and consultants. The different payment options require a strong understanding of the project's objectives, scope, risks and approach.

6. Public bodies must be smarter when it comes to understanding how consulting firms operate and in sharing information about their performance. Public bodies should have regular, senior-level discussions with their consultants to discuss openly medium- to long-term objectives and plans. Public bodies should also use their understanding of suppliers' objectives to maximize their purchasing advantage. Public bodies need to have a clear understanding of who their key suppliers are, how they are organized, their incentive mechanisms (which might focus on selling further work), and commercial practices.

7. Public bodies need to provide sufficient incentive to staff to make the consultancy project a success. Recent research has shown that the further removed people are from the decision to use consultants the more likely they are to feel confused about project responsibilities and accountabilities and frustrated because they don't know what the consultants are doing, to complain of poor communication and to be cynical about the consultants' involvement.

4.2 Lack of Local Capability: Worsening Pay and Conditions for Public Sector Workers

The use of expensive external consultants has to be understood in the context of what was happening to the economies and working conditions of local populations. The general deterioration in the economic conditions across the Global South led to a significant reduction in the real pay of public sector workers and so had a detrimental effect on the quality of public financial management across much of the Global South. Their public sectors were downsized and wage levels deteriorated significantly, leading to problems of loss of skills and capacity.

> Efficient, accountable, adequately paid and well-motivated civil servants are essential for an effective public sector, and especially to implement relatively complex reforms such as an MTEF or an IFMIS. Civil service reform was a major component of structural adjustment lending in the 1980s and the 1990s. Yet for the World Bank and IMF, such reforms primarily meant reducing the size of the civil service. At the same time, structural adjustment programmes led to a large decline in wages for civil servants who remained (Hawley, 2000).
> The IMF, for example, prompted wage reductions averaging 14 per cent in 20 African countries in the 1990s (Lienert and Modi, 1997: 18). The use of outside experts, funded by technical assistance loans, may also have hampered the growth of local expertise and capacity (Rama, 1997: 2) and demoralized the existing local professional staff, thereby adversely affecting their ability to successfully implement such complex reforms. (Wynne, 2005, pp. 31–2)

Real wages in nearly every African country were estimated to have fallen between 50 and 60 per cent since the imposition of the structural adjustment programmes of the 1980s (ILO/JASPA, 1991).

By 1990 Margaret Joan Anstee, the UN under-secretary-general, could warn that:

> The impact of recession and adjustment in the 1980s has been dealt with by economists and policy makers, within a framework of macro-analysis that pays scant attention to the people directly caught up in these economic events. These trends were inexorably leading to an ominous deterioration of sub-Saharan Africa's scarce human capital, which can be replaced only at great cost. They were setting the stage for an accelerated spiral of decline in the continent's future development. (Quoted in Brown, 1995, p. 266)

Public sector workers were not immune and in many cases suffered from reduced pay and greater insecurity. This was the result of reduced government income, but also conditionality requirements from the World Bank and the IMF. The result was that, from the early 1980s to the early 1990s, the number of people employed by central government in Sub-Saharan Africa fell from 1.8 per cent to 1.1 per cent of the population, and the average government wage also fell from 6.1 times per capita GDP to 4.8 times (Schiavo-Campo, de Tommaso and Mukherjee, 1997). In Anglophone Africa, public sector wages declined by as much as 80 per cent in real terms between the early 1970s and the early 1980s (Ayee, 2005).

Uganda provides one of the most vivid examples, with pay for civil servants in the late 1980s falling to only $10 a month (Kiragu and Mukandala, 2005). A reform programme was launched in 1993 which halved the number of public servants through the reduction in ghost workers, a voluntary redundancy scheme and a selective freeze on recruitment. Although this was coupled with significant salary increases in the early 1990s, the objective of a minimum living wage for Ugandan civil servants is far from being realized according to Mark Robinson, who concludes that:

> Failure to make progress on pay reform for the vast majority of public servants contributes to declining motivation. Large differentials between administrative grades and top civil servants, along with special treatment for senior officials in the political bureaucracy and semi-autonomous bodies like the URA, fuel resentment, undermine morale and provide a stimulus to corruption. The lack of incentives for public servants who have to cope with continuous reform initiatives and future uncertainty further runs counter to a key objective of the reform programme as set out by the 1991 presidential commission, namely the creation of a committed, responsible and results-oriented civil service, which would be better paid, more efficient, and have more effective staff. (Robinson, 2006)

Similarly, in 2002, Charles Byaruhanga could conclude that in Uganda:

> Public sector pay has improved over the last decade though pay reform remains on the public sector institutional agenda. Pay for managerial, technical and professional civil service remains un-competitive, leading to difficulties in recruiting and retaining competent staff and also negatively impacting on public service delivery.

A more recent example of the effect of economic collapse on the salaries of public officials is Liberia, where salaries of civil servants fell to a range of only $30 to $55 per month (Kumar and Brar, 2008). Many experienced and qualified staff left the public service and the country. This loss of human resources contributed to the major breakdown of government systems.

The poor pay and conditions in the African public sector has been matched by the attraction of working in developed countries: 'Approximately 20,000 skilled workers leave Africa each year. The World Bank's estimate of the share of Africa's skilled workers with a tertiary education who emigrate is more than 15 per cent, higher than any other region' (Bond, 2006, p. 89). In these circumstances, the loss of key public sector financial managers has led to the greater use of foreign consultants. However, the success of especially large-scale reforms like IFMIS and MTEF is dependent on the existence of local experts who are able to engage critically with these international consultants. The loss of this local knowledge and experience meant the strengths and challenges of existing systems are not adequately understood and so the linkages between the new and existing systems are not optimized. In addition, the absence of such local expertise has meant that the sustainability of the reforms has not been possible.

5.   USE AND CRITICISMS OF THE REFORMS

Despite the great claims made for the benefits of financial management reforms, the outcomes have often been disappointing. Many of the presumed benefits have been based more on theory and what should happen after the reforms have worked their way through the system. These reforms continue to be heavily supported by the international financial institutions and the country aid agencies. However, the 'actual level of success from their implementation has been surprisingly low. In many cases, where results have not lived up to expectations, this is not laid at the door of the "reforms" but rather at the door of the governments who have not gone far enough, or have backed off under pressure from "vested interests"' (Rosskam, 2006, p. ix). And the Danish Institute for International Studies says: 'blue-print approaches and fixed ideas about what constitutes a governance agenda can have dangerous consequences, and they demonstrate how pragmatic initiatives that do not necessarily reflect widespread ideas about "good governance" can bring about positive results' (http://www.diis.dk/sw66424.asp).

This need for a fundamental review of actual progress is supported by a former senior official of the World Bank, who said that:

> The introduction of the MTEF concept and its early application are now some 15 years old, and the time for a candid and fact-based assessment is long overdue. Given the hype the MTEF has enjoyed, its rapid expansion in the last decade, and the disregard of some fundamental considerations of institutions and capacity, a little extra emphasis in the interest of understanding the actual issues is timely. (Schiavo-Campo, 2008)

In 2005 one of the authors of this chapter (Wynne, 2005) reviewed the progress with implementation of MTEF and IFMIS reforms in Ghana, Tanzania and Uganda.

The introduction of the MTEF in Ghana appeared to have been an example of consultants and aid agencies encouraging the adoption of multi-year budgeting based on the limited experience in similar countries. This reform was thought to have been over-ambitious, as in recent years Ghana had been struggling to implement its agreed annual budget.

The Tanzanian MTEF was considered to be one of the most comprehensive in Africa (Le Houerou and Taliercio, 2002). But its success, as measured against the support for fiscal balance and in promoting the reallocation of financial resources to finance poverty eradication programmes, appears to have been rather limited. Although spending in the priority poverty reducing areas seemed to have increased more than in other areas of the government's budget, this increase had been relatively modest.

The Ugandan MTEF was considered to be one of the best examples of the success of the initiative in Africa. The introduction of an MTEF was certainly associated with improved macroeconomic stability, although it is difficult to prove the causal relationship. However, this reform has not focused on shifting funds towards poverty reduction activities. All areas of expenditure benefited equally from increased absolute funding during the implementation of the MTEF. Education, which is one of the priority areas, grew marginally, but its share in the overall government expenditure remained unchanged over the period of five years during which the MTEF was implemented.

In terms of the IFMIS, this had not been successful in Ghana. Agreed in 1997, it was re-launched in 2004, and a new project was started in mid-2010 to try to provide an integrated financial system for the central government.

In Tanzania, the IFMIS has been successful in terms of providing timely financial management information and improving commitment control. However, this only covered central government units in Dar es Salaam; budgetary information had to be re-entered once the annual budget was agreed; and the system was not linked to either the payroll or the revenue system. Despite these limitations, several other African countries have adopted the same approach as the Tanzanian government, including Malawi and The Gambia.

Uganda was at the pilot stage of a large and complex project to provide an integrated computer platform and financial system for the whole of central and at least the larger local governments. The project had suffered only limited delays relative to the original timetable. However, the risks are still considered to be significant.

This study of the implementation of MTEF- and IFMIS-type reforms in these three African countries (Wynne, 2005) concluded that:

> given the past record of limited success with the implementation of MTEFs, IFMISs and other major reforms, the need for such approaches and the evidence of their successful implementation in other countries should be rigorously reviewed. The traditional public sector concerns with regularity and probity will, if anything, become more important when major reform initiatives are being considered. Small-scale investment in basic internal financial controls may often bring greater returns than large investment in innovative reforms with their associated significant risks of failure.
>
> MTEFs and IFMISs are considered, at least by the international financial institutions to be core public financial management reforms for many developing countries. Their level of success, however, has been relatively modest and many of the assumed benefits have not necessarily been achieved. As a result, scarce resources and expertise may have been wasted on initiatives whose success in practice had not necessarily been adequately tested. (Wynne 2005, p. 32)

Both the MTEF and the IFMIS are large, complex and strategic reforms and so are high-risk projects that have actually suffered high levels of failure. Thus, for example, World Bank staff have estimated that only 6 per cent of the IFMISs they funded were highly likely to be sustainable (Dorotinsky, 2003). However, it is the strategic nature of these reforms which can be attractive to those who believe that the public sector in the Global South requires fundamental change.

A former IMF and World Bank official admitted that:

A first glimmer of recognition of these problems [with the MTEF] appeared at the World Bank's 'PREM Week' meeting of late 2000, when it was noted, among other things, that if a country cannot put together a sensible annual budget and execute it in minimally acceptable fashion it is very unlikely to have any use for a medium-term expenditure framework. One panellist (Alister Moon) gave a long list of preconditions for introducing an MTEF, including macroeconomic stability; revenue predictability; early political commitment; core capacity of the finance ministry and central agencies; supportive donor behaviour; capacity to enforce a hard budget constraint at the ministry level; executive commitment to having a transparent budget process; and capacity in sector policy analysis. (Schiavo-Campo, 2008, p. 5)

Despite these warnings of implementation difficulties, and the calls for country-led reforms, the international financial institutions and aid agencies still have a dominant role in the direction of public financial management, and MTEFs and IFMISs are still being heavily promoted as the way to improve and to modernize public sector financial management across Africa.

5.1 Sustainability of the Systems – Expensive General System Failures

There were great expectations for the MTEF and IFMIS reforms, but they have often failed in practice. The results of nearly 15 years of experience of introducing the MTEF across the Global South have been summarized by a former senior IMF and World Bank official as:

- virtually no evidence of improved macroeconomic balance
- some limited evidence of reallocation to priority subsectors
- no evidence of a link to greater budgetary predictability
- no evidence of efficiency gains in spending.

This is what the donors and the developing and middle-income countries have got in return for the billions of aid dollars, mountains of red tape, heavy burdens on local government staff, and literally centuries of full-time-equivalent technical experts. (Schiavo-Campo, 2008, p. 6)

And 'there is mounting skepticism of all MTEF concepts – seen as exhausting and expensive initiatives pushed by donors, and carried out as supply-driven self-propelled exercises conducted mainly by external consultants' (Schiavo-Campo, 2008, p. 7).

In addition, Allen Schick, a frequent presenter at World Bank public financial management events, has commented: 'Medium Term Expenditure Frameworks (MTEFs) have not proven a panacea to the challenges of budget planning, preparation and management in most countries. A possible epitaph for MTEF-type reforms would read "Died of many causes, each of which was sufficient"' (Schick, 2008).

These problems have been known for years. In a major study for the World Bank, Le Houerou and Taliercio (2002) came to the following conclusions on the progress with the introduction of the MTEF across Africa:

The limited quantitative evidence shows, thus far, that MTEFs are not yet unambiguously associated with their objectives ... In terms of macroeconomic balance, with the possible exception of Uganda, there is no evidence that MTEFs have made a significant impact. In terms of resource allocation, there is some limited and qualified evidence to suggest that MTEFs are linked to reallocations to a subset of priority sectors. With respect to budgetary predictability and consistency, there is no support for the assumption that MTEFs are associated with greater discipline and less deviation. At best, then, these cases present a mixed picture. (Le Houerou and Taliercio, 2002, p. 24)

At a major World Bank seminar to re-assess its public financial supported reforms, including a review of its experience with the MTEF, one official commented: 'The realization of the magnitude of wasted resources and dashed expectations is sobering' (Schiavo-Campo, 2008).

Another of the presenters at this event asked: 'Have certain donor-led PFM [public financial management] initiatives complicated the PFM reform landscape in countries, eg MTEF?', and a World Bank staff member said that MTEFs had become a reputational risk to the Bank. It is hoped that these reviews will lead to greater changes in practice and advice to governments. It seemed clear that the World Bank needs to put more effort into listening to local public sector financial officials, building on their expertise and understanding of the local environment to ensure that local public sector financial management reform programmes are more successful in future.

Large-scale electronic information system implementations are notoriously risky. The hope in respect of governments of the Global South was that they could benefit from the lessons of failed implementations in the developed world. In practice, this seems not to have been the case. The following three quotations indicate the huge gulf between the hype and the reality of IT reforms:

In the emerging knowledge-based economy of the 21st century, information and communications technology will likely assume an importance that dwarfs other types of infrastructure. This shift offers Africa a chance to leapfrog intermediate stages of development by avoiding costly investments in time, resources, and the generation and use of knowledge. Africa has a chance to benefit not only as a consumer in the new knowledge economy, but also as a producer. It cannot afford to miss this opportunity. (World Bank, 2000, p. 153)

E-government is difficult to implement, hard to manage and often fails. (Heeks, 2006, p. 10)

Survey and poll results produce the following working estimates about e-government initiatives in developing/transitional countries:

- 35% are total failures
- 50% are partial failures
- 15% are successes. (eGov for Development, 2007)

IFMIS in particular and IT in general have been promoted as providing the key answers to improving the quality and efficiency of a modern public sector. However, the reality has been a series of failed projects and, in many cases, the wastage of millions of dollars which are desperately needed for investment in many other areas of the public sector.

In Ghana, for example, an IFMIS was launched in 1997 by Vice-President Mills. He argued that the IFMIS would:

not only facilitate budget execution, accounting and financial reporting but will also place responsibility on the Ministers to monitor and account for resource use ... the policies we formulate, the programmes we implement, the resources we use, must all be accounted for in terms of the extent to which they help us improve our living standards. (PUFMARP newsletter, September 1997, pp. 4–5, quoted in Fyson, 2009)

However, nearly a decade later, in May 2006, the deputy controller and accountant general noted that: 'there has as yet not been one Cedi [local currency] benefit from it. I have not used [IFMIS] to generate one report yet' (quoted in Fyson, 2009).

This experience has also been replicated in industrial countries. An important book (Gauld, Goldfinch and Dale 2006) reviews a number of IT case studies in Australia, Britain, New Zealand and the United States. As a result, the authors reach the conclusion that IT is a dangerous enthusiasm. In contrast they argue that pessimism, or at least the expectation of failure, should be the guiding principle.

These conclusions appear to be even more relevant and important in Africa, where the experience has, if anything, been worse in terms of the risk of IT failure, as the following quotations demonstrate: 'the evidence does all point in one direction: towards high rates of e-government project failure in Africa' (Heeks, 2002, p. 11); 'information systems fail or under perform more often than they succeed in the public sector in Africa' (Peterson, 1998, p. 38); 'the success rate of introduced information technology systems in African state agencies has been distressingly low' (Berman and Tettey, 2001, p. 2).

One of the reasons for this high failure rate is that the economics of IT investment in Africa is different from that found in industrial countries. In Africa, labour is relatively cheap, IT hardware and skills are not available locally, and transport costs make IT more expensive to purchase and to maintain. Average public sector wage costs in Africa can be one-tenth or less of those in industrial countries. Average IT costs, in contrast, may be two to three times higher. E-governance and automation using modern IT technology therefore result in replacing cheap civil servants with costly IT (Heeks, 2002).

In late 2003, Bill Dorotinsky provided a useful overview of the World Bank's experience of providing over $1 billion to finance IFMIS projects over 17 years. The average time for completion of each project was over nine years for African projects, and the average cost of each of the 34 projects worldwide was $12.3 million (Dorotinsky, 2003).

If success is defined on the basis of being on budget, on time and delivered as planned, then only 21 per cent of these projects were successful. An even gloomier view was provided by assessments of the same projects by the World Bank staff. A quarter of the projects were considered unsustainable, 69 per cent likely to be sustainable and only 6 per cent highly likely to be sustainable, and this figure was lower for Africa than other regions (Dorotinsky, 2003).

Dorotinsky stated that the general lesson from the World Bank's experience was the requirement to have clear political commitment and ownership by the borrowing country. He also pointed out that such schemes were generally less successful in poorer countries and highlighted the following additional risks:

- Lack of capacity
- Lack of government commitment
- Too many project components
- Opposition by staff and line ministries (Dorotinsky, 2003).

In 2005 the IMF published a working paper which investigates the reason for the serious delays and frequent failure to implement and sustain IFMIS reforms in governments of the Global South (Diamond and Khemani, 2005). This paper concludes that an IFMIS should be implemented as part of a wider set of public financial management reforms. The IFMIS will require clear government commitment, support and significant resources. It should also be phased over a number of years when current and interim arrangements will still be required. Even if these recommendations are implemented, a government implementing an IFMIS can expect 'a long implementation path, and one that involves significant challenges. It will be a complex learning process for all concerned. A number of difficulties are likely to be encountered en route' (Diamond and Khemani, 2005, p. 27).

6. SUGGESTIONS FOR A WAY FORWARD

In this section we examine possible ways to assist governments of the Global South in their efforts to improve their use of information systems and accounting technologies, suggesting that local experts should take control to rebuild public sector financial management.

The international financial institutions and aid agencies may adopt suitable strategic objectives, but these are not necessarily properly implemented. They are used only as slogans and are not seriously used as a guide to action. Thus the following ideas have been correctly promoted in recent years to guide public financial management reform, but have not been delivered in practice:

- country ownership;
- getting the basics right;
- sequencing of reform.

If we accept the arguments of the previous sections, then public financial management was relatively successful, but became degraded in many governments of the Global South as a result of events beyond the control of these governments. In these circumstances, what these countries need is a rebuilding and refinement of their public financial management systems rather than the root-and-branch reform suggested by such mega-reforms as the MTEF and IFMIS. This should be led by the countries concerned and, specifically, their financial managers, who are the only experts on these systems.

6.1 Country Ownership

Country ownership has been widely accepted and considered vital for the success of large-scale public financial management reforms, especially since the OECD's Paris Declaration was adopted by over 100 ministers, heads of agencies and other senior officials in 2005. This agreement committed the donors to 'Respect partner country leadership and help strengthen their capacity to exercise it' (OECD, 2005).

The report to the follow-up meeting in Accra, Ghana in October 2008 reinforced this view, noting that:

> Country ownership and leadership are critical to success. Even when external pressures or internal crisis are the main triggers PFM reforms, the starting point for real reform must be a

country-owned response to such pressure in the form of a program of reform and a country-owned structure for managing the reform process. (Working Party on Aid Effectiveness, 2008, p. 17)

This report also noted that:

> The literature on PFM is replete with stories of failed reforms that were driven by donors rather than led by the country; such reforms may initially appear to be successful, but they are unlikely to be sustained and, in the worst cases, may be reversed after the withdrawal of donor support. (Working Party on Aid Effectiveness, 2008, pp. 18–19)

Despite these harsh warnings, the Declaration claims that it is the responsibility of each government in the Global South 'to take leadership of its development processes' (Working Party on Aid Effectiveness, 2008, p. 4), rather than the international financial institutions and aid agencies, as the most powerful partners, having the responsibility to ensure that governments of the Global South are allowed to control their own destinies.

In practice the international financial institutions and aid agencies (led by the IMF and the World Bank) maintain close control over the public financial reforms. Most public financial management projects which are funded by World Bank loans will have originated from a World Bank report. In addition, many aid projects are also micro-managed by the aid agencies; for example, all contracts let under World Bank funded projects for public financial management reform have to be screened by World Bank officials to receive a 'no objection' clearance before the contract can be awarded. In addition, the contracts may be managed by independent agencies and periodically reviewed by World Bank officials.

As a former senior official of the IMF and World Bank said at an IMF seminar in October 2008: 'There is little or no country ownership. MTEF is often pushed on to reluctant countries by donor agencies.' Despite this approach, the World Bank, for example, still has a tendency to blame the relevant country rather than the particular tools it has promoted. So in 1998 the World Bank said that 'advocates continue to suggest that the failure of these performance-orientated tools [an aspect of the MTEF] or techniques have been in implementation rather than in concept' (World Bank, 1998, p. 16). Over a decade later at a World Bank seminar Allen Schick was still claiming that 'the widespread failure of MTEF has been due to the way it has been implemented, not because of a design flaw' (Schick, 2008).

Foucault argued that political rationalities prescribe solutions and ways to achieve these prescriptions while at the same time presenting these solutions as the truth. The prescription of ways and means does not necessarily mean that political rationalities would be achieved in practice. Instead, political rationalities are congenitally failing, with their implementation the commencement of the search for ever new ways of governing a sphere (Miller and Rose, 1990; Rose and Miller, 1992).

The World Bank employs public financial management advisors in most aid-dependent countries, directly provides or supports a range of training initiatives for public financial management officials, and produces a range of publications relating to particular countries or of more general interest. Co-operative bodies for public financial management officials, for example AFROSAI-E (for auditors general), CABRI (for budget officials) and ESAAG (for accountants general), are dependent on the aid agencies for support and for the provision of international speakers for their events. All these activities tend to increase the influence of the international financial institutions and the aid agencies. In addition, these bodies are able to recruit leading public sector financial managers and officials. For example, the former federal minister of finance of Nigeria worked for the World Bank before and after her term in office; the current president of Liberia worked for the World Bank; the head of public sector financial reform in Sierra Leone went on to work for the World Bank; and the auditor general of Uganda had a spell working for the PEFA Secretariat before returning to Uganda.

The standard approach to evaluating the quality of public financial management in the Global South is now the PEFA framework. These have been undertaken in over 100 countries, with particularly high coverage in Sub-Saharan Africa (PEFA Secretariat at the 2009 International Consortium of Governmental Financial Management Miami Conference). However, very few of these assessments were undertaken with the active involvement of the public sector officials of the country under review. Most are led by the World Bank or the EU and involve international consultants. The auditor general of Uganda did undertake a PEFA-type review in 2007, but this was criticized by the PEFA Secretariat, as it was uncertain whether the donors would accept it as part of their fiduciary assessments.

6.2 Getting the Basics Right

Public financial management reform should clearly be based on firm foundations; we have to 'get the basics right', to use Allen Schick's often repeated (and then ignored) phrase. Specifically, Schick has called for the need to 'operate a reliable accounting system before installing an integrated financial management system' (World Bank, 1998) and 'focusing on the credibility of the annual budget before introducing a medium-term perspective to budget planning' (Schick, 2008).

Despite these wise words, governments have been encouraged to adopt the MTEF and IFMIS before basic internal financial controls have been brought up to an adequate standard. As an IMF working paper noted, 'MTEFs have sometimes been introduced prematurely, in the sense that annual budget outcomes and monitoring mechanisms were still quite primitive, resulting in outer-year scenarios that were inconsistent with actual budget outcomes and/or the macroeconomic framework' (Lienert and Feridoun, 2001).

Schiavo-Campo (2008, p. 7) warned against MTEF and IFMIS being seen as the basic approaches to financial management for all governments, national and local: 'The "reform" momentum is still at work, however. Especially troublesome is the notion of extending the MTEF to general government, requiring sub-national entities to go through the exercise – as currently envisaged in some countries, e.g., Tanzania.'

This is also the case in Nigeria, where both the World Bank and the Department for International Development (UK) are supporting public sector reforms in a number of state governments. The MTEF is seen as a key part of these reforms (at least by the donors), although PEFA indicators for basic internal financial controls are poor.

Somalia is well known for not having had a functioning national government for nearly two decades. Despite this, a World Bank mission to Somalia in late 2007 led to the recommendation to introduce an IFMIS. This is despite Schick's recommendation to ensure that manual systems are working well before an IFMIS is introduced. Similarly, donor-supported IFMISs have been implemented in several other post-conflict countries, including Liberia (Kumar and Brar, 2008), Sierra Leone and Southern Sudan.

6.3 Sequencing of Reform

Sequencing of public sector financial reforms is clearly important and may be another way of ensuring that basic internal financial controls are refined before wide-ranging mega-reforms such as the MTEF and IMFIS are implemented. But this approach may also be based on the assumption that donors know what is needed and it is just a question of moving there in small, easy steps. Thus the Department for International Development (UK) describes this type of approach as follows:

> The platform approach aims to implement a package of measures or activities designed to achieve increasing levels ('platforms') of PFMA competence over a manageable timeframe. Each platform establishes a clear basis for launching to the next, based on the premise that a certain level of PFMA competence is required to enable further progress to take place. (DfID, 2005, p. 1)

This approach assumes that donors know what is needed, that the main attributes of sound public financial management are well understood and that all countries should achieve this common goal. It is just a question of determining where on the development ladder a particular country finds itself to indicate what the next steps should be. However, reality is more complex. There is a variety of different approaches to public financial management, and each country and organization has, to a greater or lesser extent, developed its own approach. 'The rush for reforms, especially when driven from outside, has often wreaked havoc in vital institutions that societies had created either to foster national unity, defend disadvantaged groups and regions or support national investments' (Larbi, 2006, p. 3).

We have to start from a clear understanding of the particular priorities, demands, history and culture of each country, elements which local public financial managers are best able to understand. We then have to consider carefully how existing systems may be rebuilt, improved and refined in the light of local experience, informed, as appropriate, by the lessons and experience of other countries.

Some experiences with implementation suggest that, to reduce the risk involved in developing an IFMIS, it may be preferable for the system to be implemented in stages with, for example, the implementation of a computerized payments and budget monitoring system in the ministry of finance as a first stage and the extension to line ministries as the second stage, and only after the system has proved to be working effectively should its use by regional and/or local government be considered. An incremental approach is suggested by Peterson (2007):

> Both the Ethiopian and Tanzania experience with automating financial systems demonstrate the value of a modular approach and the need to selectively not comprehensively address core deficiencies of financial control – fixing the hole(s) in the whole. They both involved extensive customization to meet user requirements. They both put into question the need for 'high end' commercial off-the-shelf systems which are expensive, complex, difficult to customize and have features which have little or no use for the current or foreseeable needs of a government. (Peterson, 2007, p. 40)

7.   CONCLUSIONS

The economies of many countries in the Global South went into deep decline from the mid- to late 1970s with the associated rise in government debt. This was largely due to external events: the increased price of oil, increased interest rates and declining prices for their exports. These were events which governments had little or no control over and for which they were not responsible. However, it did mean that their income was severely curtailed. As a result, they were encouraged by the IMF, World Bank and aid agencies to restructure their economies, corporatize and/or privatize key sectors of the economy, adopt Western accounting procedures and systems, reduce the number of their public servants and in many cases significantly reduce their level of pay. This clearly had a detrimental effect on the quality of public services, including financial management and overall governance.

> Of course, if the developing countries had solved all of their own problems better, if they had more honest governments, less influential special interests, more efficient firms, better educated workers – if, in fact, they did not suffer from all the afflictions of being poor – they could have managed this unfair and dysfunctional globalisation better. (Stiglitz, 2006, p. 58)

However, these events have given the World Bank and aid agencies the power, through aid conditionality, to influence significantly the public sector financial management reforms which were introduced. This has often been through the use of, usually European, consultants paid significantly more than the financial managers they are retained to advise.

Public sector financial managers, far from being the cause of this decline, have in many cases struggled to try to maintain standards whilst suffering redundancies, forced retirements and dramatic cuts in their living standards. In addition, their morale has been undermined.

Global solutions do not necessarily satisfy local needs. The evidence of the previous sections demonstrate the failure of systems and procedures imported and implemented by 'experts' who may not appreciate the local history, society or culture of the countries in which they are sent to operate. The great expectations of the 'solutions' often result in expensive failures.

> Costly failures have demonstrated that – as any other institutional reform – successful introduction of a programmatic MTEF takes years of persistent efforts consistent with capacity, resources, awareness, incentives, and institutional realities. The two ingredients of the approach are therefore gradualism and selectivity, and the main conditions of success are simplicity and communication. If prematurely introduced or badly implemented, a formal and detailed programmatic MTEF causes enormous waste, frustration, and illusion – for trivial or non-existent benefits. The same is true of the informatics infrastructure for public financial management. (Schiavo-Campo, 2008, p. 26)

The authors argue that it is better to build on and enhance existing public financial management capacity, to nourish it and facilitate its development. The local officials are the international experts for the systems they are responsible for managing. For any systems the experts are the local officials. No consultant from outside the sector or country can know or understand the system as well as the public sector officials who have been managing the system for years, often in very difficult circumstances. These arose as a result of external events beyond their control or that of their governments. All public financial management reforms should be led by the relevant officials and should be subject to informed local political support.

Complex systems and reforms are always more risky than simple approaches. The authors believe that it is better to ensure that proposed reforms are kept as simple as possible.

'International best practice' has to be adapted to make it fit local conditions: international best practice is never the complete answer.

The authors would also argue for the importance of making sure that actual international best practice is being adopted and checking to ensure that the particular aspects really have been tried and tested and have been proved to be successful. Multi-year budget frameworks and programme budgeting may be good ideas, but they have been difficult to implement in practice. The UK tried for 30 years until 1997 to implement a three-year budget framework, and it is not clear that the current arrangements will survive the recent international financial turmoil. France only implemented its current approach to programme budgeting from 2006 and is only implementing a three-year budget framework with effect from 2008. The US government does not have an MTEF.

There are many other examples of reforms which were once heavily promoted by aid agencies and international consultants which time then showed were either mistaken or carried significant additional associated costs.

It would appear that the World Bank and the IMF are now slowly revising their support for mega-reforms such as the MTEF and IFMIS. In 2008 both organizations held significant seminars reviewing the evidence for the success (or more commonly failure) of such reforms.

However, there is still a long way to go. We need to gain widespread recognition that the governance and financial management problems suffered by many countries arose from global events over which they and their governments had little or no control. The international financial institutions and the donor agencies need to ensure that they use their financial power judiciously to enable public financial managers to take real leadership of their reform agenda.

The change agenda arising from the world recession and the election of Barack Obama as the US president on a programme of change should help this process. We need a move away from mega-reforms such as the MTEF and IFMIS. Public financial managers need to be provided with the political support and necessary resources to implement basic tried and tested reforms.

The World Bank says it is working for a world free of poverty. However, its prescriptions for public sector financial management are unlikely to achieve this ideal. The far more modest aims of the Millennium Development Goals are also now, as a consequence of the global recession, not likely to be achieved. The private sector free market approach of neoliberal and NPM reforms has failed. We need to change direction and build poverty reduction strategies on the firm foundations of redistributing resources from the richer to the poorer sectors of society through the use of progressive taxation and public services provided free at the point of use.

REFERENCES

Awio, G., S. Lawrence and D. Northcott (2007). Community-led initiatives: reforms for better accountability? *Journal of Accounting and Organizational Change*, 3(3), pp. 209–26.

Ayee, J.R.A. (2005). *Public Sector Management in Africa*. Tunis: African Development Bank.

Ayeni, V. (2002). *Public Sector Reform in Developing Countries: A Handbook of Commonwealth Experiences*. London: Commonwealth Secretariat.

Berman, B.J., and W.J. Tettey (2001). African states, bureaucratic culture and computer fixes. *Public Administration and Development*, 21.

Bond, P. (2006). *Looting Africa: The Economics of Exploitation*. London: Zed Books.

Brown, Michael Barratt (1995). *Africa's Choices: After Thirty Years of the World Bank*. London: Penguin Books.

Byaruhanga, Charles (2002). *Poverty Reduction and Public Sector Reform in Uganda: The Roles of Institutions in Past Experience and Challenges for the Way Forward*. Oxford: Consulting Africa.

Christian Aid (2003). *The Trading Game: How Trade Works*. Oxford: Oxfam.

Clark, T., and A. Dilnot (2002). *Measuring the UK Fiscal Stance since the Second World War*, Briefing Note no. 26. London: Institute for Fiscal Studies.

DfID (2005). *A Platform Approach to Improving Public Financial Management*, Briefing. London: DfID.

Diamond, Jack, and Pokar Khemani (2005). Introducing financial management information systems in developing countries. IMF Working Paper, Fiscal Affairs Department, http://www.imf.org/external/pubs/ft/wp/2005/wp05196.pdf.

Dorotinsky, Bill (2003). *Implementing Financial Management Information System Projects: The World Bank Experience Preliminary Results*, http://www1.worldbank.org/publicsector/egov/ReinventingGovWorkshop/dorotinsky.ppt.

Duménil, G., and D. Lévy (2005). Costs and benefits of neoliberalism: a class analysis. In *Financialization and the World Economy*, ed. G. Epstein. Cheltenham, UK and Northampton, MA, USA: Edward Elgar. (Updated version of the paper originally published as: Duménil, G., and D. Lévy (2001). *Review of International Political Economy*, 8(4), pp. 578–607, http://www.jourdan.ens.fr/levy/dle2005g.htm, accessed 29 October 2008.)

eGov for Development (2007). http://www.egov4dev.org/, accessed 24 August 2007.

FAO (2005). *The State of Agricultural Commodity Markets 2004*. Rome: UN Food and Agriculture Organization.

Fyson, Sara (2009). Sending in the consultants: development agencies, the private sector and the reform of public finance in low-income countries. *International Journal of Public Policy*, 4(3–4), pp. 314–43.

Gauld, Robin, and Shaun Goldfinch with Tony Dale (2006). *Dangerous Enthusiasms: E-government, Computer Failure and Information System Development*. Dunedin: Otago University Press.

Hashim, Ali, and Bill Allan (2001). *Treasury Reference Model*, http://www1.worldbank.org/publicsector/pe/trm.pdf.

Heeks, Richard (2002). *eGovernment in Africa: Promise and Practice*, Paper 13. Manchester: IDPM, University of Manchester.

Heeks, Richard (2006). *Implementing and Managing eGovernment*. London: Sage.

ILO/JASPA (1991). *Africa Employment Report 1990*. Addis Ababa: ILO/JASPA.

Kiragu, Kithinji, and Rwekaza S. Mukandala (2005). *Politics and Tactics in Public Sector Reforms: The Dynamics of Public Service Pay in Africa*. Dar es Salaam: Dar es Salaam University Press.

Kumar, S.M., and P.P.S. Brar (2008). Transition to IFMIS: the Liberian experience. Paper presented at the International Conference of the Controller General of Accounts of India, on Public Financial Management for Improving Programme Delivery: Issues and Challenges, New Delhi, 20–22 October.

Larbi, G.A. (2006). Applying the new public management in developing countries. In *Public Sector Reform in Developing Countries: Capacity Challenges to Improve Service*, ed. Y. Bangura and G.A. Larbi. New York: United Nations Research Institute for Public Development/Palgrave.

Le Houerou, P., and R. Taliercio (2002). Medium term expenditure frameworks: from concept to practice: preliminary lessons from Africa. Africa Region Working Paper Series no. 28, http://www.worldbank.org/afr/wps/wp28.pdf.

Leys, Colin (1996). *The Rise and Fall of Development Theory*. Oxford: James Currey.

Lienert, I., and S. Feridoun (2001). Systemic weaknesses of budget management in Anglophone Africa. IMF Working Paper 01/211.

Miller, P., and N. Rose (1990). Governing economic life. *Economy and Society*, 19(1), pp. 1–31.

National Audit Office (2006). *Central Government's Use of Consultants*, Value for Money Report. London: NAO, http://www.nao.org.uk/pn/06-07/0607128.htm.

OECD (2005). *Paris Declaration on Aid Effectiveness*. Paris: OECD.

Office of Management and Budget (2007). *Historical Tables: Budget of the United States Government: Fiscal Year 2008*, p.126. Washington, DC: Executive Office of the President of the United States, http://www.whitehouse.gov/omb/budget/fy2007/pdf/hist.pdf, accessed 17 September 2008.

Olson, O., J. Guthrie and C. Humphrey (eds) (1998). *Global Warning: Debating International Developments in New Public Financial Management*. Oslo: Cappel Akademisk Forlag.

Peterson, S.B. (1998). Saints, demons, wizards and systems: why information technology reforms fail or underperform in public bureaucracies in Africa. *Public Administration and Development*, 18(1).

Peterson, Stephen (2007). Imperfect systems: IFMISs in Africa. Harvard University.

Robinson, M. (2006). The political economy of governance reforms in Uganda. IDS Discussion Paper 386.

Rose, N., and P. Miller (1992). Political power beyond the state: problematics of government. *British Journal of Sociology*, 43(2), pp.173–205.

Rosskam, Ellen (ed.) (2006). *Winners or Losers? Liberalising Public Services*. Geneva: ILO.

Schiavo-Campo, Salvatore (2008). Of mountains and molehills: 'the' medium-term expenditure framework. Paper presented at the Conference on Sustainability and Efficiency in Managing Public Expenditures, organized by the East–West Center and Korea Development Institute, Honolulu, HI, 24–25 July, http://papers.ssrn.com/sol3/papers.cfm?abstract_id=1169783, accessed 20 September 2008.

Schiavo-Campo, S., G. de Tommaso and A. Mukherjee (1997). *An International Statistical Survey of Government Employment and Wages*. Washington, DC: World Bank.

Schick, Allen (2008). Sequencing issues in PFM reform. World Bank PFM Seminar, 21 March, blog-pfm.imf.org/pfmblog/files/thoughts_shared_by_prof_allen_schick_at_the_workshop_on_March _21st.doc.

Situmbeko, Lishala C., and Jack Jones Zulu (2004). *Zambia: Condemned to Debt*. London: World Development Movement, http://www.africafocus.org/docs04/zam0406.php.

Stiglitz, J. (2006). *Making Globalisation Work*. London: Allen Lane.

UNCTAD (2004). *Debt Sustainability: Oasis or Mirage*. New York and Geneva: United Nations.

Working Party on Aid Effectiveness, Joint Venture on Public Financial Management (2008). *Report on the Use of Country Systems in Public Financial Management*. Paris: OECD.

World Bank (1998). *Public Expenditure Management Handbook*. Washington, DC: World Bank, http://www1.worldbank.org/publicsector/pe/handbook/pem98.pdf.

World Bank (2000). *Can Africa Reclaim the 21st Century?* Washington, DC: World Bank.

World Bank (2005). *The Medium-Term Expenditure Framework: The Challenges of Budget Integration in SSA countries*, Africa Region Working Paper Series no. 82, April. Washington, DC: World Bank.

Wynne, Andy (2005). *Public Financial Management Reforms in Developing Countries: Lessons of Experience from Ghana, Tanzania and Uganda*, Working Paper no. 7. Harare: African Capacity Building Foundation, http://www.acbf-pact.org/knowledge/documents/Working%20Paper%207%20on%20Financial%20Management-Final.pdf.

12 Management control after privatization: illustrations from less developed countries

Trevor Hopper, Mathew Tsamenyi, Shahzad Uddin and Danture Wickramasinghe

1. INTRODUCTION

The effect of neo-liberal economic reform programmes in less developed countries (LDCs) upon management accounting systems is controversial. A striking facet is the pressure the World Bank and the IMF put on many LDCs to pursue privatization policies (Cook and Kirkpatrick, 1995; Craig, 2000; Parker and Kirkpatrick, 2005). Often this was an inescapable condition for loans, which LDCs often are in a weak position to decline (Uddin and Hopper, 2003; Goldman, 2005). Some LDC governments have adopted privatization programmes of their own volition but others have done so grudgingly under external pressures.

Many development economists and agents of the World Bank assume that such reforms will produce more effective controls, increase enterprise efficiency and, in turn, boost national development (World Bank, 1993, 1995, 1996c; Cook and Kirkpatrick, 1995; Toye, 1994; Goldman, 2005; Parker and Kirkpatrick, 2005). Advocates of privatisation emphasise the lack of financial accountability and transparency in state owned enterprises (SOEs), and their immunity from market discipline and the scrutiny of legal institutions (World Bank reports, 1995, 1996a, 1997). They recommend fostering an 'enabling environment' that promotes accountability, transparency and efficient companies. This entails: liberalizing domestic and foreign trade; relaxing price controls; balanced government budgets; and maintaining a legal framework and financial reporting and accountability systems conducive to the functioning of a market economy. The justification for these policies is that private ownership is more efficient than public ownership (Adam, Cavendish and Mistry, 1992; Goldman, 2005).

However, research on the effects of privatization in LDCs is inconclusive (Cook and Kirkpatrick, 1995). Some report that SOEs are less profitable than their private sector counterparts in the same industry (Killick, 1983; Ayub and Hegstod, 1986); and SOEs in LDCs fail to generate significant contributions to GDP and are less profitable than the private sector (Funkhouser and MacAvoy, 1979; Kim, 1981; World Bank, 1981, 1983; Killick, 1983; Ayub and Hegstod, 1986; IMF, 1986; Kikeri, Nellis and Shirley, 1994). However, others have found the public sector to be more efficient and SOEs outperforming private firms (Millward, 1988; Ramaswamy, 1988; Wortzel and Wortzel, 1989). Others claim that SOEs cannot be evaluated by private sector criteria because governments require them to pursue non-commercial objectives. Whatever the case, opinions are divided on the effects of privatization on the economy.

Much research on the outcome of privatizations has tended to be at the financial macro-level – examining its impact on the economy in terms of GDP and government revenue. For instance, a study on behalf of the Organisation of Economic Co-operation and Development by Megginson and Bouchkoua (1999) used economic indicators to evaluate the outcome of privatization programmes in 15 countries. Similarly, a study conducted by Bouton and Sumlinski (1997) sponsored by the International Finance Corporation on the impact of privatization in LDCs based its analysis predominantly on financial indicators. However, financial profitability may not be a good yardstick for measuring the performance of SOEs, since their objectives may be to promote social welfare and not to generate profit (Akinsanya, 1981; Cook and Kirkpatrick, 1988, 1995; Prager, 1992; Megginson, Nash and Van Randenborgh, 1994; Boubraki and Cosset, 1998). By focusing only on financial indicators, the success or failure of privatization programmes is viewed merely through one lens. Even the World Bank (2000) has recently identified the need to evaluate post-privatization performance not by short-term financial measures but by long-term qualitative analysis focusing on human, social and environmentally sustainable development. This is supported by other researchers, including Prizzia (2001), who argues for a balance of economic and social measures of performance.

In most LDCs privatization is complicated and requires a multi-dimensional analysis of its outcomes for several reasons. First, privatization is usually a condition imposed by the IMF, the World Bank and other Western donors on governments in LDCs (Uddin and Hopper, 2003). Second, most privatized firms in LDCs are sold to foreign investors with minimal participation by indigenous investors (Prizzia, 2001). Third, there are inadequate regulatory structures and weak financial markets in most LDCs. Performance measures based on financial indicators alone may distort the measurement of outcomes. Financial indicators may be adequate for reporting returns on invested capital to the parent company and hence the economic viability of the investments; and they may satisfy the IMF's and the World Bank's need to determine the ability of an LDC to repay borrowed funds. However, these measures are inadequate for assessing the full impact of privatization upon those intended to benefit from it.

Nevertheless, privatization advocates presume that the improved accounting that underpins their prescriptions will materialize (Uddin and Hopper, 2003; Wickramasinghe and Hopper, 2005; Hopper et al., 2009). But often research on this is myopic and does not capture the full impact of privatization. Despite purporting that desired results of privatization are contingent upon management control changes, development economists display little interest in studying whether this occurs at a micro-level. However, a growing number of accounting studies have incorporated micro-level analyses of management controls in privatized firms in LDCs (Uddin and Hopper, 2003; Wickramasinghe and Hopper, 2005; see Hopper et al., 2009, for a review). Even in the West such studies are sparse (Ogden, 1995a, 1995b, 1997; Ogden and Anderson, 1999; Letza and Smallman, 2001; Carter and Mueller, 2006; Cole and Cooper, 2006). They point out that accounting controls are not neutral, objective systems that unequivocally flow from rational choice or environmental determinants (Uddin and Tsamenyi, 2005). Rather, they are also shaped by other controls over production and labour, managerial choices and political conflicts within or without the organization. Moreover, accounting controls complement, interact with and are substitutable by other controls, for example internal labour markets (Hopper, Storey and Willmot, 1987; Hopper and Armstrong, 1991; Uddin and Hopper, 2001). Privatizations in LDCs may change management accounting and control systems but they can also have unanticipated and unsought consequences. Whether this induces more effective controls, improves enterprise performance, accountability and transparency in firms and government, and enhances development goals remains contested. For example, Uddin and Hopper (2003) found that only one of 13 companies privatized in Bangladesh following World Bank recommendations saw commercial success. In all but one, contributions to state revenue declined; transparent external reports required by law failed to materialize; untoward transactions affecting minority shareholders, creditors and taxation agencies emerged; and more commercial internal controls wrought declining employment, wages, quality of working life, and employee rights. Catchpowle and Cooper (1999) also present a gloomy story of privatization in South Africa, claiming that management controls bore harshly on workers, and were used to rationalize redundancies and reduced benefits. Uddin and Tsamenyi (2005) and Rahman, Lawrence and Roper (2004) recount similar stories in Ghana. This chapter examines these debates. It draws from case studies of management accounting changes by the authors following privatizations in Bangladesh, Ghana[1] and Sri Lanka to delineate whether they met policy expectations, especially with respect to accounting changes. Thus the issues are whether privatizations improved management controls and whether this not only improved financial performance but also served broader development goals with regard to employment, for example wages and job creation, and society, for example increased taxation revenues.

2.   THE NEO-LIBERAL AGENDA ON PRIVATIZATION

Arguably, the roots of privatization policies lie in the 'Austrian School' of neo-liberal economics led by the political philosopher Friedrich Hayek (Hayek, 1944). His books strongly influenced the conservative governments of Margaret Thatcher in the UK and Ronald Reagan in the USA and struggles to overthrow communism during the 1970s and 1980s in Eastern Europe. This work challenged prevailing beliefs about the benefits of 'welfare' economies, state intervention according to 'Keynesian' economic precepts, and state central planning of commercial enterprises. *Inter alia*, neo-liberals argued that state decisions are politically biased and use information contrary to market signals (Harvey, 2005). The agenda, especially by UK and USA governments, became rolling back their welfare economies and promoting market ideals (Parker, 2009). Given their prominence economically and politically, other countries followed suit, and neo-liberal discourse became more global, especially in economic institutions advising LDCs. The failures of centralized state planning and management control mechanisms within SOEs, and from SOEs to government agencies, left fertile ground for the promulgation of market solutions' incorporating of privatization to better development (Adam et al., 1992; Rose-Ackermann, 1996).

Frequently arguments for privatization rest on economic theories of productive and allocative efficiency that stress the micro-economic benefits of property rights and sound contractual relationships between agents and principals, and macro-economic benefits of private ownership and markets for public finances and capital investment (Adam et al., 1992; Cook and Kirkpatrick, 1995). Technological efficiency is a necessary but insufficient condition for efficient resource allocation (Rees, 1984). Allocative efficiency theories claim that SOEs cannot match the efficiency of private firms under market competition, as politicians, managers and workers within SOEs will divert performance into other channels to pursue their personal goals. Competition enhanced by private ownership is seen as essential, as it reveals information crucial to efficient input usage (Adam et al., 1992). Without these market references principals cannot determine the correct performance of management or the appropriate rewards. For example, falling profits could be due to lower demand or managerial inefficiency. In a market, published profits and price information from competitors helps principals to analyse this, derive input–output links that are important to internal efficiency, and design control systems accordingly. In contrast, managers of SOEs enjoy a tranquil life under monopolies that convey weak signals of managerial performance leading to inefficiency, the pursuit of non-commercial goals and even state fiscal crises due to loss-making SOEs (Adam et al., 1992).

Productive efficiency theory claims that private ownership enhances business performance because its narrower objectives facilitate devising efficiency-enhancing incentive contracts. This is fleshed out in agency and property right theories. Property right theory claims that private owners induce more efficient managers because they design management controls and incentives to maximize profits and thence the value of property rights. If they fail to do so then their business will compete ineffectively and eventually suffer market failure or a takeover. In contrast, it is alleged that SOEs lack effective links between owners and management, as no one has an incentive to design controls that align interests. The perceived costs of doing so will outweigh benefits, since benefits do not accrue to individuals (Hanke, 1986). Moreover, because public assets are not individually owned, they lack transferability characteristics (Hanke, 1986, p. 16) and are buffered from competition.

Agency theory makes similar points. Its basic tenet is that agents act in their self-interest. Therefore principals must structure incentives to make them act in congruence with their aims. This is rendered more complex by information asymmetries. Principal–agent relationships in the private sector may be simpler than in SOEs because shareholders have access to information to monitor management and sanction its actions accordingly (Adam et al., 1992). In an efficient capital market, failure to perform to potential leads to low share values, rendering the company liable to hostile takeover bids. This threat creates a self-regulating incentive scheme (Jensen and Meckling, 1976; Baiman, 1991) which is absent in the public sector. Moreover, performance-related pay systems, central to agency theory, are more difficult to implement and devise in SOEs than private sector organization (Rees, 1985).

Privatization advocates see public financing, efficiency and privatization as intertwined. Privatization is claimed to reduce net budgetary transfers, eliminate contingent external debt liabilities and reduce the adverse effects of deficit financing. In reality, neither sector conforms to these stereotypes (Adam et al., 1992). For example, such economic theorization may be relevant for classical small firms but not in the modern large limited liability corporation where the property rights of owners are diluted. This reduces owners' control over managers, who may have considerable discretionary power to further their own interests (Commander and Killick, 1988; Adam et al., 1992). Moreover, capital markets may be weak in LDCs, and the state is often the major source of capital. Finally, policy exclusively based on neo-classical economics neglects the social, political and cultural context of LDCs, may not reflect broader development goals such as health and education, reduces policy to material factors, and treats subjects as self-interested actors whose behaviour is governed solely by economic exchanges.

3.   ACCOUNTING CONTROLS AND PRIVATIZATION

3.1   Accounting in State Owned Enterprises

Accounting controls of many SOEs in LDCs are ineffective (Hopper et al., 2009). A reoccurring research finding is that management controls often become redundant and/or merely symbolic because decisions follow political rather than commercial criteria: politicians bypass formal accountability systems and intervene into operational decisions (Uddin and Hopper, 2001, 2003; Wickramasinghe, Hopper and Rathnasiri, 2004; Uddin and Tsamenyi, 2005; Wickramasinghe and Hopper, 2005; Xu and Uddin, 2008; Hopper et al., 2009). For example, Xu and Uddin (2008) found that state officials determined the costs and prices, completion of projects, availability of materials, and the production capacity in Chinese SOEs. In Bangladesh SOEs, accounting appeared to exist to legitimate state activities to external aid agencies by demonstrating the appearance, rather than the substance, of financial accountability (Hoque and Hopper, 1994; Uddin and Hopper, 2001). Apparently rational and soundly designed, if dated, accounting systems operating within central state planning were symbolically maintained to gain legitimacy from external actors such as donors and citizens. But they were irrelevant for managers, as they bore little semblance to operational realities. Managers prepared the necessary reports but perceived them to be unreliable and not reflecting the daily uncertainties they confronted – hence they often neglected them in making decisions. The running of enterprises came to rest with a fluctuating coalition of union leaders, managers and nominated outsiders, with deleterious effects. Political rather than commercial criteria drove decisions, and politicians intervened for political ends and to exercise patronage – accounting data played little part in decisions, control and accountability. The issue, examined below, is whether privatization and the management accounting changes it prompts bring about the changes anticipated and serve broader development goals. This is discussed with respect to our case studies from Bangladesh, Ghana and Sri Lanka. We do not claim that these constitute a representative sample – intensive case studies must sacrifice breadth for depth – but we believe they are illustrative of similar research elsewhere (Hopper et al., 2009).

3.2   Historical Context of the Privatized Firms

In Bangladesh the privatization programme commenced with the fall of its socialist government (Uddin and Hopper, 2003). Military governments, especially the vulnerable Ershad one, formulated market-based industrial policies to curry Western support in the face of domestic opposition. The government needed external finance from the World Bank and the IMF to cover fiscal deficits. It had little alternative but to accept loan conditions demanding privatization of SOEs (whether loss-making or not). The military governments initiated a wholesale privatization programme and established a divestment board that divested or privatized 255 SOEs, including 'abandoned' and vested properties, between 1975 and 1981 (World Bank, 1997). In 1986 many SOEs became joint stock companies in a holding company (Board of Investments) responsible for selling subsidiary companies' shares under the '51–49 Plan' (49 per cent of shares sold to private buyers and 51 per cent retained by the government). The number of privatizations was large but involved mainly small factories and mills that were economically and politically insignificant and thus easy to privatize. Most large SOEs were unionized and had strong links to political parties, and labour militancy could overthrow governments: they were not privatized because of their political sensitivity. Nevertheless, influential World Bank reports (1993, 1995, 1996a, 1996b, 1996c) argued that Bangladesh SOEs were inefficient. In 1993, the government established the Privatization Board following World Bank pressure for speedier and more independent privatizations, but from 1991 to 1996 only 13 of the 40 SOEs targeted by the Aid Group were privatized. The 1996 Awami League government promised donor agencies it would intensify privatization programmes (*Bangladesh Observer*, 1 January 1997), but from 1996 to 2001 only nine small SOEs were fully privatized. Since 2001 more than 60,000 employees of 42 SOEs (large and small) have been made redundant, but only four SOEs were handed over to private owners (*Daily Star*, 23 February 2004). Again, this fell short of expectations. The Bangladesh case involved a soap company (Uddin and Hopper, 2001).[2] It was partially privatized in 1988: the state retained a majority shareholding. Partial privatization merely increased political factionalism, bringing a sharp deterioration in performance. However, still being profitable and thus saleable made it a privatization candidate. It underwent full privatization in 1993, with one family holding 75 per cent of its shares.

Privatization in Ghana began after the fall of the socialist government of Dr Nkrumah (1957 to 1966). SOEs had been instrumental in capturing the 'commanding heights of the economy', but state ownership was also attributable to the lack of effective and capable local entrepreneurship, and fears that commercial returns from public investments would not attract private sector funding, and entrusting the economy to foreigners could bring 'quantifiable neo-colonialism' (Killick, 1978). Many SOEs were established under an import substitution programme and depended on protection and preferential access to foreign exchange. From 1957 to 1966, employment in SOEs increased tenfold, rising from 11 052 to 115 826 (Adda, 1992). These enterprises became characterized by large operating losses, low production levels due to under-utilization of capacity and low productivity, large debts, and serious liquidity problems. Most SOEs became a financial burden on the state rather than contributing to government revenue. The performance of the Ghanaian economy generally proved to be poor, characterized by high inflation, balance of payment problems, high unemployment, low productivity and GDP.

Between 1966 and 1972, successive governments pursued a policy of shifting the emphasis by developing the private sector. The military National Liberation Council (NLC) and the civilian Progress Party (PP) governments instituted IMF-/World Bank-led economic reforms in the late 1960s. The PP government recommended privatizations in 1970 but was overthrown in the backlash to its economic reforms. The military government of Colonel Acheampong that assumed power in 1972 abandoned the reforms. It encouraged private sector development but with little success. The public sector continued to dominate economic activities (the number of SOEs exceeded 350 in the late 1970s). Governments felt compelled to maintain the non-performing SOEs despite the failure of their efforts to make them profitable and viable corporate entities. By 1981, the continuous poor financial performance of SOEs threatened the economic stability and development of Ghana. Subsidies, subventions and loans to SOEs averaged around 12 per cent of total government expenditures from 1980 to 1982 (Adda, 1992); subventions increased from ¢1.1 billion in 1982 (10 per cent of government expenditure) to ¢7.35 billion in 1986 (8 per cent of government expenditure). Outstanding government loans to SOEs increased from ¢500 million in 1980 to ¢1.9 billion in 1985. Virtually no interest or principal repayments were made by these enterprises: they generated insufficient returns to sustain themselves let alone to redeem debts. The 1984 census revealed that 240 000 workers were employed in SOEs.

Killick (1978) and Pozen (1976) attributed the poor financial performance of the SOEs to poor project planning, faulty selection of product lines, inadequate working capital and undue interference by the government into their management. Adda (1992) attributed it to: an unsatisfactory policy framework such as extensive price controls and labour laws restricting lay-offs; the lack of competent managers in most SOEs; an almost total absence of management information due to poor accounting and budgetary control systems; poor remuneration packages and hence an inability to attract competent and experienced personnel; the ineffectiveness in coordinating and supervising government agencies and ministries; the lack of an effective process for monitoring and evaluating performance, resulting in poor accountability; and the large size of the SOE sector and its dispersed nature.

The inefficiency of the public sector, drought and falling export revenues, and the decline of the Soviet bloc meant Ghana had to turn to Western financial institutions, and it became one of the first Sub-Saharan African countries to adopt structural adjustment programmes. The IMF-/World Bank-led economic reforms were reintroduced in 1983 by the military government of Flight-Lieutenant Rawlings. International aid agencies encouraged his administration to adopt programmes to minimize and eliminate government interventions in markets, encourage domestic savings and foreign investment, privatize SOEs, and improve the balance of payments. A Divestiture Secretariat was established in 1987, though no sales were made until 1991 (Leith and Soderling, 2000). To date over 300 SOEs have been divested – over 55 per cent by the outright sale of assets. The mining sector, a major source of foreign exchange, and banking were particular targets for privatization.

The first Ghana case, a gold mine, was corporatized and partially privatized in the mid-1990s (Tsamenyi, Hopper and Uddin, 2011). The government's shareholding fell from 51 per cent to 20 per cent to attract more private capital and satisfy the listing requirements of the London, New York and Sydney stock markets. It became the first African company listed on Wall Street. The remaining two cases were researched because they have been proclaimed by the authorities as the most successful cases of privatization in Ghana.[3] One, anonymized as PC Ltd, is a processing firm which was partially privatized in the mid-1990s and fully privatized in early 2000s. It is now 100 per cent owned by a Western multinational. The second, anonymized as SC Ltd, is a service firm which was fully privatized in the early 1990s. It is now owned by an African multinational firm but is managed by a Western multinational under a management contract. Seven of the eight executive team members are Western expatriates. PC and SC employ approximately 700 and 350 people respectively. The performance of both companies pre- and post-privatization was evaluated by a range of financial and non-financial measures derived from the balanced scorecard framework of Kaplan and Norton (1992). Five sets of indicators so derived covered financial outcomes, customers, internal business processes, learning and growth, and serving the community.

Sri Lanka followed a similar pattern. In 1977, a new right-wing government marked a transition to market capitalism labelled the 'open economy'. It criticized its left-wing predecessor for promoting 'closed-economic policies' whereby SOEs acted as vehicles of employment and political patronage. SOEs were portrayed as loss-making entities infected with dysfunctional management control, corruption and undue government intervention. The deficits of SOEs strained the government budget: they accounted for budgetary transfers amounting to 10 per cent of GDP in the mid-1980s. Over a decade later, the privatization programme gathered momentum with a divestiture of 43 public enterprises that raised Rs. 11.6 billion by 1995 (Knight-John, 1995). The policies followed IMF and World Bank pressure (Kelegama, 1995). Even when a left-wing political party assumed power in 1994 the open economic policies and the privatization programme continued. As a result, by 2002 the government had raised Rs. 46.2 billion by privatizing 86 public enterprises (Annual Reports, Central Bank of Sri Lanka, 2003). Government statements indicate that the aims of these divestitures were to alleviate fiscal deficits and to improve enterprise efficiency by encouraging management controls based on a private sector ethos (Budget Speech, 1987). They tried to facilitate privatization by introducing an institutional framework that included new institutions such as the Presidential Commission on Privatization, the Public Investment Management Board, and the Commercialization of Public Enterprises Division (within the Ministry of Finance). The first Sri Lankan case discussed here was a textile mill that was fully privatized in 1992 and new Indian managers and owners took over (Wickramasinghe et al., 2004). The second case follows the partial privatization in 1997 of Sri Lanka state telephones – previously a government department renowned for poor service and inefficiency. A Japanese telecommunications company became a minority shareholder and undertook its management (Wickramasinghe et al., 2004).

3.3 Accounting and Accountability Changes

In general, privatizations brought improved management information systems through investments in more accurate, quicker, computerized internal controls, especially directed at improved market information, short-run planning, and matching production to market demand. In the Bangladesh soap company, the new owners computerized management information systems and linked market information to production schedules. Budgets became centralized and market oriented, and all financial information became the preserve of the owning family. The owners exercised direct and arbitrary control reinforced by their power to hire, fire and promote at whim. Physical, tighter budgets were imposed down the line and ultimately upon the labourers. Management destroyed the internal state through redundancies, installing a puppet union, and using subcontracted, low-paid, casual labour (Uddin and Hopper, 2003). Managerial actions were often justified by accounting claims arbitrarily fed downwards stating the need for cost savings, productivity and profitability. However, it is dubious whether these were internalized by workers or even supervisors, though workers could not ignore them without imperilling their jobs. The swingeing redundancy programme was justified using accounting data, and the trade union leaders permitted to remain justified their acceptance of the virtually destroyed internal state accordingly. For instance, the general secretary of the dominant trade union faction commented that redundancy programmes were necessary to revive profitability.

Despite company law and stock exchange listing requirements to the contrary, published annual reports ceased after the first year of privatization (1995) without redress. Legal problems were not confined to capital providers. Workers' claims for redundancy payments, non-payment of pensions, and other issues since privatization have been brought to the labour court by trade unions, but the state and regulatory bodies have failed to take action. Alongside allegations of irregular financial transactions and exploitation of minority shareholders, state tax officials and banks have brought prosecutions against the company for financial irregularities. The Securities Exchange Commission of Bangladesh, a government agency, has considerable powers over listed companies, but these are rarely enacted for irregularities like failing to hold annual general meetings, failing to pay dividends as promised, or making misleading statements. Executives complain of long judicial delays, and small investors have little redress over defaulting companies. Given the absence of published financial reports required by law it was impossible to discern whether performance increased after privatization.

In the Ghana gold mine, greater private ownership brought updated Western management controls. The budgeting system was computerized, and an integrated accounting software package (Business Planning and Control System) and activity-based costing were introduced. The listing on international stock exchanges and the new controls only marginally changed employees' beliefs that accounting was subservient to mining. However, with the subsequent fall in gold prices and rising production costs (due to the exhaustion of economic reserves) the company came close to bankruptcy. Management introduced cost cutting measures and emphasized the role of accounting controls: budget performance reports constituted the major part of managerial performance evaluation; courses in budgeting were introduced for all managers; and redundancies and reduced benefits ensued justified mainly using accounting data. Regular accounting reports required by law were maintained. However, regulation of the mining sector had been reduced to attract foreign investors (Canadian Council for International Cooperation, 2003), bringing neglect of pollution, land degradation, and health problems associated with mining by government and mining companies alike. For instance, the gold company shifted from underground to cheaper open mining, which has more negative environmental impacts. The Canadian Council for International Cooperation report (2003) notes: 'The weak regulatory regime, which is so attractive to investors, often results in a situation where government is unable to create local benefits or protect the environment and their people's rights.'

In PC and SC, organizational objectives changed after privatization. Under state control, there had been little emphasis on cost control and profitability – the organizations just prepared aggregated budgets to estimate government subventions and subsidies. There were no budgets for sales, production, cash and other activities. After privatization, both firms automated their accounting and information systems to support planning and to monitor results. Both implemented commercially oriented budgetary control systems and formed budget committees, comprising all department heads and the finance staff. Department heads became responsible for preparing their departmental budget estimates and implementing and monitoring their agreed budgets, which were linked to the strategic plans of each firm. Decisions on issues like investments, products and pricing became guided by cost and accounting information.

The preparation and auditing of financial reports improved following privatization. Information on their activities and annual financial statements became available on a regular and timely basis, something considered alien under state control. For example, both firms regularly prepared quarterly financial statements. Before privatization, the Audit Service was responsible for auditing the SOEs (including PC and SC), but they often failed to do so or did so two or three years in arrear. Upon privatization, both organizations have had their accounts audited periodically by one of the big four accounting firms. They have also established internal audit departments: these were not in place under state control.

The privatization programme in Sri Lanka relieved fiscal burdens on the government budget, but the money saved was diverted to defence (Knight-John, 1995). There were no severe labour redundancy issues (redundancy packages were offered), but privatization removed state subsidies and brought price increases in many public services such as transport and telecommunications. Accounting became more visible in post-privatization regimes in Sri Lanka. State-led 'good governance' campaigns induced more market-based management control systems, organization structures and performance evaluation systems in the focal cases and beyond. This was manifested in the two case studies. The Indian owners of the Sri Lankan textile mill changed its organization structure and controls considerably. A corporate planning manager at headquarters became responsible for revitalizing management accounting practices and budgeting emphasizing commercial rather than legal and bureaucratic criteria. After preparatory meetings with key managers, heads of departments were briefed on the forthcoming budget and new policy decisions. Department heads sent their draft budgets to the cost accountant and finance manager, and a budget committee reviewed these with heads of departments to check their feasibility and whether they conformed to corporate policies, and to recommend remedial alterations. The cost accountant circulated the eventual master budget to heads of departments. The mill manager, a long-standing Sri Lankan manager in the mill, became responsible for short-run budget adjustments and budget targets. He was assisted by a new production planning manager who collected information on daily production, quality, and finished goods inventories, which was forwarded daily to headquarters by a courier who brought back market information from the marketing division. Production schedules were adjusted accordingly. Machine utilization and cost budgets became the main controls in production. Machine and labour utilization forms, and shift production formats recorded daily performance against budget. Daily instructions were issued to production managers and supervisors, who modified budgets in ad hoc meetings as necessary. Each head of department prepared monthly reports highlighting variances prior to a monthly accountability meeting with top managers. Budgetary control now appeared impeccable from an accounting perspective.

In the Sri Lanka telecommunications firm its post-privatization Japanese chief executive exercised a directive but consultative style of management, worked within the prevailing trade union structure, and changed performance appraisal and rewards to recognize achievement. This was a drastic change. The rule-bound bureaucratic management controls were replaced by a more efficiency-oriented system that appraised performance. The company became a more flexible organization that provided efficient and customer-friendly services. Prima facie, in each instance, privatization appeared to induce management control changes consistent with expectations of proponents of market solutions. However, as is discussed below, these changes proved to be transitory for cultural and political reasons.

3.4   Capital Investment

In each instance, private capital brought significant investment in technology. In the Bangladesh soap factory, capital investment was limited, possibly owing to the indigenous owners having inadequate access to capital. Instead they intensified work practices. In the Ghana gold mine, considerable mechanization had occurred before majority private ownership. However, a World Bank/IFC loan guaranteed by the government financed further capital investment and operational improvements, encouraged by a new minerals law that allowed it to retain 45 per cent of its export earnings. In PC, upon privatization, long-term finance from three major Ghana banks supplemented additional capital from the foreign shareholder. This was invested into research and development, product development and market research, and long-term assets, such as additional production plants, delivery vans and trucks. This significantly improved sales growth, market share, operating profits, returns on assets, lead-times between order and delivery, and reliability of deliveries. The company entered the top 10 of the 2003 list of Ghana's Club 100. Similarly, following SC's privatization, capital injected by the foreign owners and loans from international financial institutions enabled it to address the deplorable and unattractive state of its premises, the poor attitude of employees, and low customer satisfaction and retention. This produced improvements similar to those in PC.

In the Sri Lanka telecommunications firm, massive capital investments were made after privatization, especially in new technologies and expanded service centres. This required the hiring of younger, more technically qualified staff, often from the private sector. The Indian owners of the Sri Lankan textile mill also invested in new machinery. They hired Indian managers with engineering backgrounds and strong beliefs in technical solutions, who began to overhaul and modernize its machinery and improve operations, especially quality. Loans from a state bank were given to further these improvements. However, when the owner fled the country having fraudulently used the loans to invest in machinery in other ventures abroad, the company collapsed and returned to state control.

In summary, privatization brought greater investment from private and state funds. This tended to be greatest and most effective when the new owners were large corporations with dispersed ownership. The privatizations resulting in ownership concentrated in families were more susceptible to a lack of capital and financial irregularities, though we would not wish to infer that this is invariably the case.

3.5   Employee Relations and Culture

Changed accounting practices reflecting and reinforcing market relations post-privatization can conflict with employees' traditional cultural beliefs on what constitutes legitimate rights and obligations. In the Bangladesh case, culture was not a major issue, partly because the factory was in an urban area and, given the precarious economic position of workers, managers could stamp out any vestiges of traditional culture and obligations, such as worker absenteeism during harvests. Cultural issues were not studied in the cases of PC and SC, but in so far as they existed they appeared surmountable. However, in the Sri Lanka textile mill and the Ghana gold mine, ethnic tensions intertwined with cultural issues fused with and permeated industrial relations conflicts that were intertwined with persisting issues of political patronage.

In the Ghanaian gold mine, traditional cultural values still permeated production relations, but the new mining equipment isolated miners and thus weakened cultural bonds. Moreover, whites and 'southern' Ghanaians continued to dominate management, and they received more fringe benefits and enjoyed better working conditions than predominantly 'northern' miners (northern and southern miners tend to have different ethnic identities). After the listing, the culture and language of mining continued to dominate that of accounting. Hence management gaming involving overstated budgets, understated production targets, and spending budget allocations to avoid budget cuts persisted despite accounting gaining greater prominence. The General Mines Workers Union's power diminished: miners recognized their dependence upon international capital, and the union became less confrontational. Management tried to facilitate negotiation, transparency and cordial relations by appointing two union representatives to the board. On the other hand, it also tried to infiltrate the union, and it established an industrial relations unit in each mine to monitor and discipline miners, and report imminent strikes. Miners viewed industrial relations officers with suspicion, seeing them as spies and controllers. Although the company could dismiss individual miners, the major redundancy programmes often brought strikes and government interventions. The financial crisis in the late 1990s when gold prices collapsed brought tighter controls that allegedly bore more heavily on miners. Following checks by metal detectors at the mines, miners sought compensation for the loss of previously smuggled gold, which they had traditionally perceived as legitimate rewards. This led to further strikes with ethnic overtones.

However, in PC, despite new controls linking rewards to performance, increased labour cost efficiency and lower job security, labour relations were not a major issue, possibly because of increased training, growing employee numbers, and a more favourable public image of the company following its increased effectiveness, community involvement, and contributions to government revenue. Prior to privatization, SC had poor labour cost control, an information system not conducive to meaningful planning and control, weak supervision, and no means of disciplining employees or channelling their grievances other than through the government ministry. After privatization, the new management emphasized discipline and introduced formally defined responsibilities and reporting structures. Labour costs were better controlled and became a smaller proportion of total revenue. Employees received more competitive but performance-based remuneration and improved benefit packages (for example, for health, education and clothing). Schemes were introduced to recognize outstanding employees, provide training and career development and, whenever possible, fill vacancies through internal promotions. However, some employees alleged discrimination against indigenous managers in appointments and promotions compared to 'Westerners'; and others complained of restrictions on forming a union or association, especially given the general manager's absolute power to fire staff, few means of challenging this, and the cessation of guaranteed job security.

The effect of culture was most marked in Sri Lanka. In the telecom firm, older employees were habituated to the slow pace of work in a public enterprise, rule-bound behaviour, minimal performance evaluation, and exploiting delays to customers to gain undue rewards. Following the partial privatization, by exploiting their powers within legislation, trade union and political leaders continued to exercise patronage and intervene in everyday management on behalf of disgruntled workers, though it became more difficult and less prominent. After initial hostility to privatization, trade union leaders at first undertook little direct militant action against the Japanese management, who took pains to gain their confidence. However, ensuing management changes precipitated bitter and violent clashes between the 'younger' and 'older' (often previously civil servant) workers.[4] As will be discussed, the politicians intervened to block the changes and remove the new manager. In the rural textile mill, traditional values had influenced working practices since its foundation in the 1950s. Indigenous managers reciprocated 'kingship' expectations of workers and enabled traditional obligations to be reciprocated through padded budgets. This continued after privatization but was supplemented by ethnic tensions. Workers attributed the sale of the textile mill to Indians to politicians' desire to placate Tamils. Allegations (unsupported) that the owners supported Tamil rebels precipitated an alliance of workers and indigenous managers against the new owners. The mill workers were not normally militant, but they still expected trade unions and their political affiliates to intervene on their behalf post-privatization. When the mill failed, employees successfully (but ephemerally) got political and trade union leaders to intervene and reopen it. In Sri Lanka, the trade unions remained influential after privatization, and the party-based trade union structure remained intact.

Industrial relations were an issue in the Bangladesh case. SKOP (the combination of all trade union federations) dropped their opposition to privatizations (whether in part or in full) and concentrated on protecting worker interests. Their efforts to prevent worker layoffs had little success in the soap factory. The new private owners exploited inadequacies in the drafting and enforcement of the Industrial Relations Ordinance (1969) to the full, assuming its managerial prerogative to hire and fire at will, but ignored its protections of temporary contract labour and their trade union rights. A government trade union appointed to mediate labour and capital conflicts within the firm proved to be a puppet that acted at the behest of the new owner-managers. In this instance privatization broke collective bargaining systems and revoked improvements in worker rights or conditions.

In summary, in each case, except for the Sri Lankan textile mill, privatization brought a rationalization and sometimes a reduction in employment, and tighter controls over labour. As in most organizations, managing the change was difficult, especially when it challenged employees' traditional cultural beliefs and expectations of political patronage. Employment changes associated with cost reduction could amplify industrial relations conflicts. This is not surprising given that privatization seeks to increase performance in arguably inefficient SOEs with bloated labour forces. However, such conflicts appeared more prevalent when employees perceived few of the benefits stemming from privatization percolating down to society in terms of government revenue and community support, or to employees in terms of increased employment and remuneration, and employee rights. Drives for greater efficiency are a policy aim of privatization, but they are particularly worrying when accompanied by a denial of worker and trade union rights under existing legislation. Moreover, if politicians retained powers over the firm they could reassert political intervention and patronage and thence potentially overturn many management reforms.

3.6   Political Intervention

In the Bangladesh company political influence persisted after privatization. Political agents acting as employees at the behest of politicians disappeared, but political influence took new forms. Politicians used their powers within regulatory frameworks to favour investors amenable to granting political favours. The new owner-managers of the soap company had to reward political support for ousting trade unions and militants by recognizing a token government party trade union and appointing staff recommended by ministers. Privatization brought family control exerted through direct, physical and sometimes coercive controls, but to maintain their ultimate power within production the owners had to accede to political power.

Despite the Ghanaian mine company's listing on international stock markets, the government's minority share ownership and strong board representation (a government minister is the chairman of the board of the company) enabled politicians to veto decisions, and intervene in labour relations, explorations for new mines, and mining methods. Party disputes spilt over into organizational matters. For example, the chief executive was at loggerheads with the president of Ghana because of allegations that he was a member of the opposition political party and supported a traditional chief objectionable to the government. Government probes were frequent. For example, in 1993 the head of state, Jerry Rawlings, inspected the mine and by midday he had expressed his dissatisfaction with conditions and immediately replaced the deputy managing director. The government, through its minority holding, vetoed financiers' and private shareholders' attempts to merge the company with another large foreign mining company to avert a financial crisis. In December 2001, dissatisfied with political interventions and constraints, the company demanded the government relinquish its 20 per cent shareholding. However, in PC and SC no major issues concerning continued political intervention after privatization were raised, and the regulatory structure appeared to be working effectively. The difference between the gold mine and PC and SC may in part be attributable to the government having fewer means of intervention following full rather than partial privatization.

In Sri Lanka political interventions continued in the telecommunications company but took a different form after partial privatization. The new management could not eliminate the politicized trade union culture, and subsequently a new government and its trade unions formed an alliance to act on behalf of mainly older, previously civil servant employees. Several board members and the chairman were political appointees, and the new government used its power to replace the chairman with a party supporter critical of management changes. Major conflicts with the chief executive ensued. The management reform programme was halted when a coalition of recalcitrant workers, some trade unions, state officials, and government-nominated directors eventually overthrew the Japanese chief executive. This was made possible through political capture of the regulatory process and remaining state regulations over the enterprise. Politicians can use their powers within regulatory frameworks to favour investors willing to grant political favours. If regulatory bodies are so captured, and enforcement is weak, then political interventions, disputes between firms and government agencies, and the growth of political links between owner-managers and regulators are exacerbated. For example, the head of the Telecommunications Regulatory Commission was an ex-MP appointed by the minister. Managers of the telecom company complained that the Commission refused their requests to reduce prices of products and new connections to protect small telecom service providers. Moreover, fully privatized enterprises can find that political support is still essential (Uyangoda, 2000). For example, when the textile mill was fully privatized the minister responsible for the sale helped the new owners secure loans from the state bank. Thus whilst the diminished political intervention into enterprises expected following privatization could be reduced considerably, especially in full privatizations not subject to market regulation, it did not necessarily disappear totally and could reappear through new conduits. For example, privatization of the Sri Lanka telecommunications company did not remove political interference – rather it shifted it from operations to regulatory issues.

In addition, greater accountability and governance induced by more developed capital markets did not invariably materialize as anticipated. In at least two cases weak regulation by the state and market institutions led to failures to publish financial information as stipulated, which may have encouraged corrupt financial practices. The privatizations of the Bangladesh soap factory and the Sri Lanka textile mill culminated in financial malpractices fostered by weak enforcement of reporting requirements based on statute and/or stock exchange rules. In weak capital markets with poor governance, accurate financial information and regulatory enforcement may be absent, leaving creditors and minority shareholders with little protection.

4.   CONCLUSIONS

This chapter set out to evaluate the changes to management accounting controls in the context of structural adjustment programmes in LDCs drawing on the existing literature and empirical illustrations from Bangladesh, Ghana and Sri Lanka. In each country prior research indicated major economic problems with SOEs due to dominance of political rather than commercial criteria in decisions and a lack of accountability and control. We do not wish to assert that this is inevitably a corollary of public ownership, but to date it has been a recurring finding of the small but growing accounting research on SOEs in LDCs. The aims of privatization were to alleviate the fiscal burden and to improve enterprise efficiency through adopting a private sector ethos of management control. Our examination suggests that the anticipated changes and positive outcomes, especially to accounting systems, tended to occur after privatization. These included: the recruitment of new staff capable of establishing a private sector management ethos; improved management information systems and performance appraisal methods; enhancement of market-friendly products and services; greater investment in operations and marketing; and greater staff development. However, these outcomes could have unintended consequences. These include: cultures and ethnic tensions at odds with the expectations of the new management rationality; state bureaucratic controls that reassert continuous political intervention (especially within partial privatizations) rather than the state shifting its efforts to supply-side economics and regulation; increased volatile industrial relations;

and financial irregularities during the privatization process and after. Throughout our research we have failed to find any examples of formal management accounting systems in large to medium-sized organizations that significantly differ in design and intent to those in similar Western organizations. Differences in practice have lain in their usage, which is a product of the socio-political context. Management controls following privatizations in LDCs have tended to improve and be more commercially oriented. They are a necessary but not sufficient condition for effective privatizations to materialize. However, as with their predecessors in SOEs their effectiveness remains susceptible to cultural and political ramifications. Without pertinent changes in regulation by the state and capital markets, careful and legal handling of industrial issues affecting employees who can feel the brunt of changes, and a transparent privatization process that encourages ownership with the necessary capital and ethical management expertise to bring about commercial improvements, then the anticipated accounting changes may not materialize.

NOTES

1. Ghana is particularly interesting, as it was an early implementer of such reforms in Africa and is often cited by the World Bank as a 'success' story.
2. Thirteen other companies privatized in the same tranche as the soap company were also examined subsequently, though in less detail (Uddin and Hopper, 2003).
3. Both companies as SOEs exhibited poor performance in terms of operating profit, return on capital, asset turnover, customer satisfaction, sales growth, contributions to community including no contribution to government revenue, and internal management controls.
4. Post-privatization the firm recruited newer, younger and more technically qualified staff, often from the private sector, who were often superior to staff recruited during its civil service era.

REFERENCES

Adam, C., W. Cavendish and P.S. Mistry (1992). *Adjusting Privatization: Case Studies from Developing Countries.* London: Currey.
Adda, W.A. (1992). Management of the privatization process: the Ghanaian experience. Paper presented at the Conference on Privatization, sponsored by MDPEA Division, Commonwealth Secretariat, Islamabad.
Akinsanya, A. (1981). The former Western Nigeria Development Corporation: a framework for performance evaluation. *Public Administration Development*, 1, pp. 225–33.
Ayub, M., and S. Hegstod (1986). *Public Industrial Enterprises: Determinants of Performance*, World Bank Industry and Finance Series no. 17. Washington, DC: World Bank.
Baiman, S. (1991). Studies on accounting institutions in markets and organizations. *Journal of Accounting Research*, 29, pp. 55–9.
Boubraki, N., and J.-C. Cosset (1998). The financial and operating performance of newly privatized firms: evidence from developing countries. *Journal of Finance*, 53(3), pp. 1081–1110.
Bouton, L., and M. Sumlinski (1997). Trends in private investments in developing countries. *USIA Electronic Journal*, 2, pp. 4–97.
Canadian Council for International Cooperation (2003). *Crossroads at Cancun: What Direction for Development? Focus on: Saying No to the New Singapore Issues*, www.ccic.ca.
Carter, Chris, and F. Mueller (2006). The colonisation of strategy: financialisation in a post-privatisation context. *Critical Perspectives on Accounting*, 17(8), pp. 967–85.
Catchpowle, L., and C. Cooper (1999). No escaping the financial: the economic referent in South Africa. *Critical Perspectives on Accounting*, 10, pp. 711–46.
Cole, B., and C. Cooper (2006). Deskilling in the 21st century: the case of rail privatisation. *Critical Perspectives on Accounting*, 17(5), pp. 601–25.

Commander, S., and T. Killick (1988). Privatisation in developing countries: a survey of the issues. In *Privatisation in Less Developed Countries*, ed. P. Cook and C. Kirkpatrick. New York: Harvester Wheatsheaf.

Cook, P., and C. Kirkpatrick (1988). Privatisation in less developed countries. In *Privatisation in Less Developed Countries*, ed. P. Cook and C. Kirkpatrick, pp. 3–31. New York: Harvester Wheatsheaf.

Cook, P., and C. Kirkpatrick (1995). *Privatisation Policy and Performance: International Perspectives*. New York: Prentice Hall/Harvester Wheatsheaf.

Craig, J. (2000). Evaluating privatisation in Zambia: a tale of two processes. *Review of African Political Economy*, 85, pp. 357–66.

Funkhouser, R., and P.W. McAvoy (1979). A simple observation on comparative prices in public and private enterprise. *Journal of Public Economics*, 11(1), pp. 353–68.

Goldman, M. (2005). *Imperial Nature: The World Bank and Struggles for Social Justice in the Age of Globalization*. New Haven, CT: Yale University Press.

Hanke, S.H. (1986). The privatisation option: an analysis. *Economic Impact*, 3(55), pp. 14–20.

Harvey, D. (2005). *A Brief History of Neoliberalism*, 1st edn. New York: Oxford University Press.

Hayek, F. (1944). *The Road to Serfdom*. London: Routledge.

Hopper, T., and P. Armstrong (1991). Cost accounting, controlling labour and the rise of the conglomerates. *Accounting Organizations and Society*, 16(5–6), pp. 405–38.

Hopper, T., J. Storey and H. Willmot (1987). Accounting for accounting: towards the development of a dialectical view. *Accounting, Organizations and Society*, 12(5), pp. 437–56.

Hopper, T., M. Tsamenyi, S. Uddin and D. Wickramasinghe (2009). Management accounting in less developed countries: what is known and needs knowing. *Accounting, Auditing and Accountability Journal*, 22(3), pp. 469–514.

Hoque, A.K.M.Z., and T.M. Hopper (1994). Rationality, accounting and politics: a case study of management control in a Bangladeshi jute mill. *Management Accounting Research*, 5(1), pp. 5–30.

IMF (1986). *Fund Supported Programmes, Fiscal Policy and Income Distribution*, Occasional Papers 46. Washington, DC: IMF.

Jensen, M.C., and W.H. Meckling (1976). Theory of the firm: managerial behaviour, agency cost and ownership structure. *Journal of Financial Economics*, 3, August 1975 – May 1976, pp. 305–60.

Kaplan, R., and D. Norton (1992). The balanced scorecard: measures that drive performance. *Harvard Business Review*, 70(1), pp. 71–9.

Kelegama, S. (1995). The impact of privatization on distributional equity: the case of Sri Lanka. In *Privatization and Equity*, ed. V.V. Ramanadham. London: Routledge.

Kikcri, S., J. Nellis and M. Shirley (1994). Privatization: lessons from market economies. *World Bank Research Observer*, 9, pp. 241–72.

Killick, T. (1978). *Development Economics in Action: A Study of Economic Policies in Ghana*. London: Heinemann.

Killick, T. (1983). The role of public sector in the industrialisation of African developing countries. *Industry and Development* (UNIDO), 7, pp. 47–76.

Kim, K. (1981). Enterprise performance in the public and private sectors: Tanzanian experience, 1970–75. *Journal of Developing Areas*, 5(3), pp. 471–84.

Knight-John, M. (1995). Privatization in a developing country: the Sri Lankan experience. Paper presented at the Asian Productivity Organization Symposium on Privatization, Bangkok (July).

Leith, J.C., and L. Soderling (2000). Ghana: long term growth, atrophy, and recovery, pp. 1–128. Report for the OECD Development Centre Project Emerging Africa, June.

Letza, S., and C. Smallman (2001). Est in aqua dulci non invidiosa voluptas: in pure water there is a pleasure begrudged by none: on ownership, accountability and control in a privatized utility. *Critical Perspectives on Accounting*, 12(1), pp. 65–85.Megginson, W.L., and M.K. Bouchkoua (1999). *Privatization and the Financing of the Enterprise: A Comparative Overview of the Evidence*. Paris: Organisation for Economic Co-operation and Development.

Megginson, W., R. Nash and M. Van Randenborgh (1994). The financial and operating performance of newly privatized firms: an international empirical analysis. *Journal of Finance*, 49(2), pp. 403–52.

Millward, R. (1988). Measured sources of inefficiencies in the performance of private and public sector enterprises in less developed countries. In *Privatisation in Less Developed Countries*, ed. P. Cook and C. Kirkpatrick. New York: Harvester Wheatsheaf.

Ogden, S.G. (1995a). Transforming frameworks of accountability: the case of water privatization. *Accounting, Organizations and Society*, 20(2–3), pp. 193–218.

Ogden, S.G. (1995b). Profit sharing and organisational change: attempt to promote employee commitment in the newly privatised water industry in England and Wales. *Accounting, Auditing and Accountability Journal*, 8(4), pp. 23–47.

Ogden, S.G. (1997). Accounting for organizational performance: the construction of the customer in the privatized water industry. *Accounting, Organizations and Society*, 22(6), pp. 529–56.

Ogden, S.G., and F. Anderson (1999). The role of accounting in organisational change: promoting performance improvements in the privatised UK water industry. *Critical Perspectives on Accounting*, 10, pp. 91–124.

Parker, D., and C. Kirkpatrick (2005). Privatisation in developing countries: a review of the evidence and the policy lessons. Journal of Development Studies, 41(4), pp. 513–41.

Parker, L. (2009). Photo-elicitation: an ethno-historical accounting and management research prospect. *Accounting, Auditing and Accountability Journal*, 22(7), pp. 1111–29.

Pozen, R. (1976). *Legal Choices for State Enterprises in the Third World*. New York: New York University Press.

Prager, J. (1992). Is privatisation a panacea for less developed countries: market failure versus public sector failure. *Journal of Developing Areas*, 26, April, pp. 310–22.

Prizzia, R. (2001) Privatization and social responsibility: a critical evaluation of economic performance. *International Journal of Public Sector Management*, 14(6), pp. 450–64.

Rahaman, A., S. Lawrence and J. Roper (2004). Social and environmental reporting at the VRA: institutional legitimacy or legitimation crisis. *Critical Perspectives on Accounting*, 15(1), pp. 35–56.

Ramaswamy, R.I. (1988). The privatization argument. *Economic and Political Weekly*, 12 March.

Rees, R. (1984). *Public Enterprise Economics*. London: Weidenfeld & Nicolson.

Rees, R. (1985). The theory of principal and agents. *Bulletin of Economic Research*, 37(1), pp. 3–26.

Rose-Ackerman, S. (1996). Altruism, nonprofits, and economic theory. *Journal of Economic Literature*, 34(2), pp. 701–28.

Toye, J. (1994). *Dilemmas of Development*. Oxford: Blackwell.

Tsamenyi, M., T. Hopper and S.N. Uddin (2011). Management accounting in a gold mining company in Ghana. Paper presented at Critical Perspectives on Accounting Conference, Florida, July.

Uddin, S.N., and T.M. Hopper (2001). A Bangladeshi soap opera: privatisation, accounting, consent and control. *Accounting, Organizations and Society*, 26(7–8), pp. 643–72.

Uddin, S., and T. Hopper (2003). Accounting for privatisation: testing World Bank claims. *Critical Perspectives on Accounting*, 14(7), pp. 739–74.

Uddin, S., and M. Tsamenyi (2005). Public sector reforms and the public interest. *Accounting, Auditing and Accountability Journal*, 18(5), pp. 648–74.

Uyangoda, J. (2000). A state of desire? Some reflections on the unreformability of Sri Lanka's post-colonial polity. In *Sri Lanka at Cross Roads: Dilemmas and Prospects after 50 Years of Independence*, ed. S.T. Hettige and M. Mayer, pp. 93–118. New Delhi: Macmillan India.

Wickramasinghe, D., and T. Hopper (2005). A cultural political economy of management accounting controls: a case study of a textile mill in a traditional Sinhalese village. *Critical Perspectives on Accounting*, 16(4), pp. 473–503.

Wickramasinghe, D., T. Hopper and C. Rathnasiri (2004). Japanese cost management meets Sri Lankan politics: case study of a Sri Lankan public utility. *Accounting, Auditing and Accountability Journal*, 17(1), pp. 85–120.

World Bank (1981). *Accelerated Developments in Sub-Saharan Africa: An Agenda for Action*. Washington, DC: World Bank.

World Bank (1983). *World Development Report*. Washington, DC: World Bank.

World Bank (1993). *Bangladesh Implementing Structural Reform*, Report No-11569-BD, 24 March. Washington, DC: World Bank.

World Bank (1995). *Bangladesh: Privatization and Adjustment*. Washington, DC: World Bank.

World Bank (1996a). *Bangladesh: Government that Works: Reforming the Public Sector*. Dhaka: University Press.

World Bank (1996b). *Annual Economic Update: Recent Economic Developments and Medium-Term Reform Agenda*, Country Development I, July. Washington, DC: World Bank.

World Bank (1996c). *Bangladesh: An Agenda for Action*. Washington, DC: World Bank, South Asia Department I.

World Bank (1997). *Global Development Finance*. Washington, DC: World Bank.

World Bank (2000). *The Quality of Growth*. New York: Oxford University Press.

Wortzel, H., and L.H. Wortzel (1989). Privatization: not the only answer. *World Development*, 17(5), pp. 633–41.

Xu, Wen, and Uddin, S. (2008). Changing regimes of control, public sector reforms and privatisation: a case study from China, *Accounting Forum*, 32(2), pp. 162–77.

13 Corruption in the developing countries: 'thinking about' the role of accounting

Jeff Everett

INTRODUCTION

While corruption 'may never have been compulsory', as former British prime minister Anthony Eden once said, it certainly remains a significant problem. According to global anti-corruption organizations such as the World Bank and IMF its economic costs alone are staggering, running in the order of between $20 billion and $40 billion each year in the countries of the developing world (Wallid, 2009). With these figures, it is easy to consider corruption as a problem worth eradicating, an unwelcome disease afflicting humankind, and those engaged in the fight, whether they are policy-makers, law enforcement personnel, or even accountants, as upholders of a rather noble purpose.

Yet it may be that the definition of the problem and the solutions that follow from it are shaped in unexpected ways by the perspectives and assumptions adopted by those examining the problem.[1] Consequently, the 'global fight' (Burger and Holland, 2006) against corruption may be less virtuous, and certainly less objective, than is sometimes thought. Indeed, those who argue that the fight has an uncommon fascination for neo-liberals (Hasty, 2005) or who suggest that the fight is taking place behind a hollow veneer (Bukovansky, 2006) would be inclined to suggest that behind the fight is a politically motivated set of purposes, namely the legitimation and global spread of market practices and ideologies, and a resulting circumscription of the duties and obligations of the actors involved in it.

This chapter examines this shaping process, and the way that corruption is 'thought about' (DeLeon, 1993). It examines the premises and assumptions underpinning the definition and problematization of corruption and the way these affect the solutions that are proposed for dealing with it. The chapter specifically considers the academic literature on corruption, as this acts as the gateway for the policies and processes of the large anti-corruption organizations, including the OECD, United Nations, World Bank, and IMF, organizations that involve accountants both directly and indirectly in their policies. The chapter further focuses on the dominant way of thinking about corruption, a conceptualization that originates in the work of liberal philosophers and those who continue to promote and revise their ideas to this day. Important among the latter are free market advocates and neoclassical or 'marginalist' (Tinker, Merino and Niemark, 1982) economists, a group that has left a lasting mark on the thoughts and practices of accountants working in the industrialized world. This is not to say that alternative perspectives are not available. They are, and these are worth considering because they lead to quite different ways of seeing the problem. In considering these alternatives, one is further asked to question taken-for-granted ideas regarding the accountant's duties and obligations in this field.

The chapter includes two main sections. In the first, I consider the dominant, 'private interest' or 'orthodox' view of corruption, a view that offers both a diagnosis of the problem and a set of universally applicable one-size-fits-all solutions. In this view corruption is seen as a function of the self-interest[2] of public officials and, armed with the belief that the invisible hand of the market harnesses the social actor's natural greed, market or 'exit' solutions are proposed for dealing with the problem. In this view, and in keeping with the positivist methodology of its adherents, there is also a focus on the most obvious manifestations of corruption – the type of corruption often found in the developing world (Johnson, 2005). Akin to a scientist in a laboratory, those posing the solutions further see themselves as detached, objective observers of the problem. The important consequence of this is that corruption is seen primarily as a problem found in the developing world (Bukovansky, 2006, p. 182), a world that itself is viewed as at best separate and detached from, and at worst hopelessly reliant upon (Escobar, 1995), those in the affluent West.

A key point made in this chapter is that the dominant definition of and consequent approach to dealing with corruption contains an important moralizing component. That component is rooted in a 'public/private' distinction that is not only foundational to John Stuart Mill's 'Liberty Principle' (Cave, 2009, p. 101), and hence social liberalism, but, most importantly for accountants, also the economic approach that underlies the research and teaching of accounting. This approach in turn has the effect of reinforcing what one set of authors terms an 'ethics of exclusion', or 'beliefs and practices that facilitate the creation of boundaries around [a] community of responsibility' (Michalowski and Kramer, 2006).[3] While such an ethics has the merit of protecting certain actors like accountants from criticism – after all, most accountants directly serve private interests – this ethics also limits these actors' actions to the status quo, or idea that they should simply do 'more of the same, but better'. The (normative) belief is that accountants need limit themselves to serving only a small but elite set of interests in society, namely managers and the providers of capital (that is, shareholders). Such an ethics, unfortunately, is deficient, since it disarms accountants and renders them unable to address the needs and protect the freedoms of a large number of global citizens, particularly those in the developing world, where injustices and inequities are all-too-common features of daily life.

In the second main section, I consider an alternative way of thinking about corruption. This has us focus not on the role of individual self-interest but instead power, and, rather than it being suggested that market solutions to corruption are needed to harness the human actor's natural proclivity to greed, the benignity of the neoclassical economist's free market is challenged and the accountability of private actors is viewed with skepticism.[4] The (liberal humanist) view that the individual social actor is a locus of consciousness, freedom, and subjective preference is also challenged and the possibility raised that individual actors are shaped by and are a part of a much larger set of social relations and moral obligations. These obligations concern justice, equity, and fairness, virtues to be afforded *equal* status (not inferior status) alongside liberty, choice, and the respect of the individual (including her property and privacy).

In addition, this alternative view of corruption is not beholden to the commitments of the traditional scientific method and logical positivism, but is instead born of the insights of different ways of knowing and understanding, such as critical theory and constructivism (Chua, 1986). Here, not only does one take into account more distant global actors[5] (Kramer, Michalowski and Kauzlarich, 2002), and not only do the social actor's experiences and interpretations of the world provide a basis for addressing the problem, but so too do corruption's less obvious forms become important, specifically those forms where 'power becomes caught in the grips of money', or where the boundary between wealth and power becomes obscure (Johnson, 2005; Moore Lappé, 2007). Together, these insights and this focus on power provide a foundation for understanding corruption as a problem not limited to the developing world, but one that is also ubiquitous in the industrialized world, and to which those in the industrialized world contribute in both thought and action.

CORRUPTION: THE PRIVATE INTEREST VIEW

There are numerous definitions of the term *corruption* and yet an even greater number of acts denoted by it. Regarding definitions, most in the policy arena employ a more or less common definition, and this relates to the misuse or abuse of public office for private gain (see World Bank, 1997, p.8; Dye and Stapenhurst, 1998; International Monetary Fund, 2005; Bukovansky, 2006, p.186). This definition appears to stem from the work of Nye (1967), and is common in much of the academic literature (see Klitgaard, 1988; La Palombara, 1994, p.77; Owen, 1997, p.40; Gray and Kaufmann, 1998; Gray-Molina, De Rada and Yánez, 1999, p.8). Corruption also has 'many faces' (Campos and Pradhan, 2007), which is to say the range of acts encompassed by the term is similarly broad. For instance, the term includes fraud, smuggling, treason, conflicts of interest, bribery, embezzlement, and many other acts (see Klitgaard, 1988; IFAC, 2003). One set of authors, Caiden, Dwivedi and Jabbra (2001), in fact list no less than 60 different forms of corruption.

Focal Points and Assumptions

The literature on corruption, while quite diverse, tends to align itself with what is best termed a neoclassical, economic view (Everett, Neu and Rahaman, 2006). This 'private interest view' is premised on liberal humanist thought, which holds that the rights of the individual are sacrosanct, that the individual is free to do as he or she wants – in so far as the rights of others are not violated – and that this freedom must be supported and protected (Chambers, 2008).[6] In rewriting to focus largely on *economic* rights and freedoms, neoclassical economists have provided and promoted an attractive way of thinking for those wanting to accumulate wealth and private property. Given the manner in which corruption presents a threat to wealth accumulation and private property, it is perhaps not surprising that this 'neoliberal' way of seeing (Harvey, 2005) is so pervasive in the literature and has such a wide following (see Rose-Ackerman, 1978, 1997; Mauro, 1995).[7]

Indeed, given its predominance, one might even go so far as to suggest that this private interest view represents the field's 'orthodoxy' (Watts, 1992). This literature draws attention to and effectively renders suspect one particular set of actors, namely public officials, though admittedly this literature has recently begun to broaden and include a greater focus on private sector actors in its definitions (see Kaufmann, 2005). In keeping with the private interest perspective that informs much of this literature, public officials are seen as inherently self-interested actors who, on account of their tendency to shirk their prescribed duties and general susceptibility to capture by special-interest groups, are in need of both careful monitoring and constant incentivization (see Mbaku, 2008). In the worst cases, public officials use their power to victimize the very people who put them into office – their 'principals'. In cases where businesses are forced to pay bribes to officials in foreign countries, the bribes are seen as 'agency costs', and while these costs undermine efficiency the level of corruption is thought to eventually reach equilibrium (see Eskeland and Thiele, 1999).

An important ontological assumption found in this literature is worth highlighting, and that concerns the idea that social actors are all inherently self-interested. Moore Lappé (2007) refers to this assumption as the 'premise of a lack of goodness', the idea that actors are all motivated only by economic incentives and the force of law. This includes accountants and auditors, who are seen as 'control agents' (Tillman, 2008); however, accountants and auditors are concerned about incurring 'reputational penalties', so they are careful to perform their duties and not engage in misconduct (Tillman, 2008). And while the term *corruption* connotes a sense of lost morality, morals and ethics do not enter into the discussion in any substantive way.[8] This is not to say that there is not an inherent ethics in the neoliberal view, since considerations of justice certainly preoccupied their social liberal forebearers. For one thing, justice implies the 'freedom of exit', or the idea that individuals should be allowed to leave any group or social arrangement wherein inequality exists (Chambers, 2008, p. 9).

Even with the neoclassical economist's focus on the individual, a moral obligation does exist, but this is typically left implicit. It concerns an imputed need to commit to the aims of investors and providers of capital, the belief being that societal wealth, creativity, and greater freedom automatically follow such a commitment (Michalowski and Kramer, 2006). That said, there is a movement within this perspective between a commitment to investors or shareholders and individual freedom. Where this commitment is seen to reside with the latter, human actors become essentially moral relativists; their morality – and this follows the thinking of economists such as Friedrich Hayek (1944) (especially in his later work) – becomes purely a function of one's *individual* choice or 'preference'.

Besides being inherently self-interested, the neoclassical thinker's social actor is largely motivated by economic incentives and the rule of law. At the abstract level of interaction, there is also a belief that what motivates social actors is the twin pursuit of utility and pleasure (see Friedman, 1953). The corruption literature's conceptual premises originate and remain largely at a micro-level of human action, and at this level one sees only two economic actors engaged in a contracting exercise. For example, the analytic concern might be on a citizen (a 'principal') negotiating an (often implicit) contract with a government official (the 'agent'), as a means of furthering both the citizen's and the public official's self-interested ends. One other important assumption that is made concerns the context within which corruption occurs. That context involves social actors contracting in a world of scarce resources. Another way of saying this is that neoliberal theorists are imbued with a 'scarcity consciousness' (Perlman, 1928) and, to be sure, such a consciousness does drive capitalism, for if nothing else capitalism *needs* lack (that is, 'untapped markets' and 'niches to fill') (Deleuze and Guatarri, 1972).[9]

With this alternating emphasis on responsibility to shareholders and individual pleasure or utility, it is perhaps not surprising that a key consequence for those working in this tradition is the way corruption undermines economic growth, economic freedom, and efficiency (see Stapenhurst and Sedigh, 1999; Fjeldstad and Tungodden, 2003). Corruption is seen to be problematic because of its tendency to place wealth in the hands of those deemed illegitimate, that is, persons other than the established and legal holders of wealth. Moreover, to orthodox commentators corruption is hardly surprising: in a world where there is a lack of goodwill *and* a lack of goods, and where self-interested individuals compete in brutish, tooth-and-nail struggles over resources, one can only *expect* deceit and the violation of trust. In this world, where only the fittest survive, greed comes to be seen as a natural driving force (Tonry, 1998, p. 228). Indeed, so 'natural' are greed and corruption that many see the latter as having an equilibrium point (see Eskeland and Thiele, 1999), while still others believe corruption is even beneficial (for a critique of this functionalist argument, see Alam, 1989 and Sen, 1999).

Fighting Corruption

While corruption might be expected or even normal according to this view, the fight still needs to be fought – again, it threatens the accumulation of wealth and private property. The strategies prescribed are typically based on the idea that corruption '= monopoly power + discretion − accountability'. This formula, promoted by one well-known economist and government advisor, Robert Klitgaard (1988), suggests that in order to curb corruption it is necessary, among other things, to break state monopolies and privatize government services. Such strategies are referred to as 'exit' strategies, in keeping with the moral priorities of these commentators. However, market strategies are not the only strategies found in the orthodox literature, as control and voice strategies are also discussed.

The object of control strategies is to improve legal, electoral, educational, and other institutional systems. Making the state a credible enforcer of laws, protecting whistle-blowers, reforming tax and customs administration systems, improving reporting systems, measuring public servants' performance, and strengthening watchdog agencies (ombudsmen, auditors, and so on)[10] are all seen as important means of addressing corruption (see Galtung, 1994; Klitgaard, 1994; La Palombara, 1994; Pope, 1998). These elements form what are termed 'pillars of integrity', or the foundational core of a country's 'integrity accountability institutions' (Stapenhurst and Dye, 1998; Gonzalez-Koss and Kellner, 2002; Schwartz, 2003). Voice solutions, in contrast, are based on the idea that citizens know the consequences of corruption better than do distant and elite experts, putting them in a better position to monitor the nature and extent of the problem. It follows then that 'people need to be empowered' in the fight against corruption (Caiden, 2001), that 'homegrown strategies are needed' (Eigen, 1998), and that 'the public need to be involved' and 'mobilized' in the fight (Galtung, 1994, p. 44; Khanal, 2000, p. 4).

Accounting and its associated actors have a role to play in each of these three areas. Accounting technologies are already perfectly suited to the implementation of exit, since financial and managerial accounting and auditing have been from their inception tailored specifically for use by competitive, profit-oriented organizations. Such technologies draw attention to bottom-line performance, considered by many as an indicator of efficiency (Cooper, 1980). The problem becomes one of simply implementing a working accounting system to facilitate exit, or ensuring that the existing system is moving toward accounting's 'state of the art'.

One example of this state of the art, or perceived best practice, is full accrual accounting. For instance, Torres (2004) argues that the move from cash accounting is necessary for government organizations because 'accrual-based fiscal indicators provide better information about the sustainability of fiscal policies, provide a stronger basis for government accountability and a better measure of the effects of government policies [and they also] provide better measures of organizational efficiency and effectiveness, and reduce opportunities for fraud and corruption' (p. 447). Other commentators (see Dye and Stapenhurst, 1998; Siame, 2002) call for the measurement of achieved outcomes of government programs, or measures of their efficiency, as part of performance or value-for-money audits (Barata and Cain, 2001; Schwartz, 2003). As many have argued (see Oakes, Townley and Cooper, 1998; Guthrie, Olson and Humphrey, 1999), these practices not only reflect a normative belief in the free market, but also facilitate a general shift towards a marketized system.

Also in respect of exit strategies, accounting firms are increasingly well positioned to assist in this move on account of the extensive array of services and types of expertise that many of them now provide, such as the skills required to implement accrual-based accounting systems in public sector organizations (Christensen, 2005). Together, they further the push towards what some (Hood, 1995; Lapsley, 1999) call the new public management, or the 'reinvention' of public organizations (see Gaebler and Osborne, 1993), the idea being that these organizations, more than anything else, must become more efficient. Large, integrated accounting firms are also in a position to offer once-state-owned or newly privatized firms a variety of 'tax products' and investment options, again with the stated aim of improving overall efficiency (Sikka, 2008).

Concerning control solutions, accounting also has a major role to play. For some, the objective here is the establishment and maintenance of an integrity system (Anechiaricho and Jacobs, 1995; Espejo, Bula and Zarama, 2001; Doig and McIvor, 2003) or a more general accountability framework. In respect of countries wanting to fight corruption and improve their accountability systems, one anti-corruption organization, the World Bank (1994, p. 14), recommends:[11]

- implementing an effective and integrated financial management information system;
- developing a professional base of accountants and auditors;
- adopting and applying internationally acceptable accounting standards;
- empowering a strong legal framework for supporting modern accounting practices.

Finally, concerning voice solutions, accounting technology can be employed here as well, since accountants, particularly those working for national auditors or 'supreme audit institutions' (SAIs), are in a position to provide the public with independently derived and highly comprehensive reports on government activity and spending. SAIs are believed to contribute directly to voice through their ability to report on 'deviations from principles of legality, accounting, economy, efficiency, and effectiveness' (Stapenhurst and Dye, 1998). Non-SAI-employed accountants might also play a role in enhancing voice by ensuring, for instance, that business expenses for commissions, taxes and, where they are declared, personal assets are adequately and fairly disclosed. It is worth noting here that contributions to voice often imply well-functioning institutions, meaning that control and voice solutions are often mutually reinforcing.

Presupposing Solutions

In the orthodox literature these strategies are not equally weighted in terms of preference, and there is a discernible predilection for exit or market-based solutions (Bukovansky, 2006; Everett et al., 2006). One objection that might be raised in respect of this preference is that it is not clear why corporate business principles should dominate or trump democratic principles. In fact, given that the state provides the infrastructure, security, and other resources that businesses need to function properly (Sen, 1999), and given that corruption seems to be inversely related to the democratic functioning of a state (see Johnson, 2005), one might think the preference would be on voice options first and control options second, which would put exit or market options last.

A second, related point about this literature is that there is a dearth of evidence pointing to the effectiveness of market solutions in fighting corruption. In looking at the orthodox literature on the topic one encounters problems establishing the direction of causality (Andvig and Fjelstad, 2001, p. 42), and it appears that this literature may be plagued by 'the partial and selective use of general equilibrium models, the selective retention of conclusions, and the use of *ad hoc* explanations to choose between solutions' (Hibou, 2000, pp. 7–9).[12] Worse, the very solutions that follow from the manner in which neoclassical economists 'think about' corruption – namely, market or exit strategies – might, if implemented in the absence of a democratic, functioning state, actually *increase* corruption. Indeed, there is an emerging awareness that liberalization and economic reforms have actively fostered and promoted corruption and fraud (Uprety, 2000; Andvig and Fjeldstad, 2001, p. 23; Uddin and Hopper, 2003; Black, 2005; Johnson, 2005; Tavares, 2005).

A third and final point worth noting in regard to the orthodox view is that by allowing commentators in the industrialized world to define the problem of corruption in a specific way there is a chance that that definition and any consequent analyses will deflect attention from the corruption that exists in these commentators' own national contexts (Bukovansky, 2006, p. 198). Corruption is, after all, endemic in the industrialized world, though it is of a fundamentally different type (Johnson, 2005), a point I will return to shortly. Further, in allowing the solutions to be developed by First World commentators, there is also the chance that the proposed solutions will promote the interests of those very same individuals (Kramer et al., 2002, p. 266). Here, one might consider the well-known Corruption Perceptions Index used by Transparency International. In looking at this index one might be inclined to think that corruption is low or non-existent in the industrialized world, and that the problem resides not only in poorer nations, but more specifically in the public sectors of those nations. It involves only a short step for First World business leaders and their political allies then to argue for the privatization of these countries' national assets.

The Orthodox Role and Obligation of Accountants

To the extent that accountants consciously or perhaps unwittingly go along with the orthodox view and privilege market solutions over voice and control solutions, then the prescription for accountants is to do what the majority of them already do, namely promote the interests of those elites who are currently powerful in society (Cooper, 1980, p.164). This is the status quo option: continue catering to the decision-making needs of accounting's 'primary users', that is, shareholders and managers. With justice being defined in terms of the provision of exit and the economic freedom of the individual (Chambers, 2008), accountants are implicated in a normative project of wealth accumulation and the protection of private property. When there is a focus solely on exit or market solutions, the primacy of economic growth is accepted, the scarcity of goodness among people ingrained, and the idea that the world suffers from a characteristic 'lack' (Moore Lappé, 2007) taken as a fundamental truth. Corruption, in this view, is unfortunate, but at the same time 'something to be expected'.

CORRUPTION: A PUBLIC INTEREST VIEW

There are, however, other ways of viewing the world and the corruption that exists in it, and these are worth considering, as they imply rather different roles and obligations for accountants. I would like now to explore one such view, a public interest view of corruption. Here, power is positioned much more centrally in the analysis of socio-economic relations, and the enormous difference in economic power between the rich and poor world is highlighted. This difference has affected the capacity of the developing world to deal with corruption (perhaps even setting the stage for it, as will be discussed below), and the unwillingness of the former to address this difference in any meaningful way may itself be a factor that promotes corruption. This view also presents a challenge to the humanistic and morally relativistic philosophy that inheres in the orthodox, private interest view, a view that *on its own* similarly does little to further the latter's developmental ambitions.[13]

According to this alternative view, power is not something that is pluralistically distributed, but something that is 'wielded', divided, and unevenly distributed amongst members of society (Tinker, 1980; Cooper and Sherer, 1984; Wickramasinghe and Hopper, 2005). Those who are inclined to adopt a public interest lens are particularly interested in situations where power is 'caught in the grips of money' (Moore Lappé, 2007) and where a variety of social groups or 'classes' – the poor, people of color, and especially women[14] – are treated unjustly. This view, at least in its more social constructionist variants, also points to the possibility that the naming of social problems, such as corruption, is a function of socially embedded processes (Kramer et al., 2002). Moreover, the definition of such problems tends to reflect, or at least tends not to threaten, those who occupy positions of power (Kramer et al., 2002).

Recent work employing a public interest lens (see Tillman, 2009) further points to the possibility that markets and the rules that govern them are more a function of political processes than a feature of an invariant, natural order. One implication for accountants of this perspective is that such things as financial reporting objectives and the purposes of reporting are similarly the effect of political processes. Moreover, this literature points to collusion amongst state and market actors, going so far as to suggest the existence of a unique form of criminogenic behavior known as state-corporate crime (Tillman, 2008). Accountants and auditors, said to be inherently self-interested but still 'reputable control agents' by orthodox commentators, are seen within the public interest view as much less reputable, at least in respect of the field's elite or top accounting firms.[15] These actors, along with corporate board members, bankers, and their political allies, are said to be part of a network of 'reputational intermediaries' involved in collusion, the specific role of accountants being to give legitimacy to the corrupt schemes of corporate executives and corporate insiders (Tillman, 2008).

However, this view does not paint all social actors with the same 'self-interested brush', as it remains open to the possibility that human beings are not, as Thomas Hobbes might have us think, invariably 'wolves to one another' ('*Homo homini lupus*') (Moore Lappé, 2007, p. 7). Rather, human cruelty, greed, and corruption are seen as variant properties, conditioned by circumstance, and open to change (see also Perrow, 1986). While recognizing that social relations are inevitably prone to conflict, at the same time this perspective recognizes the ubiquity of cooperation amongst people – our 'spontaneous solidarity' – or the crucial role that trust, a sense of community, and belonging play in social order (Cooper and Robson, 2006). With this more optimistic and life-affirming view of human nature, and with its greater inclination and attenuation towards power and its abuses, one need wonder why this view hasn't itself become the orthodox or normal view of corruption.

The 'Universal' Features of Corruption

The public interest view, like the private interest or neoclassical economic view, offers up a grand narrative or universal theory of social relations, morality, and human behavior. I would like now to consider some of the universal features of corruption as viewed through a public interest lens. Following this I will consider a number of more historical and contingent factors that lead to corruption, specifically as these relate to the developing world.

Rather than beginning by envisioning a dyad consisting of two self-interested utility-maximizers voluntarily engaging in a contracting exercise, the public interest view sees an encounter between an individual who has more power and an individual who has less. Equally important, these two actors need to be seen as endogenous to, or influenced by, the world around them. Indeed, the more constructionist variants of this perspective fundamentally challenge liberal theory (classic and neoliberal) by questioning the inherent humanism of this perspective and its privileging of the autonomy of the individual. To what extent, these commentators force us to ask, is the individual really an atomistic social or economic actor? Does it make sense to privilege or prioritize the sanctity of the individual, when that individual is so deeply embedded within a collectivity of others and so much a product of the social customs, norms, and mores of others? In this regard, it is also worthwhile to consider whether liberal thinkers were perhaps mistaken in putting so much of their emphasis on supporting and protecting individual freedoms, as this may have had the (un)intended consequence of entrenching inequalities (Chambers, 2008). Rather, it would seem that a much greater emphasis should have been placed on protecting those freedoms that enable the individual to *resist* inequality (Chambers, 2008).[16]

In the context of corruption a further ontological assumption can be made in respect of this encounter, and that is that these actors are motivated not by the 'rational' desire to accumulate wealth and property or avoid work and maximize pleasure, though these things are certainly part of the equation. Rather, social actors are motivated by something more fundamental, something that is a function of both their rational minds and their 'arational' bodies. One might call these 'desires' or 'preferences' or, following Tallis (2008), one could call them 'hungers', a term that conveys both the idea of control and, for many if not most of us, the constant threat of its loss. It is this loss of control or lack of discipline that results in greed (Robertson, 2001) and, where there is deceit and a violation of trust, corruption.

The hunger that motivates human action does not relate only to physical hunger. People are also motivated by a hunger for diversion and pleasure (as Milton Friedman and his forebearers observe), and this form is what Tallis calls hedonistic hunger. On top of this is a third form, social hunger, reflected in our concern with self-image and our general urge to be around others. A fourth and final form is our hunger for knowledge and meaning, a form manifested in our propensity to inquire, study, and reflect, whether scientifically or spiritually.

An added benefit of focusing on the idea of hunger is that it becomes possible to 're-moralize' the discussion of corruption, since it is very much about moral and social limits; a person is said to be corrupt not because he or she crosses a prescribed legal limit, but because that person crosses a prescribed moral (that is, social) limit. When our hunger becomes 'out of control' we reach the point at which our wants surpass our needs, resulting again in what we have come to know as *greed* (Robertson, 2001). In suggesting that corruption and greed are about the state of 'taking too much', a moral judgment is necessarily made.

Another benefit is that hunger is by definition amenable to change. Unlike the neo-classical economist's invariant self-interest, or actor who is *always* lacking and *always* wanting more (a notion challenged by economist Herbert Simon's [1997] own empirical observations), our 'hungry' actor can much more easily be sated. Finally, and perhaps the main reason why the notion of hunger is invoked here, in the developing world hunger abounds, and one might well argue that it is disingenuous if not symbolically violent (Bourdieu, 1990) to make no distinction between wants and needs, as if the two were both merely and unproblematically functions of an individual's choice or preference. The term *hunger*, this is to say, is preferred on account of its being both relevant in the development context and more ethically meaningful.

Considering again our four forms of hunger, each can be carried to excess. However, in some cases this excess has dire consequences for ourselves and others. Our hunger for food can become gluttony, and in the absence of food hunger can lead us to protest and riot violently in the streets. Hedonistic hunger, one's necessary need for diversion and leisure, can also become excessive, as witnessed in the economist's shirking agent and free-rider. Equally if not more problematic, when this hunger becomes out of control it can lead those with great wealth to fetishize opulence and luxury – Imelda Marcos's bizarre penchant for footwear being one well-known example.

Our social hunger can also become out of control, emerging in the form of insatiable lust, narcissism, ostentation, or, in extreme cases, an uncontrollable demand for the affection, attention, and reverence of others. Finally, so too can the fourth hunger run amok; the hunger for knowledge and meaning can consume us as we immerse ourselves in thought, risking losing touch with reality in the process. The thought can become misguided ('losing sight of the forest for the trees'), the ideas corrupted (in part, by making bad assumptions), and in the extreme their upholders deluded into thinking that not only are there concrete answers to all of the difficult questions they ask, but worse that they are the only ones who have the answers.

While we alternately hunger for things, people, power, and knowledge, we can also fear the loss of, and our vulnerability to, these things, fuelling greed and corruption in the process. As the Burmese activist and politician Aung Sang Suu Kyi observes, 'it is not power that corrupts but fear. Fear of losing power corrupts those who wield it and fear of the scourge of power corrupts those who are subject to it' (in Moore Lappé, 2007, p. 122). Between this fear of losing power, or fear of vulnerability to the scourge of power, depending upon the situation, and hunger's tendency to become out of control, there exists an omnipresent threat. A greater threat, however, is found where there is an abundance of power and wealth, where these two reside together ('power in the grip of money'), where there is a fear of loss of power, and where all four hungers have become out of control. Such situations are almost assuredly corrupt.

Klitgaard's suggestion (concerning monopoly, discretion and a lack of accountability) furthers our understanding of the universal features of corruption. Yet so too do the ideas of hunger, greed, and fear, as they point towards the *person acting* rather than simply the context of action. These latter concepts 'humanize' the analysis without lapsing into a problematic form of humanism, as they show the human actor to be more susceptible to influence and more fallible than the neoclassical economist's rational actor. But then admittedly it is not always clear where these concepts apply, or if and how they are causally related. On the one hand, they seem to point us towards different institutional arenas: greed is said to be influential in the private sector (see Tonry, 1998; Huffington, 2003), corruption is thought to riddle the workings of the public sector (see Harsch, 1993, p. 43; Huffington, 2003), and hunger, we know, is found throughout the world. Others, such as Robinson (2009, p. 118), tell us that corruption is a function of greed but fail to elaborate. Then there is the billionaire Warren Buffett, who, recently appearing in a putative 'Town Hall event' with Bill Gates, says that greed, corruption, *and* fear all played a major role in the sub-prime lending crisis, though like others he didn't specify exactly how the terms are related (Crippen, 2009).

Contextual and Historical Features of Corruption

The ambiguity that surrounds these terms, along with the need to 'corporealize' or humanize the term *corruption*, suggests that perhaps we need to move away from universals towards an analysis of a number of relevant historical factors – history being methodologically important to those adopting this perspective. It also seems necessary to consider a number of contextual factors. That history, it needs to be underlined, is decidedly colonialist, and that context hardly one to be characterized exclusively in terms of scarcity and lack.

In the developing world, an important contextual factor that demands attention in any discussion of corruption is what has been called the problem of food production (Sen, 1999). While we are often alerted to what is said to be a 'food crisis' in the developing world (see World Bank, 2009), it seems that this crisis is not necessarily a result of lack, at least not in terms of the globally available amount of food and material resources. Hunger exists in a world of abundance – in terms of both food and material wealth. The problem often concerns how that food and wealth are distributed; the problem is not necessarily a function of a lack of land, labor, or inputs (such as fertilizer), but often the inability of the poor to produce food *for themselves*, the inability of the poor to pay for *their own food*, and the inability of the poor to institutionalize claims on the state to provide food when necessary (Sen, 1999). Populations starve in countries that are net exporters of agricultural products (Sen, 1997). Market freedoms by themselves do not lead to food adequacy, since the problem is very much political, and, as Sen points out, famines do not occur in functioning democracies, or countries where there are civil and political rights, an active opposition, and an uncensored press. A powerful system of values and norms is what builds a society, not incentivization or personal profit, and even less the sanctification of greed (Sen, 1999).

In respect of the abundance of wealth on the planet, consider that the *average* net worth of each man, woman, and child is roughly $26,000 (Davies et al., 2007), which it would seem would sustainably support human life, especially in environments where the cost of living is low. However, and it now seems almost a cliché to point this out, the richest 10 percent of the world's individuals hold 85 percent of its wealth (Davies et al., 2006), meaning that much of the world's 'scarcity' is a function of the dominance of private interests. It would seem that a more just and fair distribution of global wealth would go a long way to reducing hunger, and the greed and corruption that arise from it. It is further worth considering that, while corruption might cost poor countries $20 billion to $40 billion each year (Wallid, 2009), the global use of tax havens by wealthy individuals and corporations costs these countries roughly 10 times this amount in lost tax revenues (Kar and Cartwright-Smith, 2008). Defense spending in the rich countries, much of which is rooted in unfounded fear and the need of cynical politicians to garner support, also stands at over $1 trillion per year (Gostin, 2007), a figure which far outstrips the amounts these countries provide in the way of development assistance (a mere fraction of this, or $61.5 billion, is spent annually by the seven largest country providers) (OECD, 2008).

In addition, it should be recognized that many poor countries are locked into a relationship of dependency on account of having incurred debts that the people in these countries often neither knowingly nor willingly entered into – the so-called odious debts (Adams, 1991). Indeed, one has to question the rational, legal, and moral basis for demanding repayment of such debts. The economic basis is relatively clear, of course, since the people who actually incurred these debts – the corrupt moguls and kleptocrats who readily accepted the money – have fled into isolation, hidden the funds in secret bank accounts, or both.

To add to these contextual factors are a number of historical factors. For one, it needs to be remembered that many of the institutions that exist in the developing world are far from home-grown. Corruption thrives in monetary economies, and these did not always exist prior to the colonization of the developing world (Mulinge and Lesetedi, 1999). Cash-based taxation systems were also often established, and these created dependencies and accountability problems in the colonies. Immense regional variations in wealth resulted from the divide-and-conquer strategies imposed by colonial powers, a situation which only worsened during the Cold War as nations were forced into 'taking sides'. First World imperialist powers often also established excessively hierarchical models of administration based on a leader's ability to hold a crowd rather than on an ability to respect the law or due process. Finally, constitutions were also passed on that were often easily re-drafted with the aim of vesting enormous and absolute powers in the hands of a single office, institution, or individual.

Saddled with illegitimate debt, deprived of adequate development aid and foreign corporate taxes, and inheriting unwanted institutional systems, many developing countries not surprisingly are unable to meet their literacy and education, health, employment, gender-equality, environmental, and democratic goals. Nor should it be surprising that corruption is also rampant in these countries. What really should be met with surprise is claims that corruption is the responsibility of the developing countries themselves – that they somehow 'need to take ownership of it' – since it is a systemic problem implicating the private interests of those living in the industrialized world.

In regard to addressing their complicity, the industrialized countries need to start by doing more to reduce their own problem of corruption, a problem that manifests itself in a rather different form in these countries. The problem or 'syndrome' of corruption (Johnson, 2005) found in nations like the US, Canada, the UK, and Australia is not about government officials or their protégés plundering an economy with impunity, as has been witnessed in countries like China, Kenya, and Indonesia. Nor is it about the 'risky, and sometimes violent, settings of rapidly expanding economic and political opportunities and weak institutions' (Johnson, 2005, p. 3), such as have been seen in Russia, the Philippines and, most recently, Mexico. Rather, it is about 'efforts on the part of private interests to rent access and influence within well-institutionalized policy processes, often through political figures acting as middlemen' (Johnson, 2005, p. 3). In short, corruption in the rich, industrialized world is about bad politics, not bribery, and this type of corruption is hardly less pervasive or efficacious than the types found elsewhere (Johnson, 2005, p. 72).

Some commentators might go further in their analysis, implicating not only rich countries in the corruption found in the developing world, but also the neoliberal ideology that pervades the discourses and informs the practices of First World elites. As David Harvey (2005) notes, 'there is a curious penchant to pursue "corruption" as if it is easily distinguishable from the normal practices of influence-peddling and making money in the marketplace' (p. 166). The suggestion here is that the fight against corruption might itself be something of a ruse, a means of detracting attention from the problematic ideas and practices of those who see themselves as anything but corrupt, and focusing attention on the problems of others (Bukovansky, 2006).

The Role and Obligation of Accountants

To the extent that accountants question the taken-for-grantedness or privileging of private interest or market solutions, and wonder why business principles should necessarily trump democratic ones, then the prescription for accountants is to focus more on control and especially voice solutions in their fight against corruption. These latter solutions promote the interests of the wider public and those who are typically much less powerful in society. This is the alternative, public interest view: cater to the needs of accounting's 'non-primary users', that is, employees, governments, communities and marginalized members of society. In so doing accountants become implicated in a normative project of wealth *redistribution*, the general protection of the public interest, and the beginning of a much-needed debate over whether accountants have any wider duties and obligations. In focusing on control, voice, *and* market solutions, the need for a *certain* degree of economic growth is accepted, but so too is the need for greater equality (on the need to join these two concerns, see Wilkinson and Pickett, 2009). The *abundance* of goodness among people can begin to be ingrained, and the idea that the world suffers from a characteristic 'lack' (Moore Lappé, 2007) treated with the skepticism it is due. Corruption, in this view, is still seen as unfortunate, but rather than expecting it corruption begins to be seen as something that is 'never compulsory'.

ACCOUNTANTS 'THINKING ABOUT' CORRUPTION

To understand accounting adequately requires understanding the social world within which it is practiced, and that in turn necessitates a consideration of the insights of those working in the social sciences (Mautz, 1963). Taking these to include not only economics but also sociology, anthropology, cultural and communication studies, and yet others (all disciplines which, it should be added, have themselves recently turned to the humanities and liberal arts for even deeper insights) we begin to see that 'all is not as it seems', that our ways of knowing are indeed many, and that our representations of reality (including accounting representations) can at best only ever 'palpate' reality (as opposed to accurately depicting it). Moreover, we begin to realize that the reality that we study does not rise from a vacuum; rather, it is constructed by social actors on an on-going basis. Accountants, these disciplines have made abundantly clear, not only communicate reality, but also construct it (Hines, 1988). This is to say that it is important to consider the way accountants 'think about' reality, because the way they think about it profoundly shapes the way they act in it.

This is similarly the case with the 'problem' of corruption: it is in no small way a function of the way those concerned with it 'think about' it. If that thinking is premised on notions of individual self-interest and rational action, then corruption comes to be defined a certain way, and the solutions posed for dealing with it reflect the presuppositions and premises of those involved in its fight. If on the other hand that thinking is premised on an understanding of the important role of power and the manner in which such things as fear and hunger motivate social action, if human actors are seen as having an *abundance* of goodness, and if they are also seen as living in a world of abundant goods, then corruption will be defined differently, and the solutions posed for dealing with it will likewise take a different form.

The implications for accountants of these two ways of thinking are likewise different. A private interest view has accountants focusing their attention on efficiency, attained through such things as accrual accounting, bottom-line performance, cost reduction, the monitoring of productivity and waste, and value-for-money audits. This view is also rooted in competition and personal gain, and is reflected in consulting practices that benefit those to whom accountants provide advice, as well as accountants themselves, in the form of often lucrative contracts. Missing from this perspective, however, is a concern with the 'bigger picture' of corruption, specifically the role that colonial relations have played and that global income inequality continues to play in establishing and fostering corruption in the developing world. Also missing is a consideration of the power and politics that affect not only the material and economic relations between the rich and poor countries but also the way corruption and accounting itself are defined and 'thought about'. This is to say that little attention is paid in the private interest view to both the obvious coercive and the less obvious, knowledge-related or ideological forms of power that influence corruption and its fight.

From a public interest viewpoint, power is an important consideration, and accountants are seen to have a role to play in resisting its negative manifestations in a number of ways. At a minimum, they can provide the public with independently derived and highly comprehensive reports on government activity and spending, as is the case with the so-called supreme audit institutions (SAIs). Yet the potential exists for the public's 'voice' to be promoted by accountants by drawing attention to the general lack of control and discipline that fuels greed and fear, specifically where the fear of the scourge of power corrupts those who are subject to it (in Moore Lappé, 2007, p. 122). This latter potential demands that accountants become more active and adept in making institutions and organizations of all kinds not only more technically accountable, but also more *morally accountable* (Roberts, 1991). Another way of saying this is that accounting's current exclusionary ethic (Michalowski and Kramer, 2006) – its near-maniacal focus on the concerns of a small, elite set of interests – needs to become much wider and more inclusionary.

One excellent place to promote a more socially beneficial, inclusive, and 'power-attuned' form of accountability in the global anti-corruption fight is the defense industry – the social consequences of which have hardly begun to be reported and publically discussed (for an exception, see Chwastiak, 2008). That industry is profoundly corrupt (Catchpowle and Cooper, 2009). Another important area to address is the global financial services sector of countries acting as tax havens, a sector hitherto known more for secrecy than accountability (see Sikka, 2008). Of course, calls for greater accountability in the natural resources sector (that is, forestry, mining, oil and gas, and so on) have been heard for decades (see Freedman and Jaggi, 1982; Gray, Owen and Maunders, 1987), and it behooves accounting authorities and standard-setters to begin paying serious attention to them. Further fertile ground for the use of existing accountability tools and the development of improved accountability tools is where less-obvious forms of corruption exist, particularly in the rich, industrialized world, where corruption tends to be less about bribery and more about influence-peddling and bad politics (Johnson, 2005).

It should be said that the point of drawing attention to the dominant way of thinking about corruption and posing alternatives to it is not to persuade the reader that the private interest or orthodox perspective needs to be completely abandoned and replaced by a public interest alternative. For one thing, the private/public distinction is itself problematic, raising numerous questions regarding the possibility of anything being truly private. Questions also need to be asked about who exactly constitutes 'the public' (Neu, Warsame and Pedwell, 1998).[17] Rather, the point is that the dominant, private perspective is at best limited, and at worst alternately deficient and dangerously excessive. Here we are reminded of Aristotle's notion of 'the Golden Mean', or the idea that deficiency and excess together need to be carefully avoided (Crisp, 2000).

For accountants, this means recognizing that objectivity and neutrality can easily be a pretense for their own deficiency: namely, avoiding taking any responsibility for their role in furthering corruption, however indirect, or in failing to help address or prevent it. It also means recognizing that objectivity and neutrality can be a pretense for excess: notably, where accountants subscribe wholeheartedly to elitist, 'top-down' control approaches in lieu of sustained considerations of more democratic, 'bottom-up' approaches (Lehman, 1999; Wickramasinghe and Hopper, 2005, p. 474). A preoccupation with the need to monitor and control opportunistic agents and protect the needs of potentially victimized principals[18] (that is, shareholders and other providers of capital) means that excess emphasis is placed on individual economic rights and freedoms, and an insufficient amount of attention afforded to the 'norms of equality' (Cohen, 2000, p. 2) that ought to guide the standards and day-to-day practices of public interest-minded professionals.

Of course it would be naïve to suggest that accountants by themselves could ever lead the way in the fight against corruption. For one thing, accounting is only one piece in the anti-corruption puzzle (Hopper et al., 2009). Moreover, the belief that accountants are mere providers of services for economic elites has left the former largely acquiescent to the demands of the latter, with the result that accountants are unlikely to take up a leadership role in the foreseeable future in any but the most mundane areas. Moreover, even if they were to become less passive in respect of their role in the world they would still be able to do only so much against what is a daunting, serious, and, as we have seen, difficult (and difficult to define) problem. At best the accountant's actions would only ever amount to a drop in the bucket. But then, as Moore Lappé (2007) suggests, why should anyone ever expect her or his actions to amount to anything more? But then again, with enough drops all buckets eventually fill up, even very large ones.

NOTES

1. This argument is motivated by a social constructivist view, the strong form of which suggests that 'the theoretical model chosen determines, for a large part, the direction of the proposed solutions' (De Graaf 2007, p. 39). In Chua's (1986, p. 616) terms, those involved in the fight against corruption are in no small way 'people with solutions looking for problems'. In choosing the term 'shapes' over the term 'determines', I am choosing a weaker over stronger form of constructivism.
2. For Hasty (2005, p. 273), economic liberals or neoliberals view the fight against corruption as a 'campaign against rationally calculating selfish desire'.
3. Michalowski and Kramer (2006, p. 40) further argue that the ethics of exclusion 'provide frameworks governing when and where ethical mandates are presumed to be operative' and 'encourage us to see the great majority of the human species as outside of our community of moral obligation'. That community of responsibility, at least according to most textbook definitions of accounting, concerns accounting's 'primary users', namely shareholders and managers.
4. One need not be an anti-capitalist to be skeptical of the claimed beneficence of the free market. Indeed, its own advocates often question the morality of 'the invisible hand'. For example, fund manager George Soros openly admits that 'there is always somebody who pays, and international business is the main source of corruption' (*Financial Times*, 1998).
5. At this level one might speak of 'core–periphery relations' and the (core) industrialized world's contribution to (periphery) developing world poverty. Following Braithwaite (1989, p. 335) one might also suggest that the industrialized world's contribution to the misery of, or really its *infliction of misery upon*, the inhabitants of the developing world directly leads to the 'criminal attitude' that characterizes many of its corrupt actors.
6. Those who subscribe to the idea that individual freedoms must first and foremost be *preserved* are said to adopt a libertarian perspective. Those who subscribe to the idea that the emphasis should be on *creating* individual freedoms – which implies a less conservative emphasis – are better referred to as liberals. Both however see the individual as an autonomous and rational 'decision-maker' (Cave, 2009, p. 97).
7. Rose-Ackerman's work is particularly well cited. Indicative of her reliance on an 'economic prism' (Williams, 1999, p. 506), she argues, for example, that 'agent–principal relationships are at the heart of . . . corruption transactions' (1997, p. 33).
8. It is only recently that the term *corruption* has been used in a manner devoid of moral meaning, as

historically the term was used to connote moral condemnation (Williams, 1999). That this literature consciously avoids discussions of morality largely effaces the connotative sense of the term and most practical or lay definitions of it. Indeed, in some working contexts the term connotes an *extreme* sense of morality. For example, Iran's 'Bureau for Combating Corruption' – Iran's 'morality police' (Paidar, 2002) – is very much concerned with the moral consequences of corruption.

9. This scarcity consciousness is rather selective, however, as can be seen in the arguments of economist Julian Simon. For him, and others, it is unlikely that the earth will ever run out of resources, as increases in wealth and technology will simply make more resources available (see [1981] 1996).

10. The lack of strength of auditors is hardly limited to those working for watchdog agencies – the problem is pervasive in the private sector as well (see Braithwaite, 1989).

11. On the contexts where the presence of fraud is most likely, see Black (2005).

12. In reviewing the literature on corruption I found no systematic research examining the influence of income inequality on corruption, though this relationship has been suggested (see Braithwaite, 1989).

13. In introducing readers to the ideas of liberal humanism, Cave (2009, p.112) makes the liberal humanist's deference to individual rights and the private interest fairly clear: 'The dispossessed and the starving would, I suspect, prefer food to rights, shelter to tales of how sacred are their lives . . . Humanism . . . confronts the ubiquitous problem – of our being concerned for the whole of humanity, yet not *that* concerned' (emphasis in original).

14. It should be noted that corruption, like poverty, disproportionately affects women (Sen, 1997, p.18).

15. Here one might be inclined to point to Société Générale de Surveillance of Switzerland, which was found guilty of paying bribes to conduct audits in Pakistan.

16. *Contra* libertarian and traditional liberal views, it is not enough simply to preserve or create individual freedom – at the very least, efforts must be made to seek out and institutionalize opposition to injustice and unfairness, all the while remaining cognizant of the 'fallibility' of human rationality.

17. In keeping with the arguments of Wolfe (1997), I rely upon the distinction between the private and public less as a way of accurately depicting social reality and more as a way of 'helping us understand it, with the aim of ultimately changing it'.

18. It needs to be pointed out that in economic analysis the assumption is made that all problems lie with the agent, not the principal, which is a form of finger-pointing (Perrow, 1986; Williams, 1999).

REFERENCES

Adams, P. (1991). *Odious Debts*. London: Earthscan.

Alam, M.S. (1989). Anatomy of corruption: an approach to the political economy of underdevelopment. *American Journal of Economics and Sociology*, 48(4), pp.441–56.

Andvig, J.C., and O. Fjeldstad (2001). *Corruption: A Review of Contemporary Research*, R2001:7. Bergen: Chr. Michelsen Institute for Development Studies and Human Rights.

Anechiaricho, F., and J.B. Jacobs (1995). Panopticism and financial controls: the anti-corruption project in public administration. *Crime, Law and Social Change*, 22, pp.361–79.

Barata, K., and P. Cain (2001). Information, not technology, is essential to accountability: electronic records and public-sector financial accountability. *Information Society*, 17, pp.247–58.

Black, W. (2005). Control fraud as an explanation for white-collar crime waves: the case of the savings and loan debacle. *Crime, Law and Social Change*, 43, pp.1–29.

Bourdieu, P. (1990). *Logic of Practice*. Stanford, CA: Stanford University Press.

Braithwaite, J. (1989). Criminological theory and organizational crime. *Justice Quarterly*, 6(3), pp.333–58.

Bukovansky, M. (2006). The hollowness of anti-corruption discourse. *Review of International Political Economy*, 13(2), pp.181–209.

Burger, E.S., and M.S. Holland (2006). Why the private sector is likely to lead the next stage in the global fight against corruption. *Fordham International Law Journal*, 30(1), pp.45–74.

Caiden, G.E. (2001). Corruption and governance. In *Where Corruption Lives*, ed. G.E. Caiden, O.P. Dwivedi and J. Jabbra, pp.15–38. Bloomfield, CT: Kumarian Press.

Caiden, G.E., O.P. Dwivedi and J. Jabbra (2001). Introduction. In *Where Corruption Lives*, ed. G.E. Caiden, O.P. Dwivedi and J. Jabbra, pp.1–14. Bloomfield, CT: Kumarian Press.

Campos, J.E., and S. Pradhan (2007). *The Many Faces of Corruption: Tracking Vulnerabilities at the Sector Level*. Washington, DC: World Bank.

Catchpowle, L., and C. Cooper (2009). US imperialism in action: an audit-based appraisal of the Coalition Provisional Authority in Iraq. *Critical Perspectives on Accounting*, 20(6), pp.716–34.

Cave, P. (2009). *Humanism: A Beginner's Guide*. Oxford: One World.

Chambers, C. (2008). *Sex, Culture, and Justice: The Limits of Choice*. University Park: Pennsylvania State University Press.

Christensen, M. (2005). The 'third hand': private sector consultants in public sector accounting change. *European Accounting Review*, 14(3), pp. 447–74.

Chua, W.F. (1986). Radical developments in accounting thought. *Accounting Review*, LXI(4), pp. 601–32.

Chwastiak, M. (2008). Rendering death and destruction visible: counting the costs of war. *Critical Perspectives on Accounting*, 19(5), pp. 573–90.

Cohen, G.C. (2000). *If You're an Egalitarian, How Come You're So Rich?* Cambridge, MA: Harvard University Press.

Cooper, D. (1980). Discussion of Towards a Political Economy of Accounting. *Accounting, Organizations and Society*, 5(1), pp. 161–6.

Cooper, D., and K. Robson (2006). Accounting, professions and regulation: locating the sites of professionalization. *Accounting, Organizations and Society*, 31(4/5), pp. 415–44.

Cooper, D.J., and M.J. Sherer (1984). The value of corporate accounting reports: arguments for a political economy of accounting. *Accounting, Organizations and Society*, 19(3/4), pp. 207–32.

Crippen, A. (2009). Warren Buffett and Bill Gates – keeping America great. CNBC transcript, 9 November, www.cnbc.com/id/33805947/site/14081545, accessed November 2009.

Crisp, R. (2000). Introduction. In Aristotle's *Nicomachean Ethics*, ed. R. Crisp. Cambridge: Cambridge University Press.

Davies, J.B., S. Sandstrom, A. Shorrocks and E.N. Wolff (2006). *The World Distribution of Household Wealth*. Helsinki: World Institute for Development Economics Research of the United Nations University (UNU-WIDER).

Davies, J.B., S. Sandstrom, A. Shorrocks and E.N. Wolff (2007). *Estimating the Level and Distribution of Global Household Wealth*. Helsinki: World Institute for Development Economics Research of the United Nations University (UNU-WIDER).

De Graaf, G. (2007). Causes of corruption: towards a contextual theory of corruption. *Public Administration Quarterly*, 31(1/2), pp. 39–86.

DeLeon, P. (1993). *Thinking about Political Corruption*. Armonk, NY: Sharpe.

Deleuze, G., and F. Guattari (1972). *Anti-Oedipus: Capitalism and Schizophrenia*, trans. R. Huxley, M. Seem and H. Lane. New York: Viking Press.

Doig, A., and S. McIvor (2003). The national integrity system: assessing corruption and reform. *Public Administration and Development*, 23(4), pp. 317–32.

Dye, K., and R. Stapenhurst (1998). *Pillars of Integrity: The Importance of Supreme Audit Institutions in Curbing Corruption*. Washington, DC: Economic Development Institute of the World Bank.

Eigen, P. (1998). Forward. In *New Perspectives on Combating Corruption*, ed. Transparency International and International Bank for Reconstruction and Development, pp. v–vi. Washington, DC: Transparency International.

Escobar, A. (1995). *Encountering Development: The Making and Unmaking of the Third World*. Princeton, NJ: Princeton University Press.

Eskeland, G.S., and H. Thiele (1999). *Corruption under Moral Hazard*, World Bank Policy Research Working Paper no. 2204. Washington, DC: World Bank.

Espejo, R., G. Bula and R. Zarama (2001). Auditing as the dissolution of corruption. *Systemic Practice and Action Research*, 14(2), pp. 139–56.

Everett, J., D. Neu and A.S. Rahaman (2006). Accounting and the global fight against corruption. *Accounting, Organizations and Society*, 32(6), pp. 513–42.

Financial Times (1998). Fund management guru reveals doubts, 8 December.

Fjeldstad, O., and B. Tungodden (2003). Fiscal corruption: a vice or a virtue? *World Development*, 31(8), pp. 1459–67.

Freedman, M., and B. Jaggi (1982). Pollution disclosures, pollution performance and economic performance. *Omega*, 10, pp. 167–76.

Friedman, M. (1953). *Essays in Positive Economics*. Chicago: University of Chicago Press.

Gaebler, T., and D. Osborne (1993). *Reinventing Government: How the Entrepreneurial Spirit Is Transforming the Public Sector*. New York: Plume.

Galtung, F. (ed.) (1994). *Accountability and Transparency in International Development: The Launching of Transparency International*. Berlin: Laserline.

Gonzalez-Koss, M., and W. Kellner (2002). Global forum on fighting corruption and safeguarding integrity II. *International Journal of Government Auditing*, 29(1), pp. 20–22.

Gostin, L.O. (2007). Why rich countries should care about the world's least healthy people. *Journal of the American Medical Association*, 298, pp. 89–92.

Gray, C.W., and D. Kaufmann (1998). Corruption and development. In *New Perspectives on Combating*

Corruption, ed. Transparency International and International Bank for Reconstruction and Development, pp. 21–32. Washington, DC: Transparency International.

Gray, R., D.L. Owen and K.T. Maunders (1987). *Corporate Social Reporting: Accounting and Accountability*. Hemel Hempstead: Prentice Hall International.

Gray-Molina, G., E.P. De Rada and E. Yáñez (1999). *Transparency and Accountability in Bolivia: Does Voice Matter?* Washington, DC: Inter-American Development Bank, Latin American Research Network, Office of the Chief Economist.

Guthrie, J., O. Olson and C. Humphrey (1999). Debating developments in new public financial management: the limits of global theorising and some new ways forward. *Financial Accountability and Management*, 15(3/4), pp. 209–28.

Harsch, E. (1993). Accumulators and democrats: challenging state corruption in Africa. *Journal of Modern African Studies*, 31(1), pp. 31–48.

Harvey, D. (2005). *A Brief History of Neoliberalism*. Oxford: Oxford University Press.

Hasty, J. (2005). The pleasures of corruption: desire and discipline in Ghanaian political culture. *Cultural Anthropology*, 20(2), pp. 271–301.

Hayek, F. (1944). *The Road to Serfdom*. Chicago: University of Chicago Press.

Hibou, B. (2000). *The Political Economy of the World Bank's Discourse*, Les Études du CERI, 39. Paris: Centre d'études et de recherches internationales.

Hines, R.D. (1988). Financial accounting: in communicating reality, we construct reality. *Accounting, Organizations and Society*, 13(3), pp. 251–61.

Hood, C. (1995). The 'new public management' in the 1980s: variations on a theme. *Accounting, Organizations and Society*, 20(2/3), pp. 93–109.

Hopper, T., M. Tsamenyi, S. Uddin and D. Wickramasinghe (2009). Management accounting in less developed countries: what is known and needs knowing. *Accounting, Auditing and Accountability Journal*, 23(3), pp. 469–514.

Huffington, A. (2003). *Pigs at the Trough: How Corporate Greed and Political Corruption Are Undermining America*. New York: Crown Publishers.

IFAC (2003). *The Accountancy Profession and the Fight against Corruption*. New York: International Federation of Accountants, http://www.ifac.org/council/anticorruptionpaper.tmpl, accessed 16 August 2005.

International Monetary Fund (2005). *Back to Basics: 10 Myths about Governance and Corruption*. Washington, DC: IMF, www.imf.org/external/pubs/ft/fandd/2005/09/basics.htm, accessed 1 June 2005.

Johnson, M. (2005). *Syndromes of Corruption: Wealth, Power, and Democracy*. Cambridge: Cambridge University Press.

Kar, D., and D. Cartwright-Smith (2008). *Illicit Financial Flows from Developing Countries: 2002–2006*. Washington, DC: Global Financial Integrity.

Kaufmann, D. (2005). Myths and realities of governance and corruption. *Global Competitiveness Report*, 2005–06, pp. 81–98.

Khanal, R. (2000). Strategies in combating corruption. In *Transparency and Accountability against Corruption in Nepal*, ed. R. Khanal, pp. 1–18. Kathmandu: Modern Printing Press.

Klitgaard, R. (1988). *Controlling Corruption*. Berkeley: University of California Press.

Klitgaard, R. (1994). A framework for a country programme against corruption. In *Accountability and Transparency in International Development: The Launching of Transparency International*, ed. F. Galtung, pp. 55–73. Berlin: Laserline.

Kramer, R.C., R.J. Michalowski and D. Kauzlarich (2002). The origins and development of the concept and theory of state-corporate crime. *Crime and Delinquency*, 48(2), pp. 263–82.

La Palombara, J. (1994). Structural and institutional aspects of corruption. In *Accountability and Transparency in International Development: The Launching of Transparency International*, ed. F. Galtung, pp. 75–89. Berlin: Laserline.

Lapsley, I. (1999). Accounting and the new public management: instruments of substantive efficiency or a rationalising modernity? *Financial Accountability and Management*, 15(3/4), pp. 201–07.

Lehman, G. (1999). Disclosing new worlds: a role for social and environmental accounting and auditing. *Accounting, Organizations, and Society*, 24(3), pp. 217–42.

Mauro, P. (1995). Corruption and growth. *Quarterly Journal of Economics*, 110(3), pp. 681–712.

Mautz, R.K. (1963). Accounting as a social science. *Accounting Review*, April, pp. 317–25.

Mbaku, J.M. (2008). Corruption cleanups in Africa. *Journal of Asian and African Studies*, 43(4), pp. 427–56.

Michalowski, R.J., and R.C. Kramer (2006). *State-Corporate Crime: Wrongdoing at the Intersection of Business and Government*. New Brunswick, NJ: Rutgers University Press.

Moore Lappé, F. (2007). *Getting a Grip: Clarity, Creativity and Courage in a World Gone Mad*. Cambridge, MA: Small Planet Media.

Mulinge, M.M., and G.N. Lesetedi (1999). The genesis and entrenchment of corruption in sub-Saharan Africa:

a historical and international contextualization. In *Corruption, Democracy and Good Governance in Africa*, ed. K. Frimpong and G. Jacques, pp. 20–30. Gaborone: Lentswe La Lesedi.

Neu, D., H. Warsame and K. Pedwell (1998). Managing public impressions: environmental disclosures in annual reports. *Accounting, Organizations and Society*, 23(3), pp. 265–82.

Nye, J.S. (1967). Corruption and political development: a cost–benefit analysis. *American Political Science Review*, 61(2), pp. 417–27.

Oakes, L.S., B. Townley and D.J. Cooper (1998). Business planning as pedagogy: language and control in a changing institutional field. *Administrative Science Quarterly*, 34, pp. 257–92.

OECD (2008). *Aid Targets Slipping out of Reach*, ODA Statistics. Paris: Organisation for Economic Co-operation and Development.

Owen, A. (1997). Public sector ethics: some practical implications. In *Accountability and Corruption: Public Sector Ethics*, ed. G.L. Clark, E.P. Jonson and W. Caldow, pp. 36–52. St Leonards, NSW: Allen & Unwin.

Paidar, P. (2002). Encounters between feminism, democracy and reformism in contemporary Iran. In *Gender Justice, Development, and Rights*, ed. M. Molyneux and S. Razavi, pp. 239–77. Oxford: Oxford University Press.

Perlman, S. (1928). *A Theory of the Labour Movement*. New York: Macmillan.

Perrow, C. (1986). *Complex Organizations: A Critical Essay*. New York: Random House.

Pope, J. (1998). Enhancing accountability and ethics in the public service. In *New Perspectives on Combating Corruption*, ed. Transparency International and International Bank for Reconstruction and Development, pp. 123–38. Washington, DC: Transparency International.

Roberts, J. (1991). The possibilities of accountability. *Accounting, Organizations and Society*, 16(4), pp. 355–68.

Robertson, A.F. (2001). *Greed: Gut Feelings, Growth, and History*. Cambridge: Polity.

Robinson, M. (2009). *Greed Is Good: Maximization and Elite Deviance*. Lanham, MD: Rowman & Littlefield.

Rose-Ackerman, S. (1978). *Corruption: A Study in Political Economy*. New York: Academic Press.

Rose-Ackerman, S. (1997). The political economy of corruption. In *Corruption and the Global Economy*, ed. K.A. Elliot, pp. 31–60. Washington, DC: Institute for International Economics.

Schwartz, R. (2003). Breaches of integrity and accountability institutions: auditors, anti-corruption agencies and commissions of inquiry. Paper presented at the Annual Conference of the European Group of Public Administration, Oeiras, Portugal.

Sen, A. (1997). Hunger in the contemporary world. STICERD Discussion Paper DEDPS/8, London School of Economics, London.

Sen, A. (1999). *Development as Freedom*. Oxford: Oxford University Press.

Siame, F.M. (2002). Contributions and challenges in the fight against corruption – an auditor general's perspective. *International Journal of Government Auditing*, 29(4), pp. 7–9.

Sikka, P. (2008). Globalization and its discontents: accounting firms buy limited liability partnership legislation in Jersey. *Accounting, Auditing and Accountability Journal*, 21(3), pp. 398–426.

Simon, H.A. (1997). *Models of Bounded Rationality: Empirically Grounded Economic Reason*. Cambridge, MA: MIT Press.

Simon, J. ([1981] 1996). *The Ultimate Resource 2*. Princeton, NJ: Princeton University Press.

Stapenhurst, R., and K. Dye (1998). Pillars of integrity: the importance of supreme audit institutions in combating corruption. In *New Perspectives on Combating Corruption*, ed. Transparency International, pp. 109–22. Washington, DC: Transparency International.

Stapenhurst, R., and S. Sedigh (1999). Introduction. In *Curbing Corruption: Toward a Model for Building National Integrity*, ed. R. Stapenhurst and S.J. Kpundeh, pp. 1–12. Washington, DC: World Bank.

Tallis, R. (2008). *Hunger: The Art of Living*. Stocksfield: Acumen.

Tavares, S. (2005). Does rapid liberalization increase corruption? Paper presented at the European Public Choice Society Conference, University of Durham.

Tillman, R. (2008). Reputations and corporate malfeasance: collusive networks in financial statement fraud. *Crime, Law and Social Change*, 51(3/4), pp. 365–82.

Tillman, R. (2009). Making the rules and breaking the rules: the political origins of corporate corruption in the new economy. *Crime, Law and Social Change*, 51(1), pp. 73–86.

Tinker, A.M. (1980). Towards a political economy of accounting: an empirical illustration of the Cambridge controversies. *Accounting, Organizations and Society*, 5(1), pp. 147–60.

Tinker, T., B.M. Merino and M.D. Niemark (1982). The normative origins of positive theories: ideology and accounting thought. *Accounting, Organizations and Society*, 7(2), pp. 167–200.

Tonry, M. (ed.) (1998). *The Handbook of Crime and Punishment*. New York: Oxford University Press.

Torres, L. (2004). Accounting and accountability: recent developments in government financial information systems. *Public Administration and Development*, 24(5), pp. 447–56.

Uddin, S., and T.M. Hopper (2003). Accounting for privatisation in Bangladesh: testing World Bank claims. *Critical Perspectives on Accounting*, 14(7), pp. 739–74.

Uprety, H. (2000). Chaos and complexity of corruption. In *Transparency and Accountability against Corruption in Nepal*, ed. R. Khanal, pp. 27–37. Kathmandu: Modern Printing Press.

Wallid, T. (2009). Corruption costs poorer states up to $40 billion a year. Thomson Reuters, www.reuters.com, accessed 7 November 2009.

Watts, M.J. (1992). Capitalism, crisis, and cultures I: notes toward a totality of fragments. In *Reworking Modernity: Capitalism and Symbolic Discontent*, ed. A.R. Pred and M.J. Watts, pp. 1–20. Chapel Hill, NC: Rutgers University Press.

Wickramasinghe, D., and T. Hopper (2005). A cultural political economy of management accounting controls: a case study of a textile mill in a traditional Sinhalese village. *Critical Perspectives on Accounting*, 16(4), pp. 473–503.

Wilkinson, R., and K. Pickett (2009). *The Spirit Level: Why More Equal Societies Almost Always Do Better*. London: Allen Lane.

Williams, R. (1999). New concepts for old? *Third World Quarterly*, 20(3), pp. 503–13.

Wolfe, A. (1997). Public and private in theory and practice: some implications of an uncertain boundary. In *Public and Private in Thought and Practice: Perspectives on a Grand Dichotomy*, ed. J.E. Weintraub and K. Kumar, pp. 182–204. Chicago: University of Chicago Press.

World Bank (1994). *Governance: The World Bank's Experience*. Washington, DC: World Bank.

World Bank (1997). *Helping Countries Combat Corruption: The Role of the World Bank*. Washington, DC: World Bank, http://www1.worldbank.org, accessed 21 September 2005.

World Bank (2009). *Food Crisis: What the World Bank Is Doing*. Washington, DC: World Bank, http://www.worldbank.org/foodcrisis/, accessed 8 October 2005.

14 Taxation and accounting issues in development policies

Kevin Holmes

INTRODUCTION

In less developed countries (LDCs) direct and indirect tax systems[1] are often a relatively new innovation or are in need of reform. It is not uncommon to find in these countries that the level of tax compliance is at best disappointing and at worst abysmal. This outcome may result from poor policy formulation, inadequate legislation, inept administration of the tax law, or a combination of those factors. The upshot is that many 'taxpayers' (meaning those individuals and entities that should be paying tax but are not, or are not paying their full liability) are not engaged with the tax system.

Taxation in LDCs is examined in this chapter at the policy, legislation and operational levels. In these respects, the focus is on effective ways to achieve equity between taxpayers, legislative simplicity, cost-effective implementation, and enforcement, with the objective of achieving greater levels of taxpayer compliance.

In a real sense the development of good tax policy, legislation and administration in LDCs is very much dependent on a well-developed level of accounting knowledge and all that goes with that: accounting education, basic record-keeping skills, accounting and auditing standards, ethical standards, and an information technology infrastructure. Without that, try as we might to introduce viable income and consumption tax regimes, we are not very successful in practice. Therefore the link between proper tax assessment and robust accounting information is vital, and still needs to be firmly established in many LDCs.

Generally this chapter considers the interrelationship between accounting and taxation in LDCs by reference to the nature of the taxpayer with which the tax system is concerned. For this purpose we can conveniently classify taxpayers into four broad groups: (i) employees and passive investors; (ii) subsistence workers (whether or not they are employees); (iii) small entrepreneurs; and (iv) large enterprises. In this context there are three general areas to be addressed in the development of an effective tax system: (a) formulation of robust tax policy; (b) writing tax legislation to transpose that policy into law binding upon all taxpayers; and (c) developing a tax administration that effectively implements the letter and intention of the legislation. The development of each of the above three elements of the tax system must take cognizance of the nature of the taxpayer and the extent to which the taxpayer is able to rely on accounting to achieve the objectives of the tax system.

The first component addressed is *tax policy formulation*. Tax legislation and its implementation are ultimately ineffective if they are not founded on rigorous underlying policy initiatives and reasoning. For example, there is little point in an LDC enacting sophisticated income tax law to calculate precisely taxable profits derived by business taxpayers if the majority of businesses in the country consist of small one-person or family operations, the owners of which have no or very little record-keeping skills, and may even be illiterate.[2]

Policies governing direct taxation in LDCs therefore generally require stratification of taxpayers based on the disparity in income distribution, the level of taxpayer sophistication, and ease of collection of tax. This means that policies to address the income taxation of more sophisticated business taxpayers can embrace a greater degree of integration of accounting principles and measurements in the determination of taxable income, while those applicable to smaller, cash-based businesses and people living at a subsistence level cannot.

At an international level tax competition is discussed, because many LDCs are obsessed with introducing tax incentives supposedly to protect their economies in the face of global competition. In addition, in duplicating Western practice, LDCs have attempted to embrace transfer pricing regimes to ensure that they collect their 'fair share' of tax from multinational enterprises (MNEs) which carry on business in their jurisdictions.[3] Arm's length pricing based transfer pricing regimes have problems of application in all countries, and more so in LDCs, the tax administrations of which typically have inadequate resources to effectively deliver what the policy demands. This chapter advocates a much more efficient approach for LDCs, utilizing greater use of extant accounting information.

The second topic is *tax legislation*. This subject canvasses the stamping on some LDCs of the International Monetary Fund (IMF) model income and VAT tax code templates,[4] even though, as a Western-based prototype, it is not always entirely appropriate to the economic and cultural circumstances of the recipient country. This section also focuses on the need for simplicity in an LDC's tax law, particularly in so far as it applies to small businesses and individuals.

The final area of concern is *tax administration practices*. In all countries, and most notably in LDCs, the supremacy of the rule of law must be a precursor to the fair and sustainable administration of the tax system. This chapter discusses different ways in which tax law can be applied in practice effectively within the framework of the cultures and prevailing economic circumstances of LDCs.

TAX POLICY FORMULATION

Fundamental Tax Policy Objectives

It is fairly well settled that the generally accepted fundamental policy objectives of an income tax regime are to:

- collect revenue from taxpayers to contribute to the financing of government expenditure;
- influence a taxpayer's economic behaviour; and
- effect income redistribution.

To achieve these three objectives successfully, the income tax must be fair and enforceable upon all people and entities that fall within its ambit. The modern approach is to encourage taxpayers to participate voluntarily in the tax system, rather than forcing the system upon them, although enforcement measures are, of course, implemented against those people and entities that do not voluntarily comply.

Tax Equity

Tax equity (or fairness) requires, as far as practicable, taxation of all benefits that are derived by a taxpayer, without differentiating between the nature of separate items of income. That means embracing benefits in kind, as well as monetary income, in a taxpayer's taxable income.

Tax equity also means taxing all (geographical) sources of a taxpayer's income in the same way, that is, taxing the taxpayer's worldwide income. In other words, fairness in taxation requires a comprehensive measurement of taxable income.[5] In a business context, in particular, accounting income measures address the tenet of tax equity better than conventional measurements of taxable income. Since accounting profit measurement is more comprehensive than income measurement for tax purposes in most countries, greater use of the accounting approach broadens the income tax base. Accounting profit embraces *all* gains, including capital gains. Adoption of the accounting approach in countries that do not tax capital gains automatically brings those gains within the tax base. To the extent that a country does not tax capital gains,[6] which are always included in accounting income measures, its tax system is unfair: it is biased in favour of the well-off members of a society (both individuals and companies), which are more likely to derive the tax-free gains.

If the income tax system is not only fair, but also perceived to be fair, a greater number of taxpayers will engage in the system, that is, they will be more willing to comply with their obligations to pay tax. The key here is for taxpayers (i) to understand that they are treated equally with other taxpayers who are in similar circumstances, and (ii) to see the benefits, in the form of public expenditure outcomes, which are financed by their tax payment contributions to the State. This requires public education.

Personal Tax Deductions versus Tax Credits

An example of insufficient consideration to taxpayer equity is the common international practice – too readily adopted by LDCs with fledgling personal income tax regimes – of allowing deductions in respect of personal or family circumstances in the calculation of a taxpayer's taxable income where a progressive income tax rate scale operates. From a tax equity perspective, tax credits are superior to tax deductions where the underlying policy objective is to offer some tax relief in recognition of taxpayers' need to incur basic living costs for themselves and their families. The problem with the tax deduction approach is that those taxpayers facing higher marginal personal tax rates obtain a greater tax benefit than those facing lower marginal personal rates. And yet the policy objective is to give relief to those in greatest need, which are the latter rather than the former group. To illustrate, assume that an LDC has the following progressive personal income tax rate scale:

Taxable income ($)	Marginal tax rate (%)
Up to 10 000	0
10 001–40 000	20
More than 40 000	35

Under this progressive scale, a low-income taxpayer (Taxpayer 1) who derives taxable income of $30 000 will pay income tax of $4000, because the first $10 000 is exempt from income tax and the next $20 000 is taxed at 20 per cent (that is, 20 per cent of the $20 000 from $10 001 to $30 000). A higher-income taxpayer (Taxpayer 2) who derives $100 000 will pay income tax of $27 000, being $0 on the first $10 000 (as for the low-income taxpayer), $6000 on the next $30 000 (at the rate of 20 per cent) and $21 000 on the remaining $60 000 (at the rate of 35 per cent).

Now, let us assume that the country wants to offer family allowances by way of tax deductions as a means of giving taxpayers financial assistance to support their families. Suppose that the deduction is $5000 per dependent family member and that the taxpayers in our illustration each have four dependants. The value of the deduction to Taxpayer 1 (measured by the dollar saving in income tax that he must pay) is $4000, because after the deduction of the allowance he has no tax to pay, that is:

	$
Taxable income before family allowance deduction	30 000
Less family allowance deduction ($5,000 × 4 dependants)	(20 000)
Taxable income after family allowance deduction	10 000
Tax payable ($10 000 × 0%)	0
Tax payable with no family allowance deduction	4 000
Less tax payable with family allowance deduction	(0)
Tax saving as a result of family allowance deduction	$4 000

However, the tax benefit (that is, saving in tax to pay) provided by the family allowance deduction to Taxpayer 2 is much greater, namely $7000, calculated as follows:

	$
Taxable income before family allowance deduction	100 000
Less family allowance deduction ($5000 × 4 dependants)	(20 000)
Taxable income after family allowance deduction	80 000
Tax payable	20 000
Tax payable with no family allowance deduction	27 000
Less tax payable with family allowance deduction	(20 000)
Tax saving as a result of family allowance deduction	$7 000

A greater financial benefit from the family allowance assistance by way of a tax deduction is provided to the high-income earner than to the low-income earner, which is not the desired outcome if equity between taxpayers is a basis on which the income tax system is founded: it is the low-income earner who requires the greater amount of financial assistance. Why should the rich be subsidized by the State (in terms of lost tax revenue) to a greater extent than the poor?

The tax equity objective can be attained if the family assistance is given by way of a tax credit, which is offset against the taxpayer's income *tax liability*, rather than by way of a deduction from the taxpayer's taxable income.

Let us assume that the financial assistance is a tax credit of $1000 per dependant.[7] The low-income taxpayer again pays no tax, which leaves him in the same position as under the deduction method, that is:

	$
Taxable income	30 000
Prima facie income tax liability	4 000
Less family allowance tax credit ($1000 × 4 dependants)	(4 000)
Tax payable	0
Tax payable with no family allowance tax credit	4 000
Less tax payable with family allowance tax credit	(0)
Tax saving as a result of family allowance tax credit	$4 000

Now the tax benefit (that is, saving in tax to pay) provided by the family allowance tax credit to Taxpayer 2 is the same as that obtained by Taxpayer 1, namely $4000, calculated as follows:

	$
Taxable income	100 000
Prima facie income tax liability	27 000
Less family allowance tax credit ($1000 × 4 dependants)	(4 000)
Tax payable	23 000
Tax payable with no family allowance tax credit	27 000
Less tax payable with family allowance tax credit	(23 000)
Tax saving as a result of family allowance tax credit	$4 000

Therefore the tax credit methodology provides a fairer outcome between taxpayers with the same number of dependent family members. Broadly, taxpayers in the same circumstances are treated in the same way: horizontal equity is achieved. If this sort of fairness is evident in the personal income tax system, the tax system is more favourably disposed towards taxpayer engagement.

Taxpayer equity in personal income tax regimes is imperative in LDCs, where the distribution of income between the rich and poor tends to be more skewed than is the case in developed countries. Nevertheless, one typically finds an adherence to the deduction approach when the tax system is used to provide social support, even in LDCs, such as China and Vietnam, where the political system is premised upon equity between citizens.

Of course, the tax equity problem described above arises whenever tax deductions are permitted within the framework of a progressive marginal tax rate scale, that is, whether or not the first tranche of a taxpayer's income is exempt from tax.[8] It should be noted at this point that a basic exemption, or total exclusion from the income tax system, is often necessary in underdeveloped countries simply because it is inequitable to subject many poor people to income tax in the first place. Here, the tax exemption is driven by the pragmatic need to ensure that people with merely subsistence incomes are not made (more) destitute as a result of the levy of an income tax upon them. In short, we are concerned about implementing an income tax on people who can afford to pay it, and an exemption for income below a predetermined threshold separates those who can bear the tax burden from those who cannot.

Flat Tax Rate

Adherents to the notion of vertical equity (that is, that people on higher incomes should pay *proportionately* more of those incomes in tax than people on lower incomes) argue that vertical equity is necessary to achieve fairness among taxpayers. However, the problem discussed above does not arise under a flat tax rate regime. In fact, much of the problem of tax avoidance arises from the adoption of progressive marginal tax rates. Progressive marginal rates induce taxpayers into income splitting arrangements between associated parties.

A flat tax rate is also attractive for other reasons. It avoids the disincentive effect inherent in progressive tax rates on earning additional income that falls into a higher tax bracket, especially if the marginal rates are steeply progressive. It is simple and therefore easily understood by taxpayers. Subject to revenue target constraints, tax policymakers should consider implementation of a low flat personal income tax rate as a quid pro quo for the prohibition of deductions for non-business expenditure in calculating taxable income. To fully appreciate the benefits of such an approach, the savings in tax administration costs also need to be properly taken into account.[9]

Accounting Information

Comprehensive income tax legislation is, in its practical application, entirely dependent on reliable accounting information. This expectation is quite valid for large domestic enterprises and MNEs which conduct business in an LDC. Their level of sophistication justifies the expectation that they can properly calculate their taxable income and resultant tax liabilities to facilitate the smooth functioning of the income tax system. They typically engage qualified accounting staff, if only primarily to correctly ascertain internally their financial performance and positions for their own benefit. However, investors and governments also expect those enterprises to follow accepted national or international accounting practices for various external financial reporting purposes, including the calculation of profit for income tax purposes.

The same cannot be said of farmers, hawkers, artisans and small shopkeepers, who constitute the larger part of the private economy of most LDCs. Although it seems implausible to impose on such business people tax obligations premised on a know-ledge of bookkeeping, that is exactly what most governments of LDCs do when they embrace model tax legislation promulgated by largely Western-influenced international organizations such as the IMF. Such documents are commendable and, indeed, an ideal prototype on which to base national tax legislation, provided that they are applied in the right circumstances, namely where accurate accounting income or profit informa-tion pre-exists. To illustrate, consider the way in which sophisticated business taxpay-ers in most developed countries calculate their assessable income. The starting point is typically accounting net profit before taxation. To that figure permanent and timing differences are added or subtracted to account for items that are treated differently from the accounting approach to arrive at taxable income. But taxable income is ascertained not by applying accounting standards and conventions but by applying legislative rules. Thus the standard approach to calculate taxable income in accordance with income tax legislation is to apply the following 'formula':

Accounting net profit before taxation	xx xxx
Add items expensed for accounting purposes but not deductible for tax purposes	x xxx
Add items assessable for tax purposes but not included in revenue for accounting purposes	x xxx
	xx xxx
Deduct items deductible for tax purposes but not expensed for accounting purposes	(x xxx)
Deduct items not assessable for tax purposes but included in revenue for accounting purposes	(x xxx)
Taxable income	xx xxx

This illustration makes three points. First, accounting knowledge is necessary to get to the starting point, accounting profit before tax. Second, accounting knowledge (and, indeed, knowledge of the prevailing income tax law) is necessary to carry out correctly the adjustments to transform accounting net profit before tax into taxable income. The third point, which is often overlooked by tax policy- and lawmakers, is that tax legisla-tion typically adopts one method to calculate taxable income while in practice account-ing-savvy businesses use a different method to calculate the same figure. Generally tax legislation prescribes a list of items that are to be included as (gross) income and a list of items that are to be treated as deductible expenditure, and requires that the latter be deducted from the former,[10] that is:

Total gross income items	xx xxx
Less total deductible expenditure items (including special allowances, if applicable)	(x xxx)
Taxable income	x xxx

For obvious reasons of efficiency, businesses that are capable of determining their accounting net profit do not adopt a dual accounting system to record largely the same items of income and expenditure for tax purposes. They adopt the 'adjustment to accounting net profit' approach. This methodology of course means that the taxable income base is totally dependent upon the correct determination of accounting income – after all, in many cases the monetary values of the adjustments will be minor relative to the underlying revenue and expenditure figures used to determine that accounting income. Therefore it is a pre-requisite in an LDC that adopts the Western-style income tax template (expecting it to produce a reliable taxable income figure) that an accounting profession is established, which embraces comprehensive accounting standards and generally accepted accounting principles and practice, together with the appropriate regulatory institutions to monitor those standards and compliance with them. Unfortunately, the reality is that there is only a fledgling accounting profession in most LDCs to perform the sophisticated role demanded of it.

To compound this issue, large enterprises with in-house accounting personnel require monitoring by qualified external accountants to ensure that they comply with professional standards for financial reporting purposes (which, of course, is the traditional audit function), but also to instil public confidence in the accuracy of the calculation of their tax liabilities. A paucity of accounting professionals to do that job potentially allows those organizations to manipulate their tax obligations, which ultimately undermines the integrity of the tax system.

The problem of a lack of properly qualified accounting practitioners is exacerbated where the income tax law is premised on self-assessment. The general expectation in developed countries is that, along with large businesses, smaller enterprises and their owners prepare their own tax returns and self-assess their tax liabilities. If they are not capable of doing so themselves, or choose not to do so, we expect them, at their own expense, to engage the services of a tax professional to perform the tasks on their behalf. That is because in developed countries even small business people are generally reasonably well educated about basic bookkeeping methods and taxation matters, and there is usually a plethora of qualified accountants available to provide the accounting service upon which proper application of the tax law depends. But that level of familiarity with accounting and availability of accounting professionals is simply not yet present in most LDCs. In practice, few small businesses retain sufficiently comprehensive business records to meet the statutory requirements. Furthermore, typically there is not widespread effective policing of the statutory requirements by the tax administration.

So where does this leave our developing country's farmer, hawker, artisan and shopkeeper? Assuming that they earn sufficient income to warrant their paying tax at all, their government's largely wholesale adoption of the Western income tax and value added tax (VAT) models means that they must either engage accountants to calculate their taxable income and tax or VAT liability or work the calculation themselves. Even if the professional services were available, their cost is likely to make the first option impractical for many (if not most) small businesses. The latter alternative places unrealistic demands upon most small business people in LDCs. It requires retention of records, time and effort in transforming those records into a taxable income figure in the required form and, probably most idealistically of all, a knowledge of the tax law so that gross income, deductible expenses and their difference can be accurately determined. Remember, unlike large enterprises, these small business people do not undertake adjustments for timing and permanent differences to accounting net profit before tax, since they have not already predetermined that figure for financial accounting purposes; they must use the 'net method' of taxable income prescribed by the legislation.

Taxpayer Stratification

The tax system must therefore recognize that the level of sophistication between taxpayers varies and, therefore, must deal with different taxpayers in different ways to ensure that an appropriate amount of tax is collected from all taxpayers. This requires stratification of taxpayers depending on their ability to meet the objectives of the tax system. This stratification is most obvious in the case of salary and wage earners and recipients of passive income. Since the efficiency of the tax system is enhanced if taxpayers can be assessed to income tax without the need to file tax returns, there is little point, from both a policy and an administrative perspective, in requiring these groups of taxpayers to maintain records of earnings, obtain a knowledge of the tax law, and file annual tax returns. Instead collection of income by way of source deductions of tax from employees' wages and salaries and from passive income is far more efficient and has the added advantage of governments receiving this income tax revenue on a timely basis.

Source deductions are a widely practised means of tax collection in both developed countries and LDCs. They require employers (for wages and salaries), companies (for dividends), borrowers (for interest) and technology acquiring businesses (for royalties) to maintain sufficiently robust accounting systems to calculate correctly the required source deduction amounts. In LDCs, large-scale entities are generally in a position to employ systems, knowledge or assistance to enable the source tax deduction regimes to operate reasonably well. However, the same level of confidence cannot be attributed to the correct source deduction tax collections and determination of taxable income in the small business sector, which is typically immersed in an LDC's cash economy.

Cash Economy

The cash economy thrives in LDCs. Official record keeping is an anathema in a cash economy. Yet the Western-style income tax model, which is so dependent on an audit trail, is expected to perform its function in the cash-based environment. Despite the tax laws of LDCs usually imposing an obligation on business taxpayers to keep proper accounting records, the reality is that many small business taxpayers – maybe most – do not. Those that do may not keep complete records of all transactions and economic events that are related to their businesses, the most patent examples being the omission of selected cash sales and the payment of cash remuneration to employees, which ultimately reduces tax liabilities. These practices undermine the integrity of the tax system in terms of both fairness and economic efficiency.[11]

Tax evasion is not confined to income tax. A government can also lose VAT revenue as a result of taxpayer evasion. VAT registered people periodically pay amounts of VAT to the government, calculated as the difference between VAT imposed on their sales (sometimes called 'output tax') and VAT paid on their business purchases (sometimes called 'input tax'). Businesses will always want to maximize their claims for input tax, because the higher that deduction from output tax, the lower the amount of VAT that they are required to pay to the government. In addition, if they do not record all of their (cash) sales they can reduce the amount of their output tax and therefore also reduce the amount of the difference between output tax and input tax, payable to the government.

There is a further disturbing aspect about the application of a conventional income tax model in an LDC with a prevalence of cash transactions. Often there is an acknowledgement by tax officials (at least those who operate in the field) that it is simply not possible in practice to tax all cash transactions because of the absence of an audit trail and limited resources to police the tax law. So here we have a fundamental dichotomy. Governments, on the advice of (often foreign) tax policymakers, introduce income tax and VAT regimes which are wholly reliant on an evidential trail into environments that are alien to such trails, while tax officers in the field confront the reality that they are not (nor can they be expected to be) capable of ensuring that the regimes are implemented in practice to determine the correct amount of tax payable. A tax system is under significant threat when the tax law purports to do one thing but in reality is incapable of doing so consistently and equitably. Such a situation is ripe for bribery and corruption. Eventually the tax system will break down, with the inevitable political consequences.

To the extent that business is conducted on a cash basis, and inadequate records of transactions are maintained, some method of presumptive taxation is necessary to ensure that liable taxpayers pay their fair share of the tax burden – at least until the level of accounting practice has matured and become more widespread, both in terms of business record keeping and the development of the accounting profession as a service to small enterprises.

Presumptive Taxation

Presumptive taxation offers a sound alternative approach to bring small accounting-illiterate businesses comprehensively within an equitable and efficient tax net. It can ensure that the tax impost upon those small business owners is sustainable.

Although comprehensive periodic tax returns, which contain information based on a taxpayer's record keeping of business transactions, can produce a highly accurate measure of income, and hence a more precise calculation of the amount of the taxpayer's tax liability, there is a trade-off between that accuracy and the efficiency or ease of getting taxpayers to comply with the tax system. In other words, we can make it easier for taxpayers to comply (and reduce the costs of compliance with the system for taxpayers, and simultaneously the costs and strain on the capabilities and resources of the tax administration) by compromising on accuracy. In the small business context presumptive taxation means allowing certain taxpayers to determine their business income on a presumptive basis, rather than having to comply with the detailed requirements of the tax legislation. That simplifies the tax system, thereby engaging a greater number of business taxpayers, and reducing opportunities of potential bribery and corruption in the administration of the system.

Generally, presumptive taxation has not been strongly advocated by international advisors to tax policymakers in LDCs. Nevertheless, the IMF has observed that:

> Presumptive taxation is a highly effective method for taxing small businesses, which cannot reasonably be expected to maintain full business records. The implementation of the new [personal income tax regime in Vietnam] is an appropriate opportunity to improve the current presumptive taxation approach for small taxpayers by establishing an appropriate turnover threshold, below which the taxpayer is entitled to adopt the presumptive method and relieved from the responsibility of maintaining full business records.[12]

Presumptive taxation is a concession to taxpayers. Business taxpayers who qualify for the presumptive tax basis can still comply with the general requirements of the tax law if they choose to do so, by keeping proper accounting records and determining their tax liabilities on the basis of that information.

There is extensive international empirical evidence to demonstrate that the costs of compliance with an income tax system weigh disproportionately more heavily on small business enterprises than on larger ones.[13] The compliance burden on small businesses and the administrative burden on the tax authority are alleviated if small businesses adopt a presumptive basis of taxation based on turnover, rather than calculating their net profit as the basis for determining their income tax liability. Presumptive taxation can adopt other bases depending on the nature and circumstances of the taxpayer and the economic activity undertaken, for example land area occupied by the business or number of cattle (particularly apposite in subsistence agricultural sectors, if they fall within the tax regime at all), or number of employees.

Where a small business presumptive tax regime based on turnover applies, a threshold level of turnover below which the presumptive tax regime is triggered needs to be determined. The threshold level is dependent on various interdependent factors, including the number of taxpayers expected to benefit from a presumptive income basis of taxation, the tax rate applicable to the presumptive income, the expected average profit margin of the businesses to which the presumptive tax is to apply, and the estimated impact on tax revenue of allowing taxpayers to opt out of the 'standard' income tax calculation and into the presumptive basis. To determine the threshold, revenue forecasting experts need to undertake a sensitivity analysis of various tax thresholds at different tax rates to ascertain the revenue impacts.

International Tax Competition

LDCs often institute special regulatory regimes to facilitate foreign investment in order to increase economic growth, local employment, and foreign exchange earnings. These regimes commonly take the form of a package of incentives, including sharply reduced effective tax rates or 'tax holidays', offered to enterprises that conduct specified business activities within designated special economic zones (SEZs) in an LDC, that is, geographically delimited areas in the country within which goods and services are produced primarily for export.[14] The main objective behind the policy is to minimize (tax) costs for operators, thereby making an attractive channel for greater inward investment flows.

The measures vary among different countries. Many countries offer incentives to foreign-based enterprises that locate their export-oriented activities in the country. Until the advent of its Enterprise Income Tax Law in 2008, China offered foreign investors in certain activities a tax exemption for up to 10 years.[15]

Although individual economic advantages can be identified in relation to SEZs,[16] the critical policy question is whether, on an overall cost–benefit analysis, the advantages outweigh the disadvantages to produce a net benefit to an LDC in terms of national welfare, which justifies its adoption of an SEZ. In other words the multiplier effect from such foreign-driven investment must outweigh the net cost to the government of funding the infrastructure and other activities associated with the establishment of the SEZ and the opportunity cost of forgone taxation and other revenue as a result of the concessions made available to the investors in the favoured activities.

The literature on the successes and failures of SEZs, and their associated tax concessions, in LDCs is extensive. The general conclusion is that, from the viewpoint of national wealth maximization, most SEZs have failed.[17] The IMF has raised several objections to tax incentives for such investments:[18]

- They are inefficient and inequitable because they discriminate between different economic activities.
- Tax revenues decrease, which may necessitate increased taxes (and thus increased distortions) elsewhere in the economy, although this tendency may be partially mitigated if indirect effects are significant.
- Taxes are not the most important factors in determining the location of investments: certainty and simplicity in the operation of the tax system, a sound infrastructure, market size, labour productivity, and institutional factors and regulatory policy are (more) important.
- If repatriated income is taxed, tax incentives may not matter anyway.
- When new businesses are not immediately profitable, tax holidays and tax exemptions are impotent.
- Tax incentives offer fertile ground for evasion and avoidance of taxes.

Consequently typically nowadays SEZs have fallen out of favour with economic policymakers. Economists generally see free trade policies as a more desirable policy option.[19]

Governments need to obtain a reasonable return on the infrastructure and other investments they make, which is required to establish and operate SEZs. However, as they find it harder to attract and retain foreign investors, they can get trapped in a situation where they fear that they will lose investments in their country if they do not extend the tax concessions and other incentives which attracted the initial investments in their SEZs. They become locked into continuing the regime when it is no longer in the best national interest. This comes about simply because investments in the SEZs are based on the incentives available, rather than on any inherent competitive attributes. If the zone is unable to develop those attributes, investment may well flow out when the incentives expire or more generous incentives appear elsewhere: LDCs fear tax competition from neighbouring countries which offer similar incentives. Ultimately that tax competition forces all of the competing LDCs into a sub-optimal national welfare position. This is the so-called 'race to the bottom'.

Furthermore the tax incentives may not be covered by the tax sparing provisions of double tax treaties concluded by the host State. The current international trend is to omit tax sparing provisions from tax treaties. For example, the United States does not permit them in its treaties and, in a more limited way, 'the UK has not provided matching relief for relief given under legislation specifically designed to promote exports'.[20]

Where a foreign investor cannot incorporate the advantage of tax concessions granted by a host State into the calculation of its tax liability in its State of residence, the advantage of the concessions is eliminated.[21] In that case, the credit for foreign tax paid in the host State, allowed by the home State in the calculation of tax payable to the home State, is diminished by virtue of the tax concession in the host State. The upshot is that the benefit of the concession is passed not to the foreign investor, but to its home State, which collects more tax from its resident than if it had paid tax in the host State. *Ceteris paribus*, investors do not care to which government they pay a given amount of tax, but the offer of tax incentives by a host State has little attraction to an investor if it cannot retain the benefit of the incentives for itself but must pass it on to its own government.[22]

Generally a government's approach of 'picking winners' in the selection of its economic policies has largely failed in both developed countries and LDCs. While some sort of government intervention to stimulate economic performance often appears necessary, it can be better achieved by identifying and promoting the fundamental economic rationality underlying investment in areas in which the country has a comparative advantage. For example, the country may be well placed – or better placed – geographically, technologically and educationally to be a banking, insurance or distribution centre for countries in its region, or there may be particular (eco-)tourism advantages that could be capitalized upon.

Economic growth and national wealth maximization (and, indeed, tax harmonization) are better achieved by introducing a low standard corporate tax rate[23] as a means of attracting foreign (and domestic) investment in a tax-neutral way, without the need for the government to impose its subjective preferences. The success of low corporate tax rates in many countries, the tax-neutrality attractions (as between foreign and domestic investors), and the general failure of special incentive regimes make this policy a preferable route to economic growth and international tax harmonization.[24]

Nevertheless a policy of extremely low or zero-rated corporation tax should not extend to extremely low or zero-rated non-resident withholding tax on dividend distributions from the LDC's resident companies to their foreign shareholders. The reason that non-resident withholding tax should be imposed by the LDC is that, in most cases, foreign investors would obtain a tax credit in their home jurisdiction for their payments of source State non-resident withholding tax. To exempt such dividends from non-resident withholding tax in the source State simply transfers tax revenue from it to the investor's home country.

TAX LEGISLATION

Simplicity

One of the most frequent criticisms of income tax legislation in Western jurisdictions is its complexity – and even its incomprehensibility.[25] The resultant lack (or even absence) of Western legislative simplicity is sometimes imported into the tax legislation of LDCs.

The surfeit of often ad hoc statutory rules (including incentive provisions, such as special allowances) drives a wedge between taxable income and accounting income. Within a business framework, simplicity – and the accompanying reduction in compliance costs – can be improved by adopting a closer alignment of accounting profit measurement with the measurement of taxable income.[26]

Chiefly for reasons of ease of understanding and compliance, income tax legislation should be relatively simple. In addition, simplifying the personal income tax system facilitates increased taxpayer engagement. At the legislative level that means that the personal income tax law must be comprehensible to the lay person. A greater degree of complexity might be justified in the corporate income tax law, where the players are more erudite and the transactions are more intricate or convoluted.

To achieve comprehensibility, tax legislation must be:

- understandable;
- uncomplicated;
- logical; and
- linguistically simple.

Some countries[27] have embarked successfully on long-term projects to rewrite their income tax legislation in a 'user-friendly' style, using relatively informal language (by comparison with traditional 'legalese') to enable taxpayers (as lay people) and their advisors readily to understand what the law is trying to say. This approach has gone so far as to embody 'purpose provisions' to assist taxpayers – and ultimately the courts in resolving disputes about the application of the tax law – to determine the purpose behind what particular sections of the legislation are trying to achieve.[28]

Simple legislation also reduces opportunities for tax evasion, tax avoidance and corruption. The more complex the legislation, the greater the likelihood of inconsistencies between different provisions, which offers greater opportunities for tax planners to drive a wedge between those differences. That in turn leads to increased policing costs and therefore higher costs to government to administer the tax system.

Furthermore, if tax legislation is complex, people will not comply with it because they simply do not understand it or they are frustrated by it and essentially 'give up' on it. In these circumstances, opportunities for bribery and corruption can arise, because taxpayers might be happy to reach a compromise with a (perhaps supposedly knowledgeable or at least relatively powerful) tax official as an effective way to resolve a problem based on something they do not (fully) comprehend.

At least in the early stages of development of a tax system, it may well be better for the government of an LDC to forgo some revenue at the margin because of the absence of complex rules that are specifically targeted to a particular, relatively small group of taxpayers, in favour of a widely comprehensible and accepted tax law. In that respect a closer alignment of the measurement of taxable income to accounting income is also desirable.

TAX ADMINISTRATION

The third pillar of a successful tax system is its effective administration. In recent years in many countries there has been a political bearing on reducing the costs of public sector administration, which has included the goal of eliminating inefficiencies in tax assessment and payment procedures. This requires the streamlining of administrative procedures and ensuring that bureaucratic obstacles are not placed in front of taxpayers which would deter their willingness to comply with the tax law. The modern catch-phrase in this connection is the provision of 'taxpayer services' to taxpayers by the tax administration. The *raison d'être* is the expedient collection of tax: in other words, making life as easy as possible for taxpayers to determine their tax liabilities correctly and to pay their tax by the due date. This means ensuring that the administrative processes do not involve unnecessary and inconvenient steps which jeopardize the efficiency of the tax collection process. It also means having mechanisms in place that allow for the timely collection of tax on a provisional basis, where appropriate.

Self-Assessment

Modern tax systems usually rely on taxpayer 'self-assessment', which simply means that the onus falls upon taxpayers to calculate their tax liabilities correctly and to pay the resultant tax on time. The accuracy of their calculations depends on taxpayers implementing adequate accounting information systems and periodic post-self-assessment audits by the tax administration. To the extent that there are deficiencies in the taxpayer's systems and calculations, the detected shortfall in tax paid, together with (deterrent) penalties, becomes payable.

The 'old-fashioned' approach is for the taxpayer to file a tax return and await an assessment from the tax administration of the taxpayer's tax liability, based on the return filed and any other information at the disposal of the tax administration. Often the tax payment would be due only after the tax administration's assessment was issued to the taxpayer. The disadvantage with that approach is the enormous resource commitment required by the tax administration to check returns, and compile and process assessments. In effect, the self-assessment system shifts the tax compliance costs from the tax administration on to the taxpayer, and correspondingly allows cost savings to the tax administration, which can then allocate its resources to the audit of taxpayers, rather than to the assessment of taxpayers.

To operate effectively, self-assessment systems require that (i) taxpayers are sufficiently literate and knowledgeable about income tax and accounting to be able to calculate their tax liabilities accurately, and (ii) they are buttressed by a comprehensive penalties regime to ensure that those taxpayers who do not comply are adequately punished so that they will comply in future and that others who are tempted not to comply are deterred from that temptation. Often in LDCs, in which an income tax system may be novel, literacy levels are low,[29] and record keeping is not sophisticated (or is even non-existent in a cash economy culture), adoption of the self-assessment system, at least upon the introduction of an income tax system, may well be asking too much of taxpayers. It should be remembered that, for most Western countries, income tax was a well-established institution long before the introduction of self-assessment.[30] Nevertheless, in general the ideal candidates for self-assessment are business taxpayers and taxpayers who derive capital gains, since they are likely to be more commercially astute, and therefore understand taxation rules better, than the general body of taxpayers (in particular, wage and salary earners).

Periodic Payments

From a government's revenue-gathering perspective, it is crucial that regular payments of tax are made by taxpayers. This is most effectively achieved by the requirement that payers of taxable income to taxpayers must deduct tax at source and pay it to the relevant government agency soon after the time of the source deduction. This is most readily achieved in the case of payments of salaries and wages and passive income.[31]

In the case of individuals who are in business, and who account for profits and tax on an annual basis, a provisional tax system needs to be implemented, which requires those taxpayers to make instalment payments of their estimated tax liability for the year at regular (say, quarterly) intervals. Such payments can be based on the previous year's actual tax liability, maybe grossed up by a factor of (say) 10 per cent to take account of a growing economy in which it is expected that a taxpayer's profits will increase from year to year. Alternatively, taxpayers might make (quarterly) estimates of their tax liabilities for the year in question as they progress through that year and get a better idea of the profitability of their businesses for the year. In this case, however, sufficient penalties must be in place to deter a taxpayer from deliberately underestimating the profits and thereby underestimating the provisional tax to be paid.

These sorts of rules work in practice only if the business taxpayer maintains proper accounting records. Hence there is the need, particularly in LDCs, for an awareness and education programme that addresses basic bookkeeping practice to go hand in hand with education about the taxation per se of business undertakings. It therefore follows that a focus of the tax administration's audits of business individuals should be on the adequacy of their accounting records, as well as their treatment for tax purposes of the income that they derive, the expenditure that they incur, and the timing of recognition of that income and expenditure.

Withholding Taxes at Source

Withholding taxes at source also facilitate a regular tax revenue cash flow to the government throughout an income year, rather than the government having to wait to collect the tax owing by taxpayers until after the end of the year when each taxpayer's annual tax liability is crystallized. As well as speeding up and evening the government's collection of tax revenue, source deductions of tax also ensure that the government receives at least part of the tax that is owing to it. If a taxpayer fails to file an annual return and pay any amount of tax owing at the year-end, the government has already collected the source deduction amount of the tax liability, which, although it may be less than the full amount of the liability, is nevertheless better than collecting nothing at all in the absence of a source deduction regime.

Such withholding taxes can be assessed on a provisional basis whereby the taxpayer files an annual return in which its actual tax liability is calculated for the year and a credit is given against that amount for the taxes deducted and paid at source during the year. Successful implementation of a withholding tax regime requires (i) a properly instituted tax identification number system;[32] (ii) reliable payment mechanisms and procedures; (iii) monthly reconciliations of withholding tax paid by payers and received by the tax administration; and (iv) annual reconciliations of a taxpayer's gross income from which withholding tax was deducted at source and the total amount of withholding tax deducted and paid to the tax administration. These requirements in turn depend on:

- comprehensive record keeping and general accounting systems, and accurate calculations of withholding tax by payers of income subject to the withholding tax deductions;
- a high level of payer compliance;
- severe penalties imposed on payers who do not comply, especially when they deduct the tax from the payee's gross income but fail to pay it over to the tax administration; and
- correct taxpayer tax code declarations made by payees where the payer must take into account the marginal tax rate (under a progressive tax rate scale) faced by a payee with multiple sources of income, tax deductions or tax credits.[33]

A critical factor in reducing tax administration and taxpayer compliance costs is to remove the compliance obligations from as many taxpayers as possible. Final withholding taxes empower this objective by removing salary and wage earners[34] and earners of passive income (other than capital gains) – that is, primarily, interest and dividend income – from the requirements to file tax returns and make tax payments. This means that taxpayers automatically have their tax paid on their behalf by the payer of their income, so that the payees do not have to be concerned about filing tax returns, self-assessing their own tax liabilities, and paying their tax by the due date.

The final withholding tax approach works particularly well where the individual income tax rate is a flat rate, rather than a progressive scale, and there are no (or few) exemptions, deductions or credits, although it can operate when these factors are present, but is more vulnerable to error and abuse. Thus the effectiveness of the final withholding tax mechanism requires a trade-off between the (possible) objective of vertical equity (manifested in a progressive tax rate scale) and minimization of taxpayer compliance and tax administrative costs.

The compliance and audit focus of the final withholding tax regime falls upon the *payers* of the income – not the recipients. Overall, compliance and tax administration costs are reduced significantly because in this context there are far fewer payers of income than there are payees. Thus the tax administration's audit spotlight shines on employers and payers of passive income, rather than the multitude of employees and investors. With far fewer participants calculating tax liabilities, and using better accounting records, the scope for error and fraud is reduced: greater accuracy in calculations and collections ensues.

The greatest efficiency benefits of regular payments of withholding taxes deducted at source require automatic reconciliations of tax paid on behalf of, with tax payable by, the taxpayer via maintenance of an individual account with the tax administration for each taxpayer. Ultimately, with adequately developed accounting information systems, the tax administration can calculate unilaterally each taxpayer's annual tax liability based on the information provided to it.

Tax Audits

The self-assessment system requires post-assessment audits to ensure taxpayer compliance. Taxpayers should be aware that such audits are necessary for that reason and do in fact take place. The tax administration must adopt predetermined audit strategies, and taxpayers should know, in general terms, that on average they can expect to be audited (say) once every five years.

The focus of audit risk assessments should be on payers of income, especially income subject to final withholding taxes, as well as on business taxpayers and taxpayers who derive capital gains.

Inevitably limited tax administration resources mean that policing of compliance with the tax law is limited and must be targeted towards particular (groups of) taxpayers. While ample tax audit strategies have been developed to do that,[35] they do not resolve the fundamental problem of collecting the correct amount of tax owing by taxpayers who operate in an LDC's cash economy. At best the traditional audit and investigation approaches can home in on some taxpayers, engage (sometimes considerable) resources in an attempt to estimate the taxpayers' incomes from cash transactions, impose taxes and penalties accordingly, and hope that other tax evaders are deterred by the prospect of their being investigated and punished. However, even with the imposition of sometimes quite stringent penalties (for example, in China the death penalty is imposed for very serious cases of tax evasion[36]) and taxpayer education programmes, tax evasion in the cash economy continues to thrive in most LDCs.

The implications for tax policymakers are clear: if an income tax system predicated on record keeping to facilitate an audit trail is to be instituted successfully, taxpayers must possess the requisite accounting knowledge and accounting information systems. That is normally the case for large enterprises, which therefore lend themselves to the conventional audit approach. It is not the case for small business enterprises operating in the cash economy of LDCs.

Where presumptive taxation on the basis of business turnover is adopted for those businesses it must be buttressed by effective policing of the taxpayer's sales records and rigorous implementation of a penalty regime in cases of detected tax evasion and fraud. The policing aspect necessary to counter the risk to the government's tax revenue base requires effective audit strategies which focus on business sector turnover in different localities and business taxpayer asset accretion investigations.

Taxpayer Services

To engage taxpayers (particularly, but not exclusively, business individuals) in the tax system, the tax administration must adopt a service industry focus. This means encouraging compliance by providing easily accessible information and assistance services, and education, to taxpayers to make it easy for them to engage. In practical terms, such assistance can take the form of counter enquiry help desks, call centres, interactive web pages (which are especially attractive to 'Generation Y' taxpayers), easily accessible (including Internet downloadable and executable) forms and explanatory documents (encompassing the liberal use of colour, diagrams and illustrations), assistance with business record keeping, offering a range of tax payment options, and establishing 'new business' teams to visit new business taxpayers to help them to become acquainted and to register with the tax system, and to put suitable accounting systems in place. Most of these services can be offered through a 'one-stop shop', whereby taxpayers can obtain all the information and assistance that they require, and carry out their taxpaying duties, at one point.

The tax administration needs to implement taxpayer education campaigns and training programmes to facilitate taxpayer engagement. Ideally, such programmes should start in schools so that by the time pupils become taxpayers they understand and accept why there is an income tax system and what it is designed to achieve, and in particular appreciate that the provision of public goods and services is dependent on the collection of taxation. The more immediate education focus should be on small traders and accountants who will be responsible for the filing of tax returns for many business individuals.

The tax administration staff itself also requires ongoing education and training – ongoing because of (i) staff turnover, and (ii) changes in law and practice over time. Such training must embrace the need for integrity and ethics in the administration of tax laws, and underlying tax concepts for all professional staff to obtain a general understanding of the tax law and to recognize tax issues when they arise, in addition to training on technical tax issues at appropriate levels.

Bribery and Corruption

Education of tax officials is one weapon in the arsenal to attack bribery and corruption, which are endemic in the tax administrations of some LDCs.[37] However, the problem is typically exacerbated by the fact that the corruption is not confined to tax administration officials, but is entrenched throughout the whole public service and right up to the political elite. The problem needs to be eradicated, because it strikes at the heart of the way in which we try to achieve the tax policy goals of equity, efficacy and administrative efficiency.

Simplicity of tax legislation and administrative procedures go some way to combat corruption by tax officials by eliminating points of complexity, for example by imposing source deduction withholding taxes rather than the need to file tax returns, which triggers the intervention of a tax official.[38]

The typical Western approach to corruption advocates transparency and punishment. However, workable solutions to the problem require a deeper analysis of the part that bribery and corruption play in the wider social and economic composition of local communities. That means addressing the causes, extent and influence of corruption in a cultural context, particularly in those cultures based on social or extended family collectiveness. Where corrupt activities constitute the basis of the economic activity within a culture of collectiveness, it may well be that the benefits of the Western approach of exposure and punishment are outweighed by the private and social costs of a total breakdown in the community's economic base, such that the Western remedy does not produce a long-term solution to the problem. Rather, the approach to the long-term eradication of corruption may well lie not where an individual's misdemeanours are carried out for personal gain, but where the benefits of corrupt activities form the whole or significant part of the economic fabric of a community. As a member of the Hong Kong Independent Commission against Corruption warned more than a decade ago, 'an anti-corruption strategy will not be complete unless it addresses [the legal, political, economic and social] implications fully and deals with them on all fronts'.[39] Viewed this way it is not surprising that the traditional Western 'slash and burn' approach during the intervening period has failed to rein in the problem.

Tax Agents

The tax administration should encourage the use of tax agents, that is, private enterprise tax professionals (such as accountants) who act on behalf of their taxpayer clients. From a tax administration resource perspective, the use of tax agents brings about efficiencies, which in effect pass some of the costs of tax administration on to the private sector.

The use of tax agents reduces the number of taxpayers that the tax administration must deal with directly. In addition, the information provided to the tax administration by tax agents should be of a higher standard than that obtainable from taxpayers directly, since the agents are themselves tax accounting professionals. The quality of tax agents can be assessed and monitored by the tax administration, with delinquent agents being denied taxpayer representation status with the tax administration. From the private sector perspective tax agencies provide new business opportunities, which encourage accountants and other tax professionals to engage as tax agents to the mutual benefit of themselves and the tax administration.

Administrative Costs

Imposing upon small business taxpayers an obligation to complete and retain records and spend time and effort condensing those records into information to be disclosed on tax returns to arrive at the business's taxable income and the taxpayer's tax liability, which requires soliciting knowledge of tax law, imposes administrative costs on taxpayers. From the taxpayer's perspective these costs are typically referred to as 'compliance costs'. Sometimes the costs can be considerable and out of proportion to the amount of tax ultimately payable by the taxpayer, particularly small business taxpayers.[40]

Compliance costs are normally thought of in monetary terms. But compliance costs also involve less tangible, ethereal elements, such as the taxpayer's psychic costs of coping with the stress that the tax system imposes on individual taxpayers. All of these imposts, particularly if they are perceived by taxpayers to be unreasonable, serve as an inducement to disengagement with the tax system and even to tax evasion. In other words, they contribute to the undermining of the integrity of the tax system. It is therefore vital that tax policymakers in LDCs are cognizant of the consequences of imposing unrealistic obligations on taxpayers, including burdening them with disproportionate compliance costs. This means looking at the sustainability of a conventional income tax regime relative to other taxing options.

Administrative costs are not confined to taxpayers. The tax administration also incurs costs in endeavouring to ensure that taxpayers meet their legal obligations. Tax administrations the world over carry out their tasks with limited resources, and that is no more evident than in LDCs. In particular the level of formal education qualifications and job-focused training, as well as availability of physical resources, is less pervasive in tax administrations in LDCs in comparison to developed countries – and yet the application of the Western tax models makes no distinction between the capabilities of tax administrations in different countries.

Tax officials in LDCs often face the added difficulty that tax advisors in the private sector (particularly those in the large international accounting and law firms with specialist tax practices) have a better grasp of the tax law than they do (especially in the field of international tax), with the consequence that the tax officials may not be as robust as they should in challenging some of the (aggressive) tax positions taken by taxpayers on the advice of their tax advisors. Where the accounting skill set rests with MNEs and other large enterprises, rather than with the tax administration, that sector comes to dominate the outcomes of tax disputes, if indeed a challenge is raised by the tax administration.

The current global transfer pricing issues are a timely example of the power imbalance between tax administrations of LDCs, which lack adequate accounting skills and other resources to determine true arm's length prices for intra-group transactions, and MNEs, which typically possess those skills and resources in greater abundance, to argue at both the conceptual and the practical level for the adoption for tax purposes of the MNE's intra-group transfer pricing position. Small Pacific Island nations especially illustrate how the MNEs have the upper hand, resulting in potentially enormous losses of tax revenue to the LDCs. To overcome this problem it would be preferable for LDCs to adopt a unitary approach to the allocation of an MNE's taxable income between the countries in which it operates, that is, using a formula apportionment basis of taxing an MNE's worldwide profits broadly based on international accounting standards adopted in the compilation of the MNE's group annual audited financial statements.[41]

Ultimately these problems can be resolved only by active recruitment by the tax administration of appropriately qualified accounting and legal staff to confront confidently the positions taken by their colleagues engaged by the large national enterprises and MNEs. That inevitably means that the tax administration must offer competitive remuneration packages and working conditions to attract the necessary qualified staff. A cost–benefit[42] analysis typically drives home the point.

CONCLUSION

LDCs can learn much from past Western experience, but that does not mean embracing its mistakes or methodologies that are not appropriate to the economic, cultural and social circumstances of the LDC. Ideally the best features of the Western income tax models should be transposed to the fledgling taxation systems of LDCs, after making appropriate adjustments that take account of the particular characteristics and circumstances of the State in question.

It is fairly well established in the literature that an upshot of more widespread and freer trade in goods and services as a result of globalization since the 1980s has been a reduction in tariff barriers.[43] That has resulted in a fall in government revenue, particularly for LDCs, which hitherto imposed high levels of customs duties relative to developed countries. The loss of that revenue needed to be compensated for by raising government revenue from other sources. An initial popular source in LDCs was VAT, often introduced as a condition of much-sought-after IMF loans.[44] In largely the same circumstances the introduction of the Western income tax template followed. Perhaps in the rush to find alternative sources of revenue and to obtain IMF and other international institutional funding the governments of LDCs – and their foreign advisors – failed to take adequate account of the contextual differences between their countries and the developed countries from which the models were drawn and in which they work reasonably well.

For their own sake LDCs must resist what might be described as 'tax imperialism': imposing the notion that what is good for the West must be good for everyone. It is not sufficient simply to duplicate Western tax models 'warts and all' in LDCs. We need both to modify those models to take only the relevant good parts and to adopt a fresh approach, looking for new, simpler, more cost-effective, and evasion-proof ways of raising tax revenue equitably. This chapter has highlighted some of the models' relevant features and alternative approaches for further serious consideration by tax policymakers in LDCs.

NOTES

1. Although indirect taxation is mentioned from time to time, the focus of this chapter is on direct taxation.
2. According to the United Nations Statistics Division, the adult (that is, people aged 15 years or older) literacy rate in Bangladesh is 55 per cent, Benin 41 per cent, Bhutan 53 per cent, Burkina Faso 29 per cent, Central African Republic 55 per cent, Chad 33 per cent, Côte d'Ivoire 55 per cent, Ethiopia 36 per cent, The Gambia 45 per cent, Guinea-Bissau 51 per cent, Mali 26 per cent, Niger 29 per cent, Senegal 42 per cent, and Sierra Leone 40 per cent: http://unstats.un.org/unsd/demographic/products/socind/literacy.htm (accessed 7 August 2010).
3. Transfer pricing is addressed in detail in Chapter 15.
4. See http://www.imf.org/external/np/leg/tlaw/2000/eng/sym.htm, http://www.imf.org/external/np/leg/tlaw/ 2000/eng/stan.htm and http://www.imf.org/external/np/leg/tlaw/2003/eng/tlvat.htm (accessed 7 August 2010).
5. For a comprehensive discussion of this point, see Kevin Holmes (2001), *The Concept of Income: A Multi-Disciplinary Analysis*, Amsterdam: IBFD Publications, especially Chapters 2 and 13.
6. Countries that do not tax capital gains include Belize and Vanuatu (see http://www.lowtax.net/lowtax/ html/jbzpetx.html, accessed 7 August 2010), Costa Rica (generally), Gaza/West Bank, India (subject to long-term asset holding periods), Jamaica, Jordan, Kenya, Malaysia (except for real property), Namibia, Papua New Guinea, Sri Lanka and Zambia (see http://www.deloitte.com/view/en_GX/global/services/ tax/international-tax/international-tax-and-business-guides/index.htm, accessed 7 August 2010).
7. This amount is chosen for illustrative purposes to leave the low-income taxpayer in the same position whether the family assistance is offered by way of a tax deduction or a tax credit. This gives us a constant reference point from which to measure the effect on the high-income taxpayer of the tax deduction and tax credit methods.
8. Administrative simplicity is enhanced if deductions are abandoned altogether.
9. The Russian Federation is an example of a transitional economy that has adopted a low flat personal income tax rate of 13 per cent, which applies to its tax residents.
10. In some jurisdictions this methodology is applied separately to different classes of income, usually based on the source of the income. The net taxable income result from each source is aggregated to produce the taxpayer's total taxable income.
11. Since a tax evader's costs of doing business are lower than those of an honest competitor (because the

former does not incur the cost of taxation, whereas the latter does), tax evaders can reduce their sales prices by the amount of tax otherwise payable, to obtain a market advantage, and still receive the same amount of 'after-tax' profit. So long as such a situation prevails, resources will be allocated by the market towards the tax evader, contrary to the intent of the underlying tax policy.

12.   J. Brondolo, K. Nakayama, F. Bosch, A. Foubister and J. Tomaso (2008), *Vietnam: Implementing the Personal Income Tax*, May, p. 36, Washington, DC: International Monetary Fund, Fiscal Affairs Department.

13.   See, for example, F. Chittenden, S. Kauser and P. Poutziouris (2003), Tax regulation and small businesses in the USA, UK, Australia and New Zealand, *International Small Business Journal*, 21(1), February, p. 85; C.T. Sandford, M. Godwin and P. Hardwick (1989), *Administrative and Compliance Costs of Taxation*, Bath: Fiscal Publications; and C.T. Sandford and J. Hasseldine (1992), *The Compliance Costs of Business Taxes in New Zealand*, Wellington: Institute of Policy Studies.

14.   Other terms that are sometimes used in place of SEZs include 'free trade zones', 'free trade areas', 'free economic zones' and 'export processing zones'.

15.   This incentive is now being phased out. One reason is that it induced tax avoidance activities on the part of Chinese residents, which, rather than undertaking taxable business activities directly in China, established offshore entities that reinvested in China to qualify for the exemption.

16.   For example, SEZs can improve the efficiency of the tax system by reducing the 'dead-weight' costs associated with its administration, that is, to the extent that complicated tax rules, which are costly to implement in terms of money and time, are inapplicable, those costs are saved.

17.   See, for example, M. Tekere (2000), Export development and export-led growth strategies: export processing zones and the strengthening of sustainable human development [SHD], Discussion Notes, ICTSD Globalisation Dialogues – Africa Meeting, Windhoek, 10–12 May. The International Labour Organization also has concerns about the impact of SEZs on employee well-being. It advocates wider application of human resource management techniques amongst companies operating in SEZs, which instil more modern approaches to the labour–management relationship, including provision for better remuneration and working conditions, profit-sharing arrangements, greater skills training, housing, transport, child care facilities and the adoption of codes of conduct by multinational companies and their suppliers that carry on business in the SEZs: see International Labour Organization (1998), Export processing zones: the cutting edge of globalization – global production and local jobs: new perspectives on enterprise networks, employment and local development policy, International Workshop, Geneva, 9–10 March.

18.   International Monetary Fund (2004), *East Africa Community: Investment Tax Incentives and Harmonization*, January, Washington, DC: IMF.

19.   See, for example, P. Krugman and M. Obstfeld (2003), *International Economics*, 6th edn, Boston, MA: Addison-Wesley.

20.   M.H. Collins (1992), Brief survey of the development and main features of the United Kingdom's double taxation agreements with LDCs. In *Double Taxation Treaties between Industrialised and LDCs: OECD and UN Models, A Comparison*, ed. IFA, pp. 27, 29, Deventer and Boston, MA: Kluwer Law and Taxation Publishers.

21.   Assuming that its home State taxes its residents on their worldwide income, which is normally the case for capital exporting countries.

22.   This investor predicament is often overcome by an investor either structuring its investment through entities in jurisdictions that do not tax on the basis of a resident's worldwide income or using conduit entities, which ensure that the investor's home State will not tax the income in a way that eliminates the benefit of the host State's tax concessions.

23.   Until recently, Estonia successfully adopted a zero per cent corporate tax rate, so that only corporate distributions were taxable (in the shareholders' hands). Simulations by Funke and Strulik show that the long-term consequences of such a policy are positive for investment, but can be negative for welfare, as consumption has to decrease in order to finance higher investment. However, if foreign investment is (mostly) used to finance investment, the net effect on welfare may be positive: see M. Funke and H. Strulik (2003), Taxation, growth and welfare: dynamic effects of Estonia's 2000 Income Tax Act, Bank of Finland Discussion Paper 10/2003.

24.   Of course, the immediate impact on the level of the country's corporate tax receipts needs to be analysed before such a policy is adopted.

25.   See, for example, John Prebble (1994), Why is income tax incomprehensible? *British Tax Review*, 4, p. 380.

26.   Slovakia is an example of a country that has embraced the accounting measurement of income as the basis of income measurement for tax purposes.

27.   For example, Australia, New Zealand and the United Kingdom.

28.   In part, this approach is intended to facilitate application of the so-called 'purposive approach' to

statutory interpretation by the courts, that is, in determining how tax legislation should apply in a disputed case, the courts should look to the legislature's purpose in enacting the particular provision at issue, and not confine themselves to a strictly literal interpretation of the words of the statute.

29. See note 2.
30. Indeed, some Western countries, such as the Netherlands, with very sophisticated income tax systems have not yet chosen to embrace the self-assessment regime.
31. Such as dividends, interest and royalties.
32. Which is paramount for any tax system, whether or not it encompasses a withholding tax regime.
33. Tax code declarations are declarations made by taxpayers who receive source deduction payments advising the payers of their relevant circumstances (for example, the number of dependants if source deduction tax payments are to take account of family allowances), to enable the payer to calculate and to deduct the taxpayer's correct amount of tax at source. The need for taxpayers who receive source deduction payments to make tax code declarations to payers of their income is removed under a flat tax rate regime with no tax deductions or tax credits, which considerably enhances the simplicity of the regime and reduces opportunities for error and fraud.
34. In many, if not most, countries, salary and wage earners make up the largest single group of taxpayers.
35. See, for example, Margaret E. Cotton (2007), Selecting cases for audit – getting it right, *Asia-Pacific Tax Bulletin*, 13(1), February, p. 11.
36. For various accounts of the application of the death penalty in China for non-violent offences, such as tax evasion and corruption, see http://www.dailymail.co.uk/debate/article-1239060/China-shot-tax-evasion. html, http://www.nytimes.com/2009/07/30/world/asia/30china.html, http://www.jstor.org/pss/654154, http:// www.amnestyusa.org/document.php?lang=e&id=ENGUSA20060419001, http://www.unesco.org/couri er/1999_10/uk/ethique/txt1.htm, and http://www.telegraph.co.uk/news/worldnews/asia/china/7204197/ Chinas-Supreme-Court-stresses-mercy-in-death-penalty.html (accessed 7 August 2010).
37. This topic is addressed comprehensively in Chapter 13.
38. For a range of remedies, see, for example, M.M. Jaramillo (1995), Current strategies for combating corruption: a study of corruption in the tax administration, Problems in the Struggle against Corruption in the Tax Administration: Technical Papers of the 29th Inter American Center of Tax Administrations (CIAT) General Assembly, Lima, 27–31 March.
39. B.E.D. de Speville (1995), Experiences and forms of struggle against corruption, Problems in the Struggle against Corruption in the Tax Administration: Technical Papers of the 29th Inter American Center of Tax Administrations (CIAT) General Assembly, Lima, 27–31 March.
40. See note 13.
41. Such an approach is currently being advocated within the European Union in respect of MNEs that derive income from more than one Member State.
42. Where the benefits are measured in terms of the additional tax revenue collected as a result of the qualified employee's investigative tasks, which revenue would otherwise have been forgone
43. See, for example, US International Trade Commission (1998), *The Economic Implications of Liberalizing APEC Tariff and Non-Tariff Barriers to Trade*, Publication 3101, April, Washington, DC: US International Trade Commission; Maurizio Bussolo and John Walley (2002), *Globalization in LDCs: The Role of Transaction Costs in Explaining Economic Performance in India*, http://unpan1.un.org/intradoc/groups/ public/documents/APCITY/UNPAN015820.pdf; and Chandrasekaran Balakrishnan (2004), *Impact of Globalisation on LDCs and India*, http://economics.about.com/od/globalizationtrade/l/aaglobalization. htm, accessed 7 August 2010.
44. See Miranda Stewart and Sunita Jogarajan (2004), The International Monetary Fund and tax reform. *British Tax Review*, 2, p. 146.

FURTHER READING

Chittenden, F., S. Kauser and P. Poutziouris (2003). Tax regulation and small businesses in the USA, UK, Australia and New Zealand. *International Small Business Journal*, 21(1), February, p. 85.
Collins, M.H. (1992). Brief survey of the development and main features of the United Kingdom's double taxation agreements with LDCs. In *Double Taxation Treaties between Industrialised and LDCs: OECD and UN Models, A Comparison*, ed. IFA. Deventer and Boston, MA: Kluwer Law and Taxation Publishers.
Cotton, Margaret E. (2007). Selecting cases for audit – getting it right. *Asia-Pacific Tax Bulletin*, 13(1), February, p. 11.
Holmes, Kevin (2001). *The Concept of Income: A Multi-Disciplinary Analysis*. Amsterdam: IBFD Publications.
Jaramillo, M.M. (1995). Current strategies for combating corruption: a study of corruption in the tax adminis-

tration. Problems in the Struggle against Corruption in the Tax Administration: Technical Papers of the 29th Inter American Center of Tax Administrations (CIAT) General Assembly, Lima, 27–31 March.

Kobetsky, Michael (2008). Transfer pricing measures and emerging developing economies. *Asia-Pacific Tax Bulletin*, September/October, p. 363.

Prebble, John (1994). Why is income tax incomprehensible? *British Tax Review*, 4, p. 380.

Sandford, C.T., M. Godwin and P. Hardwick (1989). *Administrative and Compliance Costs of Taxation*. Bath: Fiscal Publications.

Sandford, C.T., and J. Hasseldine (1992). *The Compliance Costs of Business Taxes in New Zealand*. Wellington: Institute of Policy Studies.

Speville, B.E.D. de (1995). Experiences and forms of struggle against corruption. Problems in the Struggle against Corruption in the Tax Administration: Technical Papers of the 29th Inter American Center of Tax Administrations (CIAT) General Assembly, Lima, 27–31 March.

Stewart, Miranda, and Sunita Jogarajan (2004). The International Monetary Fund and tax reform. *British Tax Review*, 2, p. 146.

15 Exploring the transfer pricing conundrum
Clive Emmanuel

THE SIGNIFICANCE OF TRANSFER PRICING

Originally transfer pricing was explored in a domestic situation where profit centre management created tensions between managerial motivation, viable measures of economic performance and economically efficient operating decisions. Joel Dean's classic analysis begins with 'The transfer pricing dispute was settled by a fist-fight in the boardroom' (1955). Those issues persist but, with the growth in multinational companies (MNCs), the value placed on intra-group transactions has attracted the attention of many other interested parties, especially when goods, services and intangibles are transferred across national boundaries. One group of interested parties are emerging or less developed countries (LDCs) that wish to attract MNC inward investment. Fiscal authorities in distinct national jurisdictions are also acutely aware of the effect transfer pricing exerts on their capacity to raise revenue. The potentially conflicting motives within and between these parties, together with MNCs, is explored to reveal the broad dimensions of the transfer pricing conundrum.

The choices facing host governments, including LDCs, national fiscal authorities and MNCs, take place in a world trade landscape where the Organisation for Economic Co-operation and Development (OECD) and the United Nations Conference on Trade and Development (UNCTAD) provide Model Conventions whose main aim is to remove obstacles to the development of economic relations between countries. We will make use of these on a selective basis in our exploration of the conundrum.

In a paraphrase of Wells (1968), a transfer price is the monetary expression of a movement of goods, services or intangibles between parts of the same company that may or may not be located in different countries. The movements can therefore include: raw materials, semi- or finished goods, and components; legal, managerial and technological services; and intellectual property, know-how, brands and patents. When parts of the same enterprise interact, the supplier may expect a revenue in the form of the transfer price, whilst the recipient usually pays the same transfer price as a cost. In addition, the interacting parts can be headquarters staff, subsidiaries, branches, affiliates, projects or whatever operation the enterprise chooses to identify.

No one has been able to quantify accurately the value of trade involving transfer pricing, although the OECD estimates that 60 per cent of world trade involves intra-group transactions of MNCs (*OECD Observer*, 2008). More recently, UNCTAD (2009) reported there are 82 000 MNCs (44 500 in 1997) with 810 000 foreign affiliates (275 000 in 1997) worldwide, suggesting that the World Trade Organization estimate of intra-group transactions accounting for $1.6 trillion (Mehafdi, 2000) has been substantially exceeded. This lack of reliable data is partly due to accounting regulators regarding these types of transactions as internal policy issues and not necessarily subject to external disclosure. IFRS 8 on segment reporting, for example, pays scant attention to transfer pricing disclosure, as does IFRS 24, which deals with related party disclosure. The net result is that existing and prospective investors are unaware of whether an enterprise is manipulating transfer prices to shift income to low tax jurisdictions and thereby reduce global tax liability. Historically, there may be grounds for this position taken by financial disclosure regulators, because accounting has focused on the enterprise in total, not the individual parts, and in any event each MNC organizes its activities to meet its specific strategy and objectives. Despite this dearth of disclosure, there is a growing awareness that transfer pricing abuse occurs (Sikka and Willmott, 2010), but the scale of the problem remains opaque.

Since the 1990s, the fiscal authorities in developed countries have strengthened, and those in LDCs have introduced transfer pricing regulations either in response to OECD and UNCTAD guidance or, in the case of the Internal Revenue Service in the USA, ahead of guidelines being agreed. These developments are on-going, but generally fiscal authorities are wary of breaching taxpayer confidentiality unless a dispute comes to court. As a result little information appears in the public domain. Investigative journalism, such as the series of articles in the *Guardian* (2009), offers some evidence of transfer pricing abuse by MNCs but can only speculate on how widespread the practices are relative to the total of global intra-group transactions. Undoubtedly the lack of reliable information publicly available contributes to the conundrum.

The argument we intend to demonstrate is that each of the major parties – host governments, fiscal agencies and MNCs – face within their spheres of influence competing choices that may subsequently result in conflict between the parties. LDCs, in particular, face policy choices that impinge on economic growth, sustainable tax revenues, membership of the international fiscal community and resource constraints. Some of the tensions underlying the transfer pricing conundrum are shown in Figure 15.1, and these demonstrate the complex inter-relationships that can influence the positions taken by host governments, national fiscal authorities and MNCs.

ECONOMIC GROWTH AND LDCS

All host governments including LDCs are aware that transfer pricing can be used to shift profit to subsidiaries in low tax countries. If all countries had the same tax regimes and income tax rates the benefits of income shifting would be substantially reduced. Unfortunately, this is not the case, and not all LDCs in particular will have regimes that include excise, import, repatriation of dividends, withholding taxes or foreign exchange controls as well as income tax regulations. In addition to these there are income tax rate differentials that each country can decide independently as incentives host governments offer to attract MNCs to locate within their territories. The creation by individual host governments of economic enterprise zones can offer low set-up costs, tax moratoria, a choice of acceptable legal forms (wholly owned subsidiary through to joint venture) and various other 'sweeteners' that may differentiate one LDC from another. These incentives to encourage foreign direct investment (FDI) appear to be effective in that pre-tax profitability of MNC foreign affiliates is negatively correlated with host country tax rates (Hines and Rice, 1994). In other words, the lower the corporate income tax rate, the

Source: Elliott and Emmanuel (1998).

Figure 15.1   Tensions in international transfer pricing

higher is pre-tax profit. Glaister and Frecknall Hughes (2008) provide survey evidence that MNCs incorporate tax in a 'highly deliberate and intended' manner when considering strategic location decisions about foreign affiliates, although fiscal aspects do not take priority.

There are numerous empirical studies (Grubert and Mutti, 1991; Oyelere and Emmanuel, 1998; Glaister and Frecknall Hughes, 2008) providing indirect evidence of tax planning influencing the location decision of MNCs. However, the host government FDI policy creates at least two implications. Will the incentives it offers result in tax haven status and will its own fiscal agency be constrained in obtaining a 'fair' tax take from the MNCs within its jurisdiction?

In terms of the second of these, lowering corporate tax rates may increase host government tax revenues when broad tax reductions succeed in attracting relatively few major employers to locate within its jurisdiction. Locating in low tax jurisdictions also creates a multiplier effect in the local economy through the increased demand for support services. Ireland, Puerto Rico and Singapore are examples where low tax rates have stimulated economic growth without a decline in tax revenue (Webber, 2011). When the MNC locates the most profitable of its activities, whether in terms of manufacturing or intellectual property generating, in these low tax jurisdictions, there is a mutual benefit to host government and MNC. However, to support this strategy the most profitable activities and their legal entities must accept the most business risk. The identification of a country as a low tax jurisdiction also implies that the government is promoting itself as a tax haven.

Tax haven status in itself is not illegal, but the potential for MNCs to evade taxation by shifting income to low tax or zero tax countries resulted in sufficient concern for the OECD to issue the Project of Harmful Tax Practices (1998). Chapter 2 of this report identifies four key factors to identify and assess harmful preferential tax regimes. The key criteria are:

1. low or no effective tax rates;
2. the 'ring-fencing' of regimes;
3. the lack of transparency;
4. the lack of effective exchange of information.

The presence of low or zero tax rates alone does not make a preferential tax regime harmful, but it does make it necessary to investigate whether any of the other criteria are present. The harmful practices report forged the development of tax information exchange agreements (addressed in the next section), but there is an important implication.

Falling foul of the harmful practices guidelines risks identification of the LDC host government being a tax haven and therefore limiting the possibility of participating in bilateral treaties to avoid double taxation. The recommendations of the OECD and UN contained in the Models of Double Tax Convention (DTC) on Income and on Capital (UN, 2005; OECD, [2005] 2010) have the stated aim of removing obstacles to economic relations between countries. Essentially both Models argue that two or more governments using the same base to recognize tax for the same taxpayer (MNC) will harm international trade. Many countries therefore seek to comply with the OECD Model DTC or the UN Model DTC. Adoption of the Models arguably helps to secure bilateral tax treaties that are attractive to MNCs in reducing the risk of double taxation and give host governments credibility as international trading parties.

The Model Conventions of both the OECD and the UN are used to develop bilateral tax treaties and, although they are not strictly binding on individual governments, the level of similarity in treaties involving OECD member countries appears to act as a benchmark for 'good practice'. Under a treaty, the OECD Convention, amongst other guidance, allocates taxing rights between the parties and defines permanent establishments, important aspects influencing an individual country's tax take. The Model Conventions are not mandatory, and the sovereignty of individual states remains paramount, but adoption of these guidelines offers some defence against recognition as a tax haven. The presence of double taxation agreements offers the MNC some security in that procedures are known when a dispute arises. For example, when one jurisdiction makes an adjustment to the transfer price and can justify in principle and amount that adjustment, Article 9(2) of the OECD's Model DTC requires that the amount of tax charged on profits subject to double taxation should be correspondingly moderated by the other jurisdiction. Where a bilateral tax treaty does not exist, the MNC may seek redress to transfer pricing adjustments by means of the mutual agreement procedures, but these can be time-consuming and costly, and the burden of proof is placed on the country making the adjustment or the MNC itself.

The choices facing LDC governments are to adopt the Model Conventions of the OECD or UN on double taxation and gain a measure of control over MNCs and their pricing policies through established procedures or, at the extreme, to be recognized as a tax haven and, by using tax incentives, aggressively promote inward investment to further economic growth. In the latter case the MNC's transfer pricing policy is unlikely to be subject to stringent examination or control. This outcome is likely when the resources, expertise and organization of fiscal authorities, especially in LDCs, are limited relative to those of more developed countries.

A FAIR SHARE OF TAX REVENUES BETWEEN FISCAL AUTHORITIES

A sound domestic tax system is believed to exhibit equity and neutrality (Eden, 1998) – neutral in the sense that the tax system should not influence the taxpayer's choice of legal form, location of the tax base and choice of pricing policy. Horizontal equity requires that two taxpayers in similar economic circumstances should pay the same tax and, likewise, taxpayers in different circumstances should pay appropriately different taxes (vertical equity). It is worth remembering these criteria when examining some of the detail surrounding acceptable transfer pricing methods.

For all countries but especially LDCs, Chapter V of the OECD Transfer Pricing Guidelines provides 'general guidance for tax administrations to take into account in developing rules and/or procedures for documentation to be obtained from taxpayers in connection with a transfer pricing enquiry' (para. 5.1).

Many countries subscribe to the recommendations of the OECD Model Tax Convention ([2005] 2010), which contains in Article 9 the 'arm's length' principle. The article argues that intra-group prices charged within an MNC must be comparable with those that would be charged between independent enterprises. The clear intention is to prevent artificial manipulation of profits earned in various countries by transfer pricing and so achieve a fair share of the MNC's profit for all the tax jurisdictions in which the MNC operates. Whilst there is wide support of the arm's length principle by the world's fiscal agencies, each agency reserves the right to interpret the principle and to determine the evidence required to justify a transfer price being acceptable. This can pose a further difficulty for fiscal agencies in LDCs that face the problem of limited fiscal authority resources.

The US has developed and continues to develop highly detailed requirements to ensure compliance with its interpretation of the arm's length principle (United States Internal Revenue Service, 1995). These include:

1. contemporaneous documentation, that is, the taxpayer is assumed to have readily available information on any intra-group transaction the Internal Revenue Service enquires about;
2. part of the documentation to include a functional analysis of the transaction, as shown in Table 15.1;
3. a road map of the interactions between parts of the enterprise, the value chain and, by degree, the strategy being followed;

Table 15.1   List of questions in a functional analysis

What was done?
What economically significant functions were involved in doing it?
Who performed each function?
How was the function accomplished?
Are there any valuable intangibles used in performing the given function?
Why were the transactions structured the way they were?
Where and when did the transactions occur and which entities were involved?
What economic risks were assumed?

Source: Fuller (1994).

4. the choice of transfer pricing method (comparable uncontrolled price, resale price, cost plus, comparable profit method, profit split, unspecified methods) to be based on the 'most reliable measure'.

Associated with these requirements are penalty regulations that require the MNC to make a reasonable effort to evaluate alternative transfer pricing methods to that chosen. The regulations distinguish between a substantial and a gross valuation misstatement, respectively 20 per cent and 40 per cent, which determine the level of penalty that can be imposed. These are in addition to any adjustments made to the income tax assessment. With some variation these requirements under s. 482 and the penalty regulations apply to services and intangibles.

This gives a flavour of the transfer pricing rules in the US, their detail and complexity. The Australian Tax Office (ATO) has experimented with more principle-based requirements, whilst Her Majesty's Revenue and Customs (HMRC) attempt to recognize the need for judgement in examining transfer pricing, but both have written rules for compliance. All three fiscal agencies adopt the OECD Model Tax Convention but through their domestic interpretation of the arm's length principle can and do obtain much more information than under the Convention's general requirements. This arguably places the fiscal agencies of LDCs at a disadvantage when a transfer pricing dispute is examined under double taxation treaties or mutual agreement procedures.

To provide substantiating evidence of the arm's length principle, comparable transactions or business operations in the host LDC may be required. One observer (Durst, 2010) estimates that a single search for an MNC can cost $100000, and for those with many global transactions the overall annual spend on accounting, law and economic consultants will easily be expressed in millions. It is highly questionable whether comparable transactions will be undertaken in the LDC, whether databases of these transactions are available and whether they are accessible. There is also the significant question of whether the fiscal authority of an LDC has the resource to develop or subscribe to these databases. This lack of comparable data to justify any of the acceptable transfer pricing methods (comparable controlled price, resale price, full cost plus, comparable profit method or transaction net margin method, profit split) has led Emmanuel and Cools (2007) to suggest that a highest common denominator effect exists when disputes arise between national fiscal authorities. The detailed regulations and databases of developed countries cannot be matched by LDC fiscal authorities.

Leaving aside whether a host LDC's domestic tax system provides neutrality, the equity heavily depends on determining whether taxpayers (MNE subsidiaries and indigenous companies) operate in similar economic circumstances. The exchange of information article of a tax treaty complying with either the OECD or the UN Model of DTC or in a tax information exchange agreement is legally a two-way street. Both fiscal authorities can request information from each other about taxpayers. The exchange of information can be on request or automatic, but all tax authorities are wary of 'fishing expeditions', that is, requests for information not merited under domestic regulations. The OECD indicates that over 300 tax information exchange agreements have been concluded and, in theory, these should benefit both LDCs' and developed countries' fiscal authorities. The major difficulty is that the LDC domestic tax system is unlikely to be as comprehensive or sophisticated and therefore is at a disadvantage in identifying similar circumstances, the cornerstone of equity. Without similar circumstances being defined, will the LDC fiscal authority be able to identify and justify the comparables under acceptable transfer pricing methods? Will the LDC fiscal authority be capable of questioning a transfer pricing adjustment by a developed country's fiscal authority that, under a bilateral tax treaty, reduces the tax take in the LDC?

Adjustments do occur. Between 2007 and 2009, HMRC raised £2.1 billion through adjustments. ATO audits between 2000 and 2005 resulted in an additional tax take of A$2.5 billion. In just one case, involving GlaxoSmithKline, the IRS successfully recouped US$3.4 billion.

Empirical findings on relative profitability of companies operating under similar economic circumstances in LDCs are difficult to discover. Alba and Lozano's (2009) study, using profitability measures and ranges consistent with the comparable profit method, show higher profitability in emerging countries and associate this with country risk. However, none of the 27 countries are obvious low tax jurisdictions or LDCs. The study does demonstrate that cross-country comparability is no easy task. The lack of representative LDCs in the analysis possibly reinforces the database gap between LDC fiscal authorities and other authorities worldwide.

The LDC fiscal authority therefore faces a number of choices. Within the constraints placed upon it by the LDC government's FDI policy, it is required to obtain a fair tax take from MNC subsidiaries operating within its jurisdiction. Bilateral tax treaties and mutual agreement procedures when they exist place the LDC fiscal agency at a disadvantage unless it has equally detailed regulations as developed countries, even if it has information exchange arrangements in place. When the LDC fiscal agency has inadequate national statistics on the profitability of indigenous companies, it is placed in a disadvantaged position to question the comparables given as evidence by other better resourced fiscal authorities operating under more detailed tax systems. Will the tax take in the LDC be fair?

The choices facing LDC fiscal agencies are therefore problematic. If their ability to demonstrate equity is limited, that is, comparables are unavailable, they either accept the adjustment of the other fiscal authority and possibly lose tax revenue or develop their own rules, regulations and statistics to be able to question any adjustment. Sustaining or improving the LDC 'fair' tax take seems remote. Without satisfactory resourcing the latter option of developing restrictive regulations is unlikely to occur, and brings into sharp focus the expertise, trained human resources and systems that LDC fiscal authorities have at their disposal. There is every likelihood that this under-resourcing will adversely affect the tax take of LDCs.

MULTINATIONAL COMPANY OPTIONS AND LDCS

Within the incentives LDC countries may offer for efficient tax planning and the differential requirements of national fiscal agencies, the MNC appears to have great discretion in making transfer pricing policy decisions. Despite double tax treaties and stated commitments to OECD mutual agreement procedures, the scope for MNCs, especially with regard to LDCs, to set advantageous transfer prices seems to be unassailable. This advantage is exaggerated by the versatility of the roles transfer pricing can serve. The academic and practitioner literature has long recognized these multiple roles (Radebaugh and Gray, 1997). For example, MNC transfer pricing policy can:

1. concentrate cash centrally;
2. minimize global tax liability (dependent on different countries' tax regimes and rates of taxation);
3. reduce exposure to risks of inflation and exchange rate fluctuations;
4. help avoid restrictions placed on the repatriation of dividends from other parts of the enterprise;
5. improve competitive advantage by providing 'cheap' finance, sometimes termed thin capitalization of subsidiaries;
6. ameliorate the management of joint ventures involving foreign partners;
7. promote or maintain good relations with the host country of residence;
8. promote or maintain good relations with the host countries overseas;
9. provide an ethical and good international citizen status with the public in general;
10. comply with fiscal agencies' regulations and, increasingly, corporate governance regulations;
11. provide relevant financial performance measures for segment or subsidiary management for managerial motivation.

Several of these roles are not simultaneously achievable, as Lin, Lefebvre and Kantor (1993) have demonstrated, and, despite press coverage of individual transfer pricing abuse and evidence of startlingly different import and export prices taken from customs data (Pak and Zdanowicz, 2002), there is some doubt whether MNCs actively manage pricing for individual transactions. Anecdotal and limited case studies (Elliott and Emmanuel, 2000) suggest that loss carry-backs or carry-forwards, accumulated tax credits and FDI-type incentives are major considerations in minimizing global tax liabilities.

Nevertheless, transfer pricing is regarded as one of the top three concerns of MNC finance or tax directors in Ernst and Young's biennial worldwide survey since 1997. The fear of audit, loss of reputation, and the cost of defending against fiscal claims are some of the reasons given (Ernst and Young, 2009). The potential of fiscal enquiry or audit has led consultants to recommend MNCs review their existing transfer documentation and consider using one set of accounting records for internal and fiscal purposes. Having more than one transfer price for the same transaction will require further documentary justification to explain the reasons for the difference (Baldenius, Melumad and Reichelstein, 2004).

Several implications can arise from adoption of one fiscally acceptable transfer price for internal managerial purposes. Although a choice of pricing methods is available, some are not available, for example negotiated transfer prices. The use of an arm's length price for internal pricing decisions, trading volumes, make-or-buy decisions and performance measurement may ignore the commercial reality. A product in the maturity stage may be manufactured in an LDC because of low labour costs. All output is transferred to a downstream subsidiary on a full cost basis consistent with the MNC's allocation methods. The host fiscal agent may regard this transfer price as breaching the basic tenets of equity and neutrality, because no profit is declared in this jurisdiction, and consequently raise the transfer price. This is an over-simplified illustration perhaps, but it raises the question whether one transfer price can satisfy both commercial and fiscal objectives (Eden, 1998).

There is a limited but growing literature based on case studies that describes the far-reaching effects of individual MNCs adopting a policy of being fully compliant with fiscal regulations. In one case, this resulted in structural re-organization along functional lines, increased centralization, reduced emphasis on key financial performance measures, and the internal tax and audit functions becoming instrumental in changing the internal control system (Cools, Emmanuel and Jorissen, 2008). Similar effects are reported when an MNC adopts an internal cost allocation system consistent with fiscal regulations (Rossing and Rohde, 2010). The degree of commitment to fiscal compliance is unlikely to be uniform, and the potential commercial distortions resulting from compliance are yet to be fully examined.

To avoid the negative claims of abusive transfer pricing, one option available to MNCs is to apply for an advance pricing agreement (APA). Each fiscal agency can set its own procedures and documentation requirements. Submission in the US is dependent on a fee being paid; in the UK a submission will be evaluated and only if deemed appropriate will it be admitted to the process; in Australia, prelodgement meetings are arranged to help clarify the aims of both the ATO and the MNC and to pinpoint the information required.

When the APA is bilateral, involving two countries' fiscal agencies, the likelihood is that the MNC will first approach the one located where the group headquarters reside, but both agencies will be privy to the information supplied. The level of disclosure in the submission is likely to reflect closely that required under a functional analysis (Table 15.1), but because the APA involves face-to-face meetings additional information can be requested by the fiscal agencies. A successful APA results in the range of prices using the agreed methodology for the arm's length prices being part of the agreement, normally with annual monitoring. The APA can apply for five years and provides the MNC with a level of certainty that this particular transaction will not be audited, as long as the transfer price falls within the arm's length range of results.

Given that an APA is needed for each transaction or series of similar transactions, the take-up rate suggests that MNCs are not convinced of the merits of submitting to the process compared to the costs of gaining agreement. In the UK, seven new APAs were signed and 18 were in force for 2005–06. In the US, 537 APAs were agreed between 1991 and 2004, 234 being unilateral, 238 bilateral and 20 multilateral (Drake, Rode and Wright, 2005). It is difficult to gain insights into the APA process. The ATO, for example, states that 'The information generated by the APA process relates directly to the income tax affairs of the taxpayer and will therefore be subject to the same secrecy and privacy safeguards as if it was obtained during an audit or advising process' (Australian Tax Office, 2005).

The many roles transfer pricing can play provides a huge choice for MNCs. With tax planning, several may be legitimately attained to minimize global tax liability, but certain roles may be mutually exclusive, such as shifting profit to low tax jurisdictions only to suffer withholding or repatriation taxes or high customs and excise rates. Adoption of fully compliant transfer pricing can result in far-reaching changes in the internal operations and control system of the enterprise. At the other extreme, the potential for tax evasion through abusive transfer pricing cannot be ignored as an alternative MNC policy. Developed countries have strengthened fiscal regulations in the past 15 years, but the effectiveness of these changes is opaque because of the confidentiality all fiscal authorities provide to taxpayers. For those MNCs operating at neither extreme of the compliance continuum, the introduction of APAs provides a level of protection from audit for the taxpayer but at a cost of providing detailed and sometimes sensitive information. There appears to be no clear-cut decision that can be justified in terms of maximizing shareholder wealth in the long term, at least partly because of the versatility of transfer pricing. When this is combined with the imperfections provided by LDC FDI policies and imbalances between domestic regulations as well as each fiscal authority seeking its own fair share of tax revenue, we begin to gain an appreciation of the MNC's powerful position. At one extreme, it may avoid tax audit and adverse publicity by complying with OECD, UN and domestic fiscal authorities' guidelines and regulations. Alternatively, the MNC may plan strategic and operational decisions to minimize global tax liabilities and maximize shareholder value. There are obviously many intermediate positions between these extremes that the MNC may choose.

POTENTIAL CONFLICTS BETWEEN THE PARTIES

The OECD has recommended that binding arbitration should apply when disputes arise between fiscal agencies and between a fiscal agency and an MNC within a two-year period. Exactly how this will be administered remains to be seen, but the intention is to be supported, because many disputes currently extend for several years. This brings into focus the relationship between the MNC and individual fiscal authorities. For countries with an established, resourced fiscal agency negotiating with an established MNC there is limited evidence to indicate that 'cherry picking' of transfer pricing transactions is the norm (Elliott and Emmanuel, 2000). That is, the MNC provides annually a listing from which the relevant agency can choose to enquire. Deliberations can be long drawn out over several years and may involve the fiscal agency having a semi-permanent office at the MNC headquarters or the MNC providing an electronic model of the specific transaction in order that the agency can apply its own sensitivity analysis to determine whether market, technological and other factors merit a change in transfer pricing outside the accepted range. Can these be regarded as efforts to comply with tax regulations or defence mechanisms to convince the fiscal agency that the transfer price can be justified? There is a whole sub-culture yet to be examined.

From an individual fiscal agency view, it is necessary to interpret regulations to MNCs, but additionally the agency needs to extract information from the MNC (Hasseldine, Holland and van der Rijt, 2010). Is the use of whistleblowers and the incentives they are offered conducive to this process when transfer pricing abuse is suspected? HMRC has announced that, effective from 1 April 2010, tax evaders, whether individuals or companies, run the risk of being publicly identified, in addition to paying the 'lost' tax, interest on tax and a penalty of up to 100 per cent on the lost tax. The relationship between fiscal agent and MNC or its affiliates is nothing if not complex. It would be interesting to discover whether fiscal authority tax inspectors are attracted to employment in MNC tax departments.

The OECD and UN's shared intention is to encourage international trade by recommending Model Conventions and double taxation agreements and promoting the arm's length principle in order that a fair allocation of tax base is provided to fiscal authorities in the relevant jurisdictions. Draconian fiscal regulations can harm world trade and adversely affect individual countries' balance of payments and gross domestic product. Therefore efforts to make binding arbitration effective when transfer pricing disputes arise between fiscal agencies and MNCs depend, in part, on the existence of double tax agreements between the parties with appropriate mutual agreement procedures and procedures for information exchange. These procedures in the Model Tax Conventions are recommendations only, and each double tax agreement can be tailored for specific countries. Whilst the OECD and UN recommendations may provide persuasive guidance, domestic fiscal regulations can vary or ultimately over-ride them. The Model Tax Convention provides a skeletal framework for international trading relationships and, whilst members of the OECD may recognize economic sustainability particularly in LDCs as a significant transfer pricing issue (Silberztein, 2004), there is a lack of detail. Only suggestions can be made regarding the joint responsibility for LDCs, developed countries, investors and MNCs 'to promote fair and efficient tax systems, administrations and attitudes that will ensure each country derives the fruit of its own economic growth' (Silberztein, 2004, p.6). Fiscal outcomes have dominated transfer pricing regulation and guidelines to the virtual exclusion of more ethical considerations such as sustainability, environmental protection and anti-corruption practices. There is however some doubt as to whether the fiscal outcomes themselves can be justified in terms of equity and neutrality.

The arm's length principle applies to transactions where a functional analysis should reveal the risk–return profile of all the parties. Emphasis is placed on prices charged to unrelated parties involved in similar transactions, but adjustments are made for differences in volumes, bad debt provision, advertising, transportation and other costs to gain a comparable uncontrolled price. The resale price method relies on an appropriate gross profit being deducted as the return for the internal buying affiliate when the service or good is ultimately sold to independent third parties. The appropriate gross profit focuses only on the internal buyer and requires comparable sales or distributions undertaking similar transactions in similar circumstances to be identified. Eden (1998) provides a masterful analysis of other acceptable transfer pricing methods, such as cost plus, comparable profits, profit split, and transaction net margin method, to demonstrate either that only one party's involvement is examined or that idiosyncrasies embedded in the transaction render comparables misleading. The idiosyncrasies may be covered by patents, special processes, a unique mix of resources, or specifications that represent the MNC's competitive advantage. For intangibles and services these idiosyncrasies are commonly encountered.

Transaction cost economics may provide a theoretical justification for tax regulations to concentrate on particular types of transaction, and Spicer (1988) has argued that certain methods of transfer pricing are relevant dependent on frequency of transactions, asset specificity and uncertainty. For example, when the transaction involves assets (including intangibles) that have no readily available alternative use, where there is uncertainty in the final or intermediate markets and when the interaction between affiliates is infrequent, actual cost should be used as the transfer price. Where asset specificity is low, frequent interaction occurs and uncertainty is reduced because of substitute providers of the service or intermediate products, a market price is argued to be relevant. Intermediate circumstances may merit a standard cost transfer price with negotiation between the segments of the enterprise. Negotiated transfer pricing is not accepted by the OECD or the majority of fiscal agencies as an acceptable method. Spicer's (1988) analysis applies to domestic interactions involving transactions between units of the same enterprise but not to international cross-border transactions. Transaction cost economics therefore seeks to explain why enterprises adopt particular activities within their structure or to use the market or a hybrid where parts of the enterprise service internal and external buyers. However, for the MNC, international interactions result in the introduction of fiscal rules and regulations that can test the most intricate analyses employing transaction cost economics.

An alternative theoretical explanation of why certain enterprises expand to be MNCs is offered by Dunning (1988). Advantages associated with ownership, location and internalization enable expansion via horizontal integration, benefiting from the technology, intangibles, and patents of the parent, to establish replica businesses overseas or via vertical integration to establish different parts of the value chain in locations that offer resource, cost or quality benefits. The frame of analysis is not necessarily the individual transaction but strategic. The key ingredient to a successful multinational business is therefore a competitive advantage that has no comparable in the geographic location or cannot match the value chain synergies of the MNC. If indigenous companies contained similar advantages to the MNC there would be limited opportunities to expand successfully overseas.

Arguably, the Dunning explanation of the growth of MNCs renders comparability inappropriate. Can the costs, revenues or profit of an indigenous company undertaking similar functions to those of an MNC affiliate be comparable when it does not operate with the same patents, technology or know-how? For the vertically integrated affiliate of the MNC whose output is destined for a sister subsidiary overseas, are the domestic market conditions influencing the performance of the indigenous company relevant in providing a comparable benchmark? Some fiscal authorities appear to accept or require indigenous comparables in examining certain transfer pricing methods; others do not, but prefer to use their domestic companies as comparables. When the tax compliant

MNC determines a global transfer price for a specific transaction, other fiscal agencies will suggest adjustments to take into account the peculiarities of its own jurisdiction, for example population dispersion or transportation costs.

Concentration on the individual transaction may allow the search for comparables to be legitimized. Functional analysis, organization structure, or an alternative method of transfer pricing selection, especially if transaction cost economics are applied, can offer justification to a limited extent. Constraints are posed by the complications of tax regimes and the detailed rules of individual fiscal authorities. The focus of the OECD, UN and many fiscal authorities is therefore on the transaction. On the other hand, MNC expansion in theory is based on comparables not being available or being irrelevant when available. It is precisely the lack of similar transactions or interactions undertaken by indigenous companies, at either the host or the home territory, that explains the success of MNCs. It is the particular uniqueness that gives the MNC a competitive advantage and allows a strategy of growth overseas to be successful. Unfortunately this success may in part be due to efficient tax planning or transfer price abuse.

UNRAVELLING THE TRANSFER PRICING CONUNDRUM

Maintaining the arm's length principle appears difficult because:

1. alternative acceptable transfer pricing methods can give different taxable profit results;
2. comparables are interpreted differently by fiscal agencies;
3. bilateral tax treaties are likely to favour those tax jurisdictions that have the most detailed rules;
4. fair tax take dominates all other aims, including sustainability, environmental protection and corporate governance considerations;
5. OECD guidance is secondary in importance to rules established in domestic tax jurisdictions;
6. host and home jurisdictions and MNCs have potentially conflicting alternative motives before interacting with each other;
7. there is no one economic or other theory that helps to inform policy.

LDCs are in a disadvantaged position when dealing with MNCs and other countries' fiscal authorities because their domestic tax and administrative control systems for customs, imports and exports may be inadequate, the tax regime is incomplete, financial statements of indigenous and MNC affiliates in their jurisdiction are unavailable and the costs of complying with OECD guidelines are high. LDCs are not necessarily tax havens, but underdeveloped domestic tax systems coupled with tax breaks to attract foreign direct investment may give this impression.

Limited empirical evidence (Borkowski, 1997) suggests tax haven countries are as concerned as other countries about income shifting. This may be partly explained by increased scrutiny from non-haven fiscal authorities suspecting that income is shifted from their jurisdictions to tax havens, with the consequence that treaty negotiations will be jeopardized. For example, Spencer (2009) quotes a senior US tax official who categorically argues that information exchange is a pre-condition before negotiations on a bilateral tax treaty can begin. If the other country has bank secrecy rules that prevent or seriously inhibit the exchange of information, no treaty will be concluded. Tax haven countries appear to recognize this problem. The Borkowski survey found that LDCs preferred more restrictive transfer pricing regulations that favoured transaction-based methods like comparable uncontrolled price, resale price or full cost plus with a specific order of preference. Several countries recognized that the absence of regulation and lack of accounting and auditing expertise made assessment of the extent of price manipulation difficult to gauge.

However, some progress is apparent, such as the formation of the African Tax Administration Forum (ATAF) (*OECD Observer*, 2009), consisting of 25 fiscal authorities many of which are classified as operating in LDCs. With the near stagnation of development aid, ATAF seeks to develop best practice by sharing experiences between fiscal authorities. Items on the agenda include widening the tax base, removing FDI incentives and controlling the illicit flight of capital from LDCs estimated to be in the region of $500 billion to $800 billion per annum (Sikka and Willmott, 2010). Whether this and other similar initiatives will improve cooperation between fiscal authorities and redress the current disadvantageous position of LDCs remains to be seen. There are more structural changes that may benefit LDCs.

FUTURE DEVELOPMENTS

If the danger of double taxation is an influence on reducing world trade, then it is worth revisiting earlier suggestions to find a solution that modifies or replaces the present system. Shoup (1985) argued for a permanent board of arbitration under the United Nations to adjudicate transfer pricing disputes. LDC countries may benefit from such an organization, but developed countries can argue that their tax sovereignty is jeopardized. If there is no international arbitration board with authority, there is a question mark hanging over transfer pricing regulation contributing to the principles of equity and neutrality.

An interesting development concerns the European Arbitration Convention under which the fiscal authorities of member states involved in a dispute have two years in which to reach agreement. After that time an advisory committee must be established and should deliver an opinion within six months. The advisory panel comprises members or representatives of the two governments and 'independent members of standing'. The fiscal authorities of the two member states have a further six months to either adopt the recommendations of the advisory panel or reach mutual agreement on other terms. Little is known about the operations of the European Arbitration Convention, as it appears to be seldom used, but perhaps its very existence is sufficient to induce fiscal authorities to expedite resolution of disputes. Whether such a body operating on a global scale would have a similar effect is moot.

A more drastic suggestion is to abandon the arm's length principle entirely and replace it with a formulary apportionment system. The US and Canada have many years' experience of using this approach, because different states and provinces set different tax rates. Within the federal tax jurisdiction of the USA, individual states, notably California, have argued for a worldwide tax assessment of MNCs that would include the revenue of affiliates that do business within a specific fiscal jurisdiction. The tax base is the unitary enterprise, which may not match the consolidated accounts owing to affiliates overseas adopting different ownership and legal forms. Unitary taxation normally calculates one affiliate's share, based on certain factors like payroll, property value or sales, as a percentage of worldwide MNC amounts, weighted in some way, and applies the ratio to worldwide income to compute the tax to be paid in a particular jurisdiction. Canada and the US have used and continue to use this approach for taxation of profits within their federal territories.

Formulary apportionment has been accepted in global trading APAs and has similarities with cost sharing agreements, but generally it switches the emphasis from transfer price determination to income separation. Consistent with this approach, the EU is currently investigating a common consolidated corporate tax base (CCCTB) to simplify and improve effectiveness of the corporate tax system in order to stimulate cross-border activities of MNCs. Schon, Schreiber and Spengel (2008) identify four steps to be taken. Each affiliate of the MNC needs to compute taxable profit by the same rules. Then the individual tax bases can be aggregated to the consolidated tax base. Thirdly, an apportionment formula is applied to the consolidated tax base to determine each affiliate's share. Lastly, the individual member state's fiscal agency can apply its own tax rate to its apportioned share of the consolidated tax base.

The underlying premise of the apportionment is that the location of the factors used in the division of the consolidated tax base, namely payroll, property values and sales, but not exclusively confined to these, should have an intrinsic relationship with profit generation. As some of the empirical evidence demonstrates, home countries, whether LDCs or developed countries, obtain little tax revenue from MNC affiliates operating within their jurisdictions relative to indigenous companies (Grubert and Mutti, 1991; Oyelere and Emmanuel, 1998; Pak and Zdanowicz, 2002). Why would MNCs continue to operate in overseas jurisdictions when those operations are apparently unprofitable?

Adoption of formulary apportionment would be a drastic change not without major repercussions. For example, unitary taxation is not universally acceptable and potentially violates bilateral tax treaties. The danger of double taxation may increase. It is uncertain whether the administrative burden placed on fiscal authorities and MNCs will increase, creating further inequity for LDCs. Defining a unitary business and deciding on the appropriate factors and their weighting in the apportionment formula are non-trivial issues that may encourage dysfunctional game-playing in order to shift income to more benign fiscal territories.

In terms of the theoretical underpinnings, there may be some merit in modifying the existing reliance on the arm's length principle. If the theoretical reasons for MNC expansion are justified, then the search for comparables under any transfer pricing method is likely to be time-consuming, fraught and, ultimately, judgemental. MNC competitive advantage is transient over time, and its impact, whether in the form of patents, specific assets or intellectual capital, will change. APAs offer the opportunity for competitive advantage to be evaluated on an annual basis, with a reassessment being undertaken at the end of the normal five-year period before an extension on the agreement is offered.

With bilateral APAs the fiscal authorities of both countries' fiscal agencies have the opportunity to exchange information and to learn about each other's tax regimes and regulations as well as the operations of the MNC. Embedding bilateral APAs within bilateral tax treaties grants certainty for the taxpayer, the MNC, and host governments can more easily plan their tax revenues into the medium term. With this measure of assurance, the need for host governments to offer incentives for FDI may be mitigated.

Making APAs compulsory in order to establish bilateral tax treaties may create an overwhelming administrative burden for MNCs and fiscal agencies alike, but this would depend on the competitive advantage claimed. Justification will vary by tangible, service or intangible transaction and, for those perceived as low risk by the fiscal authorities, a generic, limited justification APA may be all that is necessary. Transactions with higher degrees of risk may merit more extensive information. At least one MNC provides a model of transfer pricing methods used on CD to the home fiscal authority with all assumptions clearly stated. The tax authority can then satisfy itself that price changes within the range are acceptable by conducting its own sensitivity analysis.

The take-up of APA applications is not great, and the reasons for this need further investigation, but if, as is likely, the fear of retrospective investigation or inability to gain agreement or the provision of sensitive information is prevalent, this should be managed by means of a more transparent process that recognizes different information requirements to satisfy different types of APA. Binding arbitration arrangements may also need to be modified consistent with the APA and the bilateral tax treaty. Effectively the APA becomes necessary for bilateral tax treaties to be fully operationalized, and the taxpayer is safeguarded from double taxation and transfer price audit for a certain period of time. In addition, the LDC is able to plan on a given tax take, and fiscal authorities may converge their rules towards common regulations.

COOPERATION OR COMPETITION?

Within a framework of international trade that admittedly has emphasized transfer pricing to the exclusion of other aspects, it has been inevitable that conjecture has influenced the analysis. The choices available to LDC host governments and their fiscal authorities have been explored relative to the inferred aims of MNCs and the tax regulations of developed countries, notably the IRS. Within the OECD and UN guidelines, there remains considerable scope for disagreements to arise between host and home governments, between fiscal authorities and between MNCs and fiscal authorities. In all these potential conflicts, LDCs are disadvantaged because their domestic regulations cannot provide information to match that available in well-resourced developed countries. But it doesn't necessarily need to remain like this.

If fiscal authorities globally are seriously committed to extract their 'fair' tax take, if MNCs genuinely seek to comply with tax regulation and value certainty in legitimately avoiding double taxation, and if host governments wish to moderate tax differentials to reduce market imperfections, then some sensible solution should be forthcoming to satisfy all the parties. Transnational bodies like the OECD and the UN have a definite role to play, but instead of concentrating on the minutiae of acceptable methods an emphasis on the process of reaching agreement and evaluating outcomes, not exclusively economic, may enhance the reputation of all the main players. It may also mean that a transnational regulator would be charged with setting the agenda for reform. Alternatively, tinkering at the edges will continue to stimulate tax planning and tie up a sizeable proportion of resources that LDCs can ill afford in an endeavour that adds little to global wealth creation and economic development in LDCs.

REFERENCES

Alba, C.R., and M. Lozano (2009). Transfer pricing analysis for developing countries: reviewing market data. *Tax Notes International*, 21 September, pp. 1039–43.

Australian Tax Office (2005). Applying the arm's length principle, Guide NAT 2726-04.

Baldenius, T., N. Melumad and S. Reichelstein (2004). Integrating managerial and tax objectives in transfer pricing. *Accounting Review*, 79(3), pp. 591–615.

Borkowski, S.C. (1997). The transfer pricing concerns of developed and developing countries. *International Journal of Accounting*, 32(3), pp. 321–36.

Cools, M., C. Emmanuel and A. Jorissen (2008). Management control in the transfer pricing tax compliant multinational enterprise. *Accounting, Organizations and Society*, 33(6), pp. 603–28.

Dean, J. (1955). Decentralization and intracompany pricing. *Harvard Business Review*, July–August, pp. 65–74.

Drake, J., A. Rode and D.R. Wright (2005). IRS APA initiatives. *International Journal of Transfer Pricing*, September–October, pp. 210–16.

Dunning, J.H. (1988). *Explaining International Production*. London: Unwin Hyman.

Durst, M.C. (2010). Making transfer pricing work for developing countries. *Tax Notes International*, 13 December, pp. 851–4.

Eden, Lorraine (1998). *Taxing Multinationals: Transfer Pricing and Corporate Income Taxation in North America*. Toronto: University of Toronto Press.

Elliott, J., and C. Emmanuel (1998). International transfer pricing: searching for patterns. *European Management Journal*, 16(2), pp. 216–22.

Elliott, J., and C. Emmanuel (2000). *International Transfer Pricing*, CIMA Research Monograph, pp. 1–97. London: CIMA.

Emmanuel, C., and M. Cools (2007). Transfer pricing: the implications of fiscal compliance. In *Handbook of Management Accounting Research*, vol. 2, ed. C. Chapman, A. Hopwood and M. Shields, pp. 573–86. Oxford: Elsevier.

Ernst & Young (2009). *Global Transfer Pricing Survey*. London: Ernst & Young, http://www.ey.com/Global/download.nsf/International/Tax_-_Global_Transfer_Pricing_Survey.pdf.

Fuller, J.P. (1994). US tax review. *Tax Notes International*, 25 July.

Glaister, K.W., and J. Frecknall Hughes (2008). Corporate strategy formulation and taxation: evidence from UK firms. *British Journal of Management*, 19(1), pp. 33–48.

Grubert, H., and J. Mutti (1991). Taxes, tariffs and transfer pricing in multinational corporate decision making. *Review of Economics and Statistics*, 73(2), pp. 285–93.

Guardian (2009). Tax gap, 2–7 and 9–10 February.

Hasseldine, J., K. Holland and P. van der Rijt (2010). *The Management of Tax Knowledge*, ACCA Research Report no. 112. London: Association of Chartered Certified Accountants.

Hines, J.R., and E.M. Rice (1994). Fiscal paradise: foreign tax havens and American business. *Quarterly Journal of Economics*, 109(1), pp. 149–82.

Lin, L., C. Lefebvre and J. Kantor (1993). Economic determinants of international transfer pricing and the related accounting issues, with specific reference to Asian Pacific countries. *International Journal of Accounting*, 28(1), pp. 49–70.

Mehafdi, M. (2000). The ethics of international transfer pricing. *Journal of Business Ethics*, 28(2), December, pp. 365–81.

OECD (1998). *Harmful Tax Competition: A Global Issue*. Paris, OECD.

OECD ([2005] 2010). *Articles of the Model Tax Convention on Income and Capital*. Paris: OECD, available at www.oecd.org.

OECD Observer (2008). Transfer pricing: keeping it at arm's length, 3 July.

OECD Observer (2009). African tax administration: a new era, 22 November, http://www.oecdobserver.org/news/printpage.php/aid/3133/African_tax_administration.

Oyelere, P., and C. Emmanuel (1998). International transfer pricing and income shifting: evidence from the UK. *European Accounting Review*, 7(4), pp. 623–35.

Pak, S.J., and J.S. Zdanowicz (2002). US trade with the world: an estimate of 2001 lost US federal income tax revenues due to over-invoiced imports and under-invoiced exports, http://dorgan.senate.gov/newsroom/extras/pak-zdan.pdf.

Radebaugh, L., and S. Gray (1997). *International Accounting and Multinational Enterprises*, 4th edn. Chichester: John Wiley.

Rossing, C.P., and C. Rohde (2010). Overhead cost allocation changes in a transfer pricing tax compliant multinational enterprise. *Management Accounting Research*, doi:10.1016/j.mar.2010.01.002.

Schon, W., U. Schreiber and C. Spengel (2008). *A Common Consolidated Corporate Tax Base for Europe: Concept and Necessity of a Common Tax Base – an Academic Introduction*. Berlin: Springer.

Shoup, Carl (1985). International arbitration of transfer pricing disputes under income taxation. In *Multinationals and Transfer Pricing*, ed. A. Rugman and L. Eden, pp. 291–309. London and New York: St Martin's Press and Croom Helm.

Sikka, P., and H. Willmott (2010). The dark side of transfer pricing: its role in tax avoidance and wealth retentiveness. *Critical Perspectives on Accounting*, 21(4), pp. 342–56.

Silberztein, C. (2004). The role of taxation in sustainable development: a shared responsibility for developing and developed countries. Institutional Approaches to Policy Coherence for Development, OECD Policy Workshop, 18–19 May, pp. 1–6.

Spencer, D. (2009). Cross-border tax evasion and Bretton Woods II. *Journal of International Taxation*, 20(5), pp. 44–81.

Spicer, B. (1988). Towards an organizational theory of the transfer pricing process. *Accounting, Organizations and Society*, 13(3), pp. 303–21.

UNCTAD (2005). *Model Double Taxation Convention*. Geneva: UNCTAD.

UNCTAD (2009). *Handbook on Statistics*. Geneva: UNCTAD.

United States Internal Revenue Service (1995). *Development of IRC Section 482 Cases*, http://www.irs.gov/irm/part4/ch46s03.html.

Webber, S. (2011). The tax-efficient supply chain: considerations for multinationals. *Tax Notes International*, 10 January, pp. 149–68.

Wells, M.C. (1968). Profit centres, transfer prices and mysticism. *Abacus*, 4(2), pp. 174–81.

16 Social and environmental accounting in developing countries – challenges, conflicts and contradictions
Pala Molisa, Danaa Vandangombo and Judy Brown

INTRODUCTION

The aim of this chapter is to explore why and how environmental degradation is an important issue for developing countries and how, if at all, accounting reforms may ameliorate this. We also seek to emphasize the embeddedness of these issues in social and political relations. In one sense, such an aim is easy to justify. The deteriorating state of our global and local environments has been a major concern in Western societies in recent decades. Although the most widely publicized environmental threat is climate change, public reports from the United Nations and other international organizations make clear that many environmental health indicators show worrying trends pointing toward various forms of ecological crises (see, for example, Stiglitz, 2002; Dryzek and Schlosberg, 2005; Speth, 2008). While the situation is serious in the developed world, it is arguably even starker in developing countries. In the latter context, the countries and peoples in question often do not possess the material infrastructure or the technological resources and funding that enable them to cope as well with environmental crises when compared to more materially well-off societies.

In another sense, however, it may be asked why accountants should be involved in addressing social and environmental issues, since they have traditionally only concerned themselves with reporting on the financial situation of business organizations. If this traditional conception is taken for granted, the role of accounting in developing countries seems to be fairly straightforward: simply to do in developing countries what has traditionally been done in developed ones. We argue, however, that the issue is not that straightforward, because accounting is more than the technical – and purely financial – discipline it is commonly portrayed as; it is, more profoundly, a deeply social and transformative practice. As such, accounting has a moral responsibility to address social and environmental issues because, as a practice, it is *already* implicated in the production and reproduction of the ecological consequences that characterize our contemporary condition. Thus a strong argument can be made that carrying out the same accounting practices in developing countries that predominate in the developed world will exacerbate current global ecological crises. This issue is also not straightforward because accounting's social function is in an important sense dependent on the historical conditions that hold at any particular time and place; and the conditions present in developing countries are not necessarily the same as those prevailing in developed ones. This makes socio-historical contextualization important in any discussion of these issues. This chapter is structured with this aim, and these issues, in mind.

First, we present examples drawn from case studies of two developing countries

– Mongolia and Vanuatu – to provide a more concrete sense of the socio-historical context of some developing countries and of the social problems arising from development projects these countries are pursuing. These countries have been chosen because they are where two of the authors come from (Danaa Vandangombo is from Mongolia and Pala Molisa from Vanuatu). Then we explore the potential role accounting could play in addressing the issues communities in developing countries such as Mongolia and Vanuatu are facing. We do this by first discussing how accounting is commonly represented as a technical and apolitical discipline in 'mainstream' discourse, and then looking at critical accounting research which aims to challenge such portrayals by illuminating the organizational and social functioning of accounting. This more politically conscious and self-reflexive approach points to the need for new forms of accounting that are very different to the orthodox ones currently used in (Western) business practice.

This discussion provides the background for a review of the work of social and environmental accounting (SEA)[1] scholars who have sought to develop new forms of accounting and accountability practice that are more conscious of socio-historical specifics and of the political consequences of accounting itself. We argue that this research offers the most value in terms of providing insights into the sorts of alternative accounting practices developing countries could construct to address social and environmental issues. We discuss the challenges SEA researchers have faced in developing alternative accounting practices and focus on an emergent stream of SEA research – that of dialogic accounting – that we consider shows particular promise in going beyond many of the limitations evident in traditional accounting and accountability practice. We argue that, while such an approach could be applied in developing country contexts as part of wider efforts to address social and environmental issues, there are also important challenges that need to be faced if it is to be practised in ways that are empowering and progressive and able to address ecological problems substantively. We thus conclude by offering some thoughts about the political and theoretical issues scholars and practitioners will need to attend to if the potential of dialogic accounting is to be realized.

Before we begin, we emphasize that we do not have any conclusive answers about 'what is to be done'. The problems we identify relating to environmental sustainability and social development are too complex for there to be any simple solutions. Rather our aim is to stimulate self-reflection in readers about the nature of accounting, the politics of development, their social and environmental consequences, and how they could begin to be addressed in developing countries.

EXPLORING THE CONTRADICTIONS OF DEVELOPMENT – ILLUSTRATIONS FROM MONGOLIA AND VANUATU

In this section, we draw examples from two case studies to illustrate how development policies are restructuring and transforming the social and economic landscapes in Mongolia and Vanuatu. The particular industry we focus on in Mongolia is that of mining and, in Vanuatu, that of tourism. The aim of these examples is to give a sense of the social changes that are taking place, their historical context, the institutional, organizational and communal actors involved, and the political and environmental effects being produced by these changes.

Mongolian Mining – Socially Responsible Development?

Mongolia is a large, landlocked country, covering about 1.5 million square kilometres, bordering two of the world's largest nations, Russia and China. It has a diversified geology, with high mountains in the west, large steppes in the east and the Gobi desert in the south, and temperatures ranging from +45 degrees C in summer to −50 degrees C in winter. Despite its large land size, it has a relatively small population of around 3 million people. Among 20 ethnic groups, 92 per cent of the population are Mongols, 4.3 per cent Kazaks and 3.5 per cent other nationalities (National Statistical Office, 2001). It is thus an ethnically diverse society with deeply embedded traditions of nomadic culture, shamanism and Buddhism, amongst others. Any accountability relationships that are established between these groups will need to acknowledge these culturally diverse traditions and to give space to the different voices and interests that make up the society.

Historically, the area of what is now Mongolia was ruled by various nomadic empires (such as the Xiongnu, Rouran, Xianbei and Gökturks), with the Mongol Empire being founded by Ghengis Khaan in 1206. By the end of the seventeenth century, most of Mongolia was under the control of the Chinese Qing Dynasty, and it was after its collapse in 1911 that Mongolia claimed independence, struggling to gain de facto independence in 1921 and in 1945 finally to gain international recognition. The Cold War provided the context for Mongolia's post-1945 independence struggles and, as a consequence, it was greatly influenced by the former USSR, with the Mongolian 'People's Republic' declared in 1924 and Mongolian politics taking much of their cue from the Soviet politics of the time. The demise of communist regimes in Eastern Europe in late 1989 facilitated Mongolia's peaceful Democratic Revolution in 1990, which led amongst other things to a multi-party system of electoral democracy, a new constitution in 1992 and a transition – still ongoing – to a market economy. Mongolia, in other words, bears the scars of histories of imperialism, colonization and, more recently, the establishment and penetration of capitalism's unequal social relations into traditional economic and political domains. Any accountability approach seeking to account for organizational activities carried out in Mongolia will need to keep in sight these socio-historical specifics.

The transition from an authoritarian socialist regime with a centrally planned economy towards a capitalist liberal democracy with an open market economy has produced wide-ranging social, political and economic changes in Mongolia and provides the context for changes and transformations currently under way in its mining industry. The earlier regime left a mixed legacy. On the one hand, Mongolia boasts a well-educated population, as reflected in a 98 per cent literacy rate, and well-developed social capital (World Bank, 2007). In 2006, the national Human Development Index attained its highest level of 0.718, making Mongolia a 'medium human development' nation with social indicators considerably more advanced than the average country with similar levels of GDP per capita (UNDP, 2007). On the other hand, as a young democracy Mongolia also confronts many challenges, including what many regard as an 'outdated' socialist mentality, nepotism, corruption and power imbalances. In terms of economic development, it is classified as a 'lesser developed' country: a product of its historical positioning in the modern global political economy as a country of the periphery rather than of the centre.

Since 2000, and the mid-2000s in particular, Mongolia has enjoyed strong economic growth, with GDP per capita increasing from $1331 in 1996 (UN Statistics Division, 2002) to $3200 in 2008, giving it a ranking of 163 out of 232 countries (Central Intelligence Agency, 2009). This overall growth, however, masks internal inequalities reflected in the unevenness of wealth distribution and increasing divisions between rich and poor, as one-third of Mongolians continue to live in poverty (UNDP, 2007). The relatively low population levels, coupled with Mongolia's mineral and natural resources, make the primary sector the main economic sector in Mongolia. The mining industry has significantly increased in importance as the sector with the greatest potential for realizing economic growth and, as such, is one of the key drivers in Mongolia's 'development' process. Given the materials it works with, the methods of industrial production entailed, and the impact these processes have on local communities and on the surrounding ecology, mining also looms large as carrying one of the highest risks for producing pollution and other forms of environmental degradation. These contextual characteristics point to the need for forms of accounting that not only render visible the physical impacts of organizational activities on the environment and how these activities enact and legitimate certain social relations, but also embrace forms of accountability that give space and voice to the wide variety of stakeholders that may be affected by these activities.

The Mining Sector and the Responsible Mining Initiative for Sustainable Development

One of the main reasons for the emergence of mining has been a growing awareness – particularly amongst 'decision makers' – of Mongolia's extensive mineral resources, the most economically significant of these being base metals, most notably copper, zinc, gold, silver, coal, fluorspar and uranium. In 2008, mining accounted for 28.2 per cent of GDP, 64.3 per cent of total industrial products and 80.7 per cent of total exports (National Statistical Office, 2009), yet it employs only 49 000 people (Tsogtbaatar, 2009) or 4.7 per cent of the labour market. Mongolia's mineral dependence was 24th highest in the world in 2000 (Ross, 2008, p. 195) owing to its sizeable mineral deposits and its relatively narrow economic base. This interest in mining has also been facilitated by government policies that have led, since the mid-1990s, to a rapid increase in mineral exploration and mining. These include the passing of legislation to attract foreign investors by promising favourable mining conditions, such as a 'first come, first served' approach and tax holiday incentives.

This growing interest in Mongolia's mining resources has been exacerbated by the increasing international demand for minerals (particularly from a rapidly industrializing China). Widely publicized discoveries of the Oyu Tolgoi copper and gold and Tavan Tolgoi coal deposits in the early 2000s have further heightened interest. With these discoveries, the number of exploration licences and the amount of land covered have increased fivefold. By 2008, there were 4644 exploration licences and 1115 mining licences, together covering 44.4 per cent of Mongolia's territory (Shiirevdamba, 2009). There are around 500 mining companies, of which 127 mine gold (Tsogtbaatar, 2009). These figures point to an industrial sector that is not only receiving a lot of domestic and international attention by business interests, transnational corporations, governments, NGOs and local social movements, but also rapidly emerging as one of the cornerstones of Mongolia's development process.

Many international mining companies and international advocacy organizations enthusiastically support mining development and emphasize mining as a source of growth for Mongolia (World Bank, 2004, 2007; World Growth, 2008). What is not so clear, however, is whether the social and economic policies being put in place to enable the development of the mining industry are self-evidently 'good' in terms of enriching the well-being of the individuals, communities and wider environment that are being affected by it. One of the challenges Mongolia faces is how to develop accountability practices that can ensure that mining is developed in a way that contributes positively to the country as a whole.

Some of the most proactive organizations that have sought to raise awareness and to influence the political and policy discourse relating to mining in ways that are socially and environmentally benign have been those of Mongolia's NGO sector, with the Responsible Mining Initiative for Sustainable Development (RMI) being an exemplar. The RMI was registered as an NGO in December 2007, and it was initiated as an outcome of multi-stakeholder forums set up to address responsible mining. As a non-membership public NGO it operates mainly in the capital city and, as its title suggests, it seeks to promote responsible mining by aligning it with 'sustainable development'. As stated in its mission statement, the NGO aims: 'to build a common framework of understanding of responsible mining in Mongolia among the public, government, industry, and investors; to provide open and transparent information; and to secure equal participation of the multi-stakeholders in these activities' (RMI, 2009).

From the outset, the emergence of the RMI has been characterized by the diversity of Mongolian civil society. The first multi-stakeholder forum was held in 2006, facilitated by the Asia Foundation's[2] Securing Our Future programme, consisting of a diverse range of interests including government, civil society, the mining industry and academia. Participants developed the definition of responsible mining and its eight guiding principles. The way the RMI defined mining was clearly normative in the sense that it said more about how mining *ought* to be rather than about how it currently *is*. As they defined it, for instance, responsible mining is 'a comprehensive and transparent minerals activity respecting the rights of all stakeholders, especially of local people, environmentally friendly and free of human health impacts, embracing the best international practices and upholding rule of law whilst generating a sustainable stream of benefits for Mongolia' (RMI, 2006).[3]

The second forum was organized in April 2007 and it agreed to organize the RMI by developing and signing a Declaration on Responsible Mining by different mining constituents. The RMI was registered as an NGO later that year. The Declaration provided the base principles of the NGO and defined its purpose, and provided general guidance for its activities and principles of cooperation for its multiple stakeholders. The Declaration acknowledges the harmful impacts of existing mining practices on the natural environment, society and the economy and recognizes the need for developing responsible mining which serves 'the core interests of Mongolia's future'. The Declaration also emphasizes the importance of multi-stakeholder engagement in promoting responsible mining by having equal rights and responsibilities to participate in order to make collective decisions based on mutual respect and information sharing. According to the Declaration, the main form of activity is meetings or dialogue among multiple stakeholders. About 60 organizations have signed the Declaration agreeing to contribute to the development of responsible mining and to follow its guiding principles.

Since 2008, the RMI has undertaken various activities including involvement in policy and standards development, knowledge building and information sharing, and development of performance indicators among its members. The NGO successfully cooperated with members of parliament to include responsible mining related clauses in mining and environmental policy sections of the 2008–12 Government of Mongolia Action Plan. To introduce responsible mining and its principles, the NGO co-organized 13 multi-stakeholder forums with the Asia Foundation. A series of panel discussions was also organized at the National University to build knowledge and share information for the public and other stakeholders. Under the facilitation of and financing by the Ministry of Environment and Tourism, the RMI participated in the development of standards that aim to regulate mining land restoration. The NGO has also started to develop measurement criteria for mining companies to measure compliance with the principles and inform the public.

One of the interesting features of the RMI's make-up is that it is composed of a mixture of NGOs representing various social and environmental interests and NGOs with mining business interests which make up more than half the RMI's board members. On the one hand, this mix of business and non-business NGOs points to the fact that NGOs are coming to be seen as 'legitimate' actors in the mining sector whose views are to be heard, respected and taken on board. On the other hand, however, the domination of the RMI by pro-business NGOs may signal its capture by economic interests. Questions arise, in any case, over how representative the RMI's board composition actually is of the wider NGO sector – not to mention the question of whether NGOs are themselves appropriate institutions for furthering democratic and emancipatory practices (Gray, Bebbington and Collison, 2006; G. Lehman, 2007). Some NGOs may have opted out of the RMI because they are unwilling to compromise with other stakeholders or may be excluded because of their overly militant stances regarding current mining practices. The Canadian mining company occupies a prominent place in the RMI board as the mining representative. Compared to other members, it seems to talk more about 'corporate responsibility' and 'sustainable development' and it has been one of the more high-profile companies in the media because of its deposits and its negotiations with the government.[4] While having it as part of the RMI board provides other members a certain amount of access and influence in trying to persuade it to adopt best standards of practice, there is considerable concern that the company might merely engage with the RMI to provide itself with good publicity and improve its public image or, more disturbingly for some, to unduly influence the RMI and its policies for its own benefit.

Vanuatu – Tourism as Panacea or Problem?

Vanuatu, like Mongolia, has a colonial history. The first peoples to the area were Melanesian, with Europeans beginning to settle in the late eighteenth century. In the 1880s France and Britain claimed certain parts of the country, and in 1906 they jointly managed the archipelago as the New Hebrides through a British–French condominium.

Vanuatu is located in the territorial boundaries of Melanesia, and its indigenous peoples are ethnically diverse, as demonstrated by the wide range of variations in their cultural practices, languages and belief systems. This diversity is mediated also by a strong sense of national identity forged by anti-colonial struggles against the British and French. When Vanuatu achieved independence from French and British colonial powers in 1980, its people and leaders enshrined a constitution that expressed the aspirations of its people for self-determination, *kastom* values of reciprocity and compassion, and Christian ethics of solidarity with people and the earth. Developments since have shown just how hard realizing and practising these values are, given Vanuatu's historical and colonial inheritance and its ongoing insertion into the global political economy. Recent developments in Vanuatu's tourism industry provide a case in point.[5]

Vanuatu has rich resources in terms of both its natural environment and its cultural attractions. This is one reason why the tourist industry provides its main source of income, accounting for 50–75 per cent of GDP (Slatter, 2006, p. 3). In recent years Vanuatu has been the fastest-growing economy amongst Pacific Island nation states, with tourism driving much of the economic growth. While GDP figures may indicate a society on the path of social and economic progress, what they do not allow us to see is the social conflicts and inequalities that are structuring this development process. This inequality comes through, for instance, in the fact that it is expatriate investors in the services sector 'who are primarily reaping the profits from tourism' (Slatter, 2006, p. 3). The institutional conditions for this economic growth were first put into place by liberalization policies introduced as part of a structural adjustment programme under the direction of the Asian Development Bank (ADB).

One part of this liberalization was the creation of the 1995 Tourism Development Master Plan (TMP), a pivotal point in the transformation of Vanuatu's tourism industry. It was drawn up for the Vanuatu government by the United Nations Development Programme and World Tourism Organization and reflected many tenets of the neo-liberal economic ideology popular at the time, such as opening national economies and their resources to foreign investors and reducing or eliminating tariffs and other barriers to entry for them (Bargh, 2007).[6] Although major resort development as outlined by the TMP did not eventuate, other aspects were operationalized as part of the ADB-directed and financed Comprehensive Reform Programme (CRP) introduced in 1997 (Slatter, 2006, p. 3). A revised version of the TMP has guided tourism development since 2003 (Slatter, 2006, p. 3).

The CRP liberalized Vanuatu's economy extensively, locking in a commitment to foreign investment through various legislative initiatives. The Foreign Investment Promotion Act (No. 15 of 1998) established the Vanuatu Investment Promotion Authority (VIPA) with the general objective to 'expeditiously facilitate, promote and foster foreign investment in Vanuatu' (Slatter, 2006, p. 3). It also established the process for the receipt and approval of foreign investment proposals, the conditions to be imposed on overseas investors, and the entitlements accompanying an approval certificate (including 'absolute entitlement to repatriate earnings and other monies'), and provided for joint ventures and similar partnerships with foreign investors (Slatter, 2006, pp. 3–4). Two further investment-facilitating laws were passed in 2000: the Electronic Transactions Act, modelled from Commonwealth of Bermuda law to facilitate the making of digital contracts, and the E-Business Act, enabling the establishment of electronic businesses in Vanuatu with the aim, as prime minister Barak Sope put it, of creating 'an Internet Free Trade Zone where businesses can conduct legitimate trading activities over the Internet and take advantage of Vanuatu's low tax structure to earn greater profits' (cited in Slatter, 2006, p. 4). Mainstream media and the Vanuatu government announced the signing of investment promotion and protection agreements with the British government in 2003 as 'a major achievement', and similar bilateral agreements have been sought with a number of other countries. VIPA itself sees these agreements 'as placing Vanuatu in an advantageous position vis-à-vis the WTO and Cotonou agreements' (Slatter, 2006, p. 4).

From 2003 the tourism sector contributed the most of all industries in terms of new investment in Vanuatu, much coming from Australian investors (Slatter, 2006, p. 5). The Vanuatu government declared 2005 as 'the Year of Tourism' and increased its budget allocation for tourism by 50 million vatu (or approximately $US500 000), bringing the total to 150 million vatu for the year (Slatter, 2006, p. 5). On the face of it, Vanuatu's GDP statistics and high levels of industry growth in the tourism sector point to developments that are improving the wealth and well-being of ni-Vanuatu (nationals and citizens of Vanuatu). These numbers, however, do not tell the story of the problems being experienced in effecting policies that on paper look 'good' or of the social conflicts that this growth is producing. These issues are playing out in the areas of regulatory enforcement (or lack thereof), in the bungalow sector and in land sales.

Lack of regulation
An example of the problems is the lack of governmental enforcement of regulations which are meant to offer some protection to ni-Vanuatu against foreign takeovers. While VIPA's overall brief is to facilitate liberalization, it also contains clauses that are supposed to safeguard against foreign takeover of its economy. One of these measures is the Foreign Investment Promotion Act's designation of 'a number of small and medium sized investments (in tourism, trade, manufacturing, services and fisheries) as "Reserved Investments"' (Slatter, 2006, p. 5). These are ostensibly off-limits to foreign investors – 'only *citizens* of Vanuatu and companies that are "wholly controlled by persons who are *citizens* of Vanuatu or have all of their shares owned or controlled by persons who are *citizens* of Vanuatu" may run these businesses or hold these jobs' (Slatter, 2006, p. 5, emphasis in original). In reality, however, these regulations are often flouted. As Slatter (2006, pp. 5–6) explains it:

> In several reserved investment areas, despite strong evidence of entrepreneurship among ni-Vanuatu and considerable external support for their efforts to get a fair share of the tourism pie, expatriate investors and Vanuatu citizens of European descent (including naturalized citizens) have set up successful businesses (sometimes with ni-Vanuatu as 'sleeping partners', to get around the reservation) and have come to dominate the market.

This domination, structured along racialized class lines, has resulted in a lot of frustration and material deprivation on the part of ni-Vanuatu.

The bungled business of bungalows
Under the TMP, the Vanuatu government and provincial councils encouraged the building of bungalows in rural areas. The rationale behind this initiative was to spread the tourism benefits to the islands beyond Efate and to draw ni-Vanuatu into the industry

as small-scale tourist accommodation providers (Slatter, 2006, p.6). In a relatively short period a significant number of ni-Vanuatu began building bungalows, often using their own resources, in anticipation of attracting enough tourists to run a profitable business. But the tourists never came. Furthermore, the bungalows were built without infra-structural development to support local tourism or preparation to ensure standards were met, and without adequate marketing support (Slatter, 2006, p.6). As Slatter (2006, p.7) emphasizes, one of the main problems facing ni-Vanuatu bungalow operators is their lack of marketing exposure both locally and abroad. Pre-paid tourism packages arranged via overseas wholesalers tend to overlook them, preferring to favour the expatriate-owned businesses that dominate the market. While a few communities have benefited from being selected as adventure tourism destinations, in the main 'investment in bungalows has not brought much income for ni-Vanuatu people' (Slatter, 2006, p.7).

Land sales and strata titling
Alongside these developments has been a land sales frenzy, in part a result of liberalization policies. In late 2005, the *Vanuatu Daily Post* reported that foreign investors had 'bought up' two-thirds of Efate, with the result that most of its coastline 'is reportedly now in foreign hands' (Slatter, 2006, p.7). This boom in land 'sales' (in fact, 75-year leases) has been prompted, in part, by proposed hotel, resort and lifestyle property developments and custom landowners' expectations of lucrative returns through lease payments and, in some cases, profit shares (Slatter, 2006, p.7). There is evidence of land speculation in many cases, with some purchasers being real estate speculators rather than genuine tourism investors. There is a current boom in land and property sales, particularly on Efate and increasingly in Santo, and, while this increased economic activity is producing impressive growth rates, it is also producing various forms of social dislocation and tensions.

On taking power in 1980, the Vanuaaku Party government constitutionally enshrined the customary ownership of land. This recognized the importance that people's access to and control of land had for the capacities of self-reliance and self-determination. Thus, while non-ni-Vanuatu may lease land for commercial use (for terms of up to 75 years) they are not permitted to own land. Government consent must be obtained for all land transactions between 'an indigenous citizen and either a non-indigenous citizen or a non-citizen' (Constitution of the Republic of Vanuatu, Chapter 12:79:1), and the government may withhold consent if the transaction is 'prejudicial to the interests' of the custom owner(s) of the land, the indigenous citizen (if not a custom owner), the local community where the land is situated, or the Republic of Vanuatu (Constitution, Chapter 12:79:12) (cited in Slatter, 2006, pp.7–8).

This historical land policy has been a target of pro-liberalization policy advisors, with pressure often exerted during WTO Working Party negotiations on Vanuatu's accession to the WTO to reform Vanuatu's land laws and through the policy documents of pro-market neo-liberal think tanks (Molisa, 2006). To date, the Vanuatu government has strongly resisted these pressures although, 'ironically, its passing of the Strata Titles Act in 2000 has effectively opened up a market in land, and is essentially paving the way to virtual dispossession' (Slatter, 2006, p.8). This land selling frenzy is the most intense on Efate but is spreading into the outer islands, where islands such as Santo, with their greater size and tourism potential, have even greater prospects for fuelling a real estate boom.

The increasing commodification of land has been accompanied by an increase in land disputes amongst ni-Vanuatu. As market relations are taking root in Vanuatu, so are market attitudes of individualism and more importantly fragmentation, separation and the dissolution of historical social bonds. In Vanuatu, there are deep-seated cultural practices, particularly in its matrilineal traditions, based on communal reciprocity, inclusiveness and solidarity (Huffer and Molisa, 1999). These ways of maintaining social cohesiveness and well-being are being undermined by the penetration of market relations and the creation and intensification of social conflicts. These are manifested in various forms, including increased disputes over land as custom owners realize the potential windfalls they stand to gain by successfully asserting their ownership rights over others. In some cases, these disputes have gone beyond the courts and resulted 'in violence, with people being killed and houses being burned down' (Slatter, 2006, p. 9).

The land sales and property development boom have also created 'a visible and widening divide between white wealth and black poverty' (Slatter, 2006, p. 9). This is a potential time bomb, especially if living conditions amongst ni-Vanuatu continue to deteriorate and the separation and alienation ni-Vanuatu may feel toward tourists and foreigners are not overcome. One of Slatter's expatriate informants observed that:

> As a social scientist, I see the possible consequences further down the track – it's a social problem which will erupt later and lead to resentment of tourism and of tourists. The signs are already there – the high fenced walls to keep people out, on the coasts one will see more and more of these exclusive zones for the privileged few; people who once had access to the sea as a source of livelihood and recreation no longer have it. (Slatter, 2006, p. 9)

A ni-Vanuatu Slatter interviewed was blunter: 'This is Condominium coming back, this is colonialism coming back . . . it won't be long before we will be slaves' (p. 9).

One way the 'white wealth/black poverty' divide is institutionally entrenched is through legislative provisions that allow foreign investors absolute repatriation of profits. This denies to local businesses and entrepreneurs the chance to absorb re-invested profits and perpetuates a dynamic of extractive and exploitative relations rather than relations based on mutual reciprocity. Slatter (2006, p. 11) observes that another way in which this division can be discerned is through the close relationship big hotels and resorts in Vanuatu have established with wholesalers. She explains that these larger enterprises are reported to rely on wholesalers for around 80 per cent of their bookings, with the three largest (Le Meridien, Le Lagon and Iririki Resort) being foreign-owned. The larger operators dominate tourism promotion (promoting their own properties), the cost of which is primarily met by the government. Wholesalers are paid substantial commissions (20–25 per cent) for selling travel and accommodation packages and are thus incentivized to privilege higher-charging service providers so as to maximize their own earnings. As Slatter concludes, the ni-Vanuatu who make up the majority of the low-cost bungalow accommodation providers 'don't stand much of a chance' in getting a share of the tourism pie (2006, p. 11).

While the alienation of land in Vanuatu by custom owners is reducing the ability of ni-Vanuatu to continue their subsistence (and in many cases sustainable) lifestyles, the processes of liberalization under way within the tourism industry and property development are arguably also leading to the increased exploitation of ni-Vanuatu workers. Trade unionist Joseph Niel suggests that an 'expatriate community versus locals' divide has emerged, with liberalization of the tourist industry not only attracting 'land specula-tors and other con-men' but also resulting in 'more exploitation of ni-Vanuatu workers' (cited in Slatter, 2006, p. 10). The industry is known for paying very low wages, with the three largest hotels and resorts reputedly paying workers more poorly than small bars and restaurants and requiring them to work longer hours without additional compensa-tion (Slatter, 2006, p. 10).

The boom in land sales can only exacerbate these conditions as ni-Vanuatu, who once had the option of subsisting off the land, become more dependent on employ-ment for their livelihood. This increase in unemployed labour in Vanuatu will act as a brake to increased wages, especially for those in areas of unskilled or low-skilled labour, with more people willing to work for less and for longer because of the scarcity of jobs and over-supply of potential workers. In discussions with Slatter (2006), Joseph Niel suggested that most hotel workers have 'been intimidated and demoralised by seeing unionised workers victimised during recent labour disputes and strikes' (p. 10). Another informant noted that, although Vanuatu's minimum wage was 20 000 vatu (or approximately $US200) a month, many workers in the tourism industry were paid much less, with some receiving only around 16 000 vatu. Le Meridien's ni-Vanuatu manager, William Pakoa, confirmed that, 'compared with all other industries, hotel workers are the worst paid' (p. 10). He said most hotel workers lived in the shanty towns at the edge of Port Vila and that the tourist industry had indeed 'contributed to the growth of the shanty town' (p. 10).

ACCOUNTING – FROM TECHNIQUE TO SOCIAL PRACTICE AND POLITICS

The case study illustrations from Mongolia and Vanuatu presented above are far from comprehensive or systematic; they are partial, selective and in many cases anecdotal in terms of their representation of the aspects of development processes we chose to focus on. Nevertheless, what should come through is insights into just how contradictory developmental processes are and the social conflicts and problems people are facing because of them. The illustrations also hint at the various roles accounting is already undertaking in facilitating these processes. Whether referring to international loan agree-ments between the Mongolian government and the World Bank, Vanuatu structural adjustment programmes set up by the Asian Development Bank, the daily operations of ni-Vanuatu bungalow operators, or accountability relationships between the RMI and social actors within the Mongolian mining industry, accounting practices are in one way or another directly implicated in their functioning.

If we look to accounting research, however, we find that much of the literature is unhelpful in aiding us to understand the social functioning of accounting practice because of the theoretical perspectives adopted. Most accounting research is informed by a positivistic ontology, making it unreflexive about accounting's (and its own) institu-tional and socio-historical underpinnings, particularly the nature of the power relations that it is enmeshed within (A. Tinker, Merino and Neimark, 1982). When the social context is recognized, it is often framed by the worldview of neo-classical economics, moral utilitarianism and liberal economic democracy, with the effect that the social world is depicted as fundamentally devoid of systemic conflicts and deeply rooted structural instabilities and as one where individuals inhabit an essentially pluralistic world (Puxty, 1986; T. Tinker, 1988; T. Tinker, Lehman and Neimark, 1991; Gray, Owen and Adams, 1996). Within this 'mainstream' discourse (Chua, 1986), accounting comes across as little more than a technical practice, since its social and transformative effects are for the most part erased and elided.

Vollmer (2003), for example, provides a description of accounting that is typical of mainstream discourse by defining it as 'a sophisticated [method] of evaluation in allocating resources' (p. 357). In line with this definition, first-year accounting students are typically presented with a view of accounting as a profession founded on the values of 'neutrality', 'independence' and 'objectivity' and a practice that serves 'the public interest' by adhering to these values and discharging its social duty to provide a set of accounts that renders organizations 'transparent'. This 'transparency' is seen to facilitate the operations of the 'free market' by increasing 'informational efficiency', which in turn leads to a more 'rational' allocation of scarce resources and ultimately an increase in profitability for the individual enterprise in question and in material wealth for society as a whole. The latter is typically measured by rises in GDP or some other utilitarian measure of social welfare which is regarded as an appropriate indicator of social progress or 'development'. This traditional view treats accounting as primarily 'a market-driven, functional practice' rather than 'a social and transformative practice' (Everett, 2003, p. 401; see also A. Tinker et al., 1982; Hopwood, 1987; Armstrong, 1991; Neu, 1992; Chua, 1995). It focuses overwhelmingly on aspects of the organization that have been ascribed a financial value through market transactions. Accounting thus gives almost sole visibility to the financial value of market transactions while largely ignoring the social and environmental effects produced by organizational activity. Following neo-classical economics, these wider effects are classified as 'externalities' and excluded from management and financial accounting practice.

Moreover, as Neu (2001, p. 321) observes, if we consider the topics that preoccupy the majority of accounting academics – share market efficiency, earnings management, voluntary disclosures and the like – they hold little direct relevance for the bulk of the world's population, who, we should keep in mind, live in countries such as Mongolia and Vanuatu which are called 'developing'. The important exception is when that research is used to rationalize and impose neo-liberal reforms on such countries (Neu, 2001, p. 321). This is why Neu argues that, 'although accounting research is a thriving industry, the majority of accounting research remains insular from the events of importance to the majority world' (2001, p. 321). In this light, it is clear that mainstream accounting research is not very helpful in assisting us to understand the role accounting is playing in developing country contexts such as those of Mongolia and Vanuatu where there are social conflicts that are the direct result of developmental policies and – in so far as accounting itself is involved in these policies – a direct result of accounting itself.

Fortunately, not all forms of accounting research have taken for granted the technical and apolitical way in which accounting is portrayed in mainstream discourse, with perhaps the best representative of alternative approaches being the field of critical accounting. One of the distinctive characteristics of critical accounting scholarship has been the consistent and systematic way it has challenged many of the theoretical presuppositions of mainstream accounting discourse and how it has sought to understand accounting more broadly as a transformative practice by interrogating its organizational and social functioning. Critical accounting research has questioned, for instance, its positivist epistemological foundations, its realist ontology, its embeddedness in neo-classical economics, and social allegiances to capital and patriarchal discourse (A. Tinker, 1980; A. Tinker et al., 1982; Lowe, Puxty and Laughlin, 1983; T. Tinker, 1985, 1988; Chua, 1986; Hopper et al., 1986; Neimark and Tinker, 1986; Armstrong, 1987; Hopper, Storey and Willmott, 1987; Hopwood, 1987; Knights and Collinson, 1987; T. Tinker and Neimark, 1987; Hines, 1988, 1989; Arrington and Francis, 1993).

As Neu (2001) observes, within critical accounting literature two streams of scholarship stand out: research into the political economy of accounting (PEA) and research into the governmentality aspects of accounting. PEA studies have challenged positivist and neo-classical representations of accounting as a 'neutral', 'objective' and 'value-free' discipline that self-evidently serves 'the public interest' by directing attention to accounting's distributive, hegemonic and ideological functions (for example, D. Cooper, 1980; A. Tinker, 1980; A. Tinker et al., 1982; D. Cooper and Sherer, 1984; T. Tinker, 1985, 1988; Knights and Collinson, 1987; C. Lehman and Tinker, 1987; T. Tinker and Neimark, 1987; Neu and Taylor, 1996). Accounting, in this light, is less an apolitical set of techniques and more 'a device for appraising the terms of exchange between social constituencies, and an institutional mechanism for arbitrating, evaluating and adjudicating social choices' (T. Tinker, 1985, cited in Neu, 2001, p. 322). This critical political-economic theorizing is a powerful lens through which to understand current accounting practices as they affect developing countries, because it renders visible the social inequalities that structure social reproduction and the role accounting plays in this process. PEA research has illuminated the ways 'in which accounting, through its distributive and hegemonic activities, helps to justify the continued appropriation of surplus value' in developed and developing countries (Neu, 2001, p. 322). It has also examined how accounting discourses are ideological in the way they mystify social reality by homogenizing, naturalizing and universalizing social practices so as to mask the underlying unequal social relations and the way they help to build a dominant class hegemony (Neu, 2001, p. 322).

Research into the governmentality aspects of accounting highlights the role accounting plays in societal governance (for example, Miller and O'Leary, 1987; Miller and Rose, 1990; Burchell, Gordon and Miller, 1991). This research starts from the premise that government can be viewed as an '"ensemble of institutions, calculations and tactics" that attempt to arrange things in order to attain specific ends' (Neu, 2001, p. 323, citing Foucault, 1991) and, in this light, examines how accounting operates as a technology of government or, in other words, as the 'actual mechanisms through which authorities of various sorts have sought to shape, normalize, and instrumentalize the conduct, thought, decisions and aspirations of others in order to achieve the objectives they consider desirable' (Miller and Rose, 1990, cited in Neu, 2001, p. 323). Work in this genre has examined, *inter alia*, the role accounting played in the Holocaust (Funnel, 1998), in respect of indigenous populations (Neu, 2000) and in international institutions such as the World Bank and IMF (Everett, Neu and Rahaman, 2007; Neu et al., 2010) by making visible the diverse sites and agents through which governance is enacted (Neu, 2001, p. 323).

It should be clear from even this brief review that critical accounting research offers important insights for scholars and practitioners concerned about developing countries and interested in developing accounting practices that can begin addressing the ecological problems faced in these countries. Firstly, this research powerfully and persuasively shows how orthodox forms of accounting are not 'neutral' but are, in fact, directly implicated in producing the social conflicts and environmental consequences that developing countries are experiencing. This implies that accounting reforms and changes will need to come up with alternative forms of accounting and accountability that are very different to those which constitute orthodox accounting practice.

Secondly, this research brings to light the way in which the micro-functioning of accounting in specific locations is always mediated by processes of hegemony, power and political economy (Neu, 2001, p. 326). One implication of this is that alternative accountability practices that aim to address environmental problems in developing countries will need somehow to develop ways of accounting that have an explicit socio-historical sense (T. Tinker and Gray, 2003) and which are able to render visible the ways in which global political-economic processes influence and mediate the local.

Thirdly, this research shows how our experiences, linguistic categories and forms of thought are to an important extent social products. In this light, accounting practitioners in developing countries need to question the way in which concepts such as 'accounting' and 'development' are interpreted and deployed in hegemonic discourses and what their social and political effects might be. Even the term 'developing' country may be problematic in that it may mask Eurocentric notions of the good life that devalue and erase subaltern worldviews and perspectives that communities in peripheral countries find of much value. Another problematic term that needs to be interrogated is that of 'the environment'. A powerful insight from critical accounting scholarship is the idea that we need to consider 'the environment' not as something separate from 'society' but as an inherently social phenomenon. We need to interrogate the politics behind the way this term is deployed, particularly in hegemonic discourses, and to try to discern the social relations that are implicit and instantiated in environmental transformations (Harvey, 1996; Everett and Neu, 2000).[7] No sharp distinction can be made between 'society' and 'environment' both ontologically and epistemologically. Problems such as over-fishing, deforestation, toxification and pollution may seem to be 'environmental' issues, but they are the consequences of social causes that include the particular mode of production a socio-economic system is built on and its power relations amongst different social constituencies which determine how environmental risks are distributed amongst the population. This point is worth stressing in case readers do not think we have discussed 'environmental' issues much in our case studies. The point made here, however, implies that all the social conflicts discussed above have their environmental effects and all environmental transformations are importantly social in origin. The Vanuatu case of generations of ni-Vanuatu being cut off from land which historically their families had always had access to or the pollution of shanty towns is clearly an 'environmental' issue, but it is the result of certain social policies and practices and is produced through the reproduction of unequal social relations. A more adequate approach to 'accounting for the environment' will need to keep in sight the dialectical interconnections between 'the social' and 'the environment' that are often erased in mainstream and 'commonsense' discourse. What this points to is therefore not so much the need for 'environmental accounting' in the sense that it provides an account of the environment but *accounts which are able to illuminate the social contradictions and conflicts that produce environmental consequences.*

Fourthly, and perhaps most importantly, critical accounting research places on the agenda the politics of emancipatory and radical social change (Gray et al., 1996; Roslender and Dillard, 2003).

In short, this research points to the fact that any form of accounting that seeks to address the environmental problems of developing countries will need to incorporate into its practices self-reflexivity, socio-historical contextualization, and attention to issues of power, exploitation, exclusion and domination, and challenge 'commonsense' understandings of accounting, organizations and society that circulate in mainstream discourse that may be legitimating elite perspectives and interests and erasing subaltern voices and perspectives (Neu, 2001).

Given this context, we can begin to appreciate the challenges scholars and practitioners face in creating alternative forms of accounting that not only can begin to 'account for the environment' in more benign ways but also seek to realize emancipatory and radical social change. Scholars have not shied away from these challenges, and the academic field that has perhaps done more than any other in taking on these problems has been that of the social and environmental accounting (SEA) literature. In the following section we review some of the theoretical approaches scholars have used to approach this challenge, the problems they have encountered in the process and the implications these raise for thinking about emancipatory accounting practices in developing countries. As part of this discussion we highlight the field of dialogic SEA research as one which we suggest offers a lot of promise.

THE POLITICS OF 'ACCOUNTING FOR THE ENVIRONMENT' IN THE SEA LITERATURE

Like the rest of accounting research, SEA is dominated by the 'mainstream' discourses of neo-classical economics, moral utilitarianism, and managerialism (Chua, 1986; Neu, Warsame and Pedwell, 1998; Gray, 2002). Such research rarely questions the socio-historical system that these perspectives take for granted and typically assumes that 'commonsense' notions of accounting such as its technical definition, its financial orientation, its privileging of market forces, and its valorization of economic growth are unproblematic and legitimate aims of accounting practice. Such research either rejects the claim that there is even a need to 'account for the environment' (Benston, 1982) or, if it does concede this point, tends to conceive of SEA as accounts that simply re-internalize the social and environmental costs that orthodox financial and management accounting practice previously excluded as 'externalities' without questioning the socio-historical presuppositions of accounting discourse itself. Over the years, various tools and techniques have been developed to develop 'triple bottom line' and 'sustainability' indicators along these lines (for an overview of different approaches, see Molisa and Wittneben, 2008). Much of this research is dominated by a 'business case' approach to SEA, and focuses on the costs and benefits of such accounting from management's perspective (Brown and Fraser, 2006).

Certain scholars within the field recognized the failings of managerialist approaches to SEA research early on and, drawing inspiration from the critical accounting critiques of accounting practice, sought to develop a 'neo-pluralist' synthesis that bridged different theoretical perspectives (both 'Left-wing' and 'Right-wing') into a 'middle-ground' position from which reforms could be effected (Gray, Owen and Maunders, 1988; Gray et al., 1996). While this approach to accounting and social reform has a lot of potential to enact change in progressive directions (T. Tinker and Gray, 2003), it has received forceful criticisms for its theoretical limitations and the ways in which its research reproduces many of the ideological presuppositions that critical accounting scholars level at orthodox accounting practice. This neo-pluralist or middle-of-the-road theorizing has thus been accused of managerialism (Neu et al., 1998), of bourgeois, first-world and middle-class allegiances (Everett and Neu, 2000), of political quietism in failing to illuminate the conflicts and contradictions of capitalism (Puxty, 1991; T. Tinker et al., 1991) and of reproducing patriarchal values (C. Cooper, 1992), amongst other things. The lesson drawn from these critiques is the need for self-reflexivity in both accounting research and practice (Everett, 2004). Some scholars have taken on board these criticisms, and SEA can now point to alternative forms of accountability that draw from communitarianism philosophy (G. Lehman, 1999, 2001, 2007), radical feminism (C. Cooper, 1992), utopian liberalism (Mouck, 1994), neo-Marxism (Everett and Neu, 2000; Neu, Cooper and Everett, 2001; C. Cooper et al., 2005), deep ecology (Birkin, 1996), Bourdieusian reflexivity (Shenkin and Coulson, 2007) and Gramscian praxis (Spence, 2009).

These later developments marked a discernible shift in the SEA literature from theoretical exploration and analysis to a more explicit concern with engagement (for example, Thomson and Bebbington, 2005; Adams and Larrinaga-González, 2007; Bebbington et al., 2007b; Owen, 2008). This 'critical turn' in the SEA literature has also been matched by research which is putting forward forms of accounting that go beyond the traditional techniques of triple bottom line reporting and environmental reports. These now include forms of full-cost accounting such as the Sustainable Assessment Model (Bebbington, Brown and Frame, 2007a), silent and shadow accounting and the ecological footprint (Bebbington et al., 2007b, pp. 370–71) that seek to problematize 'business as usual' approaches.

DIALOGIC ACCOUNTING FOR DEVELOPING COUNTRIES – A WAY FORWARD?

One of the most promising of these new SEA approaches is dialogic accounting (Thomson and Bebbington, 2005; Bebbington et al., 2007a, 2007b; Brown, 2009; Dillard and Roslender, 2011), an approach that draws on the intellectual and theoretical resources of critical thinkers such as Paulo Freire, Ivan Illich, Mikhail Bakhtin, Henri Giroux, Jürgen Habermas and Chantal Mouffe and which aims to overcome many of the limitations of orthodox accounting and accountability practice. Dialogic accounting differs from orthodox approaches because it makes self-reflexivity part of the accountability process itself, and recognizes the need to interrogate possibilities for agency and change, the politics and power inherent in language, and the need for diversity and inclusiveness, the need to interrogate the material context and power dynamics, and the need to examine the institutional frameworks and democratic models of accountability practices, the politics of underlying epistemologies, and the role of experts within the accountability process (Bebbington et al., 2007b, pp. 366–8). All these factors are points in favour of dialogic accounting, since in contrast to orthodox forms it is explicitly concerned with ensuring that all actors are included in accountability processes, identifying unequal power relations, and expanding ethics to include issues previously overlooked or excluded by identifying marginalized voices and exposing social conflicts and tensions as ways of beginning to work toward their resolution. With this in mind, we suggest dialogic accountability has real potential in terms of offering developing countries an approach with which to construct more empowering and enabling forms of accounting and accountability practice that could guide the economic, political and social initiatives being undertaken in ways that are just, democratic, sustainable and, most of all, of benefit to peoples and communities.

Brown (2009) outlines two possible approaches to dialogic accounting, one based on Habermasian deliberative democracy and the other on Mouffe's proposals for agonistic democracy. Both are based on participatory approaches aimed to promote critical dialogue and debate (for example, within and across the State, business and NGO sectors, or between employer groups and labour unions). However, whereas the former seeks to transcend difference (for example, socio-ethical backgrounds) and is geared towards reaching consensus, the latter focuses on ways for accounting to better represent ideological and cultural differences. These different approaches, in turn, are based on divergent understandings of political and social learning processes. Whereas 'Habermas's political vision is relatively smooth, believing ... that social complexity is manageable', Mouffe's is messier, 'characterized by ongoing contestation between plural social groups' (Kapoor, 2008, p. 103). Agonistic democrats charge that consensual attempts to transcend our particularities too often result in the silencing and marginalization of vulnerable groups. They seek a more multi-dimensional understanding of community and acccountings that are more responsive to the needs of plural audiences and multiple publics and that enable them to speak and debate in their own voices.

While we believe dialogic forms of accounting and accountability contain much promise, we recognize that there are real difficulties in realizing that promise. Kapoor's (2008) writings are particularly instructive here. He argues that, from the perspective of participatory development, four key issues need to be addressed to make Habermas and Mouffe's democratic theories more relevant in a developing country context, namely: 'the legacies of colonialism, the impact of socioeconomic inequality on democratic politics, the democratic participation of the subaltern, and the pivotal role of the (Third World) state' (Kapoor, 2008, p. 98). These are all also key considerations for the development of dialogic accounting, given its 'democratizing' aspirations (Brown, 2009).

Firstly, it is important to ensure that proposed theories and approaches do not merely mask new forms of Western hegemony. While Habermas and Mouffe's ideas are both Western-focused, Kapoor (2008, p. 112) notes that Mouffe in particular is suspicious of universalizing narratives and that her approach 'is non-prescriptive and open' but still critical. Many of the observations she makes about exclusion, dissatisfaction and resistance and the rise of popular protest and social movements resonate in a developing country context (particularly with the geographic spread of Western liberal democracy). We see this in both Mongolia and Vanuatu, where economic gains from neo-liberalism disproportionately favour particular groups and come at considerable social and environmental costs, creating various antagonisms.[8] Habermas's work is more ambiguous. While cognizant of crisis tendencies in late capitalism, his deliberative democracy relies heavily on Western institutions, procedures and understandings of rationality. It, and forms of dialogic accounting built on it, would require particularly careful adaption to the realities of developing country contexts.

Secondly, close attention needs to be paid to the impact of power inequalities on dialogic approaches to accounting and democratic politics. Socio-economic inequalities pose significant obstacles to establishing accountability processes that are inclusive of those with little power relative to those exercised by the foreign governments of 'centre' countries, multinationals, and international aid institutions, which are effectively controlled by the elite interests of developed countries. Within developing countries, the existence of class and other social divisions and power differences between local elites and the general population brings significant challenges to institutionalizing fully dialogic mechanisms. In emphasizing the importance of 'discursive' aspects of our social world, we also need to ensure that we do not underplay 'the material'. While many conflicts in the West may be 'post-materialist' (particularly in the middle classes), labour and economic struggles are crucial in a developing country context, where socio-economic inequalities are much more stark. Questions of identity and cultural dislocation are complexly intertwined with issues of economic justice and livelihood (and, in many cases, sheer survival). Distributional conflicts in terms of gaining access to economic and other material resources (for example, education or infrastructure) are key. As Kapoor (2008, p. 158) puts it, it is a mistake to assume 'a single logic to development discourse (i.e. development only destroys and never enables), as well as to resistance (for example all local resistance is anti-development)'. For some groups the struggle is about getting 'better access to development' (Kapoor, 2008, p. 114), and debates are extremely polarized. In conditions of extreme socio-economic inequality, risks that elites will divert resources to their own ends and 'manipulate and impose consensus are heavier and more difficult to minimize' (Kapoor, 2008, pp. 114–15).

Thirdly, we need greater understanding of the 'discursive barriers' between elites and non-elites (Kapoor, 2008, p. 113). Habermas, similarly to many social accountants, puts his faith in a rational consensus based on transparent, inclusive and undistorted dialogue. However, this ignores 'the power relationships that pervade speech-acts' (Kapoor, 2008, p. 115). It problematically assumes that people can understand and verbalize their oppression and its connections with wider political, economic and social structures, or that, as Narayan and Harding (2000, p. 6) put it, they have access to the 'texts of exploitation' (for example, pertaining to gender, class and cultural inequalities), rather than thinking they are 'personally unfortunate'. As Kapoor (2008, p. 115) observes, this is particularly challenging 'when power is so complicatedly and abstractly mediated through global socioeconomic and cultural systems', including 'expert' languages such as economics and accounting. Even more problematically, deliberative democracy too often assumes that, if subaltern voices do communicate their concerns, they will be heard by elites (Kapoor, 2008, p. 115). Monologic accounting systems and neo-classical economic theories are prime examples of the types of 'discursive apartheid' that Kapoor refers to: epistemic systems that 'filter out, deny, or suppress subaltern voices' so that even when there is dialogue 'the subaltern's views are barely intelligible or audible' (Kapoor, 2008, p. 115). Social and expert elites retranslate concerns, confidently feeling they can speak on behalf of others. Disadvantaged groups, for their part, often 'lack the sense of "entitlement" and "assertiveness" displayed by privileged groups' (Kapoor, 2008, p. 106). Kapoor cites empirical studies that found that women felt they had 'to clothe their ideas and encode their desires in particular ways to make them heard and accepted as legitimate' so that they 'resort to letting men articulate their concerns or . . . only provide the "official" story' (Kapoor, 2008, p. 106). People similarly might feel obliged to translate their concerns into monetary terms, as the language favoured by neo-liberal elites, and this results in a discourse that ignores distributional concerns. Again, any 'consensus' in such circumstances is arguably little more than 'ideological fantasy' (Kapoor, 2008, p. 115). Dallmayr (2001, p. 28) argues that for transformative and reciprocal learning to occur social actors need 'to start from local traditions and historically sedimented practices and beliefs' and open themselves 'to cross-cultural interrogation and testing'; supposedly universal standards too often reflect those of dominant Western elites. In her advocacy of agonistic pluralism, Brown (2009) provides some pointers to ways of fostering effective minority participation (for example, through developing 'safe spaces' that allow people to build accountings in their own voice and concepts of agonistic respect that might encourage elites to listen more attentively), but much remains to be done. Spivak's (1990, 2003) teachings on 'unlearning elite prejudices' and developing capacities in imagining provide a valuable resource (see also Brown, 2010 on the possibilities of visual cultural approaches to (re)visioning in accounting). Kapoor (2008, p. 116) notes that a major challenge is 'coming up with institutional forms that are flexible and responsive, capable of cross-cultural translation and much, much better listening'.

Fourthly, we need greater appreciation of the pivotal position of the State in developing countries (for example, in terms of promoting neo-liberal reforms and structural adjustments, and channelling and monitoring foreign investment) and the potentialities of transnational approaches to governance. Kapoor (2008, p. 103) highlights 'the centralized and sometimes autocratic decision-making of state bureaucracies' in many developing country contexts. Advocates of deliberative democracy emphasize the importance of strengthening civil society and political institutions 'so that state power is made more discursive and accountable' and less vulnerable to co-option by elites (Kapoor, 2008, p. 116). The geographical reach of contemporary multinational corporates has also been accompanied by growing interest in transnational governance mechanisms (for example, international codes and rules). Agonistic democrats see great potential in decentring politics through new social movements operating at local, national and transnational levels. Escobar (1992, p. 34), for example, sees such movements as having the potential to undermine authoritarian practices through their 'pluralizing and diversifying effects on dominant, homogenizing and reductionist forces' and foster 'new economic forms which transcend the rationality of the market'. Linkages to broader democratic movements reduce the risks of a development discourse 'framed in a way that champions Western priorities and interests and excludes non-Western ones' (Kapoor, 2008 p. 104), as seen in current approaches to participatory development promoted by such organizations as the World Bank and International Monetary Fund. Rather than a top-down centralized approach, democracy is pluralized and extended to multiple socio-political arenas, both 'electoral bodies and . . . multiple formal and informal networks' (Kapoor, 2008 p. 104). Such approaches also arguably require State mechanisms to address inequalities, for example the institutionalization of legal rights to information and participation that support dialogic interaction and contestation (Brown, 2009, p. 326). Furthermore, care needs to be taken to assume that the social movements themselves operate democratically and are not co-opted by elites (Gray et al., 2006; G. Lehman, 2007).

In conclusion, we believe that dialogic accounting as a more critical and politically aware version of SEA could translate well into a developing country context, but with Kapoor (2008, p. 117) we agree that important differences between the developing and developed worlds 'constrain any automatic translation'. Like all other things that communities from 'developing' countries may use, the notion of dialogic accountability itself ought to be subjected to critical scrutiny. It needs to be scrutinized for not only its enabling potentialities but also ones that may constrain the capacities of peoples and communities from being freely self-determining through the unreflective importation of languages, values and practices that may be alienating and oppressive in their effects if not intent. As Kapoor urges for participatory democratic theory more generally, we need 'to begin the task of writing the Third World into it, opening it up, prodding it to listen to the Third World "Other"' (2008, p. 117). As he elaborates, engaging with both deliberative and agonistic approaches to democratic politics helps identify and unpack tensions 'between such issues as consensus and difference, pluralism and justice, or universalism and particularity' (Kapoor, 2008, p. 111). These are all similarly crucial issues for the development of dialogic accounting theory and practice.

NOTES

1. Following Gray, Owen and Adams (2010, p. 40), we use the term 'social and environmental accounting' here generically to include 'the activities of social, environmental, ethical and sustainability accounting, accountability, reporting, auditing and responsibility and so on'. Much SEA literature is still quite traditional in approach and, as we go on to explain, we focus in this chapter on more 'critical' versions such as dialogic accounting.
2. The Asia Foundation is a USA donor NGO operating in Mongolia.
3. The eight guiding principles are as follows: secure multi-stakeholder participation; transparent and open; law-abiding and enforcing; responsible for environment and human security; investing into the future; efficient; humane and ethical; and technologically advanced (RMI, 2006).
4. The company discovered world-class copper and gold deposits in Southern Gobi and has spent five years since 2004 negotiating a stability agreement with the Mongolian government. The agreement was a hot topic of public debate, and the company organized various meetings, training sessions and press conferences to stimulate dialogue on this subject.
5. The following discussion on Vanuatu's tourism industry draws extensively on Slatter (2006), an Oxfam-commissioned report that details some of the social, political and cultural effects that trade liberalization policies – particularly in tourism – are producing.
6. The idea was to turn 'Vanuatu into a tropical paradise destination through large-scale tourism resort development' (Slatter, 2006, p. 3). Under the TMP, 'the country was to be divided into "tourism precincts", with three international gateways – Vila, Luganville and Tanna' (Slatter, 2006, p. 3). The TMP's prescriptions reflected prevailing neo-liberal economic wisdom such as changing property ownership to enable privatization of Vanuatu's beaches and reefs, establishing an investment promotion body (making the country attractive to foreign investors and facilitating investment) and offering 'tourism investors tax breaks and other concessions for development projects undertaken within the tourism precincts' (Slatter, 2006, p. 3).
7. This is Everett and Neu's (2000, p. 19) notion of 'nature-as-ideological-ingredient'.
8. In this sense, as Kapoor (2008, p. 113) observes, highlighting the West's complicity with (neo)colonialism would arguably strengthen both Habermas and Mouffe's critiques of Western liberalism.

REFERENCES

Adams, C.A., and C. Larrinaga-González (2007). Engaging with organisations in pursuit of improved sustainability accounting and performance. *Accounting, Auditing and Accountability Journal*, 20(3), pp. 333–55.

Armstrong, P. (1987). The rise of accounting controls in British capitalist enterprises. *Accounting, Organizations and Society*, 12(5), pp. 415–36.

Armstrong, P. (1991). Contradiction and social dynamics in the capitalist agency relationship. *Accounting, Organizations and Society*, 16(1), pp. 1–25.

Arrington, C.E., and J.R. Francis (1993). Giving economic accounts: accounting as cultural practice. *Accounting, Organizations and Society*, 18(2–3), pp. 107–24.

Bargh, M. (2007). *Resistance: An Indigenous Response to Neoliberalism*. Wellington: Huia.

Bebbington, J., J. Brown and B. Frame (2007a). Accounting technologies and sustainability assessment models. *Ecological Economics*, 61(2–3), pp. 224–36.

Bebbington, J., J. Brown, B. Frame and I. Thomson (2007b). Theorizing engagement: the potential of a critical dialogic approach. *Accounting, Auditing and Accountability Journal*, 20(3), pp. 356–81.

Benston, G.J. (1982). Accounting and corporate accountability. *Accounting, Organizations and Society*, 7(2), pp. 87–105.

Birkin, F. (1996). The ecological accountant: from the cogito to thinking like a mountain. *Critical Perspectives on Accounting*, 7(3), pp. 231–57.

Brown, J. (2009). Democracy, sustainability and dialogic accounting technologies: taking pluralism seriously. *Critical Perspectives on Accounting*, 20(3), pp. 313–42.

Brown, J. (2010). Accounting and visual cultural studies: potentialities, challenges and prospects. *Accounting, Auditing and Accountability Journal*, 23(4), pp. 482–505.

Brown, J., and M. Fraser (2006). Approaches and perspectives in social and environmental accounting: an overview of the conceptual landscape. *Business Strategy and the Environment*, 15(2), pp. 103–17.

Burchell, G., C. Gordon and P. Miller (1991). *The Foucault Effect*. Chicago: University of Chicago Press.

Central Intelligence Agency (2009). *The World Factbook*, www.cia.gov/library/publications/the-world-factbook/fields/2004.html, accessed 10 December 2009.

Chua, W.F. (1986). Radical developments in accounting thought. *Accounting Review*, 61(4), pp. 601–32.

Chua, W.F. (1995). Experts, networks and inscriptions in the fabrication of accounting images: a story of the representation of three public hospitals. *Accounting, Organizations and Society*, 20(2–3), pp. 111–45.

Cooper, C. (1992). The non and nom of accounting for (m)other nature. *Accounting, Auditing and Accountability Journal*, 5(3), pp. 16–39.

Cooper, C., P. Taylor, N. Smith and L. Catchpowle (2005). A discussion of the political potential of social accounting. *Critical Perspectives on Accounting*, 16(7), pp. 951–74.

Cooper, D. (1980). Discussion of Towards a Political Economy of Accounting. *Accounting, Organizations and Society*, 5(1), pp. 161–6.

Cooper, D.J., and M.J. Sherer (1984). The value of corporate accounting reports: arguments for a political economy of accounting. *Accounting, Organizations and Society*, 9(3–4), pp. 207–32.

Dallmayr, F. (2001). *Achieving Our World*. Lanham, MD: Rowman & Littlefield.

Dillard, J., and R. Roslender (2011). Taking pluralism seriously: embedded moralities in management accounting and control systems. *Critical Perspectives on Accounting*, 22(3), pp. 135–147.

Dryzek, J., and D. Schlosberg (eds) (2005). *Debating the Earth: The Environmental Politics Reader*. Oxford: Oxford University Press.

Escobar, A. (1992). Imagining a post-development era? Critical thought, development and social movements. *Social Text*, 31–32, pp. 20–56.

Everett, J. (2003). Globalization and its new spaces for (alternative) accounting research. *Accounting Forum*, 27(4), pp. 400–424.

Everett, J. (2004). Exploring (false) dualisms for environmental accounting praxis. *Critical Perspectives on Accounting*, 15(8), pp. 1061–84.

Everett, J., and D. Neu (2000). Ecological modernization and the limits of environmental accounting? *Accounting Forum*, 24(1), pp. 5–29.

Everett, J., D. Neu and A.S. Rahaman (2007). Accounting and the global fight against corruption. *Accounting, Organizations and Society*, 32(6), pp. 513–42.

Foucault, M. (1991). Governmentality. In *The Foucault Effect*, ed. G. Burchell, C. Gordon and P. Miller, pp. 87–104. Chicago: University of Chicago Press.

Funnel, W. (1998). Accounting in the service of the Holocaust. *Critical Perspectives on Accounting*, 9(4), pp. 435–64.

Gray, R.H. (2002). The social accounting project and *Accounting, Organizations and Society*: privileging engagement, imaginings, new accountings and pragmatism over critique? *Accounting, Organizations and Society*, 27(7), pp. 687–708.

Gray, R., J. Bebbington and D. Collison (2006). NGOs, civil society and accountability: making the people accountable to capital. *Accounting, Auditing and Accountability Journal*, 19(3), pp. 319–48.

Gray, R., D. Owen and C. Adams (1996). *Accounting and Accountability: Changes and Challenges in Corporate Social and Environmental Reporting*. London: Prentice Hall.

Gray, R., D. Owen and C. Adams (2010). Some theories for social accounting? A review essay and a tentative pedagogic categorisation of theorisations around social accounting. In *Sustainability, Environmental Performance and Disclosures*, Advances in Environmental Accounting and Management, vol. 4, ed. B. Jaggi and M. Freedman, pp. 1–54. Bingley: Emerald Group.

Gray, R., D. Owen and K. Maunders (1988). Corporate social reporting: emerging trends in accountability and the social contract. *Accounting, Auditing and Accountability Journal*, 1(1), pp. 6–20.

Harvey, D. (1996). *Justice, Nature and the Geography of Difference*. Oxford: Blackwell.

Hines, R. (1988). Financial accounting: in communicating reality, we construct reality. *Accounting, Organizations and Society*, 13(3), pp. 251–61.

Hines, R. (1989). The sociopolitical paradigm in financial accounting research. *Accounting, Auditing and Accountability Journal*, 2(1), pp. 52–76.

Hopper, T., D. Cooper, T. Capps, E.A. Lowe and J. Mouritsen (1986). Financial control in the labour process: managerial strategies and worker resistance in the National Coal Board. In *Managing the Labour Process*, ed. D. Knights and H. Willmott, pp. 109–41. Aldershot: Gower.

Hopper, T., J. Storey and H. Willmott (1987). Accounting for accounting: towards the development of a dialectical view. *Accounting, Organizations and Society*, 12(5), pp. 437–56.

Hopwood, A.G. (1987). The archaeology of accounting systems. *Accounting, Organizations and Society*, 12(3), pp. 207–34.

Huffer, E., and G. Molisa (1999). In search of the Nakamal way: state, society and governance in Melanesia. Discussion Paper 99/4, Research School of Pacific and Asian Studies, Australian National University, Canberra.

Kapoor, I. (2008). *The Postcolonial Politics of Development*. New York: Routledge.

Knights, D., and D. Collinson (1987). Disciplining the shopfloor: a comparison of the disciplinary effects of managerial psychology and financial accounting. *Accounting, Organizations and Society*, 12(5), pp. 457–77.

Lehman, C., and T. Tinker (1987). The 'real' cultural significance of accounts. *Accounting, Organizations and Society*, 12(5), pp. 503–22.

Lehman, G. (1999). Disclosing new worlds: a role for social and environmental accounting and auditing. *Accounting, Organizations and Society*, 24(3), pp. 217–41.

Lehman, G. (2001). Reclaiming the public sphere: problems and prospects for corporate social and environmental accounting. *Critical Perspectives on Accounting*, 12(6), pp. 713–33.

Lehman, G. (2007). The accountability of NGOs in civil society and its public spheres. *Critical Perspectives on Accounting*, 18(6), pp. 645–69.

Lowe, E.A., A.G. Puxty and R.C. Laughlin (1983). Simple theories for complex processes: accounting policy and the market for myopia. *Journal of Accounting and Public Policy*, 2(1), pp. 19–42.

Miller, P., and T. O'Leary (1987). Accounting and the construction of the governable person. *Accounting, Organizations and Society*, 12(3), pp. 235–65.

Miller, P., and N. Rose (1990). Governing economic life. *Economy and Society*, 19(1), pp. 1–31.

Molisa, P. (2006). Aid must fit with values of the community. *Dominion Post*, 12 April.

Molisa, P., and B. Wittneben (2008). Sustainable development, the clean development mechanism and business accounting. In *Economics and Management of Climate Change: Risks, Mitigation and Adaptation*, ed. B. Hansjürgens and R. Antes, pp. 175–92. Berlin: Springer.

Mouck, T. (1994). Corporate accountability and Rorty's utopian liberalism. *Accounting, Auditing and Accountability Journal*, 7(1), pp. 6–30.

Narayan, U., and S. Harding (eds) (2000). *Decentering the Center*. Bloomington: Indiana University Press.

National Statistical Office (2001). *2000 Population Census: Key Results*. Ulaanbaatar: National Statistical Office.

National Statistical Office (2009). *2008 Statistical Yearbook*. Ulaanbaatar: National Statistical Office.

Neimark, M., and T. Tinker (1986). The social construction of management control systems. *Accounting, Organizations and Society*, 11(4–5), pp. 369–95.

Neu, D. (1992). The social construction of positive choices. *Accounting, Organizations and Society*, 17(3–4), pp. 223–37.

Neu, D. (2000). Accounting and accountability relations: colonization, genocide and Canada's first nations. *Accounting, Auditing and Accountability Journal*, 13(3), pp. 268–88.

Neu, D. (2001). Banal accounts: subaltern voices. *Accounting Forum*, 25(4), pp. 319–33.

Neu, D., D.J. Cooper and J. Everett (2001). Critical accounting interventions. *Critical Perspectives on Accounting*, 12(6), pp. 735–62.

Neu, D., A.S. Rahaman, J. Everett and A. Akindayome (2010). The sign value of accounting: IMF structural adjustment programs and African banking reform. *Critical Perspectives on Accounting*, 21(5), pp. 402–19.

Neu, D., and A. Taylor (1996). Accounting and the politics of disinvestment. *Critical Perspectives on Accounting*, 7(4), pp. 437–60.

Neu, D., H. Warsame and K. Pedwell (1998). Managing public impressions: environmental disclosures in annual reports. *Accounting, Organizations and Society*, 23(3), pp. 265–82.

Owen, D. (2008). Chronicles of wasted time? A personal reflection on the current state of, and future prospects for, social and environmental accounting research. *Accounting, Auditing and Accountability Journal*, 21(2), pp. 240–67.

Puxty, A.G. (1986). Social accounting as immanent legitimation: a critique of a technicist ideology. *Advances in Public Interest Accounting*, 1, pp. 95–111.

Puxty, A.G. (1991). Social accountability and universal pragmatics. *Advances in Public Interest Accounting*, 4, pp. 35–45.

RMI (2006). *Declaration of Responsible Mining*. Ulaanbaatar: Responsible Mining Initiative for Sustainable Development.

RMI (2009). *Responsible Mining Initiative for Sustainable Development*. Ulaanbaatar: Responsible Mining Initiative for Sustainable Development.

Roslender, R., and J.F. Dillard (2003). Reflections on the Interdisciplinary Perspectives on Accounting Project. *Critical Perspectives on Accounting*, 14(3), pp. 325–51.

Ross, M.L. (2008). Mineral wealth, conflict, and equitable development. In *Institutional Pathways to Equity: Addressing Inequality Traps*, ed. A.J. Bebbington, A.A. Dani, A. de Haan and M. Walton. Washington, DC: World Bank Publications.

Shenkin, M., and A.B. Coulson (2007). Accountability through activism: learning from Bourdieu. *Accounting, Auditing and Accountability Journal*, 20(2), pp. 297–317.

Shiirevdamba, T. (2009). The legislative framework of the Mongolian mining sector. Paper presented at the Fourth Mining Rehabilitation Seminar.

Slatter, C. (2006). *The Con/Dominion of Vanuatu? Paying the Price of Investment and Land Liberalisation: A Case Study of Vanuatu's Tourism Industry*. New Zealand: Oxfam.

Spence, C. (2009). Social accounting's emancipatory potential: a Gramscian critique. *Critical Perspectives on Accounting*, 20(2), pp. 205–27.

Speth, J.G. (2008). *The Bridge at the End of the World: Capitalism, the Environment, and Crossing from Crisis to Sustainability*. New Haven, CT: Yale University Press.

Spivak, G.C. (1990). *The Post-Colonial Critic: Interviews, Strategies, Dialogues*, ed. S. Harasym. London: Routledge.

Spivak, G.C. (2003). A conversation with Gayatri Chakravorty Spivak: politics and the imagination, interview by Jenny Sharpe. *Signs: Journal of Women in Culture and Society*, 28(2), pp. 609–24.

Stiglitz, J.E. (2002). *Globalization and Its Discontents*. New York: Norton.

Thomson, I., and J. Bebbington (2005). Social and environmental reporting in the UK: a pedagogic evaluation. *Critical Perspectives on Accounting*, 16(5), pp. 507–33.

Tinker, A.M. (1980). Towards a political economy of accounting: an empirical illustration of the Cambridge controversies. *Accounting, Organizations and Society*, 5(1), pp. 147–60.

Tinker, A.M., B.D. Merino and M.D. Neimark (1982). The normative origins of positive theories: ideology and accounting thought. *Accounting, Organizations and Society*, 7(2), pp. 167–200.

Tinker, T. (1985). *Paper Prophets: A Social Critique of Accounting*, New York: Praeger.

Tinker, T. (1988). Panglossian accounting theories: the science of apologising in style. *Accounting, Organizations and Society*, 13(2), pp. 165–89.

Tinker, T., and R.H. Gray (2003). Beyond a critique of pure reason: from policy to politics to praxis in environmental and social research. *Accounting, Auditing and Accountability Journal*, 16(5), pp. 727–61.

Tinker, T., C. Lehman and M. Neimark (1991). Falling down the hole in the middle of the road: political quietism in corporate social reporting. *Accounting, Auditing and Accountability Journal*, 4(2), pp. 28–54.

Tinker, T., and M. Neimark (1987). The role of annual reports in gender and class contradictions at General Motors: 1917–1976. *Accounting, Organizations and Society*, 12(1), pp. 71–88.

Tsogtbaatar, C. (2009). The current state of mining. Paper presented at the Fourth Mining Rehabilitation Seminar.

UN Statistics Division (2002). GDP per capita (PPPs), http://unstats.un.org/unsd/cdb/cdb_years_on_top.asp?srID=29922&Ct1ID=&crID=496&yrID=1996%2C2006, accessed 24 January 2008.

UNDP (2007). *Employment and Poverty in Mongolia*, Mongolia Human Development Report. Ulaanbaatar: United Nations Development Programme.

Vollmer, H. (2003). Bookkeeping, accounting, calculative practice: the sociological suspense of calculation. *Critical Perspectives on Accounting*, 14(3), pp. 353–81.

World Bank (2004). *Mongolia: Mining Sector Sources of Growth Study*. Washington, DC: World Bank.

World Bank (2007). *Mongolia: Sources of Growth*. Washington, DC: World Bank.

World Growth (2008). *Averting the Resource Curse: Path to Prosperity, Project Mongolia*. Arlington, VA: World Growth.

Index

Abd-Elalam, O.H. 130
Aborisade, P.A. 83
accounting firms *see* international accounting firms
accounting professionalization 66, 74–5, 89–90, 103, 135, 252
  Bangladesh 113, 114–16, 117
  donor support 17–18, 20, 21, 22, 23, 24, 30, 32
  historical legacies of empire 76–85
  patrimonialism 87–9
  way forward 85–7
accounting standards 20–21, 22, 63, 64, 65, 66, 70
  financial development and *see under* financial development
  true and fair view 43–4
  see also IASB; IASC; IASs; IFRSs
accounting technicians 85, 86, 87
accrual accounting 28–30, 229
ActionAid 143, 144, 145
Adam, C. 206, 208, 209
Adams, C.A. 303
Adams, D.W. 169
Adams, P. 235
Adda, W.A. 211, 212
Africa 21, 37, 40, 54, 75, 88–9, 158, 182, 283
  see also individual countries
agency theory 86, 125, 126, 127, 209
Agg, C. 146
Aghion, P. 120, 122
Agyemang, G. 149, 150, 155
Ahluwalia, M. 122
Ahmed, K. 130
aid funding 36, 37, 64, 128, 145–8, 207, 235
  donor support for improved accounting *see separate entry*
  NGOs *see* accounting and accountability *under* non-governmental organizations
  tax revenues and 39
Akhtaruddin, M. 130
Akinsanya, A. 207
Alam, M.S. 228
Alamgir, D. 166
Alawattage, C. 108
Alba, C.R. 276
Algeria 37, 71

Ali, M.J. 128, 129, 137, 138
Amegashie, R. 78
Amnesty International 143
analysts 117, 128
Andvig, J.C. 230
Anechiaricho, F. 229
Anguilla 45
Anibaba, M.O. 83
Annisette, M. 65, 66, 70, 71, 76, 77, 78, 79–80, 81
Anstee, Margaret Joan 192
arbitration: transfer pricing 283, 285
Aristotle 238
Armendariz de Aghion, B. 122
Armstrong, C.S. 128
Armstrong, P. 299, 300
Arnold, P.J. 64–5, 81
Arrington, C.E. 300
ASEAN (Association of South East Asian Nations) 101
Ashraf, J. 136
Asian Development Bank (ADB) 97, 101, 294, 298
Association of Chartered Certified Accountants (ACCA) 69, 74, 79, 81, 83–4, 85, 89
Athukorala, P. 120
Atkinson, A.B. 147
auditing/auditors 54, 62–3, 65, 71, 76, 83, 97, 215, 227, 252
  accountability of NGOs: social 155
  audit exemption 85–6
  corruption 88, 228, 229, 231–2
  donor support 21, 22, 26, 30, 33
  globalization of auditing standards 108–9, 117–18
    Bangladesh 109, 111–17
    caveats for harmonization 114–17
    ISAs 21, 108, 109–11, 117
  legal environment and 127–8
  tax self-assessment 259, 260, 261, 262
Aung Sang Suu Kyi 234
Australia 29–30, 95, 96, 98, 197, 236
  transfer pricing 275, 276, 278–9
Avi-Yonah, R. 45, 52
Awio, G. 182
Ayee, J.R.A. 192